The International Encyclopedia of Gambling

The International Encyclopedia of Gambling

VOLUME 2

William N. Thompson

A B C • CLIO

Santa Barbara, California • Denver, Colorado • Oxford, England

Copyright 2010 by ABC-CLIO, LLC

All rights reserved. No part of this publication may be reproduced, stored in a retrieval system, or transmitted, in any form or by any means, electronic, mechanical, photocopying, recording, or otherwise, except for the inclusion of brief quotations in a review, without prior permission in writing from the publisher.

Library of Congress Cataloging-in-Publication Data

Thompson, William Norman.
  The international encyclopedia of gambling / William N. Thompson.
    p. cm.
  Includes bibliographical references and index.
  ISBN 978-1-59884-225-8 (alk. paper) — ISBN 978-1-59884-226-5 (ebook) 1. Gambling—
Encyclopedias. 2. Gambling—Social aspects. I. Title.
  GV1301.T474 2010
  306.4'8203—dc22   2009048274

14 13 12 11 10   1 2 3 4 5

This book is also available on the World Wide Web as an eBook.
Visit www.abc-clio.com for details.

ABC-CLIO, LLC
130 Cremona Drive, P.O. Box 1911
Santa Barbara, California 93116-1911
This book is printed on acid-free paper

Contents

Section Two: Games, 239

Section Three: Biographies of Leading Figures in Gambling, 289

Volume 2

Section Four: Venues and Places, 355

Section Four

VENUES AND PLACES

Africa

Africa is one of the world's largest continents, with over 20 percent of the global land mass. More than 50 independent countries share its vast territory. Although most of the countries do have legalized gambling, the official activities are intense, indeed they are quite limited in scope. Lotteries are found in most countries, and while half or more do have casinos, these are mostly confined to single facilities in major cities. The major force in confining the existence of officially recognized gambling is the abject poverty found in most corners of the continent, especially in lands below the Sahara Desert. Poverty is manifest in phenomenon such as players "pooling" resources in order to have a single play on a slot machine or casinos paying employees on a daily basis in order to ensure that they will return for work the next day. In Togo, at one time the government was so poor that it could not furnish coinage for play in its casino's slot machines. The casino purchased its own tokens and these worked their way outside to the general economy, where they were accepted as currency for trade.

Along with poverty, conditions of external as well as internal violence and the accompanying political instability and authoritarian rule make those who would invest in casinos wary of such ventures. There are exceptions, but these are mainly found in North Africa and in the Union of South Africa.

EAST AFRICA

National lotteries made their appearance in East Africa in 1961 when Ethiopia started a passive game. That lottery has since expanded to include sports betting, and sales are now made over the Internet. More recent decades saw the arrival of lotteries in Burundi, Kenya, Mauritius, Mozambique, Rwanda, Tanzania, and Uganda. Casinos are less pervasive. In East Africa, Kenya has the strongest casino establishment; Kenya achieved independence from British colonial rule in 1963. A modicum of political stability has fostered development of casinos, the largest of which is the Paradise facility at the Safari Park Hotel in the capital city of Nairobi. It has over 300 slot machines and 24 tables. Nairobi has another casino, Malindi has one as well, and there are four in the coastal city of Mombasa. The casinos are regulated by a National Betting and Licensing Control Board. Casinos pay a tax of 13.5 percent on money they win from players.

The interior country of Uganda has not enjoyed the same political stability as found in Kenya. Nonetheless it has three casinos in the capital city of

Kampala. Tanzania also has three casinos in Dar es Salaam. Mozambique offers two casinos, and there are three in Madagascar. One casino is found in Addis Ababa, Ethiopia, while there is also one in Djibouti's Oceanside Sheraton Hotel. Four Indian Ocean islands off the coast of East Africa also have casino gambling. The Seychelles have four facilities, Reunion Island (a French possession) has one, and Comoros has one casino with table and slot games, and another with only slot machines. The multiethnic Republic of Mauritius gained independence from the British in 1968. In 1973, its Gaming Act provided for casinos in resort hotels under control of a Gaming Control Board. There are nine casinos and each pays a tax of 50 percent on its gaming revenues.

NORTH AFRICA

North African countries have populations which are predominately Muslim Arabs whose religion offers a general condemnation of gambling activity. Casinos do exist in three of the six countries; however, they do not let their local residents play in the facilities. Morocco has six casinos. It is also the only country of the region with a lottery and horse race betting. Tunisia has seven casinos. Egypt has 26 casinos, with 20 of them located in major hotels in Cairo. These cater to visiting businessmen, mostly from Saudi Arabia but also Europeans and Americans. Saudis mostly patronize the four casinos at resort complexes in Sharm el-Sheikh on the Red Sea. Also on the Red Sea is Taba, a border town next to Eliat, Israel. Most of the players at the town's casino in the Hilton Hotel are Israelis. The successful Egyptian casinos share their wealth with the government, which collects 50 percent of their table and slot revenue in taxation.

SOUTH AFRICA

The history of South Africa has witnessed horse racing gambling for many generations. However, casino gaming emerged in South Africa only in recent years. In a sense the emergence paralleled U.S. developments with Native American casinos. However, the history may also be labeled as quite unique for a country now coming out of its apartheid policies of racial divisions.

European settlers of Dutch and English origins came to the southernmost regions of Africa several centuries ago. In some cases, they occupied vacant lands even before indigenous African peoples made migrations to the same area. The Dutch and English participated in wagering on horse races in the 19th century and earlier. However, other games were banned by the colonial governments. After the English settlers dominated the Dutch in the Boer Wars, a new government called the Union of South Africa was established in 1910. The new government maintained the bans on gambling except for race bets. The policy was reiterated in laws of 1933 and 1965. The latter National Gaming Act, however, neglected to impose all its social policies on certain territories for indigenous African peoples, which were created in the 1970s.

The Union of South Africa has been a federal state from its inception. In an attempt to cope with its policies of racial separation several "homelands" were set up so that tribes in South Africa could exercise political control to some degree. While the homelands Transkei, Bophuthatswana, Venda, and Ciskei—like Native American reservation lands—were generally very poor and lacking in natural resources, they discovered the value of one political resource: the tribes were given a semisovereign authority over domestic policies. About a decade before a similar discovery was made by American tribes, homeland leaders in South Africa discovered that they could permit the existence of casino gambling—something prohibited everywhere else in the South Africa. In doing so they soon realized the value of having casino monopolies.

As with the Native American casinos, outside nontribal entrepreneurial interests took the lead in developing homeland casinos. The leading "white" entrepreneur pushing homeland casinos was Sol Kerzner. In 1979, he created the lavish Sun City resort complex, located in Bophuthatswana, only a few hours' drive from Johannesburg, the third-largest city in South Africa. Throughout the 1980s, the casino facilities were greatly expanded, and another 16 casinos were developed in the four homeland regions. The Sun casino organization, while bringing resources to the subjugated tribes of the homelands, were nonetheless criticized severely as being agents perpetuating the separatist apartheid policies of the South African regime. As the properties grew, they stimulated boycotts from many in the world's entertainment establishment. This was ironic, as these casinos became islands of racial equality and integration within the very segregated South Africa.

But all this changed in the 1990s as forces of reform compelled the white leadership of South Africa to yield to majority sentiment, and a new majority (nonwhite) democratic government was created. The homelands were abolished as a new constitution set up a regime of racial equality. The new central government with its nine states decided that casino gaming should remain and be expanded. Part of the motivation to authorize casinos in the 1996 National Gambling Act came from the fact that in the years of transition between apartheid and democracy, several hundred illegal casinos (some say thousands) began operation. New legal casinos were needed to become a force to allow strong government action to close down illegal gaming. The 1996 act created a national lottery and also permitted up to 40 casinos, assigning a number (three to six) to each of the nine provinces.

The homelands were part of the nine states, but the established casinos of the homelands were not automatically guaranteed licenses. After the first round of licensing, 9 of the 17 homeland casinos remained operating. The 1996 act also created a National Gambling Board, which established uniform standards for casinos, as well as an inspection authority. The nine separate provinces of South Africa were authorized to grant licenses and to set rules for operations consistent with the national standards. The provinces determined rates of taxation, ranging from 10 percent to 25 percent of gaming revenues.

Outside the boundaries of South Africa, nearby governments have also permitted casinos. Zimbawbe and Zambia have casino facilities near the Victoria Falls tourist attraction; Lesotho and Swaziland also have casinos. All the countries of the region of southern Africa also offer lottery gaming.

WEST AFRICA

Lotteries are found in most venues of West Africa including Benin, Burkina Faso, Ivory Coast, Gambia, Ghana, Mali, Niger, Nigeria, Senegal, Sierra Leone, and Togo. There are only a few racetracks, notably in Senegal, Nigeria, and Ghana, while casinos are very small facilities.

Nigeria has nearly 100 million people, and also a viable business establishment, much of it tied to the oil industry. Casinos are supported mostly by visiting business people. Four are found in the capital of Lagos, one each in Ibadan and Port Harcourt, and two in Abuja. Less viable casinos are found in Benin (1), Cameroon (2), Congo (Zaire) (1), Gambia (1), Ghana (2), Ivory Coast (1), Liberia (1), Niger (1), Senegal (4), Sierra Leone (1), and Togo (1).

References

"African Casinos." www.gamingfloor.com/ African _Casinos.html.

Cabot, Anthony N., William N. Thompson, Andrew Tottenham, and Carl Braunlich, eds. 1999. *International Casino Law.* 3rd ed. Reno: Institute for Study of Gambling, University of Nevada, 483–511.

Casino City's Global Gaming Almanac. 2006. Newtown, MA: Casino City, 5–30.

Asia

China (Including Hong Kong and Macau)

The Chinese people are often considered to be the most frenzied gamblers in the world. (See Essays, "The World's Best Gamblers.") Nonetheless China, as a country, has prohibited almost all gambling for more than 60 years. The ban has been consistent with the Communist Party philosophy and public policy advocated in China following the success of the Maoist revolution of 1949. For instance, a large horse racing track in Shanghai was immediately converted into a public park after the takeover.

The new Chinese regime did relent somewhat in the 1980s as the economy opened up to the world and revenue advantages of lottery play were recognized. In 1987, a national charity lottery was instituted, followed in 1994 with a national sports lottery. Originally prizes were modest so as not to overly excite the population. However, in 2008, a single grand prize of more than US$11 million was awarded in the sports lottery. The sale of tickets has grown rapidly every year. In 2006, sales exceeded US$4 billion.

China has had a long historical relationship with the horse. There are records of horse racing that date back 2000 years to the Han Dynasty. The renowned Terra Cotta warriors buried near Xian conducted military maneuvers with horses. Genghis Kahn's Mongol hordes conquered China on horseback. Interest in horses never waned. And so horse racing interests were able to persuade Communist authorities to approve the establishment of the Beijing Jockey Club in 2001. A Hong Kong business group financed the effort. The club is active in breeding thoroughbred horses, and they have constructed three tracks in the Beijing area for conducting races. They had hoped to be the venue for equestrian events at the 2008 Olympic Games, but that honor instead went to the Hong Kong Jockey Club, discussed below. Large international races have been conducted with prizes that have attracted the best locally bred horses as well as horses from Australia. The question of how patrons conduct betting on the races remains a bit tricky. Rules against gambling have been skirted by having Jockey Club members purchase large shares of the racing product—in terms of specific horses—and then receive dividends if the horses are winners. There can be little doubt that there is much "private" betting on the races. A Beijing University report on gambling in China estimated that well over US$100 million is wagered on games each year—with 90 percent or more of that amount being wagered illegally.

The national authorities were confronted with a policy dilemma in the 1990s as plans were made for British and Portuguese authorities to cede the colonial territories of Hong Kong and Macau along the South China Sea. Hong Kong was placed under the Chinese flag in 1997. So too were the operations of its lotteries and the Hong Kong Jockey Club. As the former colony was given status as a Special Autonomous Region for 50 years, officials in Beijing danced around the gambling question. Hong Kong could maintain its gambling operations. One Web site relates that "Hong Kong's favorite sport is making money, and in horseracing you have Hong Kong's favorite money sport" ("Hong Kong's Favorite Sport"). The Hong Kong Jockey Club has operated tracks from 1884 to the present time. By the 21st century, the club had become the largest tax contributor in Hong Kong, giving over US$130 million a year to the local government—this represents 11 percent of the local budget. There are two tracks: Happy Valley, which had been developed by the British in 1846, and the Sha Tin track, which has been operating since 1978. The two tracks offer more than 700 races a year. Betting turnover at the two tracks passed the US$100 billion mark in 2007.

The fate of the gambling operations in Macao also passed into the hands of the officials of the People's Republic of China when the sovereignty of the Portuguese enclave in the South China Sea was transferred to the Chinese in 1999. Macao comprises a small peninsula and two tiny islands totaling about 12 square miles of land lying 40 miles from Hong Kong by water.

As an enclave beyond the reach of the Chinese government, Macao became the site of many so-called sin activities. Gambling was illegal but operated openly until 1934, when the Tai Xing Company was given a concession to develop casinos and hotels. The company was led by Fu Tak Yam until his death in 1962. After that, operations were taken over by Stanley Ho, a Macao native. Ironically, Ho went on to purchase the largest casino in Portugal, at Estorial.

At the time the territory went under Chinese control, there were five large casino-hotel operations, as well as a floating casino docked in Macao. Additionally there were two machine-only casinos. A greyhound racetrack has one of these casinos. Macau also has had a horse track and lottery both controlled by Stanley Ho's company Sociedade de Turismo e Diversões de Macau (STDM). The casinos offer Western games such as roulette, baccarat, and blackjack, as well as slot machines of every variety. They also offer a wide assortment of Asian games such as fan tan, pacapio, tai-sai, pai gow, and mahjong. Macao has been called both the "Monte Carlo of the Orient" and the "Las Vegas of the Orient." The Portuguese authorities ruling the enclave were glad to offer the sins of Macao to the Hong Kong community. And so it was that the new Chinese rulers were content to let gambling persist as a way to appease fears that they were going to destroy the economy of the former colony, as a way to channel Chinese gambling desires into a legal pathway, and as a means to attract foreign capital—both with investments and with wagers on games.

To this latter end, the Chinese decided to revise the system of distribution of casino licenses for Macau. The executive of the new Macau Special Autonomous Region was authorized to issue three gaming concession. Each concession would operate according to a specific contract for a term of up to 20 years, a term which could then be renewed. A tax schedule required that casinos pay the Macau government 40 percent of their gross gaming wins. Concession holders would be permitted to build and operate as many casinos as the market could support, each one being approved by the government. Also the three could assign subconcessions with governmental approval. In 2000, the three "winners" were selected. Stanley Ho's STDM was selected, and he was authorized to operate 11 existing facilities in addition to his lottery and racing interests. Steve Wynn's Wynn Resorts won a second concession, and Galaxy Gaming won a concession in partnership with Sheldon Adelson's Venetian Macau. Ho's concession was later permitted to grant a subconcession to the MGM Grand Company. The Galaxy operation was split into two separate concessions a year later. In 2006, with the approval of the government, Wynn Resorts sold a subconcession to an affiliate of Publishing and Broadcasting, Ltd., for $900 million. The effect of the new licensing process was immediately felt, with large capital investments. The first new casino was the Macau Sands, under control of Venetian Macau. Galaxy then built the Waldo. Soon, Ho had a new Macau Jockey Club casino and also the Greek Mythology Casino. The Wynn Resort opened in 2006, featuring 700 rooms and a casino that included 380 table games and 1270 slots. Its position as the leading new casino was quickly challenged, however, by the Venetian Macau, which featured 3,000 suites, a casino with 870 table games and 3,400 slots, and 16,000 employees. In 2008 there were 29 casinos in Macau. The year before, their collective revenues had exceeded the revenues of the Las Vegas Strip. They were projected to exceed the $12 billion revenues of the entire state of Nevada within a few years, making Macau the leading casino venue in the world.

References

"Hong Kong Gambling." 2008. www.happy valleyracecourse.com.

"Hong Kong's Favorite Sport Is Making Money." Flixya. http://www.flixya.com/post/guoweiggad/662748/Hong_Kongs_favorite_sport_is_making_money.

"Macau." 2008. gamingfloor.com/Macau_Casinos.html, accessed June 13, 2008.

Rochelle, Dawn. 1999. "Macau." In *International Casino Law*, 3rd ed., edited by Anthony N. Cabot, William N. Thompson, Andrew Tottenham, and Carl Braunlich, 523–525. Reno: Institute for the Study of Gambling, University of Nevada.

Tegtmeier, Ralph. 1989. *Casinos*. New York: Vendome Press, 164–175.

Hong Kong. *See* China (Including Hong Kong and Macau).

THE INDIAN SUBCONTINENT (INCLUDING BHUTAN, GOA, NEPAL, SRI LANKA, AND SIKKIM)

The India subcontinent consists of the nation of India, with its 1.1 billion people, and a number of smaller countries: Nepal (population 8 million), Bhutan (population 1 million), and Sikkim (population 540,000) to the north, and the island nation of Sri Lanka (population 20 million), to the south.

Up to 75 percent of India's population may be classified as "poor." Half earn less than $1 a day. However, a small middle class, with disposable incomes of about $5,000 to $20,000 per year, numbers 50 million and is rapidly growing. Poverty has been a major factor in the country's decision to outlaw most gambling. There are state-run lotteries in 14 of 28 states, and there are racetracks in seven locations. Casino gambling is banned in all but one of the states—Goa. As more and more Indians are venturing to casino sites located in other regional countries as well as Macau, the state and federal governments of India are being besieged with proposals to legalize more casinos. With the exception of proposals for expansion of casino gambling in Goa, the efforts have been futile.

After Portuguese explorer Vasco da Gama set foot in India in 1498, other Portuguese arrived in the coastal region of Goa and took control of the subcontinent's leading trading port. The Portuguese governed Goa as a colonial outpost for 450 years until 1961, when 40,000 military troops from India reclaimed the land. Goa was governed by India as a "union territory" until 1987, when it became one of the country's 28 states. By then Goa already had its reputation as a land of temples and World Heritage architectural sites, and also for its risqué nightlife that attracted both international and domestic tourism. In the 1960s, the region attracted many hippies seeking alternative life styles. The local authorities had to keep a balance with the desires of the India central government which was strongly influenced by Hindu religious traditions. Therefore they passed a law in 1976 that prohibited all gambling. After achieving statehood, however, they allowed slot machine gaming in five-star hotels. This was followed by provisions in 1996 for machines and table games on ships. However, in its implementation in 1997, only machines were allowed. In 2001, table and machine gaming was permitted for Casino Goa, a gaming facility located aboard the *M.V. Caravela* located offshore near the main city of Panji. The facility is owned by the Advani Pleasure Cruise Company as a joint venture with Casinos Austria. The ship has to pay an annual license fee, and players are charged high entrance fees as well, as a means of discouraging casual gamers.

In 2007, the government authorized the granting of an additional five licenses for gambling ships. They have also encouraged an increase in machine gaming in hotel facilities. The array of machines now includes automated games of blackjack, roulette, and dice games, as well as poker machines and traditional slots. Additionally there are active proposals for full-scale land-based casinos, which may compete with new casinos in Macau and Singapore.

To the south of India is Sri Lanka, an island country densely populated with 20 million people of diverse religions (Hindu, Buddhist, Muslim, and Christian) and ethic groups. The island was governed as the British Colony of Ceylon until 1948. Since independence the many divisions coupled with a Marxist movement have led to an ongoing civil war.

Casino gaming was first authorized in 1983. The size of casinos and number of casinos expanded year by year, until there were 26 in 1992. Almost all were located in the capital city of Colombo as well as beach resort areas. While they were designed to attract tourists, those goals were frustrated by the civil conflict. As a result of a serious outbreak in hostilities, all the casinos were closed by the government in 1992. For most of a decade they remained closed. However, in the quest to regain taxation revenues, openings were permitted in the first decade of the new century. By 2008, 10 casinos were in operation.

Also to the south and east of India is Bangladesh. This Muslim country has a constitutional prohibition on all gambling.

To the north of India is Nepal, a landlocked country of 8 million people most known for its pathways up Mt. Everest. Nepal's relatively new casino industry has undergone expansion from four to seven facilities in the early 21st century.

These years have also seen a palace massacre led by a disgruntled prince, and a Maoist rebellion that ended with the abolishment of the monarchy and the achievement of a democratic republic with elections in 2008.

A member of the royal family started casino gaming in Nepal in 1968 with a gaming room (the Nepal Casino) at the Oberoi Soaltee Hotel in Kathmandu. In 1992, three new casinos were opened, the Anna, the Everest, and the Royale. All four casinos came under the ownership of a Hong Kong–based company, Nepal Recreation, Ltd. From 2005 to 2008, three new casinos were created, the Tara, Rad, and the Shangri-la. Ownership shifted into the hands of American entrepreneur Richard Doyle Tuttle.

As a Buddhist country, the government prohibits gambling by local residents. Foreign patrons must be 21. Over 90 percent of these patrons come from India. Gaming is conducted in the English language with Indian rupees and American dollars. The Minister of Finance oversees the casino activity. There are flat fees charged to the casinos in addition to regular business taxes; there is little outside auditing of the gaming operations.

In 2004, the tiny Himalayan country of Sikkim passed a law authorizing casinos. Regulations for the games were issued in 2007. The rules allow casinos in five-star hotels that cater to foreign guests—the only people allowed to gamble. In 2008, the first casino opened, at the Hotel Royal Plaza in Syari. As tourism was already the major revenue source for the country, it is expected that casinos will make significant additions to the economy

Nearby Bhutan holds its national identity and Buddhist cultural heritage in such high regard that they severely restrict outside influences. On an index of "Gross Domestic Happiness," they rank near the top for the world. They want to keep it that way. They severely restrict visits by foreigners. They are the only country in the world to ban smoking. Gambling is illegal; however, authorized lotteries are not considered gambling. For several years—until 2007—the sale of certain India lottery tickets was allowed. No casino gambling has been allowed. Nor is there betting on their national sport—archery.

References

"Bhutan Gambling." World Gambling Review. www.worldgamblingreview.com /gambling/bhutan, accessed June 18, 2008.

Casino City's Global Gaming Almanac. 2006. Newtown, MA: Casino City, 36, 45, 51.

Kelly, Joseph, and A. Uppal. "India." In *International Casino Law,* 3rd ed. Edited by Anthony N. Cabot, William N. Thompson, Andrew Tottenham, and Carl Braunlich, 517. Reno: Institute for the Study of Gambling, University of Nevada, Reno.

Kelly, Uppal, Thompson. "Nepal. 1999. In *International Casino Law,* 3rd ed. Edited by Anthony N. Cabot, William N. Thompson, Andrew Tottenham, and Carl Braunlich, 527. Reno: Institute for the Study of Gambling, University of Nevada, Reno.

Sarikah Atreya. 2008. "Sikkim Set to Lure Tourists with Casino." Hindu Business Line, January 4. http://www.thehindu businessline.com/2008/01/05/stories/ 2008010552072100.htm, accessed June 18, 2008.

Thompson, Uppal, and Kelly. "Sri Lanka." In *International Casino Law,* 3rd ed. Edited by Anthony N. Cabot, William N. Thompson, Andrew Tottenham, and Carl Braunlich, 532. Reno: Institute for the Study of Gambling, University of Nevada, Reno.

JAPAN AND PACHINKO PARLORS

The Japanese are known in Las Vegas as "prized customers," "top-rated quality players," and "high rollers." Deservedly, they are given first-class treatment whenever they hit the Strip. Moreover, it is well recognized that Japanese manufacturers such as Konami, Sega, and Aruze supply some of the best gaming equipment for U.S. casinos. Japanese have even owned gambling halls in the United States. Although it is known that the Japanese people are very attached to gambling enterprise, there may be a false notion that the Japanese do not gamble very much at home. Nothing could be further from the truth. Per capita gaming in Japan far exceeds that in the United States (Tanioka 2000, 13).

Over the years, trade journals have given only the slightest attention to the games of Japan. International gaming charts indicate that the country has lotteries and pari-mutuel racing, but no casinos. Comments on what various countries are doing regarding gaming almost always leave Japan out. In the history of the now defunct *Gambling Times,* there was only a short article on motorboat racing in Japan and another one on amusement machines. The lead-

Japan has as many as 20,000 pachinko halls—this is one.

ing trade journal, *International Gaming and Wagering,* devoted only one short survey article to Japan gaming, in 1994. It would be helpful if the literature gave more attention to this gambling-intense country, perhaps elaborating on the 1994 piece.

Gambling, as we would call it, or entertainment with prizes, as the Japanese police would call it, is very big in Japan. Japan has nearly 130 million people, yet the total gambling revenue of Japan is more than equal the gross win of U.S. casinos, lotteries, and pari-mutuel racing venues.

Part of the illusion that Japan does not gamble comes from the fact that there are no casinos in Japan—that is, casinos in the U.S. sense of the word. But make no mistake about it, there are gambling halls in Japan—thousands of them. They offer players opportunities to win prizes by playing "skill" games on pachinko and pachi-slo machines. Even though

there are elements of skill in pachinko, luck is a major factor in the game (Tanioka 2000). Thirty million people play on the 4 million machines around the country. The machines produce wins equivalent to US$21 billion each year (Tanioka 2000, 9). In other words, the entertainment machines with prizes win more money than is won by all the casinos—commercial, Indian, and charity—of the United States.

Pari-mutuel wagering is permitted both on- and off-track for motorcycle, motorboat, bicycle, and horse racing. Japan is unique in being the only place where wagering is offered for bike, motorcycle, and boat races. Large stadium structures permanently line banks of rivers where the boat races take place. As there is "skill" in making wagers, the government denies that there is gambling involved in the enterprise. The race betting may not be "gambling," but make no mistake about it, it is big-time wagering. The Japan Derby

(Imperial Cup) horse race each fall (November) produces a handle exceeding the collective handle of the Triple Crown races in the United States.

Lotteries are in a growth phase. Until recent years, the games were passive weekly draws that were slow and did not permit the player much involvement in selection of numbers. Instant games have been played since the late 1980s, however, and in 1995 a numbers game in which the player selects the number was added. A national lottery run through the Mizuho Bank has been one of the world leaders in sales for a single lottery.

THE PACHINKO PARLORS OF JAPAN

Pachinko may be a funny sounding word. Actually it is derived from the sound—"pachin-pachin"—that is made by balls as they bounce down the face of the game board toward winning or losing positions. It may be a funny-sounding game, but it produces some serious wins.

Pachinko has its origins outside of Japan. Some suggest that the game comes from Europe, but most find its beginnings in the United States. The modern game of pachinko shares similarities with a game called Corinthian, which was played in Detroit in the early 1920s. The game was played with a board placed on an incline. Balls were shot up one side of the board and then fell downward onto circles of nails (arranged like Corinthian architecture) and bounced into winning slots or fell into a losing pool at the bottom. Players were given scores and awarded prizes for their play.

The game developed in two different directions. In the United States it evolved into the popular pinball games that were found in recreation halls across the land until computerized games replaced them in the 1960s. The Corinthian game moved to Japan, and in the 1930s parlors were developed offering play. The game board was placed upright into a vertical position to save space. Machines were also converted so that the balls could come out of the machine in increased volumes if winning placements were made.

Soon the machine was the most popular recreational game in Japan. In 1937, however, Japan commenced military action in China, and the nation assumed a wartime posture. The game was made illegal as plants making the games were converted into munitions factories. The government did not want individuals to waste time at play, and many of the players were drafted for military service.

After the war, the machines were made legal once again. The government now encouraged play, as the occupying armies used play as a means to distribute scarce goods to the public—cigarettes, soap, chocolate. Players "won" balls from the machine and then exchanged the balls for merchandise. No cash prizes were allowed (which is still the case). In ensuing decades the machines were refined. Shooting mechanisms enabled players to put over 100 balls per minute into play. Pachinko machines incorporated new games within the game. Slot machine–type reels were placed in the middle of the playing board. As balls went into winning areas, the reels spun, enabling greater prizes to be won if symbols could be lined up in winning combinations.

Machine operators have the opportunity to make payouts greater or smaller by moving the nails on the surface of the playing boards. Players find that when the nails are farther apart, the balls are more likely to fall into a winning position. Experienced players will look for such machines. Also, they will play on certain days when the weather may cause the nails to be loosened. Particular players may be consistent winners; however, even a very inexperienced player can achieve wins when a ball activates the slot-type reels and they end up in a jackpot position. Typically the machines pay out a maximum of balls worth $160 or more for a top jackpot.

A new variation of the game, called pachi-slo, has been introduced. The game is essentially like the reel slot machines found in casinos all over the world. After the reels are activated, however, they may be stopped individually by the player's pushing buttons. With a special skill the player is supposed to be able to line up symbols in winning patterns. The reels spin so fast, however, that almost all winners claim their prizes through luck. Although pachinko wins are conveyed in balls from the machine, pachi-slo machines use tokens for play, and tokens come out for winners.

With both types of machines, the balls and tokens are converted by a weighing machine into tickets that have winning amounts written upon them. The tickets are traded for prizes at a special booth within the parlor. Popular prizes include cigarettes, music tapes, and compact discs.

Well over 90 percent of the winning players, however, choose to trade tickets for small plastic plaques, which ostensibly have value in and of themselves. Usually they include small pieces of gold or silver. But no player wants the little bit of precious metal. Instead, they take the plaques to a designated money exchange booth that is usually very near the pachinko parlor. There they receive cash payments. The process of converting balls or tokens into tickets, then into prizes, and

finally into cash costs the player about 25 percent of the prize. That is, 100 balls for play will typically cost 400 yen (about $5). If a player wins back the 100 balls, the ticket will enable him to trade the win for a prize worth 400 yen retail. The plastic plaque may be traded at the money exchange for 300 yen cash. The parlor does not really care which way the player goes. After all, the retail merchandise costs the parlor only 300 yen. The exchange booth operators may take a portion of the win when they sell the plaque, as they are a separate business. Even so, the parlor owners sometimes have close ties to the exchange businesses.

About 80 percent of the machines in Japan are pachinkos and the rest pachi-slos. The parlors may also have rooms with other kinds of amusement machines that give prizes. Each machine earns revenue averaging more than $5,000 per year, substantially less than the slot machines of U.S. casinos. The machines cost only about $1,000 each, however, and halls choose to have an excess of machines so that experienced players as well as others can have the opportunity to select machines for play. The United States has about one slot machine per 400 residents, but Japan has one gaming machine per 30 residents. And that makes for a lot of gambling.

The reluctance of Japan to embrace casino-type gambling in part derives from a feeling that gambling enterprise is closely connected to bad influences—in Japan, that might mean the Yakuza, or organized crime. There is a fear that the Yakuza has ties to the pachinko industry.

Like the democracy of Pericles and the Golden Age of Athens, citizenship privileges in Japan are for the most part reserved for people of Japanese origin. Residents with Korean or Chinese family ties may be excluded from entrance to the major corporations of the land, and for some of the time after World War II, their children were not allowed into the universities. Those with entre-preneurial spirit had to "go it alone." These "foreign" (so considered even if native born) Japanese developed mom-and-pop retail businesses, and they also gravitated toward pachinko. At first, most parlors were small and independ-ently owned. Also, pachinko, although very popular, was considered somewhat unclean—perhaps like pool, pinball, and slot machines were in years past in the United States. The traditional Japan-ese did not want to associate with the business. Organized crime groups also moved into the industry, many with Korean ties. Today the police worry that some pachinko parlor funds are utilized to support drug activities and gun smug-gling. There is an ongoing fear that funds are skimmed and sent to North Korea where the Communist regime uses them to purchase nuclear materials.

These suspicions have led various members of the industry to band together to form an association with the goal of cleaning up the industry as well as the image of the industry. The group is hop-ing that the government will revise the prize structure of the games so that players can win cash prizes directly from the machines. The police are reluctant to do so, because, as one National Police director said during an interview in Tokyo on August 10, 1995, "We don't want gambling in Japan."

The editor thanks Kotaro Fugimoto and Ichiro Tanioka for assistance with research for this entry

References

Bybee, Shannon, and William N. Thompson. 1999. "Japan." In *International Casino Law,* 3rd ed. Edited by Anthony N. Cabot, William N. Thompson, Andrew Tottenham, and Carl Braunlich, 518–520. Reno: Institute for the Study of Gambling, University of Nevada, Reno.

Tanioka, Ichiro. 2000. *Pachinko and the Japanese Society.* Osaka, Japan: Institute of Amusement Industries, Osaka Univer-sity of Commerce.

Thompson, William N. 2006. "Gambling in Japan." In *Casino Industry in Asia Pacific*, edited by Cathy H. C. Hsu, 59–76. New York, London: Haworth Press.

KOREA

Casino gambling came to the Republic of Korea (South Korea) in the late 1960s as a result of intense lobbying of the government by businessman Rak Won Chun. His efforts led to the 1967 decree from President Park Chung-hee author-izing the licensing of casinos. Chun received the first license for his Paradise Company casino in Incheon, which opened in 1968. Chun soon won a license for a second casino in Seoul at the Walker Hill Hotel resort. This facility became the largest of the "first wave" of Korean casinos. Other casinos were developed in successive decades on the resort island of Cheju, where there are eight casinos, in Korea's second city, Busan (Pusan), and in mountain areas of Songni-San and Mt. Sorak National Parks. These 13 casinos, plus three new "Lucky 7" Corporation casinos (two in Seoul, one in Busan), operate with severe restrictions on who is allowed to play. Identification is checked at the door, and only non-Koreans are allowed to enter. (Korea does not apply the rule banning local nationals from play to its lottery or its racetrack wagering—there are three tracks and 27 off-track betting centers.)

The casinos cater to Japanese, Taiwanese, and Hong Kong patrons. They have also sought players from mainland China, but Chinese policies restricting international travel for gambling purposes have put a damper on this market. Originally there were no special gambling taxes imposed upon the casinos. In lieu of taxes, the government maintained ownership and control of all profits on the slot machines. This control was relinquished in 1993, and the casinos now pay a 10 percent tax on their gross gaming winnings.

The largest of the "first wave" casinos at the Walker Hill employs a staff of 860. The casino has 78 tables and 162 slot machines. It has attracted as many as 2,500 players a day and produces annual wins of US$200 million. On average, players lose about $500 per visit, a figure that is much higher than losses by players in American casinos. As all players are "foreigners," the government takes essentially a hands-off approach to regulation. They only monitor the entrance policies and the flow of money. The casinos set all policy for the operation of games, such as gaming limits and hours of play. Most of the casinos are open 24 hours a day.

Until the 21st century, Rak Won Chun's Paradise Company, which owned Walker Hill, the Busan and Incheon casinos, and a casino in Cheju, had essentially a monopoly hold on Korean casinos. His political power was unyielding. However, following his death in 2003, the forces of change moved into high gear. A plan put forth at the beginning of 2005 targeted two Paradise locations—Seoul and Busan. A casino was designated for the southern area of Seoul as a part of the Hanmoo Convention complex. The casino is by an indoor theme park called Lotte World. The casino is expected to attract many foreign visitors attending business conventions, as well as families (parents) on vacations. The Millennium Hotel, a Hilton property in the center of Seoul, was also selected as a casino site. The Lotte Hotel in Busan was chosen as the third casino site. All three casinos are owned by a government corporation designated as Seven Luck Casinos. The three new casinos operate on the model of Walker Hill and the traditional casinos. They are open only to non-Koreans.

The government takes a much more paternalistic approach to play at the one "second wave" casino—the casino at Kangwon Land, which is the most successful casino of Korea. From outward appearances it is just another big fancy casino in a large resort complex. The resort meets the standards of many upscale Las Vegas properties, and inside its gaming atmosphere is "Vegas" all the way—and more. The casino lets Koreans gamble, although they must reside outside of Kangwon Province (except for one day a month).

The philosophy behind Kangwon Land developed out of national legislation passed in December 1995 designed to bring economic development to a depressed area that formerly was a coal mining center. Officials of the Ministry of Culture and Tourism decided that a casino could be a catalyst for the development of tourist attractions such as golf courses and ski runs. But Kangwon Province was isolated, and it would be difficult to draw in foreign gamblers, especially since these players would first arrive in Seoul or Pusan. As a result, special permission was given to allow Koreans to play.

The national government insisted on being a major partner in the casino project. They own a 36 percent share in the casino, while the province and its local units own 15 percent. In 1999, shares equaling 49 percent equity in the company were sold to the public. A temporary casino opened in October. Funds from the casino were reinvested in the construction of the permanent casino resort, which opened in 2003.

The casino now welcomes 4,500 players a day. Each loses an average of $389 per visit, making the annual win of the casino in excess of $600 million. While the casino pays the same 10 percent tax on gaming wins as the other 16 casinos, they also pay an additional 10 percent development fee.

Almost all of the players are Koreans. Therefore, the government takes a protective view toward the players. Players register identities, showing addresses as they pass through metal detectors. There is a 5,000 won (US$4.50) entrance fee. Residents of Kangwon Province are banned from daily play (they are allowed to play on one Tuesday each month only—on that day 7,000 patrons enter the doors), and just about all the casino's players have made a treacherous drive of four to five hours from Seoul or Pusan over mostly two-lane twisting mountain roads. They willingly crowd into a facility that is open from 10 a.m. until 6 a.m. the next morning, except on Saturday evening when it remains open all night long.

The out-of-town guests are very lucky if they can find a room, as the new facility has only 700 hotel rooms, and the town does not have many other rooms. Many players sleep in their cars when the casino is closed. The casino does not have to advertise.

Here, unlike at Paradise Walker Hill, no alcohol is permitted in playing areas. The casino has a policy for dealing with problem gamblers. Kangwon Land may be the only casino in the world that has a gambling treatment center *inside* the casino. Players are observed to see if they have compulsive traits. Certain players are approached by casino officials. Each may be given a green, yellow, or red card. The green card is for a player who exhibits some warning sign. The player is told about problem gambling and urged to be careful. The yellow card is given to players with more serious evidence of problems, and they are urged to limit their gambling and to seek counseling, which is provided at the treatment center. Red cards go to those with the most serious traits, and they are urged to seek counseling and are banned from play at the casino for some period of time. Players also may exclude themselves from play, and there are procedures that allow family members to have someone banned from play.

The casino has 100 tables and 940 slot machines. The tables include roulette wheels, blackjack, baccarat and mini-baccarat games, a Big Wheel, and Sic Bo. There are not enough tables or machines, as the casino is full during most of its operating time. The lack of table space has been dealt with by a practice not found in Las Vegas or in the other Korean casinos. This is back betting. Although there are only seven gambling positions at a blackjack table, there may be as many as 21 players. Two players may stand behind the player seated at the table and place the maximum bet on that player's hand.

The Kangwon Land board has set the table minimums and maximums, but it is only the maximums that matter. Every play finds the maximum amount being wagered, the equivalent of 100,000 won (US$90) a play. In a VIP area the maximum limit is 10,000,000 won, or $9,000 per play. And that is the typical amount played each hand. To be admitted to the V.I.P. room, one needs to be designated a member and must put forth 30,000,000 won as a deposit in cash, the equivalent of $27,000.

There is no credit play. However, the players need not carry cash to the casino. They simply go to their bank for bank checks, which they can use to purchase chips. Simple enough. The casino has a full-service bank branch inside the facility.

Slot machine play is as frantic as the table play. The slots only accept a maximum play of five coins per play, ergo, five times US$0.45, or US$2.25. This is quite a contrast to the U.S.$90 table players throw on each bet. But the machine players have found a means of increasing action. If they wedge a paper match stick beside the button that indicates the maximum amount bet, and they wedge another match stick beside the button that says "play," the machine takes off and plays continuously without the player having to do anything but watch. Of course, they have to first insert large amounts of paper bills into the machine. The machine just keeps track of wins and losses with its credit meter. The poker machines, where this is not possible, are popular with $2.25 plays, as each time a player wins he can immediately make a double or nothing bet.

The casino attracts 63 percent of its visitors from the Seoul area and 35 percent from Pusan and other Korean areas outside of Kangwon Province, with less than 2 percent from foreign jurisdictions.

The 940 machines win up to $800 a day each, making machine revenue approximately 40 percent of the total gaming take.

The casino has instituted an interesting complimentary system. Points are given for amount of play. The points can be exchanged for hotel rooms, and at restaurants, spas and shops, and entertainment areas. The points can also be presented to merchants, motels, and restaurants in Kohan and nearby towns.

There are over 3,100 employees at the property with 1,000 of these in gaming positions; 60 percent are from the area, and many are former coal miners. The employees from "outside," mostly from Seoul or Pusan, live in casino dormitories.

The company gives preference to local providers of goods. Three quarters of the foods are purchased locally, and one half of construction activity is handled by Kangwon firms.

The complex, which was designed by the architects who designed the Las Vegas Mandalay Bay Casino Resort, offers more than gambling. There are nine restaurants, including a buffet and a "fitness" restaurant. An entertainment area features a show by Russian magicians, a

4-D Cinema with virtual rides, and a lateral elevator that moves across the bottom of a lake for a "20,000 Leagues Beneath the Sea" show. In 2004, a golf course opened, and in 2005, skiing began on slopes of a nearby mountain.

South Korea also has a modern lottery as well as three active horse racetracks—in Seoul, Busan, and on Cheju Island.

The Marxist totalitarian regime of North Korea (People's Republic of Korea) succumbed to the lure of casinos in 2001 and 2002, as they saw gambling as a way to attract foreign money to their cash-starved government. Two casinos, the Emperor and the Seaview were authorized for the Rajin Free Trade Zone at the Chinese border. North Koreans were not allowed to enter except as employees. The Chinese authorities were not amused when a local government official from China went to the casino and lost almost a half a million dollars (US) in funds he had embezzled. Pressure from the Chinese led to a closure of the casino. A third casino has appeared in the capital city Pyongyang, where it appeals to the fun-loving spirit of diplomats visiting North Korea's leaders.

References

Thompson, William N., Ichiro Tanioka, Kotaro Fujimoto, and H. E. Yang. 2005. "The Other Korean Casinos: On Jeju Island." *Gaming Law Review* 9, no. 3 (June): 215–219.

Thompson, William N., Ichiro Tanioka, and H. E. Yang. 2005 "Two Koreas: Walker Hill and Kangwon Land." *Gaming Law Review* 9, no. 2 (April): 144–152.

Whyte, Keith. 1999. "Korea." In *International Casino Law*, 3rd ed. Edited by A. Cabot, W. Thompson, A. Tottenham, and C. Braunlich, 521–522. Reno: Institute of Gambling Studies, University of Nevada, Reno.

Macau. *See* China (Including Hong Kong and Macau).

PHILIPPINES

The Philippines offers several forms of legalized gambling. There is an active lottery and horse racing at two tracks. The major gambling activity takes place in a score of casinos, most of which are smaller government-owned facilities scattered around the nation's vast array of islands. The government is considering a new complex of casino resorts, which would be built in Manila and would compete with venues in Macau and Singapore.

The Philippines were controlled by Spanish colonial rulers for more than 300 years until the turn of the 20th century, when the United States was victorious in the Spanish American War. Independence from American supervision and then from Japanese occupation during World War II was achieved in 1946. The new Philippine government made gambling illegal, but the activity persisted openly with cockfights, casino games, lottery and numbers games, and horse racing. After President Ferdinand Marcos declared martial law in 1972, he closed 28 casinos that were operating in Manila. In

1977, after reexamining national policy on gambling, he decreed that the government could issue concessions for casino gambling. He created the Philippine Amusement and Gaming Corporation (PAGCOR) to regulate all gambling in the country. The government then selected Stanley Ho of Macau to run a network of casinos. Critics of the Marcos regime charged that the president used the casinos to generate money for his own use.

The casinos were a target for closure when President Corazon Aquino seized power in 1986. Aquino had campaigned against the casinos. She closed the casinos, but only briefly. Financial shortfalls prompted the government to reconsider having casinos as vehicles for funding government programs. Aquino reconstituted PAGCOR by appointing a new board of directors and by placing ownership of all casinos in the hands of the government agency. Initially PAGCOR opened nine casinos: two in Manila, two in Cebu, and one each in Olongapo, Davao, Bacolod, Angeles, and Bagvio. While PAGCOR sought to target foreign players, most were local residents, albeit the majority of players were Chinese-Filipinos.

Although all casino profits went into government coffers, hotels in which the government casinos were located received rents as well as incentives. They were encouraged to promote the casinos, and if gaming revenues exceeded certain levels, they were allowed to share in the profits. Often they sponsored junket tours. The larger casinos are open 24 hours a day. Players must be at least 21 and well dressed. Local players either have to pay an entrance fee, or, at some of the smaller casinos, merely wave sums of "gambling" money in front of guards at the door.

In the 1990s, additional casinos were placed in Manila and Cebu as well as Tagaytay. With the closure of American military bases, a new law in 1992 authorized private investment and operation of gaming facilities in Special Economic Zones on former base lands. In 2007, 14 PAGCOR casinos and additional slot arcades employed 11,000 workers and produced revenues of almost US$800 million. The casinos were the largest source of government revenue, making up more than 10 percent of the national budget. In 2008, PAGCOR announced that another special zone on 222 acres of reclaimed land in Manila Bay would be open for private casino investment. The proposed US$15 billion complex attracted proposals from Japan's Aruze Corporation, the Genting Highlands Company of Malaysia, and Bloombery Investments of Australia, and local company SM Investments. The complex was designed to have four casinos and at least six hotels, with as many as 8,000 hotel rooms. PAGCOR announced that the project would make the Philippines "the new entertainment capital of Asia."

References

Doocey, P. 2008. "Massive Philippine Casino Project Attracts Investors." *International Gaming and Wagering Business* (May) 12.

Gushin, F., and W. Callnin. 1999. "Philippines." In *International Casino Law*, 3rd ed. Edited by A. Cabot, W. Thompson, A. Tottenham, and C. Braunlich, 528–531. Reno: Institute of Gambling Studies, University of Nevada, Reno.

"Philippines." 1991. In *International Casino Law*, 1st ed. Edited by A. Cabot, W. Thompson, and A. Tottenham, 389–391. Institute for the Study of Gambling, University of Nevada, Reno.

Rutherford, James. 2008. "God and Man in Manilla." *International Gaming and Wagering Business* (June): 23, 26–29.

SOUTHEAST ASIA

Political instability and turmoil coupled with third world economic conditions have held back significant commercial development of gambling institutions in Southeast Asia. Moreover, religious influences (Hindu. Buddhist, and Muslim) as well as Marxist ethics dampen enthusiasm for government-endorsed gambling. This has certainly been the case with Vietnam, Cambodia, Laos, Myanmar (Burma), Thailand, Indonesia, and Singapore resisting legalization of casinos until very recently. Thailand and Indonesia remain holdouts. On the other hand, nearby Macau (now in China) and Malaysia have given permission for casino play for several generations, while Hong Kong (also incorporated into China) has permitted a variety of other forms of gambling. (Hong Kong and Macau are treated under the China entry.)

That there has been a reluctance for governments of the region to embrace gambling belies the fact that the many nationalities of Southeast Asia have a fervent affinity for risk- and chance-taking involving all sorts of games. Their enthusiasm for making wagers is captured in descriptions of Chinese gambling fever found in the essay "The World's Best Gamblers" in the appendix. One report suggests that "Southeast Asians have always been gambling mad. And they have always found a way to satisfy the urge, legally or not" (United Press International).

Today, while there are legal forms of gambling, the facilities of the region are not strong. Most face restrictions on who can play, and their appeal for customers is focused upon people who must cross national boundaries. A major target for many casinos consists of players drawn from Thailand and China, where casino gambling is banned (with the exception of Macau). Additionally, many facilities operate completely outside the law as they survive in a "tolerated gray" status through bribery or unofficial ties to ruling elements.

Thailand

While there are no legal casinos in Thailand, the kingdom formerly known as Siam does have its share of gambling. In 1917, a lottery was instituted to help the country support the Allied military effort during World War I. In the early 1930s, lotteries were used to help the work of the Red Cross and later to assist local governments with their finances. A modern government-run lottery dates to 1974. It offers passive games, with two drawings a month. Approximately 14 million tickets are sold for each drawing, with profits going to support college scholarships as well as welfare programs. Horse race betting is allowed at on-track events, with the largest facility being the Royal Turf Club in Bangkok.

The banning of all other forms of gambling has not been effective. A report suggests that "Just about anything can be used as an opportunity to bet. There are transboundary lotteries, football matches, illegal bookmaking at the races, boxing matches, cockfights and fish fights," as well as hundreds of illegal "gambling dens" ("Casinos and Gambling in Thailand"). Gambling consumes over 20 percent of the economy, with over one-third of Thailand's 62 million people making underground wagers. Only about 15 percent of in-country Thai betting is with the legal lottery; over 35 percent is played in illegal casinos, 25 percent in underground lotteries, and 25 percent in illegal sports bets. Approximately $20 to $30 billion pass through illegal channels each year. Gambling is seen as a "major source" of support for a black economy, including "drug trafficking, tax evasion, illicit arms trade," as well as prostitution and "illegal logging." Thais also spend almost $3 billion a year at casinos in Cambodia, Laos, and Myanmar. For these reasons—including the recognition that many Thais are going outside the country to visit casinos—leading government officials, including the national police chief, have advocated the legalization of casinos. However, resistance to change remains.

Cambodia

In Cambodia, a 1996 law banned gambling within the country. However, the law provided for exceptions, and in 1999 guidelines were set forth for operating casinos that could only entertain patrons from other countries. Twenty-one casinos were licensed. All but one of these is located more than 100 kilometers from the capital of Phnom Penh.

Both legal and illegal casinos in Cambodia are poised to win patronage of players just across the border with Thailand. Eight casinos are in Poipet, one is in Koh Kong, four in Sihanoukville, and seven are in Bavet near the Vietnam border. Additional casinos welcome Laos players coming into Cambodia.

At one time, dozens of casinos had operated in the capital city of Phnom Penh, but they were ordered closed by Cambodian prime minister Hun Sen, who said they contributed to criminal activity, including kidnappings. The leader advocated casinos

located by national borders. One casino remains in the capital city. It is operated by a Malaysian who holds a license for 70 years, dating from the casino opening in 2005.

The only other legally recognized form of gambling in the country of 11 million residents is a national lottery that has been in operation since 1992. It offers three varieties of number games.

Laos

Laos also offers lottery games to its four million residents. These include traditional lotteries as well as sports lotteries. Games are also offered in one casino in the country. That facility is the Dansavanh Nam Ngum Resort, which is on a lakeshore about 60 kilometers from the capital city of Vientiane. The casino looks toward a nearby border with China for many of its patrons. In 2007, the Chinese government sought to forbid its citizens from traveling across its borders to participate in gambling in other countries. The Laos government indicated that they would cooperate with the Chinese enforcement of such a ban.

Vietnam

In Vietnam, the impacts of colonialism and war were felt most directly by the country's horse race operations. The reunified nation of 84 million offers horse and dog racing as well as lotteries and casino games. French colonial officials established a top-class racing facility—called Phu Tho—at the Saigon Racing Club in the city of Saigon in 1932. Racing continued through the World War II years and into the era of national division and war. Racing ceased in 1975 as the communist forces of North Vietnam overran the South. The track closed, but only for 14 years. In 1989, the old grandstands were modernized and the track was greatly improved. Since then, races have been held every Saturday and Sunday. The track is now managed by an overseas Vietnamese from Australia. The same person introduced dog racing to Saigon (now Ho Chi Minh City).

Originally the track featured thoroughbred horses in its races. However, in the latter days of the World War II occupation, Japanese forces took the racing stock to Japan. Smaller and slower local breeds replaced the thoroughbreds. In 2005, the better horses came back, as the operator imported new stock from Australia. The track is now vying to compete with leading international venues for top-class racing contests. Jockeys from Malaysia—larger in size than Vietnamese jockeys—have been imported to handle the much larger horses.

Vietnam lotteries have operated in the modern era as well. Government drawings produced earnings of close to US$300 million in 2004, with Pick 2, Pick 3, and Instant games.

The casinos of Vietnam operate under an exception to general laws banning all gaming. The casinos, unlike the lotteries and races (also allowed under exceptions), may not permit Vietnamese nationals to play. Two major casinos include the Do Son near HaiPhong, which is a joint venture between a local government agency and Macau's Stanley Ho, and the Lai Lai Hotel in Mong Cai, located in Quang Ninh Province near the borders with China. Most patrons of each casino are Chinese nationals. A smaller casino is in Ha Long City, also in Quang Ninh. Slot machines are also available for foreign hotel guests in leading hotels in Ho Chi Minh City and Hanoi. There is no specific gaming regulatory agency, and licenses are granted by the government through the Ministry of Culture.

Myanmar

The dictatorial government of Myanmar (formerly Burma) has made all gambling illegal. However, hotels with foreign investments have been permitted to allow foreign guests to make wagers in specially licensed gaming rooms. Five licensed rooms target mainly Thai players. These include the luxurious Andaman Club Casino in a town just across the border from Ranong in southwest Thailand. The Paradise Resort opposite the Thai town of Chaeng Saen is partially owned by the brother of a leading Thai political figure. The Riverside Club near Thailand's town of Mae Sot is owned by a former opium warlord, and the Wa, a Myanmar tribe with an army of 20,000, run casinos in Mong La, near the border with China's Yunnan Province.

While these casinos are major ones, they represent only the tip of an iceberg that includes hundreds of illegal gaming halls. The Mong Ma region alone boasts more than 50 casinos, while the Katchin State has at least eleven. A major listing of casinos reports that "the number of casinos . . . is unknown, however most are located near the border with China in Shan and Katchin States" ("Asian and Oceania Casinos"). A United Press International report states that "In the northeast of Myanmar, in the town of Muse on the border with China, the mainstreet is lined with bustling little casinos. . . . Outside, local police and officers of the ruling military regime amble by unperturbed" (2002).

A 2001 report by Sein Win of the Mizzima News Group indicates that the "illegal gambling business has mushroomed throughout Burma and some observers say that the ruling regime, by neglecting the growing illegal business and in fact encouraging it in some ways, is diverting the people's interest from politics to day-to-day struggle." Win continues, "Gambling and betting are at present widely spread both in major cities, such as Rangoon, Mandalay, Prome and the border areas." He suggests that authorities receive kickback and bribes, as they contently watch gambling eat away at the "spirit of the people."

Indonesia

By law no gambling is permitted in Indonesia. Unlike other Southeast Asia venues, this law of 1974 has no exceptions. While political leaders at both the national and local levels have tried to maneuver the question of legalization onto the political agenda, they have not even approached success in gaining that first step toward change. Two major forces are in place that make efforts toward legalization of casinos or other forms of gambling unlikely. First, the nation of 240 million people (fourth largest in the world) is predominantly Muslim (88 percent), followed by Christian (10 percent) and Buddhist (2 percent). The political leaders follow mandates put forth by the Indonesian Ulema Council, made up of Muslim clerics. The second force against gambling legalization is that of the politically active owners and operators of a network of tolerated—but very illegal—gambling halls. One university report identified 13 major illicit gambling casinos in the capital city of Jakarta. Their owners and their patrons are mostly ethnic Chinese who are non-Muslim. Their political influence is enhanced by a considerable level of bribery offered to public officials, particularly those with police authority.

Casino and other gaming development in the main concentrated bloc of Southeast Asian countries on the Indo-China peninsula has been retarded by third world–style governance in which operations are not allowed by law but rather are tolerated with secret handshakes and less-than-fully-transparent oversight. On the other hand, governmental and economic stability has given rise to some of the most significant casino and racing enterprises in two nearby venues, Malaysia and Singapore.

Malaysia

Both countries were British colonies from the 19th century until independence in 1963. The two regions were joined as one country from 1963 until 1965, when Singapore separated as its own sovereign entity. Malaysia has a population of 18 million, of whom 50 percent are Malay and Muslim, 33 percent Chinese, and 10 percent of India origins. The ruling authorities are clearly Muslim. Singapore's population is just under 5 million, with over 50 percent of the population of Chinese origin, 14 percent Malay, and 9 percent Indian. A majority are Buddhist, but the government is essentially secular.

The dominant figure in Malaysian gambling has been Lim Goh Tong. He was born in China in 1918, but after World War II migrated to Malaysia, where he began his business career. In 1965, he put together a project to develop a resort in the Genting Highlands, an area with an elevation of 6,000 feet located about 40 miles from the nation's capital city of Kuala Lampur. His first task was to build a road to the resort site. It was completed in 1969, and he applied for a concession to have a casino at the location. He won the license, which included monopoly rights on gambling in Malaysia. Lim Goh Tong's company Genting Highlands Berhad also operated the country's lottery.

The casino opened in 1970 at the original hotel. At first there were only 30 tables and a few hundred slot machines. However, a fantastic level of growth soon found the casino recognized as the largest gaming facility in the world. A gaming room of over 200,000 square feet came to have 330 table games and 3,400 slot machines. The casino remained the largest in the world until a Native American facility—Foxwoods—opened in Connecticut and added slot machines in the mid-1990s. (Ironically, Genting Highlands lost its number one ranking because Lim Goh Tong's company loaned the Mashantucket tribe several hundred million dollars to build the Foxwoods casino.) Genting was able to develop its hotel complex into one with 6,118 rooms (2008). *Casino City Times* designates the hotel as the largest one in the world—a designation that depends in large part on definition. When is a complex of building considered one single hotel? The combined room totals of the several towers at Sheldon Adelson's Venetian Resort Hotel Casino in Las Vegas exceed 7,000—by some definitions. A more satisfying honor came to the Genting Highlands Hotel in 2007 when it was designated the "World's Leading Casino Resort" at the 14th annual Gala Ceremony of the World Travel Awards. In addition to the casino, the Genting Highlands complex has a convention center, multiple restaurants, a major theme park, golf courses, and facilities for tennis, boating, and other sports.

The highly successful property has very strict rules about who may enter the gaming areas. The only Malaysian citizens allowed in must be non-Muslim. For the most part, this makes the local clientele Chinese. Muslims from other countries are welcome. All players must satisfy a strict dress code, and locals must pay a door fee.

In 2006, Lim Goh Tong's company successfully bid $3.5 billion to win the license for one of two new Singapore Casinos to be located on Sentosa Island. Lim died in 2007 at the age of 90. His son Lim Kok Thay now heads the Genting organization.

The Malaysia lottery is run by a related organization, Berjaya Sports Toto Berhad. It operates 681 sales outlets and offers six games, including a sports lotto with drawings three times a week. Proceeds support cultural programs and youth sports.

Malaysia has had horse racing events from the British colonial times until today. Betting activity is permitted only at the three tracks during live races. The three racing courses are the Selangor Turf Club, Perak Turf Club, and the Penang Turf Club.

Singapore

In Singapore, the Singapore Turf Club was established during the colonial era. It now offers races on Saturdays and Sundays. Singapore authorized lottery games in 1968, with sales of tickets by Singapore Pools, a government-owned private corporation set up by the Ministry of Finance. Proceeds from the first five years of play were used to finance a national sports stadium. Proceeds from its many games still go to support sports organizations.

Singapore resisted the pull toward casino gaming until they witnessed the dramatic growth in not only of the Genting Highlands facility but also of Macau gaming in the early 21st century. In 2005, Singapore prime minister Lee Hsien Loong announced the government's plan to supervise the development of two "integrated resorts" that would include casinos. One would be on the Marina Bay and the other on Sentosa

Island. In addition to casinos, each would have hotels, shopping malls, and entertainment complexes. The projects were expected to attract massive international investments in addition to creating jobs—together they were expected to bring 35,000 jobs. Projections indicated that by 2015, the two resort complexes would attract 17 million visitors to Singapore.

Under pressure from the opposition party and also from Christian and Muslim religious groups, the prime minister incorporated severe entrance requirements for local residents who wished to gamble at the casinos. They would have to pay a door charge of $100 for each visit. Alternatively they could pay $2,000 for an annual pass. On the other hand, as an incentive for investors, the gaming tax was set at a low 15 percent—a rate guaranteed for at least 15 years of operations.

The Marina Bay license was won in open bidding by the Las Vegas Sands. Sheldon Adelson's company pledged to invest US$3.85 billion in constructing a facility that would include 2,500 hotel rooms. The total cost of the project was projected to be more than $5 billion and was expected to create 10,000 jobs. The Sands Singapore is set to open in 2009.

A conglomerate of the Genting Highlands Company, Star Cruises, and Universal Studios won the license to build the Sentosa resort. They bid $3.38 billion in construction costs, and their plan called for six hotels, with a combined room total of 1,800. The project was projected to create 30,000 jobs. It is set to open in 2010.

References

Adel Awwad. 2007. "Laos Casinos." Ezine Articles, February 22, www.ezinearticles.com/?Laos-Casinos&id=464743, accessed June 10, 2008.

"Asian and Oceania Casinos." 2008. www.gamingfloor.com/AsianCasinos.html.

Bromberg, Paul D. 2006. "Gaming in Southeast Asia." In *Casino Industry in Asia Pacific*, edited by Cathy H. C. Hsu, 78–90. New York: Haworth Press.

"Casinos and Gambling in Thailand." 2008. www.amazing-thailand.com/Casinos.html.

Hartley, Terry. 2005. "New Era of Horse Racing Dawns in VN." *Vietnam News*, February 28, www.vietnamnews.vnagency.com.vn/showarticle.php?num=025P0280205.

Sein Win. 2001 "Mizzima: Illegal Gambling Widespread in Burma." *Mizzima News*, April 24, www.burmalibrary.org/reg.burma/archives/200104/msg00093.html.

"Singapore Pools—Corporate Profile." 2009. http://www.singaporepools.com.sg/en/corporate/corp_profile.html, accessed August 26, 2009.

United Press International. 2002. "A Flush of Asian Casinos." www.hawaiireporter.com/story.aspx?23423678-fdfd-464f-bf48-69b939cc70f.

Australia Pacific Region (Including New Zealand, Tinian, and Guam)

Formal legally recognized gambling has witnessed substantial expansion in recent years in the South Pacific region. Nevertheless, the gambling phenomenon has been around for quite a long time in the area.

From the time of the first European colony in Australia in 1788, gambling has been part of the fabric of life on the world's largest island. New settlers from the British Isles, many of whom were convicts sentenced with deportation orders, had participated in games in the Mother Country. Their new society demonstrated a great tolerance for the activity, and it grew throughout the 19th century. However, it was also an activity subject to the reform movements led by church groups at the end of the century and the beginning of the 20th century. The groups succeeded in having the Gaming and Betting Act of 1906 ban all gaming except that involving horse racing. However, gambling could not be kept down for long. Within a decade, lotteries returned, as did charity games. As a practical matter, many other games persisted even in the face of the law. Legalized machine gaming (slot machines are called "pokies" in Australia) appeared in the largest state (New South Wales) in the 1950s, and the first legal casino was established in Tasmania in the 1970s.

Australia now offers a multitude of forms of legalized gambling. Collectively, gaming revenues produced revenues (equated with player losses) in excess of A$12 billion—or US$9 billion—in 2006. This amounted to wagering losses of about US$650 for each adult. (Australia's overall population is 20 million, with an adult population of 14 million.) These losses are almost twice those for average Americans in legal gambling facilities in the United States.

The most active forms of Australian gambling include wagering at 13 casinos (revenues of US$2.5 billion in 2006) in addition to play at the 200,000 "pokies" found in clubs, hotels, and arcades in every state and territory of Australia. The country has more slot machines per person than any other country in the world. Their revenues are more than double those of the casinos. Australia also has hundreds of horse racetracks, which attract more than 2 million players each year. The largest race—the Melbourne Cup—is truly a national event, the likes of the American Super Bowl. The racing industry gives employment—either full time or part time—to 250,000 people. Betting takes place both on track and at off-track outlets called Totalisator Agency Boards (or TABs). The government-owned

Lasseters Casino in Alice Springs, Australia.

TABs are also sites for betting on sports games. In addition, Australia offers both government-run and private lotteries as well as authorized bingo games—called housie-housie. Special lotteries financed the world famous opera house in Sydney.

Australian gambling is regulated by six state governments (New South Wales, Queensland, South Australia, Tasmania, Victoria, and Western Australia) as well as the Northern Territory and Capital Territory governments. A major gaming breakthrough came in 1956 when New South Wales (which includes the city of Sydney) passed legislation allowing social clubs to have slot machines. Clubs were immediately formed for every conceivable social reason or cause. The stage was set for a rapid spread of gambling activity into every neighborhood of the state, and, subsequently, the entire country as well.

A casino first appeared at the Wrest Point Hotel in Hobart, Tasmania, in 1973. The voters of the state had given their approval for the casino. A motivation for legalization was to collect taxation revenues to help the government offset the financial devastation caused by major forest fires in Tasmania. In 1982, the state licensed Australia's second casino, located in the town of Launceston.

Several other venues opened casinos in the 1980s. Queensland authorized a casino at Gold Coast in 1985, followed by one in Townsville in 1986, then one in Brisbane in 1995, and another at Cairnes in 1996. The Burswood Casino in Perth in the state of Western Australia opened in 1985. South Australia's only casino opened in the renovated Adelaide Railway Station building in 1985. The establishment of the casino effectively saved the historic building from destruction. (The goal of historic preservation via casino has also been witnessed at railway stations in Regina, Saskatchewan; Baden-Baden, Germany; and at the Kurhaus in Scheveningen, Netherlands.) The Adelaide facility was originally owned by the state government, but in recent years it was purchased by the Sky City Casino group of New Zealand. Now all 13 casinos of Australia are in private hands. The Northern Territory has two casinos. A temporary casino opened in Darwin on the north coast in 1979, with a permanent facility following in 1983. It is now owned by Sky City. Lasseters Casino opened in 1982 in the remote outback settlement of Alice Springs.

The two largest states opened casinos in the 1990s. They are the largest casinos in the country. The Crown began operations in Melbourne, Victoria State, in 1994, while the Star City Casino in Sydney opened in 1995. Each of these casinos, and most of the others in Australia, are stand-alone casinos which do not operate attached hotels. They are monopolies for their cities and regions. Taxes on gambling revenues at the casinos range from a low of 10 percent to a high of 25 percent.

In the last decade of the 20th century, the casino at Alice Springs, Lasseters, began to offer gaming over the Internet. Their model of operation led several states to permit Internet gaming. However, the national government took exception to these operations. At first the central government proclaimed a five-year moratorium on new Internet gaming sites. Then in 2001, the government made Internet wagers—with the exception of bets on horse races—illegal for all Australian players. The sites in Australia

could keep up operations, but they could only offer services to foreign players.

While New Zealand experienced some of the colonial history and immigration patterns of Australia, the residents (called Kiwis) have not embraced gambling with the same fervor as their Australian cousins 1,200 miles to the northwest. Horse racing, however, left its mark on the Kiwis quite earlier in their colonial times. The first races were held in 1835, within a year of the first British settlements. The activity only grew, as there are now more than 50 tracks, with 780 race meetings per year. The popularity of racing has been tied to the pari-mutuel betting format. In 1879, a New Zealand resident was credited with developing the world's first fully mechanical totalizator. An electrical version of the totalizator was installed at an Auckland racetrack in 1913. Lotteries were also introduced quite early in colonial times, as was sports betting. Yacht races drew great attention from the betting public.

As in Australia, early 20th-century reformers in New Zealand secured laws banning all wagering activities, with the exception of betting on the horses. However, the government could not resist the urge to get into the act, and in 1929 a government-run lottery was instituted. In 1931, a government-run TAB took horse race betting off track. TABs now also accept betting on 26 different sports. Pokies—slot machines—can now be found throughout New Zealand in pubs, taverns, and clubs.

Casinos were not authorized until the 1990s. The Casino Control Act was passed in 1990, and it initially provided for two casinos, one on each of the nation's two major islands. The first casino opened in Christchurch in 1994, with 36 table games and 430 slot machines. In 1996, the second and much larger Sky City Casino opened in Auckland. It had 110 tables, and 1,100 machines. The two casinos were given local monopolies for two years. Following this monopoly time, licenses were granted for one new casino in Dunedin, another in Hamilton, and two in the city of Queensland. Currently there are no plans to expand the number of casinos beyond six.

The South Pacific Islands beyond Australia and New Zealand are generally void of gambling activity. One exception is Tinian. Since World War II, Tinian has been a territory under United States jurisdiction. It now is part of the Commonwealth of the Northern Marianas. During the war, the island gained distinction as having the American airfields from which two planes—the Enola Gay and Boxcar—launched their atomic bomb runs to Japan. Tinian has but 2,200 local residents, although there is still a military base on the island. In 1987, the residents first voted on the question of having casinos. They said "no," but proponents persisted and a vote in 1989 was positive.

The casino proposal promised many economic benefits, starting with construction activity and followed by job creation. A temporary casino opened in 1995, and a permanent facility followed in 1998. The Tinian Dynasty Casino Resort now offers a casino with 50,000 square feet of gaming space, golf courses, swimming, beaches, and a 410-room hotel. The property is owned by a Hong Kong business group. Unfortunately the economic benefits promised remain unfilled. All construction employees came from off the island, as did all materials for construction. Casino employees as well as hotel employees are also for the most part outsiders. They spend little of their wages on the island, as the property furnishes them with lodging. The high cost of power makes profits doubtful, as does difficulty of flying in Asian players for action at a single casino. The Tinian government does get 13 percent of casino winnings as its taxation share. This amount has not been as large as hoped. The entire experience demonstrates that planning is necessary if casinos are to become effective for economic life in a region.

Guam, like Tinian a U.S. Commonwealth, has also studied the proposition of having casinos. In 2004 and 2007 voters said "no" both to small casinos in island hotels and to slot machines at a dog racetrack. The track opened in 1977 and offers an active race card, as well as kennels with 700 racing dogs. In 2008, the voters considered having a single large casino located at the site of the dog track, but voted down the idea 59 percent to 41 percent.

References

Breen, Helen, and Nerilee Hing. 2006. "Casino History, Development, and Legislation in Australia." In *Casino Industry in Asia Pacific*, Cathy H. C. Hsu, ed., 3–35. New York: Haworth Press.

Cabot, Anthony, William N. Thompson, Andrew Tottenham, and Carl Braunlich. 1999. "Australia and South Pacific." In *International Casino Law,* 3rd ed. Edited by Anthony N. Cabot, William N. Thompson, Andrew Tottenham, and Carl Braunlich, 541–603. Reno: Institute for the Study of Gambling, University of Nevada, Reno.

Casino City's Global Gaming Almanac. 2006. Newtown, MA: Casino City, 443–464.

"Guam Election Results." 2008. www.kuam .com/decision2008/results/general.

Canada

The Canadian nation and its 10 provinces and several territories offer a full range of gambling opportunities. Lottery games operated by the government are available in all 10 provinces, Yukon Territory, and the North West Territories. (The new Nunavut Territory has not yet developed its own lottery.) Charity gaming is also pervasive. Pari-mutuel horse-race betting (on-track, inter-track, and/or off-track) is permitted in all jurisdictions, and casino-style gaming is legal in most of the provinces and in the Yukon Territory. All the provinces except British Columbia have video gaming available in noncasino settings, such as bars and hotels.

Lotteries and casino gaming in Canada developed during the last three decades of the 20th century. Initially, casinos were either temporary or small organizations operated on behalf of charities or provincial exhibitions. (One exception was the seasonal casino called Diamond Tooth Gerties in Dawson City, Yukon Territory, which opened in 1970.) The nature of casino gaming changed when Manitoba decided to consolidate many small facilities and open a permanent gaming hall in the ballroom facilities of the Fort Garry Hotel in Winnipeg in 1990. Quasi-commercial casinos along the order of ones found in the United States soon were authorized in Quebec. Casino du Montreal opened in 1993, and Casino de Charlevoix opened in 1994. Ontario licensed a casino for Windsor in 1994 and one at Niagara Falls in 1997. Casinos were opened in Saskatchewan and Nova Scotia in 1995.

In all cases, the provincial governments "own" the casinos; management and operations in some cases are by regular government employees (Quebec, Saskatchewan, Manitoba) or by private companies (Ontario, Nova Scotia).

The Native Americans (First Nations) of Canada also are involved in numerous gaming facilities either as owners, operators, or beneficiaries of operations. The initial First Nation casino of considerable size is the Casino Rama facility at Orillia, Ontario.

By the middle of the 1990s, the country saw significant revenue from gambling enterprises. Canadian provinces gained C\$4.7 billion in revenue from gambling in 1995, and charities and other operators won perhaps another billion dollars. The development of Canadian gambling into a multi-billion-dollar business, albeit mostly controlled and operated by provincial governments, resulted from a major change in the national law in 1969. Prior to that time, most gambling had been prohibited. The laws of Canada have incorporated the common law of England, and without positive legislation passed by the national parliament, the laws of England at the time of national confederation in 1867 remain in force. Hence, the first Canadian law on gambling is traced back to a 1338 statute passed because Edward III feared that his military was wasting valuable training time on idle pursuits, including "dice games." All games and contests except those involving archery were banned. The prohibition on the use of dice in gambling remained in place in

The "dice" wheel in a British Columbia casino. Dice were not allowed in Canada until 1999.

Canada until 1999. It was eliminated in England and Scotland in 1968.

The English laws, which generally eliminated most gaming, were enacted into the statutory law of Canada when the first Criminal Code was passed into law in 1892. For over a hundred years, that statutory prohibition on gambling has been nibbled away at by lawmakers. First, in 1900, the code was amended to permit charitable raffles with small prizes. In 1910, on-track horse race betting was allowed. It has remained legal with the exception of a short period of time during World War I. A 1922 statute specifically banned the use of dice in games, a ban that had never been lifted out of the common law. Limits on various other games of chance were relaxed in 1925 for fund-raising events at agriculture fairs.

In the 1950s, a parliamentary committee studied the gambling restrictions and in 1956 issued a report recommending major changes. These did not come to pass for over a decade, however. Financial commitments rising out of the Montreal World's Fair of 1967 provided legislative support for opening up more gaming opportunities for government budget makers. The fact that south of the border, the states of New Hampshire, New York, and New Jersey had legalized lotteries added to the support. This support led to the passage of the Criminal Code Amendments of 1969, providing the major breakthrough for the development of a modern gambling industry in Canada. The 1969 law added a new Section 190 to the Criminal Code that allowed the provincial governments and the national government to conduct and manage a "lottery scheme." Several provinces could also operate lotteries together. Provinces were permitted to license charitable, religious, or exhibition and fair organizations and bona fide social clubs to conduct lottery schemes.

The concept of "lottery schemes" soon came to encompass many casino-type games. Section 190 repeated the ban on the use of dice in games, however, and also prohibited betting on single sports events. Gaming machines were allowed only if the provincial governments operated the machines.

Lotteries were quickly established in the provinces and territories. The national government also utilized a lottery to underwrite the costs of the Montreal Olympics in 1976. A national sports lottery funded the winter Olympic Games at Calgary in 1984. In 1985, the provinces repelled the competition of the federal games. In exchange for $100 million from the provincial games (enough money to finish the debt from the 1984 games), the federal government agreed to a law relinquishing its authority to operate any gambling at all. Present policy on gambling is held entirely in the hands of provincial governments and in territorial legislatures. One area of gambling has developed without benefit of a clear jurisdictional framework, however. Policy on affairs regarding the First Nations is still held in the hands of federal authorities, yet gambling policy is not a matter for federal law. To date, the bands of First Nations have had to resolve their rights to have gambling operations on an ad hoc basis in consultation with provincial authorities.

References

Cabot, Anthony N., William N. Thompson, Andrew Tottenham, and Carl Braunlich, eds. 1999. *International Casino Law.* 3rd ed. Reno: Institute for the Study of Gambling, University of Nevada, Reno, 169–216.

Campbell, Colin, ed. 1994. *Gambling in Canada: The Bottomline.* Burnaby, BC: Simon Fraser University, v–x.

Campbell, Colin, and John Lowman. 1989. "Gambling in Canada: Golden Goose or Trojan Horse?" In *Gambling in Canada: Golden Goose or Trojan Horse?* edited by Colin Campbell and John Lowman, xvii–xxxvii. Burnaby, BC: Simon Fraser University.

ALBERTA

Alberta can lay claim to having the first legalized casino gaming in Canada, albeit in a temporary form. In 1967 the provincial government initiated several laws that seemed to open the door to casino games even though they were forbidden by the Penal Code. In the summer, during the Edmonton Exhibition, the Silver Slipper Saloon was opened as part of the two-week celebration. The general manager of the exhibition later indicated that he had taken payoffs from the carnival company that ran the games, that is, the Silver Slipper. Amendments to the national code in 1969 helped regulate Alberta gaming. The attorney general took control over licensing charitable bingo games and raffles. In 1975, the attorney general's office opened the door to casinos once again as it first approved a casino for a charity event supporting a summer camp. A license was then given for a casino at the Calgary Stampede. A flood of applications for casino events overwhelmed the attorney general, and he quickly created a special Gaming Control Section to regulate the gaming. Rules were set into place over the next two years. In 1981, a new Alberta gaming commission took over all licensing powers.

As gaming developed, Alberta adopted the model used in British Columbia. Charities could have casino events, but they had to be held in permanent facilities that were operated by private parties. In the 1990s, the number of such facilities grew to more than a dozen: five in Edmonton; four in Calgary, and others spread around the province. Until 1998, they were not allowed to have slot machine gaming, and the charities paid a fixed fee for having an event. When the government installed machines, a new revenue division based upon play was instituted. As the government owns the machines, it keeps a majority of machine revenues. Although no serious consideration is being given to the creation of large commercial casinos, proposals have been made for wide-open, large-scale casino gaming on the First Nations reserve lands. A new policy in 2001 set up a procedure for opening First Nation casinos. The first casino to be approved under the new rules was one for the Enoch reserve south of Edmonton.

Alberta has many other types of gambling, including all forms of pari-mutuel operations, both on-track and off-track. Three tracks also operate slot machines. Raffles and pull tabs are sold by charities. The most prevalent form of gambling, however, is found in the bars and taverns of the province. By 1999, more than 6,000 video lottery terminals were operating in 1,200 locations, producing about 70 percent of the gaming revenue in the province. In that year, the popular machines (which provide an average gaming revenue of $50,000 a year) accounted for a per capita gaming participation of about $1,300 per adult, the largest in Canada and North America, with the exception of Nevada. Studies have also revealed that Albertans have the highest rate of problem gambling in Canada. There were efforts to ban the terminals, with local elections called in 1998 in most of the cities. Only in a few smaller cities did the voters choose to ban the machines. Machines, however, were modified to provide for slower action and also to indicate in monetary terms the value of credits for future play. A moratorium on expansion of gaming halted all effort to increase the number of machines in use for several years in the early 21st century.

Coauthored by Garry Smith

References

Cabot, Anthony N., William N. Thompson, Andrew Tottenham, and Carl Braunlich, eds. 1999. *International Casino Law.* 3rd ed. Reno: Institute for the Study of Gambling, University of Nevada, Reno, 172–173.

McCall, William W. 1989. "Operational Review of Gaming in Alberta 1978 to 1987." In *Gambling in Canada: Golden Goose or Trojan Horse?* edited by Colin Campbell and John Lowman, 77–92. Burnaby, BC: Simon Fraser University.

Smith, Garry, Bonnie Williams, and Robert Pitter. 1989. "How Alberta Amateur Sports Groups Prosper through Legalized Gambling." In *Gambling in Canada: Golden Goose or Trojan Horse?* edited by Colin Campbell and John Lowman, 323–333. Burnaby, BC: Simon Fraser University.

THE ATLANTIC LOTTERY CORPORATION

The four Maritime or Atlantic provinces of Canada—New Brunswick, Newfoundland, Nova Scotia, and Prince Edward Island—joined together in 1976 to form the Atlantic Lottery Corporation. The purpose of the corporation is to serve as a central marketing agency for lottery products in the provinces. An eight-member board of directors is composed of two representatives from each province. The corporation offers several different games, including traditional weekly and daily draws, instant games, and lotto games.

Reference

Cabot, Anthony N., William N. Thompson, Andrew Tottenham, and Carl Braunlich, eds. 1999. *International Casino Law.* 3rd ed. Reno: Institute for the Study of Gambling, University of Nevada, Reno, 170.

BRITISH COLUMBIA

Several forms of legalized gambling are permitted in British Columbia, Canada's westernmost province. Pari-mutuel racing was permitted before the Canadian Penal Code was amended in 1969. Now telephone betting, off-track betting, and inter-track betting are allowed for gamblers, as well as slot machine play at tracks. At first, lottery games were conducted under the auspices of the Western Canadian Lottery Corporation, but British Columbia established its own independent lottery organization in 1985. The province has permitted bingo and raffle events for charities since 1970. Charities have been permitted to conduct casino events since 1978.

The casino events grew quickly in number and volume of activity. In 1984, the province issued regulations that governed private companies that were offering casino management services for charities. The charities were restricted in their ability to pay staff to operate games, but the management companies could do so. Gradually a pattern emerged of having casino events all located in permanent casino facilities that were privately owned. There are now 17 such casino buildings. Most are in Vancouver and its suburbs. The private companies are permitted to keep 40 percent of the gaming profits from a casino event of two days; the charity gets 50 percent and the government 10 percent. There are also registration fees. The private company pays the salaries of dealers and other gaming personnel, as well as all other costs. The charity only provides personnel to watch the cage. The provincial law permits up to 22 of these casino facilities; however, in 2008 there were only 19 in operation. One of these is a riverboat casino in New Westminster.

Initially, the casinos could offer only table games, with roulette and blackjack being the most popular. In 1997, the casinos were allowed to install up to 300 slot machines each under a new revenue-sharing formula. Technically, the government owns all the slot machines. Community bingo halls are also authorized under local option in 1999. There are 30 of these facilities and they offer bingo games as well as machine games. Three of the racetracks—in Vancouver, Surrey, and Sidney—also offer machine gaming. Until national law removed the ban on dice games in 1999, the casinos had unique devices for sic bow, a three-dice game. The player rolled three balls into a roulette wheel that had thirty-six slots representing face-sides of the dice. Craps and sic bow are now played with actual dice.

For many years, there have been top-level discussions regarding the introduction of destination-type casino resorts. In the early 1990s, a plan to have the Mirage resorts of Las Vegas build a casino on the Vancouver waterfront was advanced by the premier of the province. Another plan called for a casino at the Whistler Ski Resort north of Vancouver. When the plans were announced publicly, there was a major outcry from several citizen groups. The premier backed down, but the idea of having major casinos is still a matter of conversation in the province.

In 1997, the government, without sites being designated, again initiated a local option plan for 21 larger casinos. The First Nations of the province, however, were supposed to be given 13 sites on their reserves. In the process of jockeying with persons wishing to control sites, the premier was forced to resign in 1999 when he was exposed for having taken favors from some of the applicants for site licenses. The development of large commercial casinos is on hold indefinitely.

Coauthored by Garry Smith

Reference

Cabot, Anthony N., William N. Thompson, Andrew Totttenham, and Carl Braunlich, eds. 1999. *International Casino Law.* 3rd ed. Reno: Institute for the Study of Gambling, University of Nevada, Reno, 174–179.

MANITOBA

Manitoba quickly jumped into the gambling business after the Penal Code was amended in 1969. The Manitoba Centennial Lottery Act was passed in January 1970. In 1971, the province included large jackpot sweepstakes games among their product mix, and the tickets were sold locally as well as in other provinces. Soon the other provinces adjusted to meet the competition, and Manitoba decided it was better to work in tandem with other jurisdictions as it helped form the Western Canadian Lottery Corporation in 1974. Manitoba maintained a provincial lottery organization, however, that sold tickets to benefit charities and also licensed the selling of pull-tab tickets (called Nevada tickets) and the conducting of bingo events to benefit the charities. Casino events were also licensed, but soon the government found that they generated a wide range of control problems. There were three violent incidents concerning casino suppliers in the early 1980s. Accordingly, the Manitoba Lottery Foundation was created in 1984 in order to centralize all the charity casinos into one operating organization. For most of the year the casino activity was conducted out of the Convention Centre in Winnipeg; in the summer, casinos were operated on the road by the government. Only table games were permitted, although the casinos had a slot machine with two dice faces on the reels—it was used to simulate craps games.

The government brought all the charities together and formed umbrella organizations that would distribute the profits to many good causes in the community. Among the recipients of the lottery and casino revenues was the municipally owned Winnipeg Blue Bombers football team.

The casino at the Convention Centre was closed in 1988, as the government decided to open a year-round casino. The Crystal Casino in Winnipeg was created as the first permanent government-owned casino in the Western Hemisphere. The Manitoba Lottery Foundation leased the seventh floor of the historic Fort Garry Hotel, a landmark railroad hotel built in 1913. The casino opened in 1990. In 1993, the foundation built two new gaming centers that served to replace the bingo halls that they had been operating. The McPhillips Street Station and the Club Regent offered bingo and also video gaming. Later the casinos added table games, and on May 22, 1997, when the government closed its Crystal Casino, the two facilities absorbed all casino operations.

The government gaming agency also played a role in the establishment of First Nations gaming. In 1999, the First Nations Casino Project Selection Committee was established, and the next year it made recommendations for five new casinos. The first opened in 2002 at the Opaskwayak Cree Reserve. A second was operated by the Aseneskak band, while others have not yet opened.

Additionally, the province authorizes all forms of pari-mutuel wagering both on and off track.

Coauthored by Garry Smith

References

Cabot, Anthony N., William N. Thompson, Andrew Tottenham, and Carl Braunlich, eds. 1999. *International Casino Law.* 3rd ed. Reno: Institute for the Study of Gambling, University of Nevada, Reno, 180–185.

Manness, Garth. 1989. "Views from the Regulators: Manitoba Situation." In *Gambling in Canada: Golden Goose or Trojan Horse?* edited by Colin Campbell and John Lowman, 69–76. Burnaby, BC: Simon Fraser University.

NEW BRUNSWICK

New Brunswick offers several forms of gambling, including charitable bingo and raffles, horse racing, and simulcast betting. A lottery was begun in 1976 by provincial authorities; it later merged with the Atlantic Lottery Corporation. In 1989, New Brunswick became the first province in Canada to authorize video lottery terminals in convenience stores and well as in bars and restaurants. Concerns about compulsive gambling as a result of the placement of the machines led to a referendum vote to have them removed in 2001. However, the voters by a margin of 53 percent to 47 percent decided that they would stay. In 2006, there were 650 locations that offered gambling, with a total of 2,600 machines. In 2009, the province approved the licensing of a casino in Moncton.

References

Casino City's Global Gaming Almanac. 2006. Newtown, MA: Casino City, 259–260.

Hyson, Stewart. 2003. "New Brunswick's VLT Gambling Policy." Paper presented to the Canadian Political Science Association, May 30, Halifax, Nova Scotia.

NEWFOUNDLAND AND LABRADOR

Newfoundland and Labrador offer horse race betting, both on-track and by simulcast. They also have a lottery and offer video lottery terminals in conjunction with the Atlantic Lottery Corporation. There are 568 video lottery terminal locations, with a total of 2,597 machines. With a population just over 500,000 (about 400,000 adults) this means there is one machine per 155 adults, the largest per capita number in Canada.

Reference

Casino City's Global Gaming Almanac. 2006. Newtown, MA: Casino City, 260.

NOVA SCOTIA

The idea to introduce casino gaming in Nova Scotia in order to stimulate tourism first surfaced in the early 1970s, when a study of the gaming experience in the United States and Europe was commissioned. It took another 20 years before the issue of casino gaming emerged again. Other forms of commercial gaming have been big business in Nova Scotia for a long time. Lotteries, bingo, betting on horse tracks, and, more recently, video lottery terminals (VLTs) registered a total wager of approximately $500 million in 1993.

It is somewhat ironic that the momentum for casino gaming started at a time when public sentiment was divided, if not outright hostile, toward gaming. In fact, sparks literally flew in the wake of the government's decision to remove VLTs from non–age-controlled premises such as convenience stores, laundromats, and bowling alleys in February 1993. Store owners were justifiably incensed about the unexpected loss of revenue, whereas the vocal opponents of VLTs argued that this step was necessary to keep minors away from gaming. The government was somewhat caught in the middle, and it responded with a review of the gaming laws. A subsequent report struck a cautious note with a recommendation not to expand gaming in Nova Scotia until the residents had a chance to express their views on this matter. In the meantime, the Nova Scotia Lotteries Commission conducted an independent study on gaming with specific reference to VLTs, casinos, and bingo. After carefully weighing the pros and cons of casino gaming and taking into account a survey that found that 59 percent of the respondents were not in favor of introducing casino gaming to Nova Scotia, the study group made an interesting recommendation. Two casino pilot projects should be granted—one in the Halifax-Dartmouth metro area and the other one in Cape Breton—for a one-year trial period in order to monitor and assess the impact of casino gaming and its acceptance by the residents.

The interest in operating casinos was enormous: The study group received no less than 13 proposals to do so, and among them were fairly detailed project descriptions from Hilton and Grand Casinos. The Hilton proposal suggested building a casino in a Halifax landmark hotel, the 1928 Hotel Nova Scotian, which was being operated by Hilton Hotels after a complete renovation in 1988. This proposal was endorsed by the Halifax Board of Trade.

Grand Casinos suggested a large hotel–casino–resort complex in the Ragged Lake Industrial Park Area outside Halifax. It was no surprise that this proposal was supported by the Halifax Industrial Commission. What was surprising was the fanfare and promotion surrounding these two proposals, particularly the one from Grand Casinos, since it must be remembered that the introduction of casinos was not even on the drawing board.

All of this and the report itself became history with a change in government. But the casino issue did not fade into oblivion. After only four months in office, the new government resurrected the thorny issue of gaming in Nova Scotia and empowered the House Committee on Community Services to conduct hearings all over the province on the issues of whether casino gaming should be introduced and whether VLTs should be brought back to convenience stores. In its report, the committee recommended (1) that casino gaming should not be introduced in Nova Scotia or, more specifically, that it should not yet be introduced because too little was known about the socioeconomic impact of gaming, and (2) that in view of the potential harmful effect on Nova Scotia's reputation as a nature-oriented and peaceful tourist destination, VLTs should be in age-controlled premises only.

To everyone's surprise, the government did not follow the committee's line of thinking. In a complete turnaround, it was announced that casino gaming would be introduced, and the sooner the better because of its beneficial impact for the province. This meant a fast-tracking period for casino gaming. The reasons for this move could be found in the dire state of provincial coffers: Nova Scotia has one of the highest ratios of public debt per capita in Canada, and it suffers from persistent double-digit unemployment. Casino gaming as a very labor-intensive business was simply seen as an opportunity that could not and should not be missed.

After the announcement that casino gaming would be coming to Nova Scotia, the government appointed a Casino Project Committee to draft a request for proposals (RFP) for bidders and to select and recommend a proponent to the government for the license to operate the two casinos. One was to be in the Halifax Theater in Sydney. The RFP was designed in a record time of four weeks. Its most important aspects and requirements were as follows:

- The two casinos would be publicly owned and operated.
- A gaming commission would be established to regulate and monitor gaming.
- A gaming corporation would be established to operate and manage the two casinos. The day-to-day operations of both casinos would be conducted by a private company on behalf of the gaming corporation; this agent would be determined through the bidding process.
- The tax on gaming revenue (win tax) was set at 20 percent; in addition, 70 percent of the net income of the Halifax casino would go to public coffers; the remaining 30 percent would go to the private company. The Sydney casino would be a charitable casino operation, and the casino operator would receive a management fee plus a negotiated percentage of the net income.
- Two interim casinos had to be in operation within 60 days of acceptance of a proposal.

At the time of the announcement of the short list, the names of the six initial bidders were officially disclosed. They were ITT Sheraton Canada, Casinos Austria, Harrah's, Aztar, Grand Casinos, and Crystal Casinos. With the exception of Harrah's, all casino companies had entered into partnerships with local interests in order to enhance their chances. The first three bidders made the short list, and ITT Sheraton Canada eventually got the nod. Since the proposals of other bidders were not made public, one can only speculate about the reasons why it was ITT Sheraton Canada. Most likely, ITT's guarantee of a payment of C$100 million for the first four years, which ended on July 31, 1999, may have tilted the balance in its favor. These payments ensured that total provincial revenue from gaming would not be less than C$25 million in each of the first four years. In return, ITT received the license to be the sole casino operator in Nova Scotia for 20 years, after which time the casino assets along with the customer database would become property of the province for a symbolic amount of $1.

In order to enhance its chances of becoming the operator of the two casinos, ITT Sheraton Canada had formed a partnership with a Halifax-based company, Purdy's Wharf Development Ltd., on a 90 percent to 10 percent basis. This partnership would operate the casinos under the name Sheraton Casinos Nova Scotia (SCNS). SCNS became part of Park Place Entertainment Inc. (PPE) in 1999 when PPE acquired the gaming assets of Starwood Enterprises which, in turn, had acquired ITT in 1997; subsequently, SCNS changed its name to Casino Nova Scotia.

Nova Scotia is one of the four Atlantic provinces of Canada. The province has an area of 21,425 square miles and a population of 935,000 (1998). The two casino cities—Halifax, the capital of the province, and Sydney—have populations of 350,000 and 85,000 in the respective metro areas.

In a province with high unemployment and a suffocating debt load, any new business investment that creates jobs is a welcome option. Casino gaming is such an option, and the government was wise to pick this option. Casino gaming not only creates jobs just as other business investments do, but it creates many jobs and many secure jobs. In fact, casino gaming is perhaps the most labor intensive of all entertainment industries. In addition to the direct employment effect there is the indirect employment effect through the casinos' purchases of goods and services. Furthermore, there is a direct and indirect employment effect during the construction period of the casinos. Altogether, this creates an employment effect of substantial proportions.

Next in line is the tourism imperative. Tourism is a very important industry for Nova Scotia, and the government and casino proponents eagerly emphasized the enhancement of tourism through casinos. A note of caution is in order, however. Nova Scotia is known for its beautiful nature and tranquility, and that will remain the premier reason for tourists to come and see such attractions as Peggy's Cove and the Cabot Trail. It would appear very unlikely that "gaming tourists" can be attracted in the sense of tourists who did not have Nova Scotia on their map previously and excluding visitors from the other three Atlantic provinces. Nevertheless, there can be no doubt that casino gaming will represent an additional incentive for tourists. This well-to-do category of gaming patrons is a premier target group for casinos in general and for the two Nova Scotia casinos in particular. Take, for instance, cruise passengers. The number of cruise ships coming to Halifax has risen considerably in recent years, and this increase has been fueled mainly by the New Atlantic Frontier consortium of 16 East Coast ports. Cruise passengers will come to the casino, and they come in droves since the Halifax casino is only a leisurely 20 minute walk from the cruise terminal at Pier 21.

Finally, there is the monopoly aspect for the operator, which is perhaps the most powerful incentive and a lifeline for sustained profit performance in a sparsely populated province. The 20-year contract with the government provided SCNS/Casino Nova Scotia with the franchise to be the sole casino operator in Nova Scotia. In 2005, a new clause was added to the contract that would give the operator the option to have the contract extended for another 10 years until 2025 upon expiry in 2015. In fact, the monopoly extends to all of Atlantic Canada until 2010, when a new casino will begin operations in Moncton, New Brunswick. This means a monopoly in a territory the size of France, with a population of 2.4 million people. It should also be noted that the Halifax and Cape Breton gaming markets can be viewed as separate markets, since they do not intersect at the 100 mile range. Consequently, the likelihood of cannibalism is very low.

After the announcement that casino gaming would come to Nova Scotia, some bands of the Mi'kmaq Indians indicated plans to establish casinos on Native land. Consequently, the government started negotiations with the Indian bands in order to preserve the monopoly status of the two casinos. In 1995, an agreement was reached with the Eskasoni Band Council in Cape Breton regarding gaming activity on the reserve and profit sharing from the proceeds of the Sydney casino. Specifically, under the terms of the agreement, the band would regulate and monitor gaming activity on the reserve, which would include VLTs and charitable gaming but not a casino. Furthermore, 50 percent of the profits of the Sydney casino would be earmarked to go to the entire Mi'kmaq community in Nova Scotia.

Casino gaming operates under the auspices of the Nova Scotia Liquor and Gaming Authority and the Nova Scotia Gaming Corporation. The authority is in charge of the regulation and control of all legalized gaming in the province. The corporation, in turn, conducts and manages all legalized forms of gaming in the province. For casino gaming, the corporation entered into an initial contractual arrangement with Sheraton Casinos Nova Scotia to operate the two casinos as the sole appointed agent on behalf of the corporation for a period of 20 years. The arrangements have now been transferred to a partnership organization of the Great Canadian Gaming Corporation and East Port Properties.

Games of chance permitted to be played in Nova Scotia casinos are roulette, baccarat, minibaccarat, blackjack, slot machines, keno, video poker, video keno, video blackjack, pai gow, pai gow poker, big six, craps, and poker and its variations. For slot machines, the payout must not be less than 86 percent.

In accordance with the strict liquor regulations in Nova Scotia, the Gaming Control Act does not permit the provision of complimentary alcoholic beverages in casinos. From day one, Sheraton Casinos Nova Scotia made numerous attempts to have this rule changed. These efforts were successful to the extent that the operator will be able to provide free alcoholic beverages to high-end players in the designated area (Crown Club area) of the Halifax Casino Nova Scotia. In addition, high-end players from outside of the province will be able to receive credit on demand in this casino.

Halifax Casino Nova Scotia has a gaming floor space of 34,900 square feet with 40 table games and more than 600 slot machines. Casino Nova Scotia in Sydney has 10 table games and 338 slot machines on 15,200 square feet of gaming floor space. In 2008, gross gaming revenues for the casino in Nova Scotia have been in the range of C$85 million, with the Halifax Casino accounting for C$65 million, and the Sydney casino for C$20 million.

Coauthored with Christian Marfels

Reference

Marfels, Christian. 1999. "Nova Scotia." In *International Casino Law*, 3rd ed. Edited by Anthony N. Cabot, William N. Thompson, Andrew Tottenham, and Carl Braunlich, 186–191. Reno: Institute for the Study of Gambling, University of Nevada, Reno.

ONTARIO

Ontario is the most populated province of Canada, with nearly 13 million people. It also produces the largest share of gaming revenues of any province. The four commercial casinos and seven charity gaming operations in the province generate a majority of all the casino revenues in Canada, more than 3.6 billion a year. The leading racetracks of Canada are also located in Ontario. Nearly 65 percent of the racing handle in Canada is wagered in Ontario. The Woodbine track in Toronto hosted North America's premium racing card, the Breeders' Cup, in 1997. The tracks also have the most successful gaming machine operations in Canada. Moreover, Ontario also has the most profitable lottery operation in Canada.

Ontario is clearly a leader in gaming volume today, but the province trailed others in initiating gaming operations. Until the 1970s, horse race betting was a monopoly gaming operation in the province. The lottery did not start until 1975, and lotto games were not in place until five years later. Instant tickets were not sold until 1982. The Ontario Lottery Corporation was responsible for overseeing charity gaming; however, until the mid-1990s charities could only sell raffle tickets and break-open tickets (similar to pull tabs) and conduct bingo games.

The Ontario Lottery Corporation may have hesitated a bit, but in the 1990s it went into high gear. In 1993, it made a decision to develop major casinos. To "test

Caesars Casino in Windsor, Ontario, Canada—government owned and privately operated.

the waters" it authorized a pilot project for Windsor. Windsor was chosen for an obvious reason that provincial leaders made no attempt to conceal: they boasted that the Windsor casino would market its gaming products to residents of the United States, more specifically, to residents of the Detroit metropolitan area. Only a one-mile wide waterway—the Detroit River—separated Windsor from Detroit, and there were two border crossing stations—a bridge and a tunnel. It was projected that 80 percent of the casino's revenues would come from the United States. The Ontario Lottery Corporation secured a remodeled museum and art gallery building for a temporary casino. The government owned the casino, but it contracted with a consortium consisting of Caesars, Hilton, and Circus Circus companies to run the casino. The casino opened in 1994, with greater-than-anticipated success. Seventy table games and 1,700 slot machines collected more revenue per square foot than had ever been collected in a casino anywhere. Continuous crowds led the province to purchase a riverboat (the *Northern Belle*) and open it as a second Windsor casino. No longer was Windsor a pilot project. In 1998, a permanent facility was opened in a 1.2-million-square-foot facility on the riverfront. It is now called Caesars Windsor. The facility includes all the amenities of a Las Vegas casino—a hotel of 400 rooms, showrooms, multiple restaurants, and, of course, a gaming area of 100,000 square feet, with 3,000 slot machines and 130 table games. The two temporary casinos closed. A later renovation added a 5,000-seat theater and a 10,000-square-foot convention floor.

Success is measured in many ways. One thing the success of Windsor's casinos generated was a massive concern in the Detroit area over revenues leaving not only the city but also the country.

Detroit retaliated by voting in 1995 to approve a nonbinding resolution supporting casinos. Then, in 1996, the voters of the state of Michigan made it binding as they voted for a new state law permitting three casinos for the city of Detroit. The first one opened in 1999.

While things were happening in southwestern Ontario, the Ontario Lottery Corporation decided that more casinos should be located elsewhere. In 1996, temporary casinos were opened in Niagara Falls and also in Orillia (on the Rama First Nation reserve). The provincially-owned Niagara Falls casino was managed by the Navagante Group—led by several former casino executives from Las Vegas. Soon the revenues at the Niagara Falls facility came to surpass those in Windsor. In 1998, the corporation entered into an agreement with Hyatt Hotels for the construction of a permanent casino facility, with a 350-room hotel, convention center, arts center, and cinema complex, along with show rooms, restaurants, and a 100,000-square-foot casino. It now exists as a second casino for Niagara Falls, as the temporary casino was allowed to remain open.

A new project was also slated for the Casino Rama in Orillia. As would be expected, this gaming hall has exceeded expectations. It is only one hour north of the Toronto metropolitan area. Casino Rama is owned by a Chippewa band of First Nations peoples; however, it shares some of its gaming revenues with other Ontario bands.

The four commercial casinos give 20 percent of their revenues directly to the Ontario provincial treasury. In the case of Casino Rama, the revenues are placed into a fund to benefit all the First Nations' peoples of the province. The operators also take a 5 percent share of the gaming win. From the remaining 75 percent of the gaming revenues, all expenses are deducted. Most of the residual net profits go to the province, with small shares given to the local communities hosting the casinos.

The Ontario Lottery Corporation also permitted charity casinos in the early 1990s. The casino nights featured table gaming only. These had to be "roving" casinos because no more than one night of gaming could be in one location per month. The roving games were operated by management companies, and many problems surfaced. For instance, with all the moving, equipment broke down frequently. Also there could be no permanent security systems installed to ensure that all gaming was honest and that all funds went where they were supposed to go. So in 1997, the government announced that it would create 44 charity gaming sites in the province. How funds would be distributed was not clearly addressed, although most of the funds would go to the Ontario Lottery Corporation. (This presented a legal challenge, as the charity gaming laws require that most of the net revenues must go to the charity.) The casinos would each be allowed 40 tables and 150 machines. Most of the communities selected for the casino sites expressed displeasure with the idea, as citizens propelled round after round of protest at the government. In 1998, the province backed down and decreed that there would only be four "pilot" charity casinos, to be located in Thunder Bay, Sault Ste. Marie, Point Edward (adjacent to Sarnia), and Brantford. These cities were the only ones that had voted in favor of having charity casinos. Sault Ste. Marie and Point Edward were especially desirable sites as they bordered Michigan cities. One of these cities, Sault St. Marie, Michigan, boasted a very large Native American casino (the Kewadin Chippewa casino) that had been drawing most of its revenue from Canadians. Only Brantford did not have direct highway access to the United States and to potential American customers. Additional charity casinos were permitted for First Nations' reserve lands. One is in operation near Port Erie. The four pilot casinos were allotted 450 gaming machines and 80 tables for players. All are now in operation and drawing good business from players. After they opened, three additional charity casinos were opened in Kenora, Quananoque, and Port Perry—the latter two being operated by First Nation bands.

The Ontario Lottery Corporation was also dissuaded from another plan owing to the protests of the citizens. The government announced that it would authorize 20,000 video machines for bars, taverns, and racetracks in the province. In 1998, the corporation abandoned the overall plan but instead finalized plans to place up to 20,000 machines in 18 provincial racetracks, with as many as 2,000 at a single track. The operation of machine gaming began in 1999, with 800 machines being installed at Windsor Raceway. Other tracks now have machines.

Coauthored by Garry Smith.

References

Alfieri, Donald. 1994. "The Ontario Casino Project: A Case Study." In *Gambling in Canada: The Bottomline,* edited by Colin Campbell, 85–92. Burnaby, BC: Simon Fraser University.

Cabot, Anthony N., William N. Thompson, Andrew Tottenham, and Carl Braunlich, eds. 1999. *International Casino Law.* 3rd ed. Reno: Institute for the Study of Gambling, University of Nevada, Reno, 192–204.

Casino City's Global Gaming Almanac. 2006. Newtown, MA: Casino City, 262–266.

Prowse, Peter. 1994. "An Operator's View." In *Gambling in Canada: The Bottomline,* edited by Colin Campbell, 105–110. Burnaby, BC: Simon Fraser University.

PRINCE EDWARD ISLAND

Prince Edward Island is the smallest of the Canadian provinces with only 140,000 people. The province has a lottery, which is run in conjunction with the Atlantic Lottery Corporation. There are also 91 sites that offer 406 video lottery terminals for play. The Charlottetown racetrack also has 225 video lottery terminals. It did not allow Sunday play on the machines until 2008.

References

Casino City's Global Gaming Almanac. 2006. Newtown, MA: Casino City, 266.

"Gambling Revenues Declining for Prince Edward Island." 2007. CBC News, April 13, www.cbc.ca/canada/prince-edward-island/story/2007/04/13.

QUEBEC

Public officials in Quebec in a sense "jumped the gun" when a lottery was introduced in Montreal in 1968 as a device to generate revenue for the municipal government. Judicial officials in Quebec took exception to the gaming operation, as they held it to be in violation of the Canadian Penal Code of 1892. Action did not stop for long. After the Penal Code was amended, the Quebec government created Loto Quebec in 1969, and the next year Quebec became the first province in Canada to operate a lottery. A separate agency licensed a wide range of games for charities and also to support agricultural fairs: bingo games, raffles, and limited-time casino events. The agency also regulated pari-mutuel horse race wagering.

As the lottery grew along with private charity-oriented gaming, the province initiated studies of casino gaming. The studies persisted from 1978 into the early 1990s. Part of the motivation guiding a conclusion that tourist-oriented casinos should be authorized was the revelation that illegal gambling and particularly illegal slot machines were quite prevalent in Quebec. In 1993, the province opened Casino de Montreal, housed in the former French Pavilion built for the Montreal World Expo of 1967. The casino has a 90,000-square-foot gaming floor, the largest in Canada until a permanent casino was built in Windsor, Ontario. The province also authorized government-owned casinos for Charlevoix, 60 miles north of the city of Quebec, and for Hull, across the Ottawa River from the national capital city.

The three casinos welcome 10 million visitors a year, 20 percent of whom are tourists. Most of the revenue (67 percent) is derived from slot machine gaming; tables generate another 31 percent, and keno games 2 percent. The casinos have a combined 200 table games and approximately 6,000 slot machines. The casinos do not offer credit to players; however, they do have automated teller machines. Casino de Montreal actually has a branch of a major bank located on its premises. The province has also allowed slot machines to be placed at four racetrack locations in Montreal, Three Rivers, Quebec City, and Aylmer.

The mid-1990s also brought another new policy to the province. Video lottery terminals are now permitted in restaurants, bars, and taverns. The province has placed over 15,000 machines in 4,400 locations.

A major gaming development in Quebec—as well as all of Canada—occurred in 1996 when the Kahnawake First Nations Reserve, located near Montreal and governed by the Mohawk Council of Kahnawake, initiated Internet gaming services from their territory. While the council has recognized that Canada very clearly outlaws Internet gaming, they assert that they are sovereign and outside the boundaries of those legal edicts. About 250 online gaming licenses have been granted by the council at a fee of $10,000 per year. The online operators also make a $15,000 deposit, which covers costs of regulation and control.

References

Cabot, Anthony N., William N. Thompson, Andrew Tottenham, and Carl Braunlich, eds. 1999. *International Casino Law.* 3rd ed. Reno: Institute for the Study of Gambling, University of Nevada, Reno, 205–207.

Casino City's Global Gaming Almanac. 2006. Newtown, MA: Casino City, 255, 266–268.

SASKATCHEWAN

Like other provinces in Canada, Saskatchewan's gaming began with horse racing, followed by lotteries, and then, in the 1990s, casinos. Gambling activity in Saskatchewan is under the control of The Saskatchewan Gaming Corporation (SGC), which was established in 1994. The corporation consists of seven persons appointed by the lieutenant governor of the province. Three of the persons are nominated by the Federation of Saskatchewan Indian Nations.

On January 26, 1996, Saskatchewan opened its first permanent casino—Casino Regina. The casino facility is located within the historic Union Station railroad building in downtown Regina. The casino provides 25,000 square feet of gaming and entertainment space, with 500 slot machines and 41 table games, a poker room, restaurant, lounge area, and bar. Two additional commercial casinos are located in Moose Jaw and Saskatoon.

The province added three casinos on lands of First Nations peoples later in 1996. The Gold Eagle Casino opened in North Battleford. It has 8,800 square feet for gaming, with 159 machines and 14 tables. The Northern Lights Casino opened in Prince Albert in an 8,000-square-foot facility that includes 229 machines and 15 tables. The Painted Hand Casino is in Yorktown at a 1,500-square-foot facility with 108 slots and 16 tables. The three First Nations casinos are operated by the Saskatchewan Indian

Gaming Authority under an agreement with the provincial government.

Casino Regina has generated many positive economic benefits for the province. A report prepared by the Saskatchewan Tourism Authority and released in January 1997 (the most recent statistics available) found the impact of the casino has been equivalent to the hosting of two Grey Cup Canadian professional football championship games. The report suggested that annually the casino attracted 101,000 nonlocal visitors who came to Regina specifically to gamble at the casino. Non-Saskatchewan visitors spent an average of three nights in Regina, similar to visitors to Las Vegas.

When the casino was planned, an agreement was negotiated with the province's charity casinos to allow them to have slot machines. The Regina charity casino had been operating at the Exposition Park. It was first known as Buffalo Buck's and later as the Silver Sage. It agreed to have machines and give 37 percent of the revenue from the machines to Casino Regina and the Saskatchewan Gaming Corporation. In 1997, the Regina charity casino agreed to close its doors in exchange for a share of the profits of Casino Regina. Also, when Casino Regina originally opened its doors, the SGC had made an agreement with Holland Casinos, a Netherlands government corporation, for that entity to train the staff and oversee the opening of operations. Holland Casinos received part of the casino revenues as well as a fixed fee for its services.

References

Saskatchewan Tourism Authority [STA]. 1996. *Report on Casino Gambling.* Regina: STA.

Thera, Leanne, K. Maher-Wolbaum, D. Innes, and W. N. Thompson. 1999. "Saskatchewan." In *International Casino Law,* 3rd ed. Edited by Anthony N. Cabot, William N. Thompson, Andrew Tottenham, and Carl Braunlich, 208–215. Reno: Institute for the Study of Gambling, University of Nevada, Reno.

WESTERN CANADIAN LOTTERY CORPORATION

The Western Canadian Lottery Corporation (WCLC) was formed in 1974 by an agreement among the governments of British Columbia, Alberta, Saskatchewan, and Manitoba. The Yukon and Northwest territories joined the WCLC as associate members, and the products of the corporation are sold in the territories. The products include instant tickets, weekly draws, and lotto games. In 1976, the WCLC governments entered into an agreement with Ontario to run nationwide lotto games. The Inter-Provincial Lottery Corporation is now an organization encompassing all provinces and territories. Sales of the WCLC are recorded by each province, and revenues are distributed accordingly. The profits are distributed within the jurisdictions in a manner designated by the individual province or territory. In 1985, British Columbia withdrew from the WCLC, and it now conducts its own lottery games.

References

Cabot, Anthony N., William N. Thompson, Andrew Tottenham, and Carl Braunlich, eds. 1999. *International Casino Law.* 3rd ed. Reno: Institute for the Study of Gambling, University of Nevada, Reno, 154–157.

La Fleur, Terri. 1992. "Charting the Growth of Video Lottery." *International Gaming and Wagering Business* (August-September): 1, 62, 64–65.

YUKON TERRITORY

The first Canadian casino was not in a province, but instead in the Yukon Territory. Its operation received little notice. The casino is a special exception for this remote northern location and has not spawned attempts to duplicate it elsewhere. Still, the casino operates under the guidelines of the 1969 Criminal Code amendments.

The Yukon Territory had considerable gambling activity during the Klondike gold rush days of the Gay Nineties. Gaming halls offered a wide range of gambling opportunities along Dawson City streets. After the gold fever subsided, Canada annexed the territory in 1898 and began enforcing the Criminal Code. Gaming activity declined.

Under the 1969 amendments, the territory granted a special gaming license to the Klondike Visitor's Association, a division of the Yukon territorial government. The license permits casino gaming from mid-spring through the summer months at a location known as Diamond Tooth Gerties (Diamond Tooth was the name of a renowned Klondike personality). The 9,000-square-foot gaming facility offers blackjack, roulette, wheels of fortune, and poker as well as 52 slot machines. Maximum bets are as high as $100 per hand. The casino has a professional manager and gaming staff. The casino is open from 7:00 p.m. to 2:00 a.m. during the spring and summer seasons. Patrons pay an entrance fee of $3. Annual passes are available for $10. Alcoholic beverages and snacks are available, but there is no restaurant. Live productions in the style of the gold rush days entertain the patrons. A regular feature is the Ballad of Sam Magee Show. Although designed to attract tourist play, the casino draws the most play from Dawson City residents. The casino attracts annual play of about $1 million. Gross wins approach $400,000. The Canadian government under the 1994 Lottery Licensing Act and Regulations receives 25 percent of the gross win. Remaining profits minus payroll expenses go to promote tourism and preserve historical buildings. A deputy minister within the territorial Ministry of Justice regulates the casino.

Reference

Thompson, William N. 1999. "Yukon Territory." In *International Casino Law*, 3rd ed. Edited by Anthony Cabot, William N. Thompson, Andrew Tottenham, and Carl Braunlich, 216. Reno: Institute for the Study of Gambling, University of Nevada, Reno.

Caribbean and Atlantic

ARUBA

Aruba has been one of the most successful casino jurisdiction in the southern Caribbean. The island, now an independent nation, lures tourists who enjoy the warm climate along with gaming opportunities in 11 casinos. The casinos look to South America, particularly to Venezuela, for players. In the past many people have also come to Aruba from the United States via the gambling junkets offered by the casinos. The lack of adequate lodging, however, limits the potential for gaming development, as does a renewed fear of crime. Profit margins are small, as expenses are very large. Also the government extracts a 2 percent drop tax, meaning that when a player buys $100 in chips, the casino is obligated to pay a tax of $2. That amount is rather high. In addition, there is a gross gaming tax.

The casinos of Aruba are self-regulated; the island nation has no gaming board. The Ministry of Justice provides inspectors who monitor the doors of the casinos to ensure that no persons less than 18 years of age enter.

The gaming industry of Aruba suffered a major set back in 2005 when the island became the site of the murder of an American teenager on a high school senior trip to the island. She was last seem in public at one of the casinos. As a result of a sensationalized investigation that resulted in no final resolution, many American tourists have removed Aruba from their list of potential vacation destinations.

Reference

Cabot, Anthony N., William N. Thompson, Andrew Tottenham, and Carl Braunlich, eds. 1999. *International Casino Law.* 3rd ed. Reno: Institute for the Study of Gambling, University of Nevada, Reno, 234–235.

THE BAHAMAS

The Bahamas consist of two major centers with casinos (Nassau on New Providence Island and Freeport on Grand Bahamas Island) as well as many smaller islands, the closest ones lying about 50 miles off the Atlantic coast of Florida. The country, with a population of 330,000, was fully under the political control of Great Britain until 1964; in 1973, it gained independence and became a full partner in the Commonwealth. Tourism has been the dominant product of the islands for most of the past century. The islands' resorts employ 40 percent of the workforce. Casino properties dominate the tourist offerings.

Prior to the 1960s, there was very little gambling in the Bahamas. The Penal Code in colonial statutes declared all gambling to be illegal. In the 1920s, however, the small Bahamian Club opened in Nassau on New Providence Island, having been given an exemption by the governor. Another small casino won an exemption to operate on the tiny island of Cat Key. Efforts to establish major casino facilities had been advanced by Sir Stafford Sands as early as 1945. Sands was a private attorney seeking opportunity, but he was also the minister of finance and tourism for the island colony. The timing was not right, but Sands did not go away.

Sands was still a critical player in island politics in the early 1960s when the Castro revolution in Cuba caused many gaming interests there to look in the direction of the Bahamas. Meyer Lansky was reported to have visited Sands in 1960 with a $2 million offer for the right to have casinos. The offer may have been rebuffed, but soon Sands, in a "partnership" with two Americans— Wallace Groves (a convicted stock swindler) and Louis Chesler (a major Florida land developer and compulsive gambler)—pushed a proposal for a casino in Freeport through the Executive Council. The Monte Carlo Club at the Lucayan Beach Hotel began operations in 1964. A second casino in Freeport— El Casino—opened in 1966. Lansky had a direct interest in the property, as several of his associates in Cuba took management roles. These included brothers Dino and Eddie Cellini, who also shared management in a Lansky-controlled London casino and in a casino dealers school that furnished employees

for casinos in England as well as the Bahamas. Initially, all casino employees had to be nonresidents, a rule that has since changed. From the beginning, no local resident has been allowed to be a player at any of the casinos in the Bahamas. A local resident is fined $500 if caught playing.

Sands was also instrumental in pulling together the principals who negotiated to establish a casino near Nassau. These included James Crosby and Jack Davis of the Mary Carter Paint Company, Wallace Groves, and Huntington Hartford, a millionaire with grandiose dreams for development of Paradise Island, which was very near Nassau. A silent partner in the organization was Lynden Pindling, whose political party had won control of the government in the parliamentary elections of 1967. It was the first time in the history of the island that the Black party had won an election. The effort to gain a license for a new property included the purchase of the license that had been held by the Bahamian Club. In 1968, the Mary Carter partnership was reorganized as Resorts International, and they opened the Paradise Island Resort and Casino. The company had to actually move the Bahamian casino building onto their grounds to gain its license. Today the old casino facility is the restaurant within the new casino structure. Resorts International also took over the management of the El Casino in 1978. In 1983, the license for the El Casino was sold to the London-based casino company (Lonhro) that built the Princess Casino in Freeport.

A second casino in Nassau was licensed on Cable Beach in 1978. It operated as the Playboy Casino until 1983. Then the license was transferred to Carnival Cruise Lines, who opened the

Crystal Casino; subsequently it has become a Marriot property. In the 1990s, the Paradise Island Resort was sold to Sun International and renamed the Atlantis. Also, the Genting casino company of Malaysia purchased the Lucayan Beach Resort. A fifth casino license has been given to the Club Med, which operates the Columbus Isle Casino on San Salvador Island, the location where Columbus first set foot on land in the Western Hemisphere in 1492. However, today only four casinos are open, the Atlantis in Nassau, the Breezes Bahamas also in Nassau, the Cable Beach Wyndham near Nassau on New Providence Island, and the Isle of Capri on Grand Bahamas Island, formerly the Lucayan Beach Resort.

Earlier patterns of organized crime involvement in Bahamas casinos have essentially been eliminated through a process of effective regulation. Moreover, the operators' connections to other jurisdictions where they must face vigorous checks for licensing preclude connections with organized crime. The Bahamas have one of the most interesting taxation systems for casino gaming—a reverse progressive tax system. The island nation wishes to use casinos to promote tourism. Because the political leaders realize that it is expensive to market gaming to high rollers and persons who will spend considerable vacation dollars in the islands, the goal is to attract players who will stay in the hotels and take full advantage of the beaches and other tourist amenities. Larger properties have a better chance to market to these players. Also, it costs more to bring in such players than it does to advertise to low-roller day trippers who take boats from the Florida coast. Hence, the reverse-progressive tax system. Casinos pay a 25 percent tax on gaming revenues up to $10 million per year. As the earnings go up, the tax rate goes down. For earnings between $10 million and $16 million, the tax is only 20 percent. It is reduced to 10 percent for earnings between $16 million and $20 million. Annual earnings above this amount are taxed at a rate of only 5 percent. Casinos pay other fees as well.

Coauthored by Larry Dandurand

References

Cabot, Anthony N., William N. Thompson, Andrew Tottenham, and Carl Braunlich, eds. 1999. *International Casino Law*. 3rd ed. Reno: Institute for the Study of Gambling, University of Nevada, Reno, 224–228.

Mahon, Gigi. 1980. *The Company That Bought the Boardwalk*. New York: Random House.

CARIBBEAN ISLAND CASINOS

Many Caribbean jurisdictions have casino gaming facilities. Lotteries are also in operation on larger islands that have major population concentrations.

Casino gambling is offered in approximately 20 jurisdictions. Major events in the expansion of casinos in the region include the closing of casino operations in other places—a crackdown on illegal casinos in the United States in the 1950s, Castro's Cuban revolution in 1959, and London's casino reforms in 1968. Each of the casino locations follows different regulations for casinos with different taxation structures and different enforcement policies. Overall, it might be suggested that there is considerable laxity in regulation. A tradition of laissez-faire oversight has been generated by the fact that casino gaming was, in several places, initiated by operators from other jurisdictions—such as Cuba and early Nevada—who operated with limited enforcement in those jurisdictions. Also, the purpose of gaming in the Caribbean region has been to draw in tourists, whose economic activity outside the casinos provided the greatest level of benefits to the jurisdiction—greater than could be provided by direct taxation. Casinos are seen as an added attraction that fill an entertainment void for the majority of tourists, particularly in evening hours. The tourists come for beach attractions and spend their daytime hours outside the casinos. The nature of their travels suggests that they have only limited hours for gaming activity. The relatively high expenses for hotel rooms and transportation also provide impediments to the development of the region as a place for mass crowds of gamblers.

Although efforts to establish casinos persist in the noncasino jurisdictions of the region, several factors seriously obstruct the opportunities for successful casinos. One factor is government stability. Financial institutions that are necessary for capital investments generally lack confidence in the island locations owing to traditional and ongoing political problems. As govern-

ments change, taxation policies also change, adding to the instability of business conditions. A second problem is that most of the jurisdictions do not have formal, specialized gaming control boards. In most cases, a minister of finance oversees gambling along with his or her other duties. Without specialized government regulation, casino management controls the honesty of games. The managers also control the size of the bank—how much money they have on hand. Cases of cheating against the players or failing to pay off wins have occurred. A third difficulty arises from a lack of a coherent policy on development of the casino industry. Governments (or politicians) may desire the fees that come with licenses for casinos, and accordingly, they may license too many facilities. Markets can be saturated, making profits very difficult for most casinos.

Several of the island nations are newly independent, and as such, the local populations resent the notion of having foreign entrepreneurs on their soil. They may resent any suggestions that the casino operators offer regarding the manner in which the casino conducts business. This situation has an impact on the labor forces available for the resorts. Jurisdictions may require that employees be hired from a native workforce that might be totally inadequate for the tasks at hand. Many of the populations have been agriculturally based, and commercial work habits, such as following daily work schedules, have been lacking. This means that the casinos have to engage in long training sessions for employees. Also, it may be very difficult for a casino operated by "foreigners" to fire or discipline local workers if they are inefficient or even if they are dishonest. The concept of *mañana* has become very much a part of some operations, causing customer service goals to trail the recreational interests of the employees. Sometimes resentment against foreign casino owners is transformed into resentment against the customers.

Another factor that causes some difficulties to gaming operatives in the Caribbean region is currency exchange. This is usually overcome by having all gambling transactions conducted in U.S. dollars. Problems may then be posed by government policies restricting exportation of dollars (either in player wins or owner's profits). Import duties can be overwhelming to the casinos during construction and furnishing phases of start-ups.

The casinos encounter marketing problems, as costs can be very high. The costs of travel are high owing to a lack of direct flights into major U.S. cities; all tourist products are expensive, as they must be imported. Moreover, tourism is seasonal in all the jurisdictions. One additional seasonal difficulty is presented by severe (and potentially catastrophic) weather at the end of the summer season each year. The weather problems only exacerbate the inadequacies of island infrastructure—airports, roads, water, and power supplies.

All of the above factors make casino gambling a risky commercial business in most of the Caribbean region. Nonetheless, many operators seem willing to give gambling a try in most places where it is legal. One exception seems to be the Virgin Islands, which legalized casinos as a result of an election in 1995. Only one company presented an application for a license in this new "wide-open" venue. The intervening years have witnessed two major hurricanes that have dampened investor optimism for more casinos.

The Virgin Islands are at the eastern end of the Greater Antilles. On the western end, Cuba has no casinos, and Jamaica has permitted gaming in 500 slot machine outlets with 3,250 machines altogether, but the island has resisted other casino gaming. Haiti has had several casinos, but severe political turmoil culminating in a U.S. military invasion and occupation in 1994 has effectively ended casino operations. There is some effective casino gaming in both Puerto Rico and the Dominican Republic. To the north of the Greater Antilles (technically outside of the Caribbean basin), the Bahamas have some profitable operations as well. Also to the north, Grand Turks Islands and the Caicos Islands have one small casino in a resort hotel. Most of the islands in the Caribbean region do welcome operators of Internet gaming beamed toward the United States and focusing upon gambling on sports events.

In the Lesser Antilles, the Leeward Islands of St. Martin, St. Kitts (formerly St. Christopher) and Nevis, Barbados, and Antigua and Barbuda all have casinos. St. Martin is a divided island: one half is a subprefecture under French control; the other part, called St. Maarten, is under control of the Netherlands Antilles. The Windward Islands of Martinique, St. Vincent and the Grenadines, Saint Lucia, and Guadeloupe have casino gaming, as do each of the "ABC" islands in the south Caribbean—Aruba, Curaçao, and Bonaire, the latter two also being part of the Netherlands Antilles. The Netherlands Antilles consist of two of the three "ABC" islands (Aruba, Curaçao, and Bonaire) of the southern

Caribbean, and the Dutch half of the island of St. Martin/Sint Maarten. These islands are autonomous in their domestic affairs, but they report to the government at The Hague in matters involving international affairs. Casino policy is in the latter category. St. Martin/Sint Maarten is an island of 37 square miles; 16 square miles (Sint Maarten) are on the Dutch side, and 21 square miles (St. Martin) are controlled from Paris as a subperfecture of Guadeloupe. The casinos on the French side have not been developed to attract large numbers of tourists; on the other hand, the Dutch casinos operate within large resort hotels. The seven Dutch casinos have gambling junkets and offer credit for high-stakes gamblers.

Bonaire and Curaçao were governed jointly with Aruba until that island won independent national status in 1986. Bonaire has had two casinos, one of which—the Diva Flamingo Beach Casino—is the only casino in the world where players may be barefoot. The dealers too may be barefoot, but they always wear black ties. The second casino, the Plaza, has closed. Curaçao has 12 casinos, all of which are in resort hotels and are located on beaches or next to the harbor. Nine are in the major city Willemstad.

Trinidad and Tobago, a country just north of Venezuela, has two small casinos in addition to a racetrack.

There have been unsuccessful efforts to place casinos on other island nations and dependencies of the Caribbean, including the Caymans, Dominica, and Grenada. Either investors with ample resources to make it all work would not step forth (considering the multiple disadvantages listed above), or the governments could not be persuaded that they wanted this kind of foreign investment and potential foreign control over their island economies.

References

Cabot, Anthony N., William N. Thompson, Andrew Tottenham, and Carl Braunlich, eds. 1999. *International Casino Law.* 3rd ed. Reno: Institute for the Study of Gambling, University of Nevada, Reno, 221–272.

Casino City's Global Gaming Almanac. 2006. Newtown, MA: Casino City, 53–74.

CUBA

During the 1950s, Cuba offered the gambler several of the leading casino facilities in the world. There was little doubt, however, that the gaming was connected to organized crime personalities in the United States as well as to military dictator Fulgencio Batista, and both entities skimmed considerable sums from the operations. Cuba also had both public and private lotteries, a first-class racing facility, and jai alai fontons. All the gambling activity came to a halt after Fidel Castro engineered a successful rebellion and took over the reins of power in 1959. Repeated attempts to negotiate a continuation of casino gaming were unsuccessful, and it has been suggested that U.S. crime interests were involved in attempts to overthrow the Castro regime, both in the abortive Bay of Pigs invasion and in several assassination attempts on the new dictator's life. The entire tourism infrastructure has slipped into decay during the four decades of Castro rule. Today there are voices suggesting that Cuba may seek to restore its tourism industry and may even contemplate reopening casinos.

The island of Cuba was colonized and controlled by the Spanish government for four centuries, until a revolution developed on a major scale in the 1890s. When the United States declared war on Spain in 1898, the revolution became successful, and independence was gained for the Cuban people. Authorities in the United States, however, sought to keep many controls over the Cuban people. War troops were not removed until 1902, and even after the Cubans elected a new government under President Jose Miguel Gomez that year, the United States "negotiated" to have a major naval base at Guantanamo Bay. Other commercial interests in the United States also maintained economic domination over much of Cuba, but these interests had been in Cuba for many years before the revolution. Many Americans looked at the seaside location called Marianao, 10 miles outside of Havana, and found it to be a desirable place to live, engage in real estate transactions, and start tourism resorts.

A local group known as the 3 C's (named for Carlos Miguel de Cespedes, Jose Manuel Cortina, and Carlos Manuel de la Cruz) formed a tourism company that sought to build a casino in Marianao. In 1910, they proposed legislation in the National Congress that would permit the casino and would also grant them an exclusive 30-year conces-

sion to operate it. At a time when the Americans in Cuba saw the casino as "opportunity," Americans in the United States were in a wave of anti-sin social reform. This was the same year that the casinos of Nevada closed their doors and the Prohibition movement was in high gear. U.S. President Howard Taft was lobbied hard by church interests to not allow gambling so close to U.S. shores. During the Spanish American War, President William McKinley had decreed that there be no more bullfighting in Cuba, calling the activity a disgraceful outrage. Taft was expected to bully the Cuban Congress to follow U.S. wishes as well. The legislation failed to pass. A second attempt was made to have casino-tied revenues to support $1.5 million in construction of facilities for tourism in Marianao. One New Yorker, who had a contract to build a jai alai fonton and a grandstand for racing, sought to change Taft's mind on the issue, but again, casinos were defeated as a result of a moralist campaign in the United States.

Gambling was in the cards for Cuba, however. In 1915, Havana's Oriental Park opened for horse racing. In 1919, the casino promoters promised that they would build the streets and plazas for Marianao if they could have casinos. President Mario Menocal, who had been elected in 1917, supported a bill for casinos. The national legislature authorized a gambling hall for the resort on August 5, 1919. The 3 C's group ran the facility. In addition to land improvements for tourism, they agreed to a national tax that was designated for the health and welfare of poor mothers and their children. At the same time, President Menocal's family won the concession to have jai alai games in Marianao. The tourism push was on, and the United States was the primary market, especially after Prohibition began for the whole country in 1919. The Roaring Twenties roared outside of Havana. Several new luxurious hotels opened, each having a gaming room. Each successive presidency endorsed tourism and welcomed all investors. Even Al Capone opened a pool hall in Marianao in 1928. Then the Depression came.

The 1930s in Cuba were years of reform thinking. Leaders openly condemned the degradation of casino gaming and other sin activities that had been widely offered to tourists. In 1933, the casinos were closed, and Prohibition ended in the United States. The economy floundered. The next year, army sergeant Fulgencio Batista was able to oust President Ramon Grau San Martin and install his own government. He ruled as chief of staff of the army while another held the presidency. At first Batista tried to bolster the notion of cultural tourism, but he could not resist allowing casinos to reopen—under the control of the military. Batista was very concerned about the honesty of the games. For sure, he would be skimming. If players were being cheated, however, there soon would be no players. The house odds could give the casinos enough profits to pay off the generals and the politicians, but not enough to pay off all of the dealers. Games had to be honest. He turned to a person who understood this and other dynamics of the casino industry very well—Meyer Lansky. Lansky took over casino operations, and he imported dealers who would work for him and not behind his back. The Mob cleaned things up. Because of World War II and postwar disincentives for foreign travel by Americans, however, the casino

activity was rather dormant through the 1940s. Nonetheless, Havana attracted more persons of bad reputation. In 1946, Salvatore "Lucky" Luciano moved in to conduct heroin trade and to be involved with the Jockey Club and the Casino Nacional. Lansky was influential in persuading the government to expel his competitor.

Fulgencio Batista won the presidency on his own in 1940. In 1944 and 1948, he permitted Grau San Martin and Carlos Prio Socarras to win open elections; however, he remained very much a controlling element. In 1952, while a candidate for the presidency, he sensed he had no chance of victory. Batista executed a coup and took the reins of power. Subsequent elections were rigged, and he remained in power until the beginning of 1959. During this latter period of rule, casino development accelerated.

The 1950s started out slowly for the casinos. Prior to 1950, only five casinos were in operation, and a brief reform spirit in 1950 led the government to close them. Commercial pressures, however, led to a reopening before Batista conducted his coup. The casinos now offered large numbers of slot machines for play. By the mid-decade, new Cuban hotels were attracting large investments from the United States, as the gambling operations were quite lucrative. Foreign operators, however, still had ties to organized crime members. A major incentive for a renewed interest in Cuban gaming came from the Senate Kefauver investigations that were exposing illegal gambling operations in the United States. Organized crime members were being run out of places such as Newport, Kentucky; Hot Springs, Arkansas; and New Orleans, Louisiana. At first, they gravitated toward Las Vegas; then Nevada instituted licensing requirements that precluded their participation in operations there. Cuba, the Bahamas, and Haiti became desired locations. Four of the five largest Havana casinos were in the hands of U.S. mobsters. As newer properties such as the Havana Hilton, the Riviera, Hotel Capri, and the Intercontinental Hotel came on line, Mob hands were involved in the action. Meyer Lansky was always the leader of the group. He kept the games honest, and he kept the political skim money flowing in the correct directions. When someone got out of line, he gave the word, and Batista could make a great show about throwing a mobster out of the country. In addition to enhancing casino gambling, Batista also improved revenues of the national lottery by inaugurating daily games.

In 1958, things seemed to be on a roll just when Fidel Castro gathered strength for his military takeover. Revelations in the *New York Times* about Mob involvement in Cuban casinos dampened tourist enthusiasm, as did the fear of impending violence. The names of Jake Lansky, Salvatore Trafficante, and Joseph Silesi were added to the list of unsavory participants in the industry.

Fidel Castro was born in 1926, the son of an affluent sugarcane planter. He attended a Catholic school in Santiago de Cuba before entering the University of Havana as a law student in 1945. There he began his career as a political activist and revolutionary. He participated in an attempt to overthrow the government of Dominican Republic strongman Rafael Trujillo and disrupted an international meeting of the American states in Bogota in 1948. He sought a peaceful way to power in 1952 when he ran for Congress; however, the contest was voided as Batista seized power and cancelled the election. In 1953, Castro took part in an unsuccessful raid on the government; he was captured and imprisoned for a year. He was released by Batista as part of a general amnesty program but kept up his revolutionary efforts, leading another unsuccessful raid in 1956. His third try was a charm, as he successfully moved through rural Cuba during 1958, attacking Havana at the end of the year and driving Batista from office.

When Castro's forces descended on Havana on New Year's Eve 1958, there were 13 casinos in Havana. The hotel casinos represented a collective investment of tens of millions of dollars. Lansky's Riviera alone cost $14 million. Owners and operators did not want to join Batista in his hasty exile out of the country, even after revolutionary rioters had smashed up many of their gaming rooms. They wanted to hold on to what had been a very good thing. That would be difficult, however. Castro had waged a revolutionary media campaign that condemned the sin industries of Cuba and their connections to the Batista government. Castro had pledged that he would close down the casinos.

Castro was as good as his word on this score, at least at the beginning. He also stopped the national lottery from operating. Meyer Lansky, on the other hand, pledged that he would work with the new government, and casinos were temporarily reopened, ostensibly to protect the jobs of their 4,000 workers. The re-openings were short-lived, however. The casinos closed for good (under the Castro regime) in late 1960. Castro's frontal attack on the Mob and its casino interests in Havana had political consequences in the United States, where the Central Intelligence Agency planned the 1961 Bay of Pigs invasion to overthrow

Castro and also may have contracted with organized crime operatives to attempt to assassinate the new leader.

The fall of the Batista regime and the end of Cuban casinos had repercussions throughout the gaming industry. Nevada lost its strongest competitive market, and Cuban operatives and owners had to move. The ones that could be licensed went to Las Vegas, as did many of the dealers and other casino workers. Others had to find unregulated or underregulated jurisdictions. Haiti and the Dominican Republic were close at hand, as were the Bahamas. Most of the gaming entrepreneurs in these jurisdictions had Cuban experiences, as did many who went to London to open casinos after 1960 legislation gave unregulated charity gaming halls a green light. Lansky, George Raft, and Dino Cellini were principals in London's Colony Club until they were expelled from the country. Former Nevada lieutenant governor Cliff Jones of Las Vegas had been active in Cuba. He had made a choice between Nevada gaming and foreign gaming when the "foreign gaming" rule was adopted in Nevada. He chose to be involved in foreign gaming and therefore could not have casinos in Las Vegas. Instead, he began campaigns in one small country after another to legalize casinos and then began operations that he would later sell to (or share with) local parties for high profits. Clearly, the activity of Castro in closing down Havana gaming caused a major spread of gaming elsewhere.

References

Lacey, Robert. 1991. *Little Man: Meyer Lansky and the Gangster Life.* Boston: Little, Brown.

Schwartz, Rosalie. 1997. *Pleasure Island: Tourism and Temptation in Cuba.* Lincoln: University of Nebraska Press, chaps. 6, 12.

Sifakis, Carl. 1990. *Encyclopedia of Gambling.* New York: Facts on File, 85.

HISPANIOLA (DOMINICAN REPUBLIC AND HAITI)

The Dominican Republic (population 9,500,000) shares the Greater Antilles island of Hispaniola with Haiti (population 8,700,000), with which it has shared many attributes, especially an impoverished condition. In the early 1800s, the country was ruled in succession by French, Spanish, and Haitian military forces. When not ruled by foreign forces, the Dominican Republic has suffered at the hands of indigenous dictatorial rule as well as having been dominated by commercial interests of the United States, aided by the U.S. military. During the rule of strongman Rafael Trujillo (1930–1961), foreign casino interests established properties that were essentially governed by the dictator, largely for his benefit as well as that of the owners. The years from 1961 to 1966 were turbulent and unstable. In 1965, U.S. troops invaded to preserve order and preclude intervention by Cuba. The troops left in 1966, and the stage was set for the installation of a democratic government. Democracy has survived over the remaining years of the 20th century and into the 21st century.

The legislature of the Dominican Republic formalized a set of rules for casino operations in a law that was passed in 1968. Under the 1968 law, casinos must be in top-rated tourist hotels that have 200 rooms. Exceptions were made for two casinos in smaller hotels that had been operating before 1968. All licensed casinos since the law was passed are in larger hotels that market their rooms to foreign tourists.

The 1968 act outlawed slot machines. Slot machines had operated in casinos before that time; however, the government felt that the machines appealed too much to poorer local residents, who did not have the resources to meet minimum play requirements of the table games. The machines were permitted to come into the casinos with a new law passed in 1988; however, the government imposed a higher tax on machine wins than on other wins. The government wished to encourage the casinos to have only higher-denomination machines ($1 per play or more) rather than nickel and dime machines that would appeal to the poorer people. In contrast, poorer people can purchase passive lottery tickets each week in order to satisfy their gaming urges. Besides that, the lottery directs its profits to programs for the poor and also employs many poor people to sell the tickets. In recent years, however, policy has been reversed and the casinos do have slot machines today.

In the 1990s, the casinos kept two sets of books, one for play in U.S. currency and the other for play in Dominican currency. There was no currency exchange. There were two sets of chips—U.S. and Dominican. There were also specifically designated chips for credit play. This provision for special chips enabled the casino to ensure that loans are repaid at the time a winning player would be "cashing-in." The casinos followed two methods of taxation. For casino wins in Dominican currency, the casinos paid a tax of 20 percent on the gross win. For players using chips valued in U.S. dollars, the tax was paid when the chips are purchased. It was a 2 percent drop tax; that is, for each $100 of chips purchased, the casino paid $2 in tax. There was no win tax. The casinos have been reluctant to offer credit to players, especially local players. They had a history of players refusing to pay back the casino owners who, for the most part, are foreigners—usually Americans (*see* the Honduras Section in the Central America entry for a discussion of the same problem). Locals have considered it an affront to be challenged in court by "rich foreigners" for repayment of money they have "already returned" to the casinos via their losing play. Therefore, the casinos contract with local residents who will "guarantee" repayment of the loans. If the player loses and does not repay the loan in a rapid fashion, the casino asks the guarantor to collect the loan. The guarantor then pays 70 percent of the loan and is given the right to collect the entire loan and to keep the 30 percent differential as a commission. The guarantor is also empowered to take the loan obligation to court, where he is well acquainted with the judicial personnel and is not subject to antiforeign accusations.

There are several premium casinos in Santo Domingo, the capital city—a city that was settled by Bartholomew

Columbus, brother of famed explorer Christopher Columbus. The leading casino is the Jaragua, which is owned by Americans. It features a Las Vegas–style floorshow and a set of fountains that was designed by the architect who designed the fountains at Caesars Palace. Koreans own the next leading property, which is located at the Embajador Hotel. Most of the dealers in these facilities are citizens of the United States, and many have had experience in Las Vegas casinos. There is no restriction on such foreign labor. Other major casinos are in the Sheraton, Concorde, Lina, and Centenario hotels. Altogether, there are a dozen hotels in the Santo Domingo area.

Santo Domingo is a historical city that should appeal to a tourist with a craving for evidence of the founding of the oldest European-settled city in the hemisphere (1496) and a desire to see buildings still standing at the oldest university in the hemisphere (founded in 1538). Most casino-oriented tourists, however, like things such as beaches and room amenities. Santo Domingo falls short. It has no sandy beaches, and its electrical supply is challenged. Every day the power in the hotel—casino and rooms—goes out for some time. The casino keeps essential functions going with backup facilities; however, tourist facilities such as Jacuzzis, televisions, restaurant areas, and telephones temporarily go down. For tourism, however, the Dominican Republic is fortunate to have another location with ample power and top-class natural beaches—the north island shore called Puerto Plata. Its golden beach extends for nearly 60 miles. Several new casino hotels have been constructed in Puerto Plata within the last decade, the leading one being a Jack Tar facility with 300 rooms and a 40,000-square-foot casino area. There are now 21 casinos in the Dominican Republic. They offer gaming on 236 tables and 907 machines.

The Dominican Republic competes with Puerto Rico for casino players—each has its advantages and disadvantages. In Puerto Rico, English must be spoken at the casinos, whereas it is not mandated in the Dominican Republic. Puerto Rico has superior airline service, whereas the Dominican Republic has limited direct flights to the United States. On the other hand, labor costs are much lower in the Dominican Republic, which translates into lower hotel costs for tourists—and lower costs for casinos that are offering free rooms to players. The other advantage of gaming in the Dominican Republic is shared with other Caribbean venues: no reports are given to the Internal Revenue Service of the United States regarding players activities—how much they wager and how much they win.

The Dominican Republic was one of the first offshore jurisdictions to enter the market for sports bettors. They now offer bets through telephone service as well as over the Internet. There is also a lottery and several hundred bookie shops taking sports bets.

Haiti achieved its independence in a revolution against the French army in 1804. Haiti is the oldest black republic in the world, and next to the United States it is the oldest independent country in the Western Hemisphere. The "independence" must be qualified, however. The people of Haiti have not enjoyed a democratic freedom during many of its years. Most of its rulers have been dictators, and the country has remained under the commercial domination of many nations during its history.

In 1915, U.S. President Woodrow Wilson feared that other countries might invade Haiti because of its foreign debt.

He sought to enforce the Monroe Doctrine before it could be breached. Therefore, he had the U.S. Marines invade Haiti. They occupied the country until 1934. Although depriving the people of their autonomous status, the presence of U.S. troops did lead to an eradication of yellow fever and also to the construction of roads and a sewage system. Governmental instability ensued when the marines left, but in 1957 stability returned with the election of François "Papa Doc" Duvalier as president. In 1964, he declared himself president for life. Upon his death in 1971, his son, Jean-Claude "Baby Doc" Duvalier, became the dictator.

In 1960, Papa Doc Duvalier guided the national legislature in passing a casino law. The timing was appropriate. Operators who were being thrown out of Cuba were seeking new venues. In truth the 1960 legislation was just a piece of paper that would justify Duvalier's invitation for new casino entrepreneurs to come on in and make an offer. One casino, the International, had been established on the waterfront in Port-au-Prince in 1949. It had a reputation of being a Mob house from the start.

The 1960 law was not intended to be followed to the letter, if at all. The law provided that casinos could only be in hotels with 200 rooms. There were no such hotels in the entire country then, and there are none now. At least two casinos, in addition to the International, were free-standing gaming halls unattached to any hotel. The casinos could have only seven table games, and the games allowed were specified. The major casinos in operation in 1989 during this editor's tour of the country had 15 or more table games. They also had games that were not authorized. Additionally, the casinos had slot machines.

Licenses for casino gaming were supposed to be granted by the minister of commerce. At the time of licensing, the operators were supposed to present a deposit of $50,000 to the government to be held in the Central State Bank. This earnest money was to be returned to the operators when the casino actually began conducting gaming activity. One of the operators in 1989 had gone through the licensing procedure for his property. When asked about the law, he laughed. He said the deposit was not for $50,000. It was for $250,000. The deposit was not given to the minister of commerce; it was given directly to Baby Doc Duvalier (when he was in power). The deposit was not returned to the casino when it began operations; it was never seen again.

The law provided that the casinos would pay an annual fee of $1,000 plus a tax of 40 percent on the gaming win. Individual casinos would work with the government to negotiate certain expenses that could be deducted from the tax obligation. The tax had been paid in the past. When Baby Doc was deposed in a coup d'état in 1985, the tax collectors no longer came to the casinos. The operator who was interviewed in 1989 indicated that he had not paid taxes since the Duvaliers had been exiled. During the earlier years of the law, an additional 5 percent tax had been levied on players when they cashed in their chips—when they won. This tax was earmarked for the construction of the Duvalier International Airport in Port-au-Prince. When the airport was finally constructed, the tax collectors no longer asked for the player win tax.

Foreigners were permitted to own the casinos; in fact, that was the desire of the government. They could have foreign dealers, but to do so, they had to get special work cards from the government for an undetermined price.

El Rancho Casino, Port-au-Prince, Haiti.

In 1989, during the editor's visit, there were five casinos in the Port-au-Prince area. One, the Club 54 in the suburb of Petionville, was owned by Haitians. It was operating but in poor condition. As the editor entered the gaming area, a hen and four little chicks walked across the floor. The leading property was the El Rancho. It was also located in Petionville and was attached to a hotel with 125 rooms. A thatched-roof casino without a hotel was located on the main square of Petionville. The Chauchon was owned by Mike McLaney, an American who had previously been involved with Cuban and Bahamian casinos. He had held the concession for the International from 1969 to 1976. In the capital city a small casino operated at a Holiday Inn, and a larger casino was at the 85-room Royal Haitian Hotel. The casino, which opened in 1973, was also owned by McLaney. The International, enclosed by a chain-link fence, was in disrepair and out of business. It had been closed since McLaney gave it up in 1976.

In 1989, there were very few players at any of the facilities. In previous times—during the stable years of the Duvalier dictators—cruise ships touring the Caribbean would stop in Port–au-Prince, but by 1989 they no longer did so. A few stopped on the northern coast of Haiti, but there were no casinos there. Cruise ships ceased stopping in Haiti at all later in 1989. One week after the editor's tour of the casinos, there was a coup d'etat, and gunfire filled crowded streets from the national palace to the International. Any chance of growing markets for the casinos ended with the gunfire.

Since 1989, there have been almost no tourists in Haiti. The editor may have been the last casino tourist. The government disintegrated into near anarchy, and in 1994, the U.S. Marines once again landed in order to preserve something, perhaps order, certainly not the U.S. casino property. The marines have left, but they did not leave anything better for the casinos. Casino gaming is no longer of any importance. Only two casinos—the El Rancho and the Royal Haitian have their doors open. There may be some play from local residents, but the outward signs of poverty suggest business is not good.

References

Cabot, Anthony N., William N. Thompson, Andrew Tottenham, and Carl Braunlich, eds. 1999. *International Casino Law*. 3rd ed. Reno: Institute for the Study of Gambling, University of Nevada, Reno, 232–233.

Casino City's Global Gaming Almanac. 2006. Newtown, MA: Casino City, 61–63, 64.

Thompson, William N. 1999. "Dominican Republic." In *International Casino Law,* 3rd ed. Edited by Anthony N. Cabot, William N. Thompson, Andrew Tottenham, and Carl Braunlich, 229–231. Reno, Nevada: Institute for the Study of Gambling, University of Nevada, Reno.

PUERTO RICO

Casino gaming came to Puerto Rico in 1948 as part of an economic development effort called "Operation Bootstrap." The casinos were allowed only to have table games until 1974. There are 16 casinos in Puerto Rico. The largest and most successful are in San Juan near the Condado Beach area. The casinos are all contained within hotels. Hours are restricted to afternoons and evenings. There is no live entertainment within the casinos. Casinos are restricted in size, with most offering less than 10,000 square feet of gaming space.

Table games, blackjack, baccarat, and craps are operated by the private casinos, and slot machines were operated by the Puerto Rican Tourism Company, a government agency that regulated the casinos, until a 1997 law privatized the operations. Up to that time, the government took the revenue from the slots and returned a portion to the casinos. However, now the machines are owned by the casinos. The only gaming tax is on machine revenues, with the government taking two-thirds of the proceeds. There is a room tax on casino hotels and a franchise fee for casinos, which is based upon revenues from games.

The most prominent casinos are the Hyatt Dorado Beach, the Wyndham El San Juan, the Wyndham El Conquistador, the Ritz Carlton, and the Inter-Continental. These properties draw tourists from the United States. The very high cost of hotel rooms and high occupancy rates limit opportunities for extensive gambling junkets, however. Local residents are permitted to gamble, although the casinos cannot advertise directly to the local market.

Puerto Rican casinos have potential marketing advantages over other regional casinos, as San Juan is a major airport hub for the Caribbean, easily accessible to other American cities, and as Puerto Rico is a U.S. jurisdiction with no currency restrictions for Americans. Disadvantages, however, include high room costs and U.S. taxation reporting requirements.

Several of the casinos in Puerto Rico have been suffering financial trouble. These problems are attributed to heavy taxation and to mismanagement,

Caribe Hilton, the first modern casino in Puerto Rico.

especially in the area of credit policies. Nevertheless, there have been several applications for new casino licenses in recent years, and new casinos have opened.

References

Gambling il dado. "Land Casinos Puerto Rico." www.ildado.com/land_casinos_puerto _rico.html.

Schiffman, Daniel, and Maria Milagros Soto. 1999. "Puerto Rico." In *International Casino Law*, 3rd ed. Edited by Anthony N. Cabot, William N. Thompson, Andrew Tottenham, and Carl Braunlich. Reno: Institute for the Study of Gambling, University of Nevada, Reno, 240–260.

Thompson, William N. 1989. "Puerto Rico: Heavy Taxes, Regs Burden Casinos." *Gaming and Wagering Business,* September, 15, 73–76.

VIRGIN ISLANDS

The Virgin Islands lie off the eastern edge of Puerto Rico. The islands are controlled by the governments of the United States and Great Britain. The U.S. Virgin Islands (USVI) consist of 50 small islands. The most populated of the USVI are St. Croix, St. Thomas, and St. John.

Together the USVI have just over 110,000 residents. In 1989, Hurricane Hugo devastated the tourist islands. Many properties were destroyed, as was much of the islands' infrastructure. A depression ensued during which many of the air flights to the islands ceased. In

1995, the two leading employers—Hess Oil and Virgin Island Alumina—cut production and downsized by 650 employees. Casino gambling, an idea that had been rejected several times before, suddenly became popular. A referendum was authorized, and the voters endorsed casinos by a narrow margin. On November 3, 1995, the Virgin Islands' representative assembly followed the popular will by passing legislation authorizing casino licenses. The law was amended on March 6, 1997.

The legislation provides for up to six casinos in hotels on St. Croix island. The first opened in 2000 at the Divi Carina Bay Resort. The resort now has 166 rooms, 20 villas, and a convention center. It offers 344 machines for play along with 16 tables. The licenses are issued by a board of commissioners appointed by the governor. Of the six licenses, one must go to a company that is obligated to build a 1,500-room hotel and have a gaming area of 20,000 square feet or more in the facility, along with convention and banquet facilities. Two licenses go to hotels with at least 300 rooms and a casino of 10,000 square feet or more, while another two go to hotels of at least 200 rooms located in two historic districts of the island. A smaller casino may be licensed in another hotel with at least 150 rooms. The Divi Carina barely qualifies. Yet to date, it has been the only property to seek a license, and the only casino to open its doors. Casinos are subject to the U.S. cash transaction reporting rules and the reporting rules of the Internal Revenue Service. They are also subject to the rules of the United States in online gaming. In a 2001 act, the U.S. Virgin Islands approved licensing for Internet gambling products. However, officials from the United States warned that such gambling—if aimed at off island persons—would be illegal. No licenses have been granted. A Virgin Island lottery dates from 1978.

References

Cabot, Anthony N., William N. Thompson, Andrew Tottenham, and Carl Braunlich, eds. 1999. *International Casino Law*. 3rd ed. Reno: Institute for the Study of Gambling, University of Nevada, Reno, 261–272.

Casino City's Global Gaming Almanac. 2006. Newtown, MA: Casino City, 74.

Divi Carina Bay Resort. www.carinabay .com.

Mayer, Martin. 1988. *Markets: Who Plays, Who Risks, Who Gains, Who Loses*. New York: W. W. Norton.

Shelton, Ronald B. 1997. *Gaming the Market*. New York: Wiley and Sons.

Europe

(*See also* European and American Casinos Compared, General Topics)

AUSTRIA AND CASINOS AUSTRIA INTERNATIONAL

When there is an entrepreneur, there is always a way to find a profit. The entrepreneur can even be a government employee seeking a profit for his agency. Casinos Austria International is a corporation controlled by public entities. After a post–World War II resurgence in casino development in Austria, the company hit a virtual brick wall. They had placed casinos in all corners of the small country. They had saturated their market. Moreover, a conservative, religious-oriented population and a timid political establishment was quite content with the existing array of rather small, restricted casinos. They did not want more gambling.

Casino profits—that is, money left over after share distributions were paid to government owners (which included local and national agencies)—were lingering without direction for investment. The leader of Casinos Austria, Leo Wallner, saw opportunities. However, the opportunities were beyond the borders of Austria. Knowing the limits of activity within a government-controlled agency, he directed the creation of a subsidiary agency, to be owned by Casinos Austria but located outside of Austria and managed separately. Since then he has led his Casino Austria Inter-national to become perhaps the leading force for the international development of casinos and other gambling activities as well. Wallner has also kept his eyes on improvements in Austrian gaming.

Private hands guided the control of many casinos in Austria in the 19th and early 20th centuries. These casinos were outside of the control of government until a national law was passed in 1933. At that time the Austrian government granted casino concessions to a single private company known as Austrian

Casinos in Belgium are among the oldest in the world.

Casino AG/Laxenburg. The company's first owners included both Italians and Canadians, but later were almost all Canadians. Their first licensed casino was in the Semmering resort region. Its roulette wheels started spinning in February 1934. By April 1934, a casino was operating at Baden bei Wien, "the grandfather of all health resorts." Here, 21 miles south of Vienna, Romans had taken "the cure" in hot sulfur springs, and later Beethoven maintained a home. Later in 1934, casinos opened at the Mirabell Palace in Mozart's city of Salzburg, and in the Tyrolian resort village of Kitzbuhel. The nearby ski resort of Bad Gastein opened a casino in 1937.

In 1938, Adolf Hitler forced his policy of Anschluss (unification) on Austria. His government imposed German gaming law on Austria, forcing all the casinos except the one at Baden bei Wien to close. It joined Baden-Baden and Sopot (near Gdansk in present-day Poland) as the only casinos meeting Third Reich gaming standards. Baden bei Wien kept its wheels spinning until August 26, 1944, when again a war defeat swept the nation.

After World War II, Austria was an occupied nation. American, British, and French forces governed western Austria, while the Russians controlled the eastern area. Vienna, which was well within the eastern (Russian) zone, was like Berlin, jointly occupied with American, British, French, and Russian sectors.

Immediately after the war, a new gaming school in Vienna provided training for dealers. Each class at the school had spots reserved for "deserving" war veterans. The veterans had hopes that they would soon be finding jobs. The Allies allowed the Austrians to hold elections in November 1945 and set up a civilian government. The government optimistically began negotiations to reopen the Baden bei Wien casino in 1946. This proved impossible. Baden bei Wien was not only in the Russian sector, but the casino building was the Austrian headquarters for the Russian Army. The casino remained closed.

In 1950, gaming returned permanently in the western occupation zone when three casinos opened in Bad Gastein, Salzburg, and Velden. Kitzbuhel reestablished its casino in 1954.

Russia showed a fleeting glimpse of glasnost in 1955 when it agreed to end the occupation of Austria. The voluntary withdrawal of the Russian, American, French, and British troops locked the country into international neutrality. Perhaps the Russian move sent a false signal to Hungary as armies retreated homeward to Moscow. Still, by the end of 1956, the Hungarians knew there would be no glasnost for them anytime soon. Baden bei Wien received a more favorable signal. The casino resumed operations in July 1955. The opening of the eastern zone also led to an authorized casino for Vienna in 1960.

The 1960s were not a stable time for Austrian casinos. Following repeated irregularities, the government decided to take the concessions from privately controlled Austrian Casinos AG/Laxenburg. A new policy decreed that Austrians should totally control all casinos. The government helped create the Osterreichische Spielbanken AG (Casinos Austria). Most of its ownership (70%) is in the hands of Austrian governmental entities, a national travel company, a provincially-owned insurance company, and public banks. Private banks and utility groups control other shares. There is no public trading of ownership stock.

The guiding hand behind the creation of the company is its operating director, Leo Wallner. Wallner expanded Austrian casino operations into eight of the nine regions of the country. He negotiated to win local acceptance of casinos in the very conservative religious western regions. In 1972, he persuaded the Vorarlberg region to allow a casino at Kleinwalsertal. In his favor, local village residents could not gamble at the casino, and the casino was accessible by road only from Germany. The casino originally conducted gaming in German marks.

Other areas also received casinos. In 1975, Bregenz, also in the Vorarlberg region, obtained a casino license. The Tyrolian ski resort town of Seefeld, just 20 miles above Innsbruck (on a 15 percent incline road), added a casino in 1969. In 1982, the industrial city of Linz, capital city of Upper Austria, placed a casino in the Schillerpark Hotel. Graz, Austria's second largest city and capital of Styria, opened a casino in its convention center in 1984. New casino facilities premiered in Kleinwalsertall in 1983 and in Bregenz in 1986. Besides locating casinos in all parts of Austria, Wallner improved many facilities. A new facility was opened in Vienna in 1992. Additional Austrian casinos include one in Kleinwalsertal and the Wals-Siezenheim casino which replaces the Salzburg facility. Austria now has 12 full-service casinos in addition to three machine-only facilities and one racetrack machine casino.

Wallner's company also looked toward other types of gaming. In 1983, they were requested by the finance min-ister to work with the Austrian Post Office Savings Bank to develop new forms of lottery games, including sports wagering and lotto games. In 1990, full responsibility for the entire Austrian lottery was given to Casinos Austria.

Austria was once an integral part of an empire with more than 50 million people. Now it is the size of Maine, and it has a population of 7.5 million. The Casinos Austria enterprise has saturated the domestic gaming market. However, its guiding entrepreneur, Leo Wallner, has always looked for opportunities for expansion. Necessity, therefore, demanded that he set his sights beyond the frontiers of his small country. His outlook became international.

In 1977, Casinos Austria founded a subsidiary company in Chur, Switzerland. At first it was called Casinos Austria Consulting AG, later becoming Casinos Austria International. In 1982, the company discovered another fertile market for its expertise when it contracted to operate casinos on cruise ships on several seas. Cruise ship operations were the recipients of the company's slot machine innovations. Casinos Austria sailed onto new seas when they signed a contract enabling the Norwegian Caribbean Line to take advantage of the Austrians' knowledge.

Casinos Austria began operating cruise ship casinos on its own under an agreement with the Royal Viking Line. Norwegian American Lines contracted for a Casinos Austria casino in 1983. Four additional lines gained company casinos in 1984, including the Royal Caribbean Cruise Line. On September 22, 1984, Royal Caribbean's *Song of Norway* became the first ship to have a casino with a fully integrated, computerized security control system for all slot machines and table games. Now, Casinos Austria runs casinos on 13 ships.

On land, Casinos Austria's first outreach exercises benefited a new casino industry in Holland. After legalization, the Dutch Casino Board decided that all its gaming personnel should be Dutch nationals. They also stipulated that dealers could not have had experience in the illegal casinos in Holland. These rules made it almost impossible for the Dutch to open casinos with an experienced workforce. To get around the problem, the Dutch invited bids from established casino organizations to help them get started. Casinos Austria won a "know-how" contract to provide both initial gaming personnel and to help train a new Dutch staff. After training the staff and allowing it to gain sufficient experience, the Austrian dealers moved out. The company remained to oversee ongoing operations, offering management advice into the early 1980s.

In 1977, the company entered a know-how contract with the first Istanbul casino. In 1978, two agreements with Spanish casinos were put into place. Belgium's Middelkerke Casino sought Casinos Austria for management help in 1980, and the new Istanbul Hilton Casino asked for know-how assistance in 1983. The Greek casino on Mt. Parnes near Athens and the island casino on Corfu became Austrian operations in 1984. In 1986, Casinos Austria took over majority ownership of the Istanbul Casino at the Etap Marmara Hotel.

In 1986, Casinos Austria, the successor to a company once almost totally owned by Canadians, presented a plan at Alberta's request for the feasibility of a casino in that Canadian province. Simultaneously, they began operating the first private casino in Argentina at the Las Lenas Ski Resort in the Andes Mountains.

The Hungarian State Hotel and Spa Corporation (Danubius) established the Hungarian Casino Corporation by entering a full partnership agreement with Casinos Austria. The joint venture in Hungary eventually encompassed six casino properties.

In 1989 and 1990, as walls and iron curtains fell, ventures in the former Eastern Bloc accelerated. Other joint operating agreements included casinos in Leningrad (now Saint Petersburg), Moscow, the Russian Federation of Georgia, and the Republic of Latvia. Under Casinos Austria's guidance, casinos opened in Czechoslovakia, Poland, the former East Germany, and Romania. Today Casinos Austria operates 54 land-based casinos in 18 different countries. The Casino Austria gaming empire controls 1,200 gaming tables and over 13,000 machines. They employee 13,000 people.

References

"Casinos Austria International." www.casinos austria.com.

Thompson, William. 1991. "Austria." In *International Casino Law*, 1st ed. Edited by A. Cabot, W. Thompson, and A. Tottenham, 317–322. Reno: Institute for the Study of Gambling, University of Nevada, Reno.

Wallner, Leo. 1999. "Austria." In *International Casino Law*, 3rd ed. Edited by A. Cabot, W. Thompson, A. Tottenham, and C. Braunlich, 329–336. Reno: Institute of Gambling Studies, University of Nevada, Reno.

"Welcome to Austria." 2008. World Casino Directory. www.worldcasinodirectory .com/austria.

THE BALTIC COUNTRIES (LATVIA, LITHUANIA, ESTONIA)

The three Baltic states, Latvia, Lithuania, and Estonia, were under control of the Soviet Union for almost 50 years, from World War II until the fall of the Berlin Wall and the events of 1990 and 1991. During this time, there was little public gambling activity in the region. Some exceptions existed, with passive lotteries run by the communist governments and, in the case of Latvia in the 1950s and 1960s, with horse racing and betting at the hippodrome in Riga. Most of those attending the races were party officials and members of the Soviet military.

The fall of the Berlin Wall and the virtual opening of the Brandenburg Gate was followed by a rush to establish all sorts of gambling opportunities as well as other activities that were previously forbidden, even if those participating could not afford the new "pleasures." The rush saw entrepreneurs opening up myriad casino facilities, as well as placing slot machines throughout the three countries. They did these things almost immediately upon finding that new freedoms permitted their actions, even though there were no laws or regulations in place governing their commercial ventures. It was almost totally a laissez-faire situation.

There could be no doubt that other matters had precedence on the political agendas of the countries' leaders. They had to set up procedures for truly democratic elections. They had to establish a financial system with "hard" currency, they had to develop procedures for having a military under civilian command,

they had to initiate independent schemes for conducting foreign trade and all other foreign relations. Gambling in the greater scheme of things was simply not that important. Indeed there were parallels with the United States during the Depression years and the years of World War II that followed, which saw the widespread unregulated (another way of saying illegal) establishment of casinos throughout the country as the political leadership were consumed with other matters.

The development of gambling laws had to wait—until 1994 in Latvia and Estonia, and 2001 in Lithuania—and the governments have had to fight a backdoor fight ever since. The barn door had been left open for a long time.

Latvia was the first venue to have formal casinos. In 1991, Casino Austria quickly found a local entrepreneur who became a partner on the first joint venture. Other companies followed shortly thereafter, with the small national population (2.3 million) being the only real barrier for continued expansion of the number of casinos. In 1994, regulations were finally put into place for oversight over the operations and also for a scheme of taxation. In 2005, a revised gaming law provided for regulation of Internet gaming. The laws have served to limit the numbers of full-service casinos. There are only 14, with most located in the capital city of Riga. However, this belies the true scope of gambling, as in 2008 there were a reported 636 gaming halls and overall 14,167 slot machines in operation. The laws have also permitted the state lottery to modernize and offer a full variety of lottery products.

Under the Lithuanian gaming law of 2001, a State Gaming Control Commission permits casinos, gaming halls with machines, betting shops, and bingo parlors as well as modern lottery games. The largest of the Baltic countries with a population of 3.5 million, Lithuania has 25 casinos, which each average 8 tables and 40 Type A machines (these machines may award large prizes). There are 70 gaming halls, with an average of 20 Type B (smaller prize) machines. The tables are taxed at a rate of 33 percent and the machines at 25 percent. In 2007, casinos produce over 67 percent of the $230 million in gaming revenues, with the gaming halls accounting for 22 percent, betting shops 10 percent, and bingos 1 percent. In 2006, the betting shops began to conduct off-track betting programs for international track races. There are three private companies that run lottery games on behalf of charities in Lithuania. The largest of these is Olifeja, which has online lotto as well as instant tickets sold in 820 retail locations.

The smallest Baltic state is Estonia, with a population of 1.3 million. The government licenses various forms of gambling, including casino table games and slot machines, poker games, race and sports betting, and lotteries. More than 70 casinos have been licensed and are found in 12 cities throughout the country. Over half are in the largest city, Tallin, including the largest one at the Park Hotel—it has 4 tables and 70 machines. In 2008, there were also 150 slot machine gaming halls. A parliamentary effort in 2009 greatly reduced the number of casinos and machine locations.

The modern lottery began in 1994 with a variety of games, among them the international Viking Lotto game. In 2004, an Internet company in Finland was authorized to conduct sports betting online to support the Estonian Olympic Committee.

References

Buinauskaite, Dovile. 2006, 2007. "Lithuania Country Reports, 2006, 2007." http://www.euromat.org/uploads/documents/15-93-lithuania_country_report_2007.pdf, accessed September 5, 2009.

"Estonia Casinos." Casinos and Gaming. www.jobmonkey.com/casino/html/estonia_casinos.html

Glickman, Leon, and Kadi Kuusk. 2004. "Estonian Gambling Regulations." *Gaming Law Review* 8, no. 3(June): 173–174.

Hobemaji, Toomas. 2008. "Half of Casinos in Estonia Set to Go out of Business." *Baltic Business*, October 15. www.balticbusinessnews.com/Default2.aspx?ArticleID=1F26E353-D633-4D3E-89.

MacDougall, Alex. 2007. "Gaming in Latvia." *Card Player Europe*, August 1. http://europe.cardplayer.com/magazine/article/65674?page=3.

Novamedia Gaming and Lottery Files. "Lithuania." www.gamingandlotteryfiles.com/novamediafile.php?file=Lithuania.htm.

BELGIUM

Belgium is a bicultural and bilingual nation situated between France and The Netherlands. It is bounded on the east by Germany and Luxembourg. The nation arose out of compromise among the major European countries in 1830. The gambling policy of the country also has arisen from a unique set of compromises.

Long before Belgium was a nation, casinos stood on the soil. A casino at Spa can be dated back to 1763. Today this casino lays claim to being the oldest existing casino in Europe.

There are now nine casinos in Belgium: four in the Flemish-speaking Flanders region (Knokke, Ostand, Blankenberge, and Middelkerke) and four in the French-speaking Walloon region (Spa, Chaudfontaine, Dinant, and Namur), and one in Brussels—the bicultural national capital.

Throughout the 19th century, casinos in several Belgium locations operated with the blessing and protection of the laws of the land. But this was not to be the case most of the 20th century. Early in the 20th century, the prime minister encountered a problem with the casinos: his son was a heavy gambler. He did not know how to deal with the problem on a personal level. Instead the prime minister sought to solve his problem by making all casino gaming illegal. Parliament acquiesced and passed legislation in 1902 that remained in effect until 1999.

Soon after the passage of the law banning casinos, Belgian King Albert was entertaining visiting royalty. He asked if he could provide the guests with some gaming opportunities. The host of the resort, which formerly had had a casino room, informed the king that gaming was illegal since Parliament had passed the law. The King sought an "arrangement." He called a meeting of the procurators (chief prosecuting attorneys who also supervise the police) of the major provinces. He asked if they could overlook the law if only the "right people" gamble. The prosecuting attorneys agreed under certain conditions. As a consequence, under the guidance of the procurators, casinos, although illegal, have remained opened since 1911.

In 1952, the procurators informally adopted specific rules, most of which still govern casino operations today: (1) only eight casinos would exist; (2) their municipalities would own the facilities; (3) the casinos would be private clubs; (4) members would have to pay fees and register identities before gaming; (5) members had to be at least 21 years old; (6) they had to declare their occupations; and (7) only "independent" persons could gamble. Lawyers, notaries, public officials (national, provincial, local), and public employees (including police and members of the Belgian military) could not gamble. These restrictions effectively barred one-third of the adult Belgian population from entering the eight casinos in the country. The procurators also decided not to allow advertising or promotion of the casinos.

The procurators decided what games they would allow. Slot machines were not among them. The rules of operation as set down in 1952 state that players had to have even chances at the games. Therefore, the house did not participate in baccarat, collecting only a 5 percent fee from winning bank bets. The roulette wheels lacked zeros. Winners paid a 7 percent fee to the house after each spin of the wheel. With the coming of new casinos in Holland and Germany in the 1970s, the fee shrank to 4 percent; later the house was allowed to use a one-zero wheel (with its 2.7 percent house advantage). Then, blackjack games with their built-in house advantages were permitted. The procurators have not been alone in setting casino policy. The minister of finance sets rates of taxation and places inspectors (whose main role is to collect taxes) in the casinos.

In hopes of competing with the slot machine casinos of Germany and Holland, the casino owners approached the provincial procurators and the minister of finance in 1982. After receiving a favorable reading for their request, several casinos purchased machines. The minister of justice, however, said he would not approve the machines unless Parliament passed a law permitting them. The procurators serve for lifetime terms, but they found it politically wise to maintain good relations with the minister of justice. They withdrew their approval.

The industry had a dilemma: that is, should they go to Parliament or not to get approval for slot machines. The casino association opposed legalization because of a "Brussels threat." Between competing Walloon and Flemish provinces in Belgium lies the neutral "bicultural" province of Brabant, which contains the capital city of Brussels. Major political players in Parliament believed it was impossible to give legal status to existing casinos without allowing business interests to obtain concessions for one or more casinos in Brabant.

Brussels was the feeder market for all eight existing casinos in the country. Several casinos ran daily bus trips to Brussels. The impact of a Brussels casino on the earning capacity of the other casinos was viewed as a serious threat. However, as the 21st century approached, the casino operators recognized that without slot machines, they could not compete with casinos in surrounding venues. The casinos also found that they were competing with slot machines that had found a way into the many arcades, bars, and taverns of the land.

When taking office in 1995, a new minister of justice indicated willingness to pursue a new law. At the end of June 1997, a draft was approved by the federal government and sent to the Belgian Parliament. In 1999, the Games of Chance Law was passed, which regulated casino gaming as well as gaming in arcades and bars.

Locations where gaming could be permitted were separated into three types: casinos, arcades, and bars. The distinction between those three types was based on the kind and number of games operated and the amount of the bets, as well as losses per player.

Only nine casinos were permitted. These included the eight existing locations plus a new one in Brussels. The casinos were permitted to have slot machines. Licensing and oversight was provided by a new nine member independent gaming board supported by annual fees to be paid by operators and manufacturers.

The process for licensing the new casino in Brussels involved two steps. First, in 2004, the Brussels city council reviewed many applications. They selected Casinos Austria International to construct and operate the casino. Then, in 2005, the new Belgian Gaming Commission granted a license to the company. In 2006, the casino opened. The strategy of legalizing slot machines and allowing the ninth casino seemed to save the Belgian casino industry from impending financial doom. In 2004, the eight facilities had produced collective gaming wins of 43 million euros. By 2007, that number rose to 115 million euros for nine casinos.

Belgium also has two tracks for betting on horse races, as well as a government run lottery. These types of games are regulated by separate agencies of the government.

References

"Belgian Casinos Post Record Turnover of EUR 115m." August 18, 2008. http://www.expatica.com/be/news/local_news/Belgian-casinos-post-record-turnover-of-EUR-115m.html.

De Smet, Joris, and Andrew Toittenham. 1999. "Belgium." In *International Casino Law,* 3rd. ed. Edited by Anthony N. Cabot, William N. Thompson, Andrew Tottenham, and Carl Braunlich, 337–341. Reno: Institute for the Study of Gambling, University of Nevada, Reno.

"Grand Casino Brussels." www.casinosaustria.com/GCB-Press-Release-25-11-2005pdf.

Central European Countries

Today there is casino gaming, as well as other gaming, in six central European states that had been part of the Soviet-dominated Eastern Bloc prior to the Soviet Union's collapse at the end of the 1980s. The six nations include Hungary, Bulgaria, Romania, Czech Republic, Slovak Republic, and Poland; of these, only Hungary and Bulgaria had casinos under the communist regime.

Casino gaming in Hungary expanded rapidly as the country emerged from its Eastern Bloc ties. New legislation in 1991 authorized several new casinos.

World War I tore the Austro-Hungarian Empire asunder as its Hapsburg rulers allied themselves with the losing German cause against the British, French, Russians, and Americans. A peace treaty led to the destruction of the monarchy and a dismemberment of the territory. The two countries, Hungary and Austria, split apart. World War II again found each country allied with a losing German effort. Occupation forces accompanied defeat this time, and the territory was separated from the rest of Europe by the Iron Curtain. The 1990s brought unity between Austria and Hungary once again and a new Vienna-Budapest axis emerged, with many joint economic ventures, including a network of casino operations.

Hungary had welcomed casino gaming in the earlier days of the 20th century. In 1928, an American group operated a legal casino on Margaret Island in Budapest. World War II, however, ended their venture. Occupation forces stymied the return of gaming enterprise there and in Austria until the 1950, when American forces, who occupied western Austria, allowed a return of casinos. After the Russians withdrew from eastern Austria in 1955, and the country became neutral, a nationwide network of casinos emerged once again.

The Hungarians took hope when they saw Russian troops leaving Austria in 1955. They, too, expected freedom. They quickly embraced political leaders who promised independence from Russian occupation and from a Marxist ideology.

Their taste of freedom was fleeting, and the Russians proved unwilling to let territory so close to their own borders slip from their control.

The fierce suppression of the Hungarian revolt of 1956 was not a likely signal that capitalism was coming to the communist state. Still, force could not sustain indefinitely the Russians' brutal imposition of the dictatorial regime of Janos Kadar on the Hungarian people. As the years passes, the Kadar regime loosened its grip. Gradually, the winds of capitalism seeped through cracks in the Iron Curtain. Controlled free enterprises were accepted more and more in the 1960s and 1970s. Communist leaders were very mindful of the historical and cultural attributes of Budapest and of the festive nature of the Hungarian people, reflected especially in their national cuisine and world-famous wines. It was not too long before they realized that a strong tourism industry could provide a needed boost to a lackluster manufacturing sector.

Danubius, the state-owned hospitality corporation, selected Hilton Hotels to manage a new hotel in Budapest, located near the Danube next to the Matthias Church and its famous statue of St. Stephen on Castle Hill. Archaeological excavations on the Hilton site uncovered artifacts from prior centuries. Public pressure on the state hotel company led to the decision that the project should incorporate these archeological finds. Walls and a tower from a 13th-century Dominican church and Jesuit monastery were preserved, as were gothic columns and Roman stonework. When finished, the 323-room hotel presented tourists with a museum inside modern glass exteriors that permitted outstanding views of the Danube. Casi-

nos Austria was selected to operate a casino at the facility.

At the beginning of the 1980s, Casinos Austria partnered with Danubius to created the Hungarian Casino Corporation. The two entities are full and equal partners in casino gaming enterprises in Hungary, with the provision that the Hungarians maintain 51 percent ownership in case an ultimate dispute should again tear this Austro-Hungarian alliance asunder. In 1981, the new casino corporation leased the fourth floor of the Budapest Hilton Hotel. A restaurant and nightclub were evicted, and the four rooms they occupied became Casino Budapest. Gaming action began on April 18, 1981.

The opening of the casino did raise some eyebrows, as the notion of a communist-controlled casino was somewhat unique. When confronted with this philosophical paradox, casino director Jozsef Somogyi responded, "It has nothing to do with ideology, it has to do with money. No casino was ever founded on ideological grounds. Ours wasn't either." The casino corporation's goal was to attract hard currency—Western money. The operators had no interest in recirculating Hungarian florins. So when the casino first opened, all Hungarians and residents of other Eastern Bloc nations were banned from gaming activities. The ban was lifted in May 1990.

All the tables originally conducted play in West German marks. There were several reasons for selecting German currency. With the ban on Eastern Bloc players, the casino found, as expected, that more players were from West Germany than from any other country. Second, many perceived the mark as the strongest Western European currency. Third, the West German paper currency was the only national currency that distinguished between each denomination with both size and color variations. The casino exchanged 22 Western currencies for mark-valued chips. The use of Western currency provided one additional barrier to locals wishing to make wagers because they cannot possess more than small amounts of "hard currency."

The casino offers gaming in four different rooms. Two American roulette, one French roulette, and a blackjack table greet the player in the cage room at the front of the casino. The main gaming room offers two French roulette, two American roulette, one blackjack, and one baccarat table. The main room has thick carpeting and brown paneling on one side. Opposite this wall is an old stone wall with stained-glass windows that let the patron know the historical value of the site. The stone represents the walls of the Jesuit Monastery, and the third gaming room is within the tower of the Old Monastery. This church room, dating back seven centuries, yields more cathedral windows and four blackjack tables. The church flavor gives a special touch to the gaming ambience. And it may not be too inappropriate: local historians claim that after prayers the monks used to gather in the upper tower and shoot dice.

Casinos Austria reports healthy growth in gaming revenues for each year between 1981 and 1987. Also encouraging are visitor figures that registered a gain of 58 percent over the same period. Until 1990, the casino organization paid a tax on gross win that ranged from 35 percent to 80 percent depending on volume of win. In 1990, the government decided that the Budapest casino and

other casinos in Hungary would pay a once-only fee of US$1 million plus 40 percent of gross win.

The success of the Budapest casino led the Austro-Hungarian company to expand westward. In 1983, their second joint venture began with a casino in the Hungarian city of Sopron, on the Austrian border on the road to Vienna. In 1984, their third casino opened within the Thermal Hotel at Heviz. In 1989, a new casino venture began on a steamer ship that was permanently docked on the Danube at Budapest.

Today the legal basis for the operation of casinos in Hungary rests upon 1991 legislation. Under the new law, the minister of finance announced the invitation to tender for 16 new casino concessions. Many of the new casinos that opened their doors found that the market was saturated, and they have subsequently closed. The concession fee is US$1,000,000, and the concession is granted for 10 years. The gaming tax is 40 percent of the gross revenue of the table games. Also tips received by employees are taxed at a rate of 20 percent with the remaining 80 percent being returned to employees according to their employee contracts.

Casinos Austria remains a dominant participant of the casino industry in Hungary. However there are now other major operators as well. The largest casinos in Budapest, Casino Las Vegas (with 25 tables and more than 70 machines) and Tropicana Casino (with 25 tables), are separately owned by others. Casinos Austria maintains control of casinos in Gyor, Kecskemet, and Sopron.

The laws of 1991 also qualified the following activities for licensing by the national Gaming Supervisory Authority:

lottery gambling, slot machines, and betting at horse races.

In 2005 the Bulgarian government organized a lottery with prizes that included a Hyundai car, high-tech television sets, and mobile phones. The entry ticket was a simple one. Players had only to vote in the national election. This unusual lottery designed to increase voter turnout was not the first lottery in the former communist state. In 1957, a sports lottery was authorized, and an online 6/49 lotto game was established in later years. In 2007, the lotto prize exceeded 1.2 million euros. Bulgaria was one of two former Soviet satellite countries (the other being Hungary) that developed casinos while under communist domination. The casinos persist today.

Bulgaria lies north of Greece and Turkey and south of Romania. It has a territory the size of Tennessee and a population of 8.4 million. Its status as a country dates back to 681 when the first Kingdom of Bulgaria was established. During the communist era following World War II, Bulgarian authorities permitted unregulated casinos to operate in the larger hotels of the capital city of Sofia, as well as in Black Sea resort hotels near Varna. All gaming had to be done by persons holding foreign passports, and play was conducted with Western currencies.

A new democratic government was installed in 1991, and they initiated rules for gaming in 1993. In 1999, a law was passed establishing a State Commission on Gambling. The commission has oversight authority for lotteries and bingo halls, as well as casinos. There are 11 casinos under the new authority. Six are in Sofia, and five in the Sunny Beach area near Varna. The casinos are generally very small, with gaming floors less than 3,000 square feet in size. The casinos pay a special gaming tax from 8 to 12 percent, depending on the specific game being played. They also pay regular corporate income taxes. All persons over 18 years old are welcome to play, and their winnings are not taxed.

Poland is the largest of the central European nations formerly in the Soviet Bloc. It is the size of the state of New Mexico, and it has a population of 38.5 million, with 27 million adults. The population gambles a lot. In 2008, wagers lost by the population reached 8 billion dollars. This amounts to about $300 per adult, very similar to the amount gambled by Americans, albeit the wealth of Poland residents is less than that of Americans.

There are several forms of gambling in Poland. There are limited opportunities for betting on horse races, as there are only three tracks. On the other hand there is a wide array of choices for lottery bets, with both government-run games and private games. There are also sports betting shops. Three types of casino gaming is found: full service casino facilities, slot machine arcades, and free standing machines in bars and restaurants.

The first casinos opened almost immediately upon Poland's release from Soviet domination in 1988 and 1989. A company called Casinos Poland was organized in 1988 with a partnership among LOT—the Polish Airlines, the Polish Airport Authority, and Century Casinos. The next year, the group opened a casino in Krakow, and the following year, one in Warsaw. Today the country has 27 casinos, which are controlled by three companies—Casinos Poland, Orbis Casinos, and ZPR—the later a company that is also the largest slot machine maker in Poland. Seven of the full-service casinos are in Warsaw, three each in Gdynia, Krakow, Lodz, and Wroclaw, two each in Katowice, Poznan, and Szczecin, and one each in Torun and Rzepin. There are 181 slot machine arcades—33 in Katowice and 21 in Warsaw. There is a formula for giving out licenses. Cities with fewer than 250,000 people may have one casino, and cities above that population may have one for each 250,000 people. Slot arcades are given to cities on the basis of one per each 100,000 persons.

The Polish casinos and arcades pay a tax of 45 percent on their winnings. Machines in bars and restaurants pay per-machine fees. There are 35,000 free-standing machines in 18,000 locations. Considerable concern has been expressed about problem gambling generated by the free-standing machines. However, the government has mixed emotions about controlling them, as they are seeking to balance the revenues produced by the machines for the government with the social dangers of the machines.

While not as large as Poland, the Czech Republic, with its 10 million people, does have many more casinos. New legislation in 1990 put gambling regulation under supervision of the Ministry of Finance. More than 40 facilities have been licensed since 1990 for the country (which in 1993 separated from the Slovak Republic). Fourteen are in the capital city of Prague. Most are quite small, with the largest being the Admiral Casino Coliseum, having but 8 table

games and 160 slot machines. A report in 2007 suggested that most machine gambling in the country is underground, being conducted in nearly 200 unregulated casinos. Overall these casinos, which include all manner of slot arcades, have nearly 50,000 machines, one for each 200 residents—the highest density of slot machines per capita in the European Union. This machine proliferation is a serious problem for the national government, as many social problems are tied to the phenomenon. The Czech Republic also has an unusual density of horse racing tracks—19 in all.

TIPOS, a joint stock company, was created shortly after the Czech Republic became a separate political entity. The company runs a variety of lottery games, including instant games, keno, lotto, and sports betting games. All beneficiaries of the lottery are Czech charities.

The new Slovak Republic has 5.5 million people. Its capital city is Bratislava, which is also its gambling capital. The city has 5 of the country's 14 casinos. It also has a racetrack and is headquarters to Sazka, the national lottery company. Nine sports-oriented civic groups came together to develop the company, as they own all of its stock. Sazka is the largest operator of lotteries in the country, offering keno, instant, bingo, lotto, and traditional passive lottery games, as well as sports betting games. Sazka has developed online capacities and at present conducts Internet games for fun, as well as providing a variety of information on gambling in Slovakia. Sazka is poised to offer Internet gambling for money as soon as the government authorizes it to do so.

The 22 million people of Romania were not strangers to gambling when their country was released from the hold of the Soviets in 1990. Lotteries had been part of their existence dating back to the establishment of a national drawing in 1906. The government operation was reauthorized in the 1990s, and now runs traditional passive games as well as lotto and instant games. In 2005, the government-owned lottery was partially privatized and equity shares were given as reparations to people who had had their properties seized illegally by the communist regime during the post–World War II years. The lotto prize exceeded 8 million euros in 2007.

Casinos came to Romania in 1991, when Casinos Austria opened a facility in the Bucharest Intercontinental Hotel. The capital city now has over 20 casinos, some of which are large slot machine arcades. Ten other casinos are found in the country's smaller cities.

References

Awwad, Adel. "Czech Republic Casinos." http://ezinearticles.com/?Czech-Republic-Casinos&id=625847.

"Czech Casinos and Gambling in Czech Republic." www.casinocity.com/cz/cities.html.

Gambling il dado. "Land Casinos Hungary." www.ildado.com/land_casinos_hungary.html.

Gambling il dado. "Land Casinos Romania." www.ildado.com/land_casinos_romania.html.

Gambling il dado. "Land Casinos Slovakia." www.ildado.com/land_casinos_slovakia.html.

Hunter, Meredith R. 2001. "Gambling." In *A Comparative Perspective on Major Social Problems*," edited by Rita J. Simon, 135. Lanham, MD: Lexington Books.

"Increasing Polish Gambling." 2008. *Extra,* September 25.

News.bg. 2007. "Bulgarian Lottery Reached 1.2 M EUR Jackpot." June 7. http://international.ibox.bg/news/id_2051766441

P.M. 2007. "Risky Business." *The Warsaw Voice*, January 24, www.warsawvoice.pl/view/13686.

Revada, Maria. 2008. "Bulgaria." In *International Casino Law and Regulation*, edited by William N. Thompson. Boulder, CO: International Masters of Gaming Law (looseleaf).

"Sazka Launches an Internet Portal that offers Casino Games." Lottery Insider, September 29, 2008, www.lotteryinsider.com/lottery/sazka.htm.

Shields, Elinor. 2005. "Ballot Box Lottery Sparks Bulgaria Row." BBC News, June 24, http://news.bbc.co.uk/2/hi/europe/4122970.stm, accessed October 21, 2008.

Thompson, William N. 1993. "Hungary." In *International Casino Law*, 2nd ed. Reno: Institute for the Study of Gambling, Reno: University of Nevada, 317–324.

CROATIA AND THE FORMER YUGOSLAV STATES

Yugoslavia was created as a nation following World War II when the previously separate kingdoms of Slovenia, Croatia, and Serbia were joined together with the provinces of Bosnia, Herzegovina, Montenegro, Macedonia, Dalmatia, and Voyvodina. The amalgamated state survived after World War II due to the strong hand of Marshal Tito. Things began to fall apart after his death in 1981, and by the 1990s civil war had torn the country apart. Slovenia (covered in a separate entry), Croatia, and Serbia became separate states, as did Bosnia, Macedonia, and Montenegro, although Serbia has struggled to maintain dominance over the latter areas. The new states surround Albania, which remained independent throughout the 20th century. Casinos have been permitted in the various areas for nearly 50 years, and they remain in the region today.

Croatia with its 4.7 million people has a major advantage in casino gaming. The country, which gained independence from Yugoslavia in 1991, has over 3,000 miles of coastline on the Adriatic Sea. The shoreline is a favorite vacation spots for Europeans. Of the former states of Yugoslavia, Croatia has the most casinos. There are 22 casinos with both machines and table games, and another 24 slot machine arcades. The interior city of Zagreb, the capital, has the most casinos (17), with six being full-service facilities. The Croatian national lottery operates six casinos, three of which are in Zagreb. Other casinos are privately owned.

Serbia has several casinos, mostly in the capital city of Belgrade. The largest, Grand Casino Belgrade is owned by a partnership between a local hotel and Casinos Austria. The HIT casino company of Slovenia holds the license for the Maestral Resort casino in Montenegro. The new state, which became independent in 2006, has three other casinos. Macedonia, independent since 1993, has four casino facilities, one of which is operated by the state lottery company. Bosnia has two casinos, both of which are in its capital city, Sarajevo. Gaming in Albania is confined to a single casino, the Regency, in Tirana.

References

"Croatia Gambling Casinos," www.ildado .com/land_casinos_crotia.html.

"Eastern European Casinos." 2008. Gaming Floor.com, August 13, www.gamingfloor .com/Eastern_European_Casinos.html.

Tottenham, A. 1999. "Republic of Croatia." In *International Casino Law*, 3rd ed. Edited by A. Cabot, W. Thompson, A. Tottenham, and C. Braunlich, 343. Reno: Institute of Gambling Studies, University of Nevada, Reno.

Tottenham, A. 1999. "Yugoslavia," In *International Casino Law*, 3rd ed. Edited by A. Cabot, W. Thompson, A. Tottenham, and C. Braunlich, 480. Reno: Institute of Gambling Studies, University of Nevada, Reno.

FRANCE

The cultural history of France is filled with the excitement of gambling. Many of today's games either had their origins in France or were commercially developed there. Decks of cards were prevalent as early as the 14th century. The ace was elevated to its prime status in the deck during the revolution against the king. Baccarat games came from France, and the roulette wheel generated its current layout as well as rules of play in the Palais Royal, an arcade for gambling located just below the quarters for the king. Of course, the game came to be known as "French roulette." Blackjack also emerged as a major game at the French court. The excesses of French Kings Louis XIV through Louis XVI made gambling ubiquitous not only near the palace but in gaming houses throughout Paris. The activity was also surrounded by criminal scams, schemes, as well as street "thuggery." Even during the revolutionary years (1789–1792) gambling activity continued, almost as if it were a diversion for the violent, crumbling society of the times. Order came with the arrival of Napoleon Bonaparte.

Napoleon in a sense cleaned up the street life of Paris, but he found that he was unable to suppress gambling. Instead he opted to control the activity and to impose taxes on the games. He instituted an 1806 law which limited casinos in Paris and confined outside gaming halls to resort communities with spas, communities which had catered to elites and the former nobility. There were continuing attempts to ban all gambling, but their success had to await the arrival of a restored monarchy and another Bourbon King, Louis Phillipe. Under his rule, an 1836 law banned casino gambling and also abolished a national lottery. (The national lottery had been instituted by Louis XIV in 1776 to replace myriad private and royal games. It continued operations with only a pause in the postrevolutionary years 1793–1797.)

While the law was enforced in a general way, much gambling continued even as French entrepreneurs (the most famous being the Blanc brothers, who developed casinos in Homburg and Monaco) left for other lands. Pressure for legal games was resisted until 1907, when the National Assembly recognized the economic pleas from spa communities hoping to restore their commercial viability. A 1907 law permitted player-banked casino games at the Paris suburban spa of Enghien as well as other spa communities. In 1920, another law decreed that casinos had to be at least 100 kilometers from Paris; however, Enghien was permitted to continue its games.

Casinos win their licenses with a system of dual application. The private organizations first seek to find a facility in a location that qualifies for a casino. They make a contract for the facility (which is sometimes owned by a local government), and the local government approves the contract. Then the national gaming commission, which is part of the Ministry of Interior, conducts a full background investigation on the applicant. If the ministry approves, the matter then goes back to the local government, which invites public comments and then gives the final approval for gambling to begin.

In 1931, in recognition that French casinos needed new games to compete with gaming houses in Monaco, Italy, and Belgium, the games of French roulette and blackjack were permitted. However, in 1937 there was a specific law which made all slot machines illegal. More games were authorized in 1959, including American-style roulette, although that game was required to have two zeros on its wheel, making it less inviting than the French game with one zero.

The 1960s and 1970s saw a major decline in French casinos as competitors emerged in the United Kingdom, Netherlands, Germany, and Spain. This editor was refused entrance to a casino at Trouville in the summer of 1986 during a research tour because according to the manager, they were embarrassed that there were no (zero) players there that evening. In 1986, Trouville was listed as the ninth leading casino in revenue for France. There were more 150 casinos in France. The socialist dominated government of the early 1980s had little sympathy for the economic plight of the casinos. Their owners were wealthy people, not socialists. And the government saw gambling activity as an exploitation of the poor. Fortunately for the casinos, the political climate changed with the election of a centrist prime minister (Jacques Chirac). In 1987, Parliament lowered taxes from 60 percent to a scale between 25 percent and 33 percent. Most important, casinos were authorized to have slot machines, as well as the house-banked variation of baccarat, punto banco.

The lingering influence of the socialists impeded the installation of machine gaming. At first, only 16 casinos were allowed to have machines, but as the 1990s unfolded all casinos became eligible to have the games. Almost immediately casino revenues doubled (and more) with the inclusion of the machines. Now machines represent over 90 percent of the winnings of most of the casinos. New laws have also allowed casinos to come into major cities. Large casinos have been developed in Bordeaux, Toulouse, and Lille. The largest French casino is the new one in Lyon, which has 400 machines. Although the casinos emphasize their machines, they have also developed new offerings for poker players, and France has also started several major poker tournaments.

The national lottery returned to France in 1933, and it now offers all modern variations of play. The popularity of the lottery has been greatly enhanced by televised drawings and programs featuring winners and their life stories. The government also conducts all horse race betting activity, although chances may be sold in 8,000 betting shops as well as at nine racetracks. The major track is Longchamp, in Paris. The pari-mutuel system developed in France, as many consider the word "pari" to be a short form of "Paris." The government organization controlling racing is called Pari Mutuel Urbain. It claims to be the third-largest betting operation in the world.

References

Schwartz, David G. 2006. *Roll the Bones: A History of Gambling*. New York: Gotham, 49, 90, 103–104

Vercher, Elizabeth, and William Thompson. 1999. "France." In *International Casino Law*, 3rd ed. Edited by A. Cabot, W. Thompson, A. Tottenham, and C. Braunlich, 359–370. Reno: Institute of Gambling Studies, University of Nevada, Reno.

"Welcome to France!" 2008. World Casino Directory, October 30, http://wwwcasino directory.com/france, accessed October 30, 2008.

GERMANY

Several of the oldest casinos in the world can be found in Germany. A facility at Bad Ems entertained players as early as 1720, while a law authorized gaming at Casino Bad Kissingen in 1746. The tables of Baden-Baden were filled with chips in 1748, and those in Wiesbaden helped change fortunes as early as 1771.

The word "bad" means water. Casinos were traditionally placed in resort communities that had medicinal waters coming from hot springs. Affluent tourists seeking "the cure" would come to the resorts and during their hours out of the waters entertain themselves by playing games. The style of play was genteel and relaxing. Casinos around the world have changed considerably over the past three centuries. However, even though they have enjoyed the greatest number of years for progress, the German casinos still cling to a style that has been passed by in most other venues. To be sure, there are some more modern gaming houses in Germany, but cultural and legal factors keep most of the casinos operating with rules from another era.

Gambling law in Germany should be understood in the context of Germany history. The Middle Ages found Germany decentralized, and certain regions encouraged gaming. For instance, the city of Frankfurt on Main used gaming houses primarily to raise revenue as early as 1378. During the Age of Enlightenment in the 18th century, the renewed power of the aristocracy led to a

Baden Baden (Germany), the most luxurious casino in the world.

revival of casino gaming in the German states in order to entice wealthy elites to visit the spas and, as always, to help raise tax revenues. By the end of the 18th century, there were about two dozen casinos at health spas.

Casino prosperity for Germany was enhanced during the 19th century, especially after King Louis Philippe closed the French casinos in 1838. However, during the German revolution of 1848, the governing rulers in Frankfurt overwhelmingly approved the closing of German casinos. The end of the revolution granted only a short interval for continued casino gambling. The hammer came down completely with the rise of Prussia and its dominance over all of Germany. The creation of the German Empire in 1871 resulted in the banning of casinos. The reasons given were that casinos encouraged immorality, superstition, and had a negative impact on family life. Casinos stayed closed for more than 60 years.

The National Socialists of Adolf Hitler gave a green light to opening the casino doors—slightly. On July 14, 1933, the minister of the interior authorized casinos in resort communities that averaged 70,000 annual tourist visits, if they could prove that 15 percent of the visits were from foreigners. The only casino allowed to open was at Baden-Baden. Its tables operated from October 1933 until August 1944, when a closing was required due to an impending Allied occupation. In 1938, after the Anschluss of Austria and the annexation of Danzig, licensed casinos opened in Baden (near Vienna) and Sopot (now in Poland). During these years of casino operation, the German government imposed uni-

form taxation measures and mandated that the casinos close on certain dates. Both the 1933 and 1938 laws survived the end of the Nazi government, and they are to some degree effective even today.

The victorious Allies allowed casinos to open by interpreting the gaming laws of 1933 and 1938 liberally. In 1948, Rheinland-Pfalz became the first German state to have casinos at Bad Neuenahr and Bad Duerkheim. Subsequently, Baden-Wuerttemberg, Bavaria, Hessen, and Schleswig-Holstein granted new casino licenses. Although the central government was somewhat hostile toward the casinos, there was little it could do to prohibit them. By the 1950s, the accepted interpretation of the new constitution of the German Federal Republic was that it delegated casino licensing matters to the states.

In the late 1950s, state interest in casinos increased considerably when, because of scandals in Bavarian casinos, the government took over four of the five casinos by 1961. The state now had an interest in ensuring casino viability, as it was a casino owner. In other areas, such as the Saarland, the government had a predominant interest in the casino ownership (four-sevenths). A sports association (Sportverband) controlled the remaining three-sevenths interest. Casinos in other states also had a shared public-private ownership scheme.

In 1973, a change in German law allowed casinos to open in areas other than the traditional resort areas. States now could permit casinos in any location. Several cities gained the right to have casinos. In the 1980s, the federal government permitted the states to control taxation. Thus, the states now decide virtually everything affecting German gaming.

Today, casinos have developed in or near many major German cities such as Hamburg, Berlin, Bremen, Dortmund and Stuttgart. With the collapse of the German Democratic Republic (East Germany) in 1990, casinos were established in former East Germany states of Saxony, Saxony-Anhalt, Mecklenburg-Vorpommern, and former East Berlin. All 16 German states now have casinos.

While the various states of Germany are permitted to set the rules for casinos, they have apparently worked closely together because the manner of operations is quite similar across Germany, especially in the most critical way—taxation. The minor variations in rates of taxation are essentially agreements to elevate tax rates above the standard 80 percent of winnings. It is this basic tax rate that has done the most to retard the development of the casinos and keep them small and quite unexciting. The casinos uniformly have dress requirements that discourage casual players seeking only the entertainment of the tables as opposed to making social statements. Most of the casinos prohibit drinking of beverages (of any type) at gaming tables. There are also admission charges and identity checks for all players.

While the number of casinos has more than doubled to about 80 since the fall of the Berlin Wall in 1989, all remain quite small, usually with 5 to 10 tables and 100 or fewer slot machines. The machines are almost always placed in separate rooms, or even separate buildings. Nonetheless revenues from slot machines often represent as much as 90 percent of the casino's winnings. That

along with the fact that casinos use tip money to pay almost all of the wages of the table dealers, allows casinos to realize net profits even after taxation.

Casinos are considered to be vehicles for cultural enhancement of their communities. They sponsor bands and orchestras with free concerts in the summertime, as well as subsidize popular culture entertainers. Two casinos that are operated by the state bank of Nordrhein-Westfalen have used their casino facilities as art museums. The casino building in Aix-la-Chapelle (now called Aachen) has provided a visual connection between tables and art works by having a "Rain of Light," a gigantic sculpture incorporating 7,000 lights moving in 256 variations at 10 different speeds. Artworks line the walls, including originals from major artists such as Salvador Dali, Andy Warhol, George Segal, and Stanley Boxer. Elvis and Brando portraits surround diners in the Gala Restaurant. The bank's second casino at Bad Oeynhausen opened in 1980. It too features unifying light displays along with art such as the magic mirrors of Victor Bonato and the life scenes by Karlos Lodenkamper and Kurt Sohns's "pictures within pictures." State and local governments allow tax credits for these casino investments.

While the history of Germany is replete with casino gaming footprints, there are other forms of gambling available to the public. Slot machines are more popular outside the casinos than inside them. Amusement with prize machines (AWP) are found in amusement centers, pubs, and restaurants. The machines are operated by vending machine companies. There are some

180,000 AWP machines and 100,000 other amusement machines in Germany.

Germany has a wide variety of lotteries, the largest ones being conducted by the state governments. Smaller lotteries are conducted for charities. There are no private commercial lotteries. Pari-mutuel betting is allowed at 50 different horse tracks, while sports betting and off-track betting may take place in shops.

References

Kelly, Joseph, Christian Marfels, and Hartmut Nevries. "Germany." In *International Casino Law,* 3rd ed. Edited by A. Cabot, W. Thompson, A. Tottenham, and C. Braunlich, 371–380. Reno: Institute of Gambling Studies, University of Nevada, Reno.

Thompson, William. 1988. "Casino at Aachen a Montage of Art, Lights and Games." *Las Vegas Sun,* February 28.

Thompson, William. 1988. "Roots of Modern European Casinos Can be Traced to 1746 German Law." *Las Vegas Sun*, February 14.

"Welcome to Germany." 2008. World Casino Directory. http://www.worldcasino directory.com/germany, accessed October 30, 2008.

GIBRALTAR

Gibraltar is a peninsula of only 2.3 square miles, with a huge limestone mass known as the Rock of Gibraltar taking up most of the area. Like its geography, the history of Gibraltar may be described as a "rocky" one indeed. The peninsula connects to the Spanish mainland, and although controlled by the United Kingdom, the Spanish still covet oversight of the land.

Gibraltar is the home of the only monkeys that inhabit the European continent—the Barbary apes. It is also home to 28,000 civilians and 5,000 British military personnel. The apes are sure of their home; the other residents are not. In 1713, the Treaty of Utrecht settled the War of the Spanish Succession by ceding Gibraltar to the British for as long as they hold it. The British wanted Gibraltar for a navy base and as a critical defense position at the entry to the Mediterranean Sea. If the British do not hold on to the enclave, sovereignty is supposed to revert to Spain. Ever since 1713, the British presence on Gibraltar has been an irritant to the Spanish people. In 1964, the British upset Francisco Franco, the Spanish leader, by revealing future plans for Gibraltar's independence.

Franco began a campaign to win back the peninsula. First, he stopped all air traffic between Spain and Gibraltar. Then, he halted all British ground traffic. Then, in 1966, he stopped all traffic. Since 1985, a decade after the death of Franco, the border has gradually reopened. However, there still is no direct air traffic between Spain and Gibraltar.

Gibraltar did not have traditional casinos until 1960, when British legislation opened the doors to casinos in the mother country. The colonists of Gibraltar wished to follow suit. British officials acquiesced at the request of the local council. In 1961, they authorized bids for a single casino concession.

Several English companies sought the license. The winner of the competition, however, did not have sufficient financial resources to complete a building project. By 1963, there still was no casino. At that point, a prominent Gibraltar attorney contacted his close friend, Herman Heyman, a German who often vacationed in Gibraltar with his wife. He had owned the casino at Forges-les-Eaux in France until 1960. His Gibraltar friend felt that he might like to apply his gaming skills to Gibraltar.

Heyman was aware that the British were not the most avid gamblers in the world, but there was a closer venue. Within a one-hour drive was the Spanish Costa del Sol. Here was a fantastic unexploited gaming market, since Spain, under Franco, would not allow casinos. Heyman purchased the concession. He constructed an elegant gaming palace costing several million dollars on the side of the Rock of Gibraltar. In 1964, it opened.

Heyman was just starting to market the casino to the high-rolling vacationers (especially Arabs) who frequented beach resorts near Marbella in Spain when the British suggested that Gibraltar could become independent. To Franco, the British had broken the 1713 treaty. He closed the border. In the aftermath, Heyman saw his multimillion dollar investment facing a market reduced from one including the world's best high rollers to one made up of 33,000 local residents to whom parsimony was a way of life.

The peninsula had an airport and boats to Morocco, but the old marketing plan had to be scrapped. The dreams of a double tower with 850 luxury apartments and a new casino disappeared. Heyman had to exercise one of two choices—to fold or to survive. He chose survival, knowing that that course demanded a radically new plan. He looked closely at the local population and quickly discovered that the parsimonious British love bingo. Bingo became the key to survival. His International Sporting Club became a very successful bingo operation.

In 1985, the Spanish reopened the border, prompting new crises. First, eight commercial Spanish bingo games were available in the border area. The crisis turned out to be a Spanish crisis, however. By concentrating on bingo as a tool to attract patrons to his casino, Heyman had developed an appealing bingo operation. Entrance fees were nonexistent, cards were inexpensive, and prizes were generous. The Spanish could not compete, and not one Spanish bingo game survived.

The second crisis was more imperative. The Heyman concession ran for 21 years, from 1963 to 1985. In 1985, a new dynamic entered the picture. As the border reopened, the International Sporting Club faced the prospect of local competition. A rival group won the right to build a new £10 million ($20 million) resort facility on Queensway Street, next to the harbor, which included a casino.

The original casino concession passed on to new ownership. Gibraltar now has two full service casinos, which include bingo games but rely more on traditional casino revenues. The casino at the Rock Hotel has 150 gaming machines and eight tables Although the casino is important for attracting tourist revenue, Gibraltar relies more on its status as a duty-free shopping venue and as a tax haven for large corporations. Gibraltar is also the site for online gaming operations for the William Hill betting enterprise.

References

"Gibraltar Casinos." http://ezinearticles.com/ ?Gibraltar-Casinos&is=636316.

"Gibraltar Gambling News." www.casino city.com/gi/cities.html.

Thompson, William N. 1999. "Gibraltar," In *International Casino Law*, 3rd ed. Edited by A. Cabot, W. Thompson, A. Tottenham, and C. Braunlich, 381–382. Reno: Institute of Gambling Studies, University of Nevada, Reno.

GREECE

The ancient Greeks were well acquainted with gambling. Their gods purportedly rolled dice to determine which would rule the heavens (Zeus won), the seas (Poseidon), and the underworld (Hades). Mortals rolled the six-sided objects as well, and they also flipped objects like we now flip coins. The Greek affinity for games was based upon appeals to luck rather than any pretense of having skills, albeit there were running races and chariot races as well. In their pantheon of deities, the Greeks of the classical era had Tyche, the goddess of fortune, and Hermes, the god of luck.

Greeks of the modern era have availed themselves of knowledge of mathematics, which precludes a total reliance on luck in their games. It also provides the rational for choosing the winning side of the table when one engages in gaming. In the early 20th century, gambling at several leading European casinos was dominated by the "Greek Syndicate," which was led by Nicholas Zographos. Zographos had the mental ability to track all the cards dealt from a six-deck shoe in baccarat (*chemin de fer*) games. His gang controlled the bank at the baccarat tables (which private gamers could do), and this enabled them to stop play whenever it appeared that a losing streak was upon them (something the casino as "bank" cannot do unless players have taken all their money—that is, "broke the bank"). With advanced money-management skills and a memory of all the cards played, the Greek Syndicate had a considerable advantage over most players they encountered, and over several years they amassed a considerable fortune.

Another Greek personality shared the advantages of sitting on the house side of the table. Basil Zaharoff (who was born in Turkey of Greek parents) used business skills to buy controlling shares of SBM's Monte Carlo casinos in 1923. The 1920s were a time of Greek dominance of gaming in Monaco. The Greeks came back for another stint in 1950, when shipping millionaire Aristotle Onassis took over majority control of SBM. He held domination over the casinos until 1966, when Prince Rainier's family regained ownership control over Monte Carlo. These years were also the years when Greek-born Nicholas Dandolos, took on the moniker of "Nick the Greek" and established a prominence in American poker circles. Nick the Greek was one of the first two players in Binion's World Championship of Poker in 1969, albeit he finished the tournament in second place.

The Greeks brought their gaming home after World War II. Casinos were established under government ownership on the islands of Rhodes and Corfu, as well as on Mont Parnes just outside of Athens. These were the only casinos until the 1990s. Greek society, although quite familiar with games, was not favorably disposed toward casinos, and they pressured the government to keep them restricted. The casinos did not improve facilities or develop the kind of amenities that would attract players from other countries. Casinos in surrounding venues gained considerable commercial advantages over the Greeks until government officials were persuaded to expand and privatize much of their casino industry.

Today there are nine casinos, and of these, only the ones at Mont Parnes and Corfu are partially state owned. The six new casinos (established in the 1990s) are in Patra, Porto Carras, Xanthi, Loutraki, and Thessaloniki. The latter two are the largest and most developed.

Casino Hotel Loutraki is partially owned and operated by Casinos Austria. It has 70 table games and 929 slot machines. The Regency Casino Thessaloniki has more than 75,000 square meters of space, and claims to be the second-largest casino facility in Europe. Its main gaming floor offers 77 tables and 900 slot machines for players.

Greece has also had a lottery organization run by the government since 1862. It runs passive games. In 1993, a private group was licensed to conduct instant games with scratch tickets. Since 1959 a private group has also run sports betting operations. Additionally, the ODIE Hellenic Horse Racing Organization has conducted pari-mutuel betting on races since 1925.

Cyprus is the third-largest island in the Mediterranean Sea. It is a Republic with a population divided between ethnic Greeks and Turkish peoples. Political turmoil has led to a partition of the island, with the Greek Republic sector being to the north. That sector has 20 casinos, plus a dog track and a horse racing track, each with pari-mutuel betting.

References

Anagnostaras, John, and Henry Melvani. 1999. "Greece." In *International Casino Law*, 3rd ed. Edited by A. Cabot, W. Thompson, A. Tottenham, and C. Braunlich, 406–408. Reno: Institute of Gambling Studies, University of Nevada, Reno.

"Gambling in Greece." www.casinocoinage .com/blogs/gambling-in-greece.html.

"Greece." www.gamingandlotteryfiles.com/ novamediafile.php?file=Greece.htm.

Schwartz, David. 2006. *Roll the Bones: The History of Gambling.* New York: Gotham Books, 24–25, 73

IRELAND AND THE IRISH SWEEPSTAKES

There have been many legal forms of gambling in Ireland during the century of its national independence. These forms now include a lottery (and its predecessor, Irish Hospital Sweepstakes), wagering on horse and dog races both on track and off track, and gambling on sports events at betting shops. Additionally, there are bingo games gambling on amusement machines, some of which are conducted in "private" casino clubs. Internet gambling is not provided for in the law, but the statutes against much (casino-type) gambling (a 1956 law and other and related laws) are not enforced against online wagers as long as the providers of the gambling services are outside of Ireland. Bingo games are permitted and regulated as lotteries under the 1956 law.

A report from the financial firm of Merriom/Landsbanki estimated that the "total Irish betting and gambling market" in terms of gross win (players' losses) was 924 million euros in 2006. By sectors the market was

Lotteries   317.0

Betting Shops   362.0

Bingo   27.1

Online Betting   83.0

On-track Racing and Other   134.9

The per person wagers by Irish adults amount to 292 euros per year (losses).

Among Europeans, only in Finland (307 euros) and Sweden (295 euros) do adults wager more. The Irish number is comparable to that of adults in the United Kingdom (289 euros) but substantially more than that of American adults (245 euros, or US$350).

In 1930, the Irish Hospital Sweepstakes lottery was established as a source of funding for the newly independent Ireland's voluntary hospitals. Most of these facilities were operated by Protestant church organizations, which relied heavily upon large contributions from English sponsors. Much of this sponsorship had been lost as a result of the Irish Revolution from 1918 through 1921. Heightened medical costs and the onset of the economic depression added to the miserable state of the hospitals

The law creating the sweepstakes established a Hospital Trust Fund under the minister of health. The minister of finance would dispense funds from ticket sales to this fund—basically the fund received 25 percent of all sales. Tickets were sold 3 times a year (later raised to 4 times and then 13 times) and drawings coincided with dates of major horse races. At first the races were run in England, but later Irish races were the events. The Irish Derby became one of the world's leading races as sweepstakes funds were put into the prize pool for the race.

The sweepstakes lottery was conducted in two phases. First, a general drawing selected tickets for each horse in the race. Then the race was run and prizes were distributed according to how each horse performed in the race.

The sale of tickets was quite legal in Ireland and was conducted by an agency under the minister of finance. However, the creators of the Hospital Sweepstakes knew well that Ireland was not an adequate market for their needs. The population was too small and too poor. The sponsors knew that the success of the endeavor would come with overseas ticket sales. They looked to England, Canada, and the United States as venues for ticket sales. There had been a tradition of selling Irish lotteries in England in the later decades of the 19th century, but while tolerated, these sales were illegal. Lotteries had been banned in England since 1823. Similarly lotteries had been banned in the United States at the turn of the 20th century.

As the sweepstakes sales were conducted by a government agency, the Irish were quite shy about selling tickets in venues where the sales were illegal. Therefore the minister of finance made a contract with a private group, Hospital Trust Ltd., to conduct all overseas ticket sales. The Irish government conveniently closed its eyes to the fact that most sales were in England and the United States.

At first the bulk of sales were made in England—over two-thirds of the tickets. This stimulated a reaction by British authorities. In 1932, Parliament appointed a Royal Commission on Lotteries and Betting, which urged stricter controls over sales. In 1934, Parliament enacted laws giving extra enforcement powers to the post office and to customs. As a result, a majority of sales permanently shifted over the ocean to the United States. The war years saw all sales fall off, but the slump abated somewhat as peace returned. British sales fell again as the United Kingdom authorized its own lottery scheme in 1956. In that year both Ireland and the United Kingdom authorized the sale of "Premium Bonds." These were bonds sold to individuals. They could be redeemed at full face value at any time, but they were interest free. Instead of receiving interest, the bond holders would be entered into periodic lottery drawings based upon the number of their bonds.

The sweepstakes produced revenues for several more decades. However, as a majority of American states and almost all European countries permitted and promoted sales of lottery tickets of their own, interest in the sweepstakes fell off considerably. By 1986, the government of Ireland realized that the two-step horse race ticket scheme used only 13 times a year was not an effective way to achieve lottery sales. In January 1986, the last sweepstake race was held.

The Irish Dail passed the National Lottery Act in 1986, and they awarded a sales contract to An Post, a subsidiary of the national post office. In 1987, the new lottery sold its first tickets, which were scratch-offs. The minister of finance directed lottery funds to many good causes, including medical initiatives, which benefited from the sweepstakes.

The National Lottery was initiated in a time of general recession, 1987, and contrary to the foresaid commentary on poverty and gambling, some saw it as an appropriate venture for state involvement. Reporter Claire Ryan wrote in the Sunday *Independent* in 2005 that the lottery "made a gambler out of mainstreet Ireland. Suddenly it was socially acceptable to gamble." She noted that the lottery "dangled the hope of instant and drastic escape of a biting depression. We clung to the hopes of a lottery won for a simple reason: we were broke. If you won, you would win big." Playing the lottery was much more dignified than wagering in "the choking betting shops with floors drenched in spent dockets, frequented by men with nowhere else to be at 2 p.m. on a Tuesday who clasped the stubby pens as tightly as they did their desire to win a few bob."

In addition to scratch-off tickets, the lottery sells several lotto jackpot products, televised bingo tickets, as well as tickets for the transnational Euro-Millions game. In 2005, an Irish woman won a super jackpot of over 115 million euros in that game—the biggest win in European lottery history to the time.

Betting shops have conducted business in a legal regulated manner since a 1926 law authorized off-track wagering. It is estimated that there are currently 1,100 betting shops in Ireland. In 2006, they won 362 million euros from their patrons. Most shops are operated by major companies.

Bingo and amusement machines are governed under the 1956 law, with bingo being treated as a lottery game. According to Casino City's *Global Gaming Almanac*, there are 13,020 licensed amusement machines in 130 locations in Ireland.

In pre-Christian times, horses were tied to an individual's venture into the otherworld after death. St. Patrick and the Christian forefathers kept the image of sacredness that surrounded the horse. With the evolution of time, church and community celebrations included races and sporting events using horses. The soils and grasses of Ireland were very favorable for breeding horses, and up to the present day, Ireland remains the third leading nation of the world for horse breeding—both for racing and other purposes.

The Irish have taken great pride in their horse racing stock. In the 18th and 19th centuries, the local populations would identify with horses in races against other entries from England or Scotland. Most races, however, were contests conducted between noblemen and wealthy landholders, and the public played only passive roles as observers. Additionally, the masses were relegated to positions on the side of things, as most races were either long steeplechases or point-to-point events covering many miles. There were no grandstands. The first Irish track that was enclosed with stands for hundreds or thousands of observers was built in 1860. Rules for circular races were set into place for the first time in the 1870s. Even then, among the mass audiences that began to attend races, very few engaged in wagering, for the obvious reason set forth above. The people were poor. The British authorities also sought to suppress betting. In 1906, they recognized a growing number of bookies were conducting organized betting, and Parliament passed the Street Betting Act, which banned all betting except that taking place at the track.

However, after Ireland gained home rule status, a new law was passed in 1926 that permitted bets to be made at licensed regulated shops as well as at the tracks. Track betting was also regulated, and in 1929 the government instituted its state-owned pari-mutuel system called "the Tote." The Tote operated alongside the private bookies on-track and in betting shops.

Today there are 26 tracks in the Republic of Ireland. Collectively they have an annual betting handle of over 2 billion euros.

Dog racing came a bit later in Irish history. The first dog races were held in 1927 in Dublin. Today there are 17 licensed tracks, 9 owned by the government and 8 private. The largest two are near Dublin at Harold's Cross and Shelbourne Park. Tracks employee 700 and draw 1.3 million visitors a year. Recent laws provide that a portion of the betting revenue goes toward building newer facilities and upgrading older ones. These efforts have resulted in an enhanced popularity for the sport.

Ireland is the largest breeder of racing dogs in the world, with 20,000 new dogs being registered each year. Ireland racing is unique in that many of the racing dogs are also household pets.

Casinos remain illegal, but interests have been chipping away at the law. In 1993, an Irish company called Sonas joined together with an American gaming company called Ogden and purchased more than 100 acres at the Phoenix Park racecourse in Dublin. Earlier the racecourse had closed down operations because it was losing money. The Sonas-Ogden group proposed rezoning the property to allow for construction of a 65,000-seat stadium, a 12,000-seat indoor arena, and a 2,500-person national convention center, in total a 375 million pounds sterling investment. Additionally, they were going to oversee construction of a 450-room, 26-story Sheraton Hotel that would house a 4,800-square-foot casino offering all casino games. The casino would be operated and owned by Sonas-Ogden, perhaps in some kind of partnership with An Post. It was essential to the

success of the project, as its profits would enable smooth financial operations of all of the facilities. In addition to winning rezoning changes from local authorities in west Dublin, which they did in 1996, the sponsors had to gain approval from the national Dail (parliament) with changes in the 1956 gaming law. This was another matter.

Subsequent to winning zoning support, a very active opposition arose, guided by key members of the Dail and also parties that wanted to see horse racing revived at Phoenix Park. The opponents gathered 20,000 signatures in opposition from local residents of the area. They claimed that the proposal would lower air quality and bring noise pollution as well as traffic congestion. A leading member of the Dail, Joan Burton, vocally condemned the project saying that it would be a magnet for organized crime activity, drug use, and prostitution.

Only a few weeks after the project won rezoning, the cabinet met and refused to discuss the proposal and refused to authorize consideration. In the course of his successful 1997 campaign for prime minister (Taoiseach) Bertie Ahern completely rejected casino gambling. The issue was dormant—for awhile anyway. Under Ahern's leadership, the Department of Justice, Equality and Law Reform initiated an interdepartmental group to make review the gaming and lotteries acts from 1956–1986. In 1999, they held hearings and collected submissions from 70 interested parties, including local authorities, elected representatives, charitable organizations, trade associations, gaming interests, and gaming suppliers. They issued a report with recommendations in 2000. Regarding casinos they were of one voice. They were adamant: "Casino gaming is illegal in this country at present." And so the situation has remained. But forces still advocate casinos.

During the first decade of the 21st century, new quasi-casinos have come onto the scene in the form of "private clubs." Their presence is rather discreet, as the owners and operators do not want to stimulate any political or legal opposition to their existence. Yet they do want to be legal. In 2003, Minister of Justice McDowell was confronted with their existence and with the apparent observation that they were operating in contravention of the 1956 act. McDowell was inclined to bring criminal prosecutions against the casino clubs, but he hesitated.

He reasoned that with criminal changes, it might be difficult to convince a jury that the violations of the 1956 act were "beyond a reasonable doubt." He said essentially that he would keep monitoring the situation for clear-cut law violations, but that in the meantime, he would ask parties to study the proposition that new laws be written to clarify the legal status of the casinos.

Potential casino owners took his statement to be words of encouragement. Several new facilities opened their doors. A few years later, McDowell began to sing a new tune.

In 2006, McDowell first announced that he intended to crack down on casinos. He claimed that casinos were illegal and he implied he would close them. A line had been drawn in the sand. Casinos responded, and 13 of them (with 3 in the Dublin area) formed an association, the Gaming and Leisure Association of Ireland (GLAI), in order to exerted pressure upon the government to repudiate the stand taken by McDowell. In a very short time, McDowell caved. He joined others in supporting the creation of a special task force to examine casino policy and to report their findings to the government. In the meantime, he vowed he would take not action.

One of the first items on the new GLAI's agenda was to offer the government suggested legislation to make their existing properties legal and to place them under government regulation. Their proposal sought to have casinos that adhered to the model of gaming that existed with their private clubs.

A special task force made its report to the government and to the public in 2008; however, no action has been taken in the Dail.

References

Casino City's Global Gaming Almanac. 2006. Newtown, MA: Casino City, 173–174.

Coleman, Marie. 2005. "A Terrible Danger to the Morals of the Country: The Irish Hospitals' Sweepstake in Great Britain, 1930–1987." *Proceedings of the Royal Irish Academy* 105, no. 5 (September).

Department of Justice, Equality and Law Reform. June 2000. *Review of the Gaming and Lotteries Acts 1956–1986: Report of the Intergovernmental Group.* Dublin: Department of Justice, Equality and Law Reform.

Gaming and Lotteries Act (Ireland), 1956.

Merrion/Landsbanki. 2007. "Paddy Power Company Update." October 30, 5, 12.

Report of the Gaming and Leisure Association of Ireland. 2007.

Ryan, Claire. 2005. "The Other National Vice." *Independent*, March 6, 2005: 23.

Smith, Brian. 1991. *The Horse in Ireland.* London: Wolfhound Press, 215–221.

Thompson, William N. 2008. "From Gray to Green," *International Gaming and Wagering Business* 29, 5 (May): 1, 39–43.

ITALY

The empire of ancient Rome was replete with gambling activity. Emperors played games at their palaces as well as with the people at chariot races or in gladiator contests at the Coliseum. The people spent endless hours playing games in taverns. Historian David Schwartz begins his history of gambling, *Roll the Bones*, with the story of players who refused to leave their games during the eruption of Mount Vesuvius near Pompeii. The spirit of gambling survived those foolish mortals and continued into the Middle Ages. The Italians left their mark upon the development of lotteries. In 1522, a commercial lottery took place in Venice as a means of distributing merchandise. The method quickly spread to other cities. The first money-based lottery was conducted in Florence in 1530. Soon afterwards, Genoa took up a lotto-style game with multiple winning numbers. The first government-approved house for games was the Ridotto on the canals of Venice in 1638. Many card games were played for the first time in the gaming houses and casinos of Italian city-states. Casinos existed into the modern era, which saw the unification of Italy in 1861. Lotteries, race betting, and casinos persist today.

The modern history of casinos in Italy involves a concept associated with casino gaming throughout the world: "guarding the borders." Italy has five casinos. One is located in Campione, an Italian enclave beyond the Swiss border. One casino is on the Grand Canal in Venice, located in a house dating to the 14th century, a house that was the residence of composer Richard Wagner in the latter years of his life. Venice is not far from Trieste and the Yugoslav border. Venice established a second casino near its airport in 2001. Another casino is in San Remo, which is on the Mediterranean Sea; the casino is near the French border and close to Monaco. The fifth casino, in St. Vincent, is in the Alps close to the French border and the Mont Blanc tunnel, the longest automobile tunnel in the world. Municipal governments own the casino buildings; however, management is private at Campione and St. Vincent. The municipal governments run the casinos of San Remo and Venice.

The strategy of locating casinos near borders came after World War I. Gambling action had slowed considerably during the war years, and the era of reform that followed brought a crack down on casinos. In 1919, raids closed 58 casinos. In ensuing years, political instability and confusion allowed Benito Mussolini and fascism to emerge. In 1923, he marched on Rome, and the king proclaimed Mussolini to be the premier of Italy. With ruthless force, Mussolini brought centralization and stability to governmental affairs. In 1923, his cabinet rejected pleas to legalize casinos and instructed the minister of the interior to suppress all gaming except the national lottery. The cabinet declared that casino gaming was inconsistent with Italian dignity and that towns should not depend on returns from gambling for revenues.

However, Mussolini was not blind to the political effects of closing casinos.

Casino at Campione, Italy.

Italians had a love for games. Moreover, the Monaco casinos were located near Italy. Italian lire escaping into the coffers of foreign casinos hampered Mussolini's policies of national economic development. His nationalistic solution was to protect the borders with an Italian casino, and in 1927, legal gaming returned to the Municipal Casino at San Remo. It can be noted that the businessmen behind the venture were staunch supporters of Mussolini.

The leader was firm in declaring that he would allow only one casino. Inquiries from other resorts drew the reply that their "wishes will not be fulfilled." He added, "The government's intentions are quite clear cut. For very strong reasons of a political and economic nature, a specific exception was made in favor of San Remo, but the exception in this case also serves but to prove the rule." Gaming at San Remo was part of a larger scheme to compete with Monte Carlo, a dream never fully realized.

Despite his earlier declarations against further casino expansion, Mussolini was susceptible to persuasion. But the process was slow. During his regime, a second casino opened in Campione in 1933, while Venice was permitted to have a return to casino gaming in 1937. The three casinos closed during World War II. They reopened under the new republican government in 1946. Since the war, the Italian governments generally have been built around Christian party coalitions. The coalitions have been consistently adamant that there should be no more casinos. The three original national casinos remain to guard the borders. So too does a new satellite casino for Venice. The facility, which emphasizes machine gambling, is located in a suburban area near the airport and also close to the train line that runs into

Slovenia, less than 100 miles away. One motivation for this new casino came from the expansion and promotion of nearby casinos in Slovenia.

The casino at St. Vincent was almost a French casino. The Aosta region lies high in the Alps. Its people have their own dialect and a distinct culture. At the end of World War II, the French looked upon the region as a possible war bounty. They urged the Aosta residents to hold a referendum to decide whether to remain with Italy or become part of France. Italy wanted to keep Aosta. The government in Rome promised that, if it voted to remain, the region could have autonomy over its domestic matters. Aosta knew that French political structures were extremely centralized, and under a French regime they would be governed from Paris, and they would be required to speak French. They voted to keep their own Italian dialect and to keep their political control close at hand. They voted to remain part of Italy. In 1947, their regional government informed Rome that it authorized a casino in St. Vincent. Rome acquiesced.

After the war, the government in Rome also gave domestic autonomy to Sicily, but when that island region tried to open a casino in 1963, the reaction of Rome was unequivocal. Four casinos were enough. In the 1960s, a two-year struggle against the opening of a new casino at Taormina, Sicily, was motivated in part by fears that uncontrolled organized criminal elements would control operations.

The Italians fought off the creation of a casino in San Marino. Here, the national government had to contest the efforts of a renegade communist government that controlled the enclave on Italian soil. Technically, San Marino is an independent country, the smallest republic in Europe. The nation covers only 24 square miles of mountain slopes in northern Italy. Italian land surrounds it. The 19,000 residents enjoy an independence dating to the fourth century. While the Republic of San Marino ceded its essential sovereignty to the force of Mussolini's fascist regime, it quickly reasserted a separate identity and political standing after World War II. In 1945, the residents elected a communist government, and the new government received aid from the Soviet Union. However, it needed more to support its economy. Self-sufficiency was difficult, because the enclave has no industry or agriculture base. The tiny republic looked elsewhere for revenues. They sought a model in the United States: the state of Nevada. The reaction in Rome was different than the reaction in Washington, D.C.; Rome did not agree to allow all San Marino's plans. In 1950, San Marino passed laws allowing easy divorce and civil marriages. They also planned a huge casino and a large radio and television station complex. This outraged the Italian Chrisian Democratic Coalition. They blockaded San Marino for 18 months until August 1951, when the communist government sought a settlement. They agreed to restrict marriages and divorces to the resident population and to abandon the casino plans. In turn, Italy agreed to finance the reconstruction of a railroad to San Marino. Still, the dispute raged on until 1954, when San Marino abandoned the plans for a television station. This concession, and the Soviet Union's suppression of the Hungarian uprising in 1956, outraged local residents. In 1957, the communist government was soundly defeated. Since then, no one has raised the casino question.

References

Interview with Carlo Pagan, director Casino di Venice, July 10, 2008, in Venice.

Schwartz, David G. 2006. *Roll the Bones: A History of Gambling.* New York: Gotham Books, 3–4, 83–84, 93–95.

Thompson, William N. 1999. "Italy." In *International Casino Law*, 3rd ed. Edited by A. Cabot, W. Thompson, A. Tottenham, and C. Braunlich, 307–314. Reno: Institute of Gambling Studies, University of Nevada, Reno.

LUXEMBOURG

Luxembourg was one of the last countries in Western Europe to authorize casino gambling. The conservative nature of the government precluded the urge to have a casino until the country was virtually surrounded by casinos operated in Belgium, the Netherlands, France, and all the states of western Germany. After nearby Saarbrucken in Germany opened a casino in 1977, welcoming among its patrons many residents of Luxembourg, the Luxembourg Chamber of Deputies said, "Enough." They passed a casino law.

The leaders of the small country (less than one half a million residents on 1,000 square miles of land) deemed that there should be a single casino. They also deemed that it not be in the largest city, the capital city of Luxembourg, as local residents would be too tempted to participate in frequent gaming activities. They also had their eyes on attracting players from other countries. Mondorf-les-Bains was the natural site for a single casino. The casino opened in 1979. The rules set down by the government permit a second casino if one would be considered desirable at a future time. That time has yet to come.

The town of Mondorf has the only thermal springs resort facility in the country, so the officials were adhering to the age-old European tradition of affixing gambling opportunities with "the cure." The Mondorf resort has exploited its mineral waters since the 1840s. In 1871, Victor Hugo spent a month healing his rheumatism in the springs of Mondorf. Train service began in 1882, and in 1886, an elaborate baths facility opened. The location soon won the reputation as a premier European resort. World War I delayed plans for more thermal facilities as German troops occupied the town. The Germans also dominated the community in World War II. After liberation, the central hotel was transformed into a prison for Nazi war criminals being tried at Nurenberg.

Placing the casino at Mondorf returned a degree of the old attractiveness to the town. Planners desired to keep the casino out of the big city (Luxembourg) where local residents might be the most frequent patrons. The city is only 20 miles away, and the casino runs buses downtown, but they make stops only at the hotels. The Mondorf location was chosen mainly with eyes directed to the road maps. The casino site is only five miles from the

Mosel River and a bridge to Germany. France is a mere 10 miles away. The casino offers good marketing opportunities for both countries, as the nearest competitor, Saarbrucken, is over an hour away. Mondorf is the most convenient casino for many Germans in the Mosel Valley. The casino also runs daily buses to Thionville, Metz, and Nancy in France. The only casino in the Alsace-Lorraine region is at Niederbronn. It can be reached from these French cities only by travelling on poor secondary roads. Mondorf is much more convenient.

A German-based company won the bid to construct the casino complex in Mnodorf. It had been involved in operating the casino at Bad Homburg. So not only does Mondorf-les-Bains share the European tradition of being a casino at a health spa, it also shares the distinction of being another child of Bad Homburg. (Bad Homburg is fond of its title "The Mother of Monaco.") Yet, tradition is not the motif of Mondorf. The casino focuses its plans not on the traditions from the past, but rather, on a vision of the future. The name of the casino reflects the mission: "Casino 2000."

The Casino 2000 facility is one of the few European gaming complexes that combines a hotel, restaurants, convention rooms, show rooms, sports events, and a casino under a single ownership. The casino offers 9,000 square feet of gaming space, with 273 slot machines and 7 tables for gaming. The hotel offers only 35 rooms and suites on 7 floors. Even with the small number, management does not encourage full occupancy so as to keep complementary services available for special patrons who may arrive without notice.

The casino pays the government of the Grand Duchy a gross win tax that is calculated on a sliding scale from 10 percent to 80 percent. Revenues keep the tax toward the lowest points on the range.

The Variety Showroom and Ballroom presents entertainment programs throughout the summer months. The grounds of Casino 2000 also include a professional horse-jumping course with obstacles and grandstands. A national horse show is an annual event which draws 35,000 spectators.

References

Casino City's Gaming Business Directory. Newton, MA: Casino City Press, 2007.

"Luxembourg." http://ezinearticles.com/? Luxembourg-Casinos&id=673729

Thompson, William N. "Luxembourg," In *International Casino Law*, 3rd ed. Edited by A. Cabot, W. Thompson, A. Tottenham, and C. Braunlich, 436-443. Reno: Institute of Gambling Studies, University of Nevada, Reno.

Monaco

For a century and a half Monaco, with its Monte Carlo casino complex, has offered the essence of classical gambling elegance. The casino, or casino complex, has been the leading European gambling facility until recent times. It was the most prominent casino property in the world until the advent of the Las Vegas megacasinos. Monaco itself is a historical throwback, a city-state of less than one square mile located on the French Riviera coast of the Mediterranean. It is surrounded by water on one side and by France on the other three sides. The state began as a semiautonomous political entity in the 13th century when an exiled clan called the Grimaldis established their independence from the Republic of Genoa on the then-barren seacoast spot. The geographical isolation and seeming worthlessness of the land (in the eyes of surrounding neighbors) helped preserve its independence. That independence has over the centuries become the reason for existence of the state of Monaco. Survival has come through isolation, treaties and diplomacy, and trade concessions, but mostly through the establishment of an economic base by means of the creation of the casino resort industry.

The gambling industry of Monaco developed mostly because its neighbors turned puritanical regarding the world of risky games in the 19th century. France closed its casinos in the 1830s, and soon afterward so did the states of Italy and Germany. An early effort to build casinos in 1861 failed in Monaco owing to the lack of capital resources. Soon Louis and Francis Blanc came to the rescue. The two brothers had been very successful in a casino venture at Bad Homburg near Frankfurt, Germany. That property was closed under pressure from the Prussian government. Francis survived Louis, and he contracted with the prince of Monaco to set up a company— Societe des Bains de Mer (SBM)—to build and operate a casino. The SBM promised to improve the harbor and to finance the building of a road to Nice.

Local opposition to casino gambling was overcome when the SBM persuaded the prince to suspend all taxes on local residents. The residents were also denied access to the casino except as employees. This restriction applies to the 25,000 citizens of Monaco, but not to the alien residents of the tax haven. (The total population is 32,000.)

Unlike other European casinos today, Monaco is a very democratic place that welcomes all visitors (just not the locals). It sets forth a philosophy of operations similar to that found on the Las Vegas Strip—gambling is considered an exported tourist product.

Francis Blanc was succeeded by his son, Camille, in 1889. Working with Monaco's Prince Albert, the SBM under Camille's leadership helped finance a ballet, as well as an oceanographic museum and research center. World War I greatly hurt business, but Sir Basil Zaharoff, a Turkish-born financier of Greek ancestry, came to the rescue. He helped Albert negotiate a new treaty for autonomy from France and generated new capital resources for the casino. Zaharoff took over the property in 1923 (Jackson 1975, 124).

The casino was able to remain prosperous through the Depression years and also through World War II as Monaco maintained a posture of neutrality. After the war, however, there was a major business downturn. While the SBM was nearly bankrupt, its control was taken over by Aristotle Onassis in 1951. Through the 1950s, Onassis worked closely with Monaco's Prince Rainier to build up the facilities. The two had a major falling out in the early 1960s, and Rainier seized the reins of control over the SBM. The prince directed the completion of a railroad tunnel that took tracks away from the seafront, and he added a new beach area, as well as developing new casino facilities. One of the facilities was an American Room that featured slot machines. Rainier also invited the Loews Hotel Corporation of New York to build a new casino complex that today represents the closest one can come to a Las Vegas–style casino in Europe. There are no door fees and no dress codes, and slot machines are adjacent to the table games.

Today the SBM offers gaming in five casino buildings including Loews, the traditional Grand Casino, the Sporting Club, Sun Casino, and the Café de Paris. Together they have more than 2,000 slot machines and 100 table games. Gaming revenues exceeded 250 million euros in 2007. The SBM also owns four hotels (with 950 rooms), 32 restaurants, a golf course, an opera house, and several nighclubs. Its current concession agreement with Monaco lasts until 2027.

While the identity of Monaco is the Monte Carlo casino resort complex, tourism provides only 15 percent of the gross national product of Monaco, with casino revenues representing less than 5 percent of the economy.

References

Embassy of Monaco, http://monaco-usa.org/embassy/travelleisure.

Jackson, Stanley. 1975. *Inside Monte Carlo.* New York: Stein and Day.

Sylt, Christian. 2008. "Monaco Looks for Windows on the World." *The Independent,* August 17, 2008, www.independent.co.uk/news.

Thompson, William. 1999. "Monaco." In *International Casino Law,* 3rd ed. Edited by A. Cabot, W. Thompson, A. Tottenham, and C. Braunlich, 441–445. Reno: Institute of Gambling Studies, University of Nevada, Reno.

NETHERLANDS

The mantra for Netherlands gaming should be "If you can't beat 'em, join 'em." The Netherlands provides many lessons for those wishing to understand the effects of legalizing gambling. Today Holland Casinos is a very successful government company operating 14 full-service casinos. Their first casino opened in the beach town of Zandvoort in 1975. The road from that time to today has been a rocky one.

If any venue could have been seen as one that could do it right, it would be the Netherlands. They are one of the most well-ordered societies in the world. And since 1726 they have had a national lottery, the oldest current operating lottery in the world. Yet even with that experience, they had a lot of trouble with casinos.

The idea of having legal casinos was presented to the government before World War II, yet it was not until 1974 that legislation for legalization was passed. The goals of the legislation were two-fold. First, the Netherlands saw much local money going to foreign casinos in surrounding areas—Belgium, Germany,

France, and Great Britain. They wanted their Dutch players to "come home." Second, an illegal casino establishment was flourishing inside their country. Lawmakers felt that the legalization process could destroy the illegal houses through competition. It was reasoned that a patron wishing to gamble would prefer to do so in a legal casino than in an illegal one—if they had a choice. While the goals of the government were admirable, they were faulty ones in execution.

For a legal casino to overcome competition from an illegal casino or from a foreign-based casino, it must at a minimum be able to provide a comparable gaming experience. In the course of doing so, it must also be able to attack the operational capacity of the competitor. In Nevada in 1931 there were many illegal casinos games. The legislature simply passed a law saying "if you want to do casino gaming, apply for a license." The illegal operators did so, and illegal gaming was ended. Not so for Holland. Consider what the Netherlands did.

A newly created government corporation was chosen to run the casinos—Holland Casinos. Three sites were selected for the casinos: Zandvoort in 1975, Valkenburg in 1977, and Scheveningen in 1979. All the sites were remote from the major cities—although admittedly everything in the Netherlands is pretty close to everything else. Nonetheless, to get to a casino a person needed ground transportation. So too did casino workers. Two of the casino locations were on North Sea beaches, and one was deep into the wooded countryside.

The illegal casinos were in the middle of cities, often being only walking distance from residential areas. The foreign casinos were mostly accessible by trains or boats leaving from city centers.

The policymakers also felt that government-run casinos should not be open all night long. There were closing hours. Moreover, they felt that it would be bad policy of a government organization to provide "comps," that is, free items for players. Hence, there were no free drinks, free food, or free transportation to and from the casino. The casinos were not allowed to advertise, as the government thought it improper for the government to promote gambling. There was also a strict dress code, and no slot machines were permitted.

On the other hand, the foreign and illegal casinos weren't confined by all these rules. They did give drinks and food to their players, and the illegal casinos operated all night long and did not have dress codes. Some of the foreign casinos had slot machines and so too did clandestine casinos in the Netherlands.

Moreover, while the illegal houses did have experienced employees, the policymakers thought that it was only proper that a person with experience in an illegal gambling establishment should be forever banned from working in a government casino. The consequences might have been predictable, but they were not predicted. The many employees of the illegal casinos needed jobs, and they became a unified vested interest in favor of keeping illegal gambling flourishing. (A parallel situation has been recorded by some as a mistake in the early stages of the U.S. military action in Iraq in 2003. American forces captured members of the enemy army, and then refused to allow them to join a new, friendly Iraqi army. They were not allowed to help in putting down an insurrection. They needed jobs—so they joined the insurrection.)

Another consequence of the Netherlands policy (and the U.S. policy) was that there were not enough "good" employees around to do the job. Holland Casinos therefore contracted with a foreign casino company to provide temporary staff and also to train new inexperienced Dutch persons for casino jobs. Some bad apples got into the barrel, as few background checks were made on the foreign workers. The foreign company did not send its best employees to Holland. Instead they grabbed whomever they could; these mostly were persons who had worked in unregulated casinos on ships in international waters. Knowing that they would not have their jobs for long (temporary generally meant one year), they started a cheating scheme and stole from the gambling tables. Unfortunately, they also recruited many of the new Dutch employees to work with them. In time the scandal was discovered and corrections were made. As a result Holland Casinos became a European pioneer in using video surveillance in casinos.

The government made no concerted frontal attack on illegal gambling. Whenever they did try to prosecute a case in court, they encountered friendly judges sympathetic to workers who needed their casino jobs to support their families, and they sympathized with arguments that the only reason the government was prosecuting them was that the government wished to protect its monopoly. Illegal casino operators argued that if they were so bad, the public would stop coming to them. The illegal casinos also found a new game that was quite lucrative, but also could be defended as not being a gambling game. It was called Golden Ten. In the roulette-like game, a ball moved very slowly around a circle before falling on a number. Operators maintained that a person with skill could predict where the ball would land, and hence players were not "gambling"—just exercising skill. Courts again were sympathetic to the argument as they required prosecutors to prove that skill could not be used in the game. It seemed that legislation against gambling left a giant loophole for Golden Ten.

The new government casinos had an initial effect of promoting illegal gambling. Indeed, at closing hour (2 a.m.), workers from the illegal (all-night) casinos would pass out flyers offering patrons leaving the legal casinos both transportation to and a good meal at the illegal casino.

The somewhat remote locations of the government casinos also retarded their ability to compete. The new product they were offering was simply mis-marketed. Policy changes were needed. These came in the 1980s, along with a new law in 1985. Advertising was permitted for the government casinos. The dress code was relaxed. Free gifts could be given to players. Slot machines were placed in the casinos. And new casinos were authorized for cities big and small. The Rotterdam Casino opened in 1985, Amsterdam's in 1986, Breda's in 1987, Groningen's 1988, and Nijmegen's 1989. Subsequently casinos were placed in Eindhoven (1993), at the national airport Schiphol (1995), Utrecht (2000), Enschede (2002), Venlo (2006), and Leeuworden (2007).

The Netherlands never fully came to grips with all the illegal gambling houses, but they did address the fact that the people of the Netherlands wanted to gamble. The government decided to permit many slot machines to open, and several were allowed to have legal—and regulated—Golden Ten games. A new government company, Fair Play, was licensed to operate more than 30 arcades, but private companies were also permitted to be licensed. The number of gambling houses—legal ones—in the Netherlands numbers in excess of 160.

The goal of "competing" with others in order to "close them down" has been dropped in favor of incorporating the competitors into a commercial model of maximizing gambling profits and maximizing government revenues from gambling operations.

References

Hoogendoorn, Chris. 1999. "The Netherlands." In *International Casino Law*, 3rd ed. Edited by A. Cabot, W. Thompson, A. Tottenham, and C. Braunlich, 446–451. Reno: Institute of Gambling Studies, University of Nevada, Reno.

Thompson, William N. 1991. "The Netherlands." In *International Casino Law*, 1st ed. Edited by A. Cabot, W. Thompson, and A. Tottenham, 287–292. Reno: Institute for the Study of Gambling, University of Nevada, Reno.

Thompson, William N., and J. Kent Pinney. 1990. "The Mismarketing of Dutch Casinos." *Journal of Gaming Studies* 6, no. 3 (Fall): 205–221.

PORTUGAL

When the editor was visiting Estorial, Portugal, in 1986, he was struck by a certain Asian flavor in the casino. Many dealers appeared to be Chinese, and prominent among the table games was an Asian three-dice game called cussec. All the writing on the green felt tables consisted of Chinese characters, along with Arabic numbers.

The casino manager who conducted the editor's tour informed him that the casino had been purchased by casino magnate Stanley Ho of Macau. Macau was a colony of Portugal, lying off the Chinese coast, and its residents were permitted to have working papers for Portugal. Ho wanted the casino of the "Mother Country" to have an aura of the "Orient," similar to that found in his famous Macau casino, The Lisboa. After

hearing more about his plans, the suspicion was aroused that just perhaps Ho had his eyes on Portugal becoming a colony of Macau, rather that vice versa.

Some things change, others don't. Macua lost its colonial status in 1999 as it was merged into the political structure of mainland China. However, Stanley Ho not only held onto his casinos, Estorial and the Lisboa in Macau, but he capitalized upon an opportunity to expand his empire even more in Portugal. In 2002, he won the right to have a new casino in the city of Lisbon. In 2006, it opened as the first "urban" casino in Portugal. Without imagination he called the casino The Lisboa. He is the majority owner of the facility. It is the ninth casino in Portugal.

The first Portugal casino was established at Figueira da Foz, on the Atlantic

Coast about 120 miles north of Lisbon. It opened in 1904 while Portugal was a monarchy. After the king and his eldest son were assassinated in 1908, a new democratic regime came to power and closed the casino.

Portugal experienced turmoil, with 44 governments over the next two decades. The casino was periodically reopened, then closed; only to be reopened permanently in 1926. During that period of instability, other casinos opened on Portugal's northern coast at Espinho and Povoa de Varzim, which are towns near the Oporto metropolitan area.

A revolt by the military that established a dictatorship achieved stability in Portugal and with Portuguese casinos. The leader of Portugal from the mid-1930s into the 1960s was economist Antonio Salazar. Salazar's adopted right-wing dictatorial policies were somewhat similar to those of his neighbor, Spanish dictator Francisco Franco. But Salazar permitted casinos. For Salazar, casinos were compatible with his notion of corporate syndicalism—a policy in which large conglomerates controlled the economic and social life of the nation.

Corporate combinations owned the casinos with local governments. Under Salazar, casinos also opened in the Madeira Islands and at Estoril near Lisbon. Before the 1960s, the casinos offered games only during summer tourist months. When Estoril and Madeira opened, these and the three other casinos became year-round facilities. Salazar suffered a stroke in 1968. He resigned his position as head of state, and he passed the mantle of dictatorship to Marcello Caetano before dying in 1970.

In 1971, Caetano embarked upon a policy of developing the southern coastal area known as the Algarve into a tourist haven. His eyes were firmly fixed upon British tourists and Arabs who frequented the nearby Costa del Sol in southern Spain. As the Spanish did not then permit casinos, Caetano saw casinos as a tool for drawing tourists away from Spain. He decreed that the Algarve would have three casinos. All were to be run by a single organization. The Anglopor group won bidding for the concession to operate three casinos. The group included American, Belgian, and Portuguese interests.

In 1973, a casino at Vilamoura on the Algarve opened. Operations began at Alvor and Monte Gordo in 1974. But soon after wheels began spinning at Monte Gordo, politics upset development plans. Military and socialist civilian forces ousted the Caetano government in a quiet, essentially bloodless, coup. A revolutionary council governed until elections brought in a socialist regime. In 1975, the new government began a campaign of nationalization; taking over first the banks, then the utilities, the chemical industry, and finally, the casinos of the Algarve.

The socialists left the northern casinos alone, while they operated the three Algarve facilities directly. They also interfered with other private corporate projects on the Algarve. Hotels that were planned were not built, and a beautiful coastal setting was held back from economic development, or exploitation, depending on one's point of view. The three casinos struggled through several losing years. They became an economic drag on a government that had plenty of economic problems already.

In 1979, after the regime of nationalization had cooled its ideological fever, the government created a private company to run the casino. And, as indicated, Portugal's ninth casino opened in Lisbon with private owner-ship in 2006. Although all nine casinos are in private hands, cities own the buildings for several.

A unique Portuguese game popular in the the region's casinos is called French Bank. There is nothing French about the game, and it is played only in Portugal. The game is similar to chuck-a-luck games that used to be popular in Nevada. The croupier throws three dice onto the center of the table. Players make one of three bets. They bet low (wagering that the three dice will total 5, 6, or 7); they bet high (14, 15, or 16); or they bet aces (that three 1s will fall). If any other combina-tion appears, the croupier very quickly grabs the dice and rolls them again. He rolls until high, low, or aces appear. There are 63 winning combinations (31 for high, 31 for low, and 1 for aces). High and low are paid even money, while aces are paid 61 to 1. The house percentage is under 2 percent. However, as the game moves very fast, the house is able to keep 18 percent of the chips sold to the players.

The casinos pay a complicated mixture of table fees (depending on the amount of time the table is open) and gaming win taxes (up to 30 percent of gross win). Casinos also pay property taxes and por-tions of admission fees to the government. The National Tourism Fund receives 80 percent of the gaming taxes.

References

"Portugal Lotteries." http://lotteryondemand .org/western-europe-lottery/portugal-lottery.html.

Thompson, William N. 1988. "Macao Gamers Give Portuguese Casinos Distinct Oriental Flavor." *Las Vegas Sun*, May 8.

Thompson, William N. 1991. "Portugal." In *International Casino Law*, 1st ed. Edited by A. Cabot, W. Thompson, and A. Tottenham, 271–273. Reno: Institute for the Study of Gambling, University of Nevada, Reno.

Thompson, William N. 1999. "Portugal." In *International Casino Law*, 3rd ed. Edited by A. Cabot, W. Thompson, A. Tottenham, and C. Braunlich, 455–458. Reno: Insti-tute of Gambling Studies, University of Nevada, Reno.

RUSSIA AND THE FORMER SOVIET REPUBLICS

When the Berlin Wall fell, the Iron Curtain came down, and the Soviet Union broke apart, its component parts along with almost all of the Eastern bloc nations abandoned a long opposition to casino gambling. Such was the case with the Russian Federation—the core unit of the former Soviet state. In all of these venues, communism with state-driven command economies was replaced with a nascent quest for all things market driven and capitalist. And what could be more capitalist than a desire to "let it roll" and double your money with a turn of a card, a pull of a handle, a roll of the dice, or a spin of a wheel?

Business entrepreneurs did not wait for niceties—like rules and regulations. Neither did their customers. A pent-up demand, bottled up by communist theory and communist authority for 70 years, sprung forth from a bottle like the proverbial genie. The genie offered the hope of instant fame and fortune. Certainly many operators did cash in on those hopes.

It is a bit ironic that in America the anticasino movement has most often been led by and associated with the right-leaning conservative position in politics, alongside other morality issues. In Europe and Russia, on the other hand, the banner of morality and opposition to casinos has most often been carried by left-leaning politicians. For instance, the communists have seen casinos as corrupting workers by depriving them of time that they could be using on productive pursuits. Casinos also were viewed as exploiting poor workers by taking their resources. Moreover, casinos have been considered by the left as rewarding entrepreneurs not for their labor but rather for their ability to exploit others.

During Soviet dominance of Eastern Europe during the Cold War era, casinos were almost universally banned. They were found in only two of the satellite countries, Hungary and Bulgaria. Things changed suddenly in 1991 as the Soviet Union collapsed. Gambling capitalists came out of the woodwork in a fury in Russia. Blackjack tables and roulette wheels appeared everywhere. Old slot machines were imported and they too flourished. Gangster elements were prevalent in the new, almost lawless, economy and they embraced gambling, surrounding it with a sex industry, drugs, and loan sharking. Some say there were hundreds of casinos with table games and more than a thousand slot machine locations. Moscow, by the mid-1990s, could boast of having more gaming locations than any other city in the world—even more than Las Vegas.

The first serious efforts to impose controls over the widespread gaming operations came in Moscow. In 1996, Mayor Yury Luzhkov oversaw enactment of rules which caused the number of casinos to be reduced from 72 to 30 in the city. The rules required each casino to have nongaming entertainment facilities. Slowly the number of casinos rose again as new operations were built to conform to the rules. Then, in 2002, a new federal law allowed licensing of facilities for a token fee that amounted to only US$45. The authority over casinos was taken away from municipal governments and transferred to a State Sports Committee. The committee authorized casinos, but they had no rules for the regulation of casinos. Once more the door was opened for a rapid expansion of casino gaming. By 2006, Moscow had 70 casinos with table games, and nearly 2,000 slot machines, located on almost every street corner, at all subway stops, and in residential complexes. St. Petersburg had 21 casinos and 570 slot machine locations. There were estimates that nationwide 250,000 slot machines operated. The Russian casino market was realizing annual gross wins of US$7 billion as 80 percent of the adult population participated in the gaming.

With a renewed expansion of gaming came recognizable problems—compulsive gambling afflicted a large portion of the population. The Moscow City Council (Duma) published a report saying there were 330,000 gambling addicts in the city. A public backlash ensued. A bit of the right-wing flavor of casino opposition came from religious organizations. Two Muslim regions of Russia (Chechnya and Dagestan) banned all gambling.

Critics of gambling suggested also that the gambling industry had become powerful politically, and that it had close ties to organized crime and to strong voices in the media. Like the lonely call from casino opponents such as Tom Grey in the United States, Russian critics faced a very tough fight. But then, they found an unlikely ally. They could not have wished for a stronger ally. In October 2006, Russian President Vladimir Putin stepped forth. He compared the Russian gambling problem with alcoholism and indicated that the problem permeated the entire population.

It would take a very strong man to put the genie back into the bottle. Putin was indeed such a man, and he set about accomplishing the task. President Putin designed a law to restrict gambling that was introduced into the national parliament. It passed the lower house in November and the upper chamber in December. On December 30, 2006, Putin signed the law into effect. The law did not ban casinos, but it went almost that far. It banned all slot machine parlors, and it banned all casinos in urban areas. The law established a schedule for closing current facilities. It also provided for licensing of casinos in four selected regions of Russia. The restrictions did not apply to bookmaker shops or existing state lotteries. On the other hand, all Internet gambling was banned everywhere.

The four regions were quite remote. One was in Primorsky Krai at Ant Bay on Russkiy Island 20 miles south of Vladivostok in Russia's Far East. It is near land boundaries to China and North Korea and has sea access to South Korea and Japan. The second region was in the Altai territory of Siberia near the Chinese border. The third was near the Sea of Azov on the border of the Rostov and Krasnodar regions. The fourth was in the Kaliningrad enclave (or exclave) located between the now independent (of Russian dominance) countries of Lithuania and Poland. Kaliningrad is well-linked by transportation facilities to Scandinavia and Central European cities.

Casino gaming in the four zones would be by licenses for five years, with a renewal period of five years. The zones could not be changed for 10 years. Each zone would have a Gaming Zone Administration, which would report both to a regional government and also to the Russian Federation Executive. Regulations would be devised in accordance with the 2006 law by both the local and national authorities. They would be enforced by the Gaming Zone Administration and, for some rules, by the zone's association of gaming operators.

License applications would require a fee, and applications would be made to local authorities. Once given, a license could be revoked only with cause, and decisions made regarding licenses could be appealed to courts. No government entity—local, regional, or national—could participate in the ownership of a casino license. However, license holders could own their facilities, but they could not own the land underneath the facilities. The land would be leased from the government in accordance with Russian Federation land policies.

In 2007, the closings proceeded according to schedule. Within months, 1,900 slot machine locations in Moscow were closed. The government of Vladimir Putin transitioned to the new president, Dmitry Medvedev, in 2008 and the reform efforts continued to move forward.

Several news accounts suggested that the goal of the 2006 law was to create several new Las Vegas–style gaming centers. This is an admirable goal, as gambling can best be a tool for economic development and not a tool of personal destruction if casinos are located some distance from major population centers, especially where they may draw in money from other countries. Nonetheless, the plans will face several obstacles.

Some point out that Russia has no tradition of gaming tourism and that players will support illegal gaming spots rather than travel by air many hours to one of the new zones. While Kaliningrad just completed a new airport complex with great connections to all points Russian and European, other zones fall short on transportation connections. This is especially the case with Altai. The *Moscow News* described Altai as "in the middle of nowhere" and reported that the "most reliable way to get there is by tractor." The town near the casino site has no sewer system and no street lights. News reports question how investors, let alone players, will find the casino locations.

Questions have been raised about why Putin took his zone approach. Some say he saw casino ownership in bad hands. In Moscow, several casinos were owned by political opponents who were Georgians; others were owned by mobsters, whom he wished to control. Cynics said he didn't like casinos because he had lost money as a player. Yet most neutral observers saw him responding to a public demand to rid neighborhoods of forces that were harming residents. His plan was introduced in time to be used as part of a platform in national elections, and polls in 2008 found 65 percent in support of the idea of taking casinos out of cities. Voices in 2008 were saying "Stay tuned for something that will be different in the gaming world—putting a Genie back into a bottle."

A house-banked game at the Taleon casino in St. Petersburg.

The 1991 breakup of the Soviet Union resulted in the creation of 12 sovereign entities, which are now affiliated with membership (or, for Turkmenistan, associate membership) in the Commonwealth of Independent States (CIS). In addition to Russia, the 12 include Armenia, Azerbaijan, Belarus, Georgia, Kazakhstan, Kyrgyzstan, Moldova, Tajikistan, Turkmenistan, Ukraine, and Uzbekistan. Several of the new countries have not authorized any gambling facilities, albeit, there is a presence of illegal gambling almost everywhere.

Kazakhstan had been the testing site for nuclear weapons during the days of the Soviet Union. After the republic—the ninth largest in land mass and the largest landlocked country in the world—achieved independence, its economic policies turned to oil production. During the boom years of the latter 1990s, casinos and casino gaming engulfed the nations 17 million residents. By 2006, there were 132 casinos and more than 2,000 slot machine arcades. There was also a public backlash against the facilities that brought bad habits and neon signs to every residential neighborhood in the land. The harmful effects of gambling were likened to drug addiction.

At the end of 2006, the National Security Council adopted the "Russian solution" to the problem of uncontrolled casino gaming. A law was passed and then signed by President Nursultan Nazarbayev in 2007. The law decreed that all casinos and slot arcades had to close by April 1, 2007. After that date, casinos could only be licensed for two cities: Kapchagai, 20 miles from the largest city of Almaty, and Shchuchinsk, near the capital city of Astana. Residents of the two cities were promised economic prosperity; however, many reacted to the notion of being the "new

Las Vegas" with disdain. They worried about increases in crime, prostitution, traffic, and addiction. They also feared that they would be hit with waves of invading Chinese gamblers. The Chinese border was only 400 miles away, and political leaders were accused of placing the casinos so as to attract the Chinese.

The new licensed casinos were required to have the most up-to-date security systems. They also had to have at least 20 tables and 50 gaming machines each. While the old casinos did actually close, gambling did not leave the major cities. Private card games were not banned, so many individual entrepreneurs set up games in coffee shops throughout Kazakhstan.

Part of the backlash to gambling in Kazakhstan resulted from the fact that Muslims are the largest religious group in the country; 47 percent of the population are Muslim, while 46 percent are Christian. Azerbaijan, with the oil-rich Baku region, has a population of 8 million, 90 percent of whom are Muslim. They had many casinos—with 12 in Baku—after independence, but all were ordered closed in 1998 by President Ilham Heydar oglu Aliyev. In Tajikistan, President Emamali Rahmonov suspended all casino operations in 2002. According to the leader, the casinos in the capital city of Dushanbe had turned into dens of gamblers and "voluptuaries." One constituent had written him that "such establishments in the Muslim country" were "immoral," and he expressed hope that they would be closed forever. The country in the far eastern sector of the former Soviet area has more than 7 million people, with over 90 percent of these Muslim.

Uzbekistan, on the old Silk Road, with a population of 27 million—88 percent of whom are Muslim—has no casinos. In contrast, 75 percent of Kyrgyzstan's 4,700,000 people are Muslim, and the country has authorized two casinos for its capital city of Bishkek. Turkmenistan is a very poor country even though it has vast natural gas resources and produces 10 percent of the world's cotton. Almost 90 percent of its 5 million people are Muslim. Nonetheless, the country permits two small casinos to operate in its capital city of Ashgabat.

In none of the countries located in the western area of the former Soviet Union does the population have large blocs of religious Muslims. The religious objections to casino gambling do not have a presence.

The small republic of Moldova, population 4 million, has more than a dozen casinos, with several in the capital city of Chisinau. Most of the casinos of Armenia, population 3 million, are in or near the major city of Yerevan. Georgia, population 4 million, has several licensed casinos in its two major cities, the capital, Tbilisi, and Batumi.

The 10 million people of Belarus are served by 25 casinos, which are open 24 hours a day. Nineteen of these are in the capital city of Minsk, while others are in Brest, Gomel, Grodno, and Vitebsk. Ukraine is the second-largest country to emerge from the break-up of the Soviet Union. Located to the south and west of today's Russia, its 48 million people live in economically depressed circumstances. Nonetheless, entrepreneurs seek to extract gambling money from their pockets and from the pockets of the few who put Ukraine on their tourist maps. The country has 33 casinos, with a majority of these located in the major city of Kiev, and the country runs a national lottery. Kiev also has a horse racetrack.

References

Casino City's Global Gaming Almanac. 2006. Newtown, MA: Casino City, 196–209.

Eurasianet.org. 2002. *Tajikistan Local Press Digest,* January 20, www.eurasianet.org/resource/tajikistan/press_digest/digest7.21.shtml, accessed June 22, 2008.

Thompson, William N. 2008 "The Russia Casino Scene: Putting the Genie Back in the Bottle." *Casino Lawyer* 4, no. 4 (Fall): 8–11.

SCANDINAVIAN COUNTRIES (ICELAND, NORWAY, SWEDEN, FINLAND, AND DENMARK)

All Scandinavian countries offer lottery gaming, while those on the European continent itself have other forms of gambling as well. This entry examines the several forms of gambling authorized in Iceland and in Norway, Sweden, and Denmark, as well as in Finland, which geographically is part of Scandinavia, although it is culturally separate.

Sweden is the largest country in the Scandinavian region, with a population of more than 9 million. While the Viking warriors from Sweden often engaged in dice games, as early as the 14th century rulers of the land instituted very restrictive laws over all gambling. In 1772 government-run lotteries were started by King Gustaf III; religious opposition to gambling, however, caused them to be shut down in 1841. Games were revived in the 20th century. In 1934, a private monopoly company called Tipstjanst started lotto games and sports pools. A state lottery company called Penninglotterietalso began operations. The two companies were merged in 1997, becoming the government-run company Svenska Spel. This company now controls all gambling in Sweden, along with a subsidiary group called Aktiebolaget-Trav och Galopp (ATG), which conducts dog and horse race betting and breeding activities. Sweden has 26 racetracks. Private charities are permitted to have bingo games.

Svenska Spel was authorized to license casinos in the early 21st century. All casinos are government owned, and their net revenues go to the national treasury. The first casino opened in July 2001 in Sundsvall, an a second in Malmo in December 2001. A third casino opened in Gottenburg in August 2002. In March 2003, the country's largest casino, Casino Cosmopol, opened in Stockholm. It is located near the railway center in an old theatre building. Its gaming floors are on three levels and occupy 37,674 square feet, with 300 machines and 31 table games. The casino employs 359 people.

In 2005, Sweden became the first government to actually open and operate an Internet poker site under the direction of Svenska Spel. The Svenska Spel monopoly also controls sports betting in off-track betting shops. Its monopoly has been challenged by large private betting shop companies that seek to operate in Sweden. The companies claim that the monopoly is operating in violation of European Community open competition laws. This issue is not confined to Sweden, and its final resolution may be several years away.

Denmark witnessed casino gambling before any other country in the region. In 1902, the king authorized a casino to operate within the Marienlyst Hotel in Helsingor, 30 miles north of Copenhagen. The operations did not persist for many decades into the new century. However, the hotel retained its casino license and after a new law permitting several casinos in Denmark passed in 1990, the casino was reopened at the hotel. Now six casinos have been licensed by the Ministry of Justice. The most elegant one is the casino at the refurbished Marienlyst Hotel. However, the largest and most profitable casino is on the ground floor of the SAS Hotel in Copenhagen. The casino has 30,000 square feet of gaming space, with 20 tables and 160 slot machines. The other casinos are in Aalborg, Aarhus, Odense, and Vejle. Each is privately owned, with Danish interests having majority control. They pay government taxes on gaming wins ranging from 45 percent to 75 percent.

Denmark also has racetracks, sports and off-track betting shops, machine arcades, and a state-run lottery. Because the limited number of licenses granted by the government go to Danish-controlled interests, the Danish gambling industry has been subject to criticism from foreign interests who claim that the arrangement, like that in Sweden, violates European Community standards.

Norway has a history marked by gambling activities, but also by a genuine reluctance to embrace gambling. Legal gambling appeared in the form of a lottery in 1719 while the land was under control of Denmark. This short-lived lottery gathered funds for charities, and the king gave land away to winners. A passive lottery returned with parliamentary approval in 1913. In 1927, horse race betting was permitted. Sports betting began in 1946, and charity bingo games flourished after the 1960s. In the 1970s, the government lottery introduced instant tickets as well as the mega-prize lotto games. The Red Cross was also given the right to operate slot machines, and they did so with a vengeance. The 1980s and 1990s also saw the spread of betting shops. The Red Cross slot machines numbered over 30,000 by the turn of the century, and although the beneficiaries were good causes, concerns were raised that problem gambling was getting out of control. By 2002, per person spending on gambling approached US$1,000 per year. In 2003, parliament made a drastic move to limit the machines. A new law gave the government lottery company, Norsk Tipping, full control over the machines. They were told to drastically cut their numbers. Moveover, parliament decreed that Norway would not have casinos. A newly created Norwegian Gaming Board was given control over all gambling. Since these measures were implemented, the number of machines has been reduced to 11,000. Efforts to maintain restrictions on gambling continue.

The Finnish Lottery Act of 1966 places all gambling in Finland under the control of government organizations and charities. The term *lottery* was defined in the act with the traditional definition of all gambling: activity wherein a player seeks a prize by putting up consideration on a chance event. Therefore even though after the law passed, Finland operated only a traditional lottery, the door was open for other gaming as well. Subsequent legislative changes authorized placement of pari-mutuel wagering under the control of the Finnish Trotting and Breeding Association, which operates several racetracks, and permitted a slot machine association, called RAY, to operate gaming for charities. In 1991, RAY made the move to open a regular casino in Helsinki in order to co-opt illegal gaming that had spread across the country.

Today the RAY casino operates as the Grand Casino of Finland. It offers players opportunities to bet on 300 machines and at 35 tables. The 29,000-square-foot facility has four restaurants and employees 200 people. In addition to the casino, RAY controls more than 15,000 slot machines in restaurants, bars, supermarkets, and gas stations throughout the country. They also operate low-stakes table games in nearly 300 locations. Some of these locations are deemed to be mini-casinos or "Club Rays." Most of RAY's revenues go to charities, although a fixed percent go directly to the government.

For gambling in Iceland, the exception is the rule. The general rule is that gambling is illegal. Under a parliamentary act of 1926, all lotteries were deemed illegal. The Ministry of Justice, however, could grant permission for a raffle or special drawing. In 1940, the criminal code made it a "punishable offense" to engage in betting or gambling or to encourage others to do so. One could not receive direct or indirect income from gambling activities.

The reality was not in keeping with the general laws. The exceptions ruled. The nation of Iceland—occupying the second-largest island in the North Atlantic Ocean—with its 320,000 residents (approximately 130,000 adults) is indeed a "gambling nation." A recent report found that the population had experienced wager losses of 83 million euros in 2005. This represents over US$400 per adult, considerably more than gaming losses in the United States. The losses were from a variety of lottery games, sports betting, slot machines (electronic gaming machines), and bingo games.

The "exceptions" began in 1933. Parliament had authorized funding for the construction of what would be the largest building for the University of Iceland. The project began. However, the encroaching economic depression meant that the state was short of funds. An educational crisis was at hand. Lawmakers seized the moment and granted the University of Iceland permission to have a lottery to raise funds to finish construction. They also allowed games to continue in order to finance more construction as well as purchase research equipment for the faculty. While the history of lotteries shows that other universities have benefited from occasional drawings, the University of Iceland Lottery is the only continuous lottery used for general university financing. Twenty percent of the money from the lottery is returned to the national treasury. The lottery operated with only a passive game for more than 50 years.

In 1949, the university's monopoly over lottery games came to an end as the Association of Tuberculosis and Chest Patients won the right to have a lottery with monthly drawings. In 1954, the priviledge was extended to the DAS, an association for elderly seamen's homes. The Heart Association started a lottery in 1959.

Sports betting games were allowed in 1972, as were stand-alone slot machines operated by Icelandic Gaming on behalf of the Red Cross and the Icelandic Association for Search and Rescue. They now have 600 machines in 280 locations. In 2004, the parliament permitted the organization to open a Website for interactive casino gaming.

In 1986 a government enterprise called Islensk Getspa was created to conduct lotto games. There is an on-island game of lotto 5/38, as well as a cross-national game called Viking Lotto. This action by the government presented a threat to the Univesity of Iceland Lottery, and in 1987 they reacted by offering instant ticket games. The games are now sold in 300 retail locations, which include vending machines for selling tickets. In 1993, the University of Iceland Lottery began using interconnected video lottery terminals for gambling. Today these machines produce 57 percent of the revenue from that lottery.

References

"Betting Markets: Sweden Gambling Industry—Questions Still to be Answered?" www.bettingmarket.com/ sverige 151172.htm, accessed October 10, 2008.

Binde, Per. 2007. "Report from Sweden: The First State Owned Internet Poker Site." *Gaming Law Review* 11, no. 2 (April): 108–115.

Casino City's Gaming Business Directory. 2007. Newton, MA: Casino City Press.

Gambling il dado. "Land Casinos Denmark." www.ildado.com/land_casijnos-denmark .html, accessed October 10, 2008.

Nevris, Hartmut. 1999. "Denmark." In *International Casino Law*, 3rd ed. Edited by

A. Cabot, W. Thompson, A. Tottenham, and C. Braunlich, 352–353. Reno: Institute of Gambling Studies, University of Nevada, Reno.

Novamedia Gaming and Lottery Files. 2005. "Iceland." www.gamingandlotteryfiles.com/novamediafile.php?file=Iceland.htm, accessed October 16, 2008.

Olav Fekjoer, Hans. 2000. "Gambling and Gambling Problems in Norway." Paper presented to the 4th Conference of the European Association for the Study of Gambling, Warsaw, Poland, September 23.

Romppainen, Esko. 1999. "Finland." In *International Casino Law*, 3rd ed. Edited by A. Cabot, W. Thompson, A. Tottenham, and C. Braunlich, 354–357. Reno:

Institute of Gambling Studies, University of Nevada, Reno.

"Sweden Casinos." www.jobmonkey.com/casino/html/Sweden_casinos.html, accessed October 10, 2008.

"Swedish Casinos and Gambling in Sweden." www.casinocity.com/se/cities.html, accessed October 10, 2008.

Vaiglova, Lenka. 2008. "More Gambling May Be Coming to Sweden." *IceNews*, September 14, www.icenews.is/index.php/2008/09/14/more gambling, accessed October 10, 2008.

"What's Gambling Laws in Denmark." 2008. *Ecommerce Journal*, March 4, http://www.ecommerce-journal.com/articles/whats_gambling_laws_in_denmark, accessed October 10, 2008.

SLOVENIA

Slovenia is the most active gambling region among the independent countries of the former Yugoslavia.

While Slovenia is one of the youngest—and smallest—nations on Earth, having been born in an "almost" peaceful revolution in 1991, the Slovene people have existed for most of two millenniums. So too, the land of Slovenia has been familiar with gambling for many a century. Yet it has only been in recent years that a formal lottery organization has conducted several games for the benefit of sports and humanitarian causes. Formal licensure and regulation of casino gambling are also of recent origin.

Slovenia has a population of almost 2 million, all of whom speak Slovene (91 percent are Slovenes, and 3 percent are Croats). The largest city, its capital, is Ljubljana, with a population of close to 300,000. Slovenes live on a 7,827-square-mile piece of land (the same land area as New Jersey) located just south of Austria and southeast of Hungary, east of Italy, and north and west of Croatia's borders.

Slovenia was exposed to Asian influences by traders going to Italy. These persons brought playing cards and dice on their journeys. The predominant Catholic Church forbade gambling on certain days, however, the practice was widespread among both laity and clergy. A fresco in the Holy Sunday Church in the town of Crngrob from around 1460 shows two eager card players at the game with the "devil's pictures." The finding of three dice by archeologists in the Ljubljana castle suggests what the lords of the castle did for entertainment. The inhabitants of Ljubljana rolled dice, played cards, and shot billiards in the inns and cafes in the early 18th century.

In the middle of the 18th century, the authorities tried to curtail gambling. They made attempts to prevent excessively high stakes and unsuccessfully forbade certain games. There was a special prohibition of gambling concerning servants. The ineffectiveness of forbidding gambling is indicated by the existence of cardmakers. The first "native" professional card painter is mentioned in the Ljubljana tax registers in 1724. In the second half of the 18th century, Ljubljana was also the seat of the guild of card painters in the Austrian provinces.

Although the authorities made efforts to stop gambling, they also tried to make some money from their subjects' weakness. They introduced a special tax on cards. Despite restrictive laws, newer games soon emerged, namely, the lottery and bingo. Systematic legislation penalizing forbidden games was introduced during the reign of Austro Hungarian emperor Franz II (1792–1806).

For more than 70 years of the 20th century, Slovenia was an integral part of the Yugoslav federation. While traditional casino resorts had been known in the Balkan lands, which were united into the SHS (Serb-Croat-Slovene) Kingdom in 1918 and Yugoslavia in 1929, gaming ceased in the period following the two world wars that engulfed the territory. In the new Yugoslavia, professional gambling was first classified as a criminal act of "unwillingness to work," together with vagabondism, harlotry, and begging.

However, a revival of the economy after World War II under communist leader Marshal Tito led to a renewal of gambling as a means to generate tourism to the beautiful beaches of the Adriatic and to the mountain cities of the interior.

The federal law regarding games of chance came into force in 1962 and was modified in 1965. The law allowed "special" games to be played in gambling houses where foreign guests were allowed to play for foreign currency. The state was more comfortable with the lottery and used it in large part to finance state entities.

In 1963, the first Yugoslav casino opened in Opatija in present-day Croatia. A casino followed the same year at the Palace Hotel in the Slovenia coastal town of Portoroz. It soon opened a branch casino in Lipica, home of the world-famous Lipizzaner stallions. A casino was established in the mountain village of Bled in 1965, as well as in the large Serbian city of Belgrade and the Croatian city of Zagreb. Nova Gorica got its casino in 1984 and created branches in Rogaska-Slatina, in Otocec, and at Kranjska Gora. In Ljubljana, a casino in the Hotel Slon began operating in 1969, died out in the 1970s and was reborn in the 1990s.

By the end of the 1980s, there were 21 Yugoslav casinos operating on a blend of European and Marxist principles. First of all, the casinos were organized like other businesses under Tito's brand of communism. They were truly self-managed by their workers (the actual workers, not Communist Party officials), but they were still a state-owned property. Second, the style of play was European. Gaming floors were very small, most with fewer than 5,000 square feet for play, and with fewer than 10 tables and not many slots. The largest casino at Portoroz had 36 tables and 150 slots. The casinos were generally in larger hotels and operated only in evening and early morning hours. The casinos banned all but passport holders from non-communist lands from play. The casinos used Western currency in all play.

The death of Marshal Tito in May 1980 in Ljubjana, now the capital city of the Republic of Slovenia, opened the doors for changes in national structures. Yugoslavia was broken up into many separate republics. After only a brief time of military struggle, independence for Slovenia became a fact that was ratified in 1992 with recognition by the European Union and with United Nations membership. In 2004, Slovenia joined the European Union and in 2007 began using the euro as its currency.

The new state called for new rules for casinos. In 1995, casino regulation and reform was moved onto the active political agenda. A new act was passed.

The Gaming Act of 1995 confined all gambling activity to the Slovenian lottery and to two types of casinos. Up to 15 major casinos were authorized. These facilities could have as many games— tables and machines—as allowed by their application and concession grant. The law also called for as many as 45 slot gaming halls, each having between 50 and 200 machines. Gaming hall machines were required to pay back at least 90 percent of their play as prizes.

An Office for Gaming Supervision was created within the national Ministry of Finance. The office was controlled by a director appointed by the government. The office had a legal department, a sector for financial supervision and analysis, a sector for technical supervision, and a department for information science. The initial function of the office was to grant concessions for casino facilities. As of 2009, 13 major casino concessions have been granted, as have 41 gaming hall concessions. The 13 casinos collectively have 246 tables and 3,317 machines, while the gaming halls have

3,377 machines. Each of the concessions also had to be approved by a municipal government. Major casinos had to be owned by public corporations, while private owners could operate gaming halls. A special commission was established within the Office for Gaming Supervision that is responsible for licensing all casino managers, croupiers and dealers, supervisors, cashiers, as well as internal security and accounting personnel. The office also certifies each gaming device as well as a centralized computer system for monitoring play. The sectors of the office supervise casino operations

Of the 13 major casinos, seven are under the ownership and control of HIT (an acronym for Hoteli Igralnice Turizem which translates to Hotels, Casinos, and Tourism). The HIT group is a public corporation with 60 percent of its shares owned by government entities—20 percent by municipalities, 20 percent by a federal government corporation, and 20 percent by public employee pension funds.

HIT has two casinos located in the city of Nova Gorica on the Italian border. The casinos are in the Perla and Park Hotels. The group is pinning its hopes on developing these facilities, especially the Perla, into major world-class tourist destinations with American-style (as opposed to European-style) casino gambling. The Perla has 250 rooms along with top amenities. Nova Gorica is located very near the prosperous northern Italian industrial region. There are 26 million people within a one-day (500 km, or 300 mile) car drive. Moreover, the city is within a one hour drive of ski resorts to the north and Adriatic beaches to the south and west. HIT boasts that the Perla is among the largest casino complexes in Europe, with close to 1,000 slot machines and 59 tables, as well as bingo games. The smaller Park Hotel (with 100 rooms) offers 528 slots and 38 tables, with bingo as well.

Other HIT properties are smaller. Two casinos are located to the north in the Alpine mountain areas. One, the Aurora Casino, is on the Italian border at Kobarid. A second, the Korona Casino, is on the Austrian border to the north at Kranjska Gora. In central Slovenia, HIT has the small Otocec Casino, and on the southeastern border with Croatia, the Rogaska-Slatina casino. At Sentilj in northeastern Slovenia at the Austrian border is their newest casino. The HIT organization also has two slot gaming hall facilities as well as several hotels and restaurants. The Slovenia HIT casinos entertain 1.5 million guests annually, producing gaming revenues of over 200 million euros. They win approximately 130 euros from each guest visit.

HIT also owns two other casinos, one in Sarajevo, Bosnia, and the other in Przno, Montenegro. A second group of three Slovene casinos is controlled by the Portoroz company. Its largest casino facility is on the Adriatic Coast at Portoroz. The casino at the Grand Hotel Metropol has 191 machines and 10 tables, along with bingo. Also in the Karst region is the Grand Casino Lipicia in the Lipa Hotel. The company's Grand Casino in the Lido Hotel at Catez, on the Croatian border, offers thermal bath surroundings along with its tables and machines. Most of its customers come from the Croatian capital city of Zagreb, only 25 miles away. Together the Portoroz company's casinos won 41.7 million euros from its players in 2005.

Three other casinos in Slovenia are operated independently. In 2004, a major casino opened in Ljubljana in the Grand Media Hotel, with 24 tables and 147 slot machines. One of the oldest casinos is on the shores of the lake in Bled, next to the Park Hotel. It has 20 tables and 85 slot machines. The casino in Maribor in northeast Slovenia has 117 slots and 11 tables.

Collectively the 13 casinos of Slovenia attracted 2,300,000 visitors in 2006. The players lost close to 2.4 million euros (104 euros per visit). Of the visitors, 86 percent came from outside Slovenia. Gaming halls had revenues of 105 million euros, with visitors numbering 2,000,000, each losing an average of 52 euros per visit. Only 55 percent of the gaming hall players came from outside of Slovenia.

The taxes on casino gambling vary according to the status of the casino and whether the win is at the tables or from machines. To start with, all gaming wins in casinos and gaming halls is subject to an across-the-board 18 percent tax. This tax goes directly to the national budget. In 2006, the casinos provided 43.2 million euros in general win taxes and the gaming halls gave 18.9 million euros.

In addition to the general win tax, there is a concession fee. The gaming halls each provide a fee of 20 percent on all their machine wins. The casinos give a concession fee of 5 percent of their table wins, plus from 5 percent to 20 percent of their machine wins on a sliding scale. The 20 percent rate is applied to machine wins in excess of 420,000 euros per month for each casino. Overall, the casinos provided 33.9 million euros in concession fees, and the gaming halls gave 20.9 million euros in fees for 2006. Total government revenues (taxes and fees) for 2006 for all gaming hall and casino wins was 117.1 million euros, or 33.9 percent of a total 344.9 million euro win.

While gaming taxes all go to the national government, concession fees are divided and sent to various sources. The national government takes 47.8 percent of the concession fees for stimulation investments in tourist infrastructure and tourism promotions. A similar 47.8 percent goes to the budgets of local governments, with 60 percent of this amount to the local city where the facility (casino or gaming hall) is located and 40 percent to neighboring communities. Of the remaining fees, 2.2 percent goes to a foundation financing disability and humanitarian organizations and 2.2 percent to a foundation for financing sports organizations.

In addition to providing revenues for governments and good causes, the casino facilities are important for their communities as sources of employment. More than 3,000 individuals are employed full time in the country's gaming establishments.

References

Thompson, William N. 2008. "Sometimes It Is Better If There's No Deal: Casino Gaming in Slovenia." *International Gaming and Wagering Business Magazine* 29, no. 10 (October): 1, 26–27.

Thompson, William N., Boris Nemec, and Carl Lutrin. 2007. "Casinos of Slovenia." *Casino Lawyer* 3, no. 4 (Fall): 16–19.

SPAIN AND "EL GORDO"

In the world of lottery gambling, Spain stands above others with its Christmas lottery, El Gordo, or, in English, "The Fat One." Each December 22, life in the whole nation of 40 million people comes to a squeaking halt for three hours as numbers are slowly drawn from a drum and are sung into television cameras by a Catholic school choir in Madrid.

The national lottery sells 66,000 numbers many times over. Each ticket costs 200 euros, and people buy whole tickets as well as major and minor shares of tickets. Villages buy tickets to be shared by each of their residents, and merchants buy tickets and give small shares to their customers. Families buy tickets, some purchasing the same number or numbers for generations.

On average, each Spanish adult spends 70 euros on tickets each December. The grand prize for a winning ticket amounts to 150,000 times the price. Prizes for a 20 euro share amount to 3 million euros. In 2007, over 2.2 billion euros were given as prizes. The Spanish public had spent almost 2.9 billion euros for their chances. The national treasury received about 700 million euros as their share of the ticket sales.

King Carlos III began the Christmas drawing in 1763, and it continued on an erratic basis until 1812. Since that date, there has been a drawing each year. The prize pool is now the largest one of any lottery worldwide.

The Spanish do not have lottery drawings only at Christmastime. The national lottery organization conducts large monthly and weekly draws as well, and other games are sold in stores and kiosks on a continuing basis. ONCE, the national organization for blind people, employs 23,000 individuals with disabilities to stand on corners and in kiosks to sell lottery tickets. These individuals have direct opportunities to support themselves with the wages they receive. The profits going to ONCE are used for other programs to aid the handicapped.

Almost as ingrained into the Spanish psyche as "El Gordo" is the spirit of the horse race. The sport of kings is especially loved in the southern Spanish province of Andalusia. There races are run along the beaches as well as at the Hipodromo Costa del Sol in Mijas Costa near Malaga and at the Hipodromo in Sevilla. It was from the stock of Andalusian horses that the famous Lippizaners of Slovenia and the Vienna Riding School descended. Spain also has a major racetrack in Madrid.

The Spanish love games, as any walk along the Grand Via in Madrid can attest. There you may find bingo parlors and lottery salespersons, as well as kiosks and store windows consumed with lottery tickets. Every block has a tavern or two offering several low-stakes slot machines for customers. Near each corner is a sharpie conducting a game with fast moving hands, while his eyes look over his shoulders for approaching policemen. A Grand Casino building stands with grandeur from the past. Here in great privacy the elite came to play card games with one another. These social clubs are unlike the casinos scattered around Spain, and have been licensed only in the last 35 years.

Formal casinos with roulette and baccarat games had operated in several Spanish cities until November 1, 1924. The day before All-Saints Day, the new dictator Miguel Primo de Rivera ordered all playing to stop, and at 11:66 p.m., croupier Don Leandro Dendariarenza took the small ball in his right hand and rolled it swiftly against the top of the bowl. As it descended toward the numbered slots, he called out "Rien ne va

plus." No more bets. The ball fell into slot number 34, red, even. The tables at the casino in San Sebastian were closed.

All the tables in Spain's legal casinos remained closed until 1978.

In the early 1930s, Miguel Primo de Rivera's right wing government fell, and King Alphonso XIII abdicated the throne. Later in the decade, Francisco Franco emerged as the victorious leader following three years of devastating civil war. Franco's theocratic dictatorship emphasized almost total opposition to every variety of "sin." In the world of gambling, only El Gordo survived unscathed.

Several efforts to get Franco to change his mind about casinos were completely frustrated. As life began to wane in Franco's feeble body, a death watch began. And, casino entrepreneurs headed the list of parties making daily inquiries about the health of Generalissimo. On November 20, 1975, death finally came.

After a respectful two weeks of mourning, the National Tourism Council presented its proposal for casinos to Franco's handpicked parliament. A study was immediately authorized. Then came legislation, rule making, selection of sites, and granting of concessions for casinos. These steps took time, but the decision had been made. Spain had legalized casino gaming.

The date was June 5, 1978. The time was 8 p.m. Croupier Don Leandro Dendariarenza took the small ball in his right hand and rolled it swiftly against the top of the bowl. As it descended toward the numbered slots, he called out "Rien ne va plus." No more bets. The ball fell into slot 32, red, even. The wheels at San Sebastian were open again. The first of 18 nationally authorized casinos had opened.

In the 1980s, additional casinos opened their doors as several regional governments were able to exercise newly granted autonomous powers over gaming activities. The casinos number more than 40 today and are located in all regions of the country.

While many of the Spanish casinos are rather ordinary, albeit well appointed, there is one that stands out among all casino facilities of the world, Casino Perelada. The casino is located in the Cataluna province near the French border, 120 miles north of Barcelona. The casino is a 14th century Spanish castle. While the casino includes the standard 100 slot machines and 15 or so table games, a restaurant, and a convention center, it offers so much more. Within the facility there is an art museum with originals by Goya and El Greco, as well as the essential collection of Vincent Lopez, palace artist in the early 19th century. There is also a winery and a museum of ancient winemaking equipment, a museum showcasing armour from the Middle Ages, a collection of rare books that includes editions of Cevantes' Don Quixote in 30 languages, and the finest collection of crystal glass on the Iberian Peninsula. And it is all in a genuine castle.

The Spanish spend about 30 billion euros a year in gambling activity, with 40 percent going to lotteries and 60 percent to private sector gaming—8.5 percent to casinos and 33 percent to machines outside casinos, which number 250,000. Other spending goes to bingo halls (12 percent), and racing and sports betting (6.5 percent).

References

Angloinfo. "The Spanish Lottery." http://costablanca.angloinfo.com/countries/spain/lottery.asp.

Geller, Rich, and Alan Campbell. 2008. "Casinos in Spain: Anticipation or Acceptance." *Global Gaming Magazine* 7, no. 7 (July), http://www.ggbmagazine.com/articles/_Casinos_in_Spain.

"Horse Riding—Andalucian Horse History." http://www.andalusia.com/rural/horseriding/history.htm, accessed September 5, 2009.

Lalandra Fernandez, Carlos, and Ana Lopez. 1999. "Spain." In *International Casino Law*, 3rd ed. Edited by A. Cabot, W. Thompson, A. Tottenham, and C. Braunlich, 465–473. Reno: Institute of Gambling Studies, University of Nevada, Reno.

Reuters. 2007. "Spain's 'El Gordo' Lottery Awards Over 1.6 Billion Pounds." December 22, http://UK.reuters.com/articles/oddlyenoughnews/idUKL221949542007122.

Thompson, William N. 1988. "Castle in Spain among the World's 'Most' Unique Casinos." *Las Vegas Sun,* April 10.

Tremlett, Giles. 2006. "Tiny Village Hits El Gordo Lottery Jackpot." *The Guardian,* December 22.

SWITZERLAND AND THE SWISS SOCIAL CONCEPT

In 2002 Switzerland embarked on a plan to have modern "casino gambling," with all the types of games that the concept implies.

Switzerland had known of casino gambling before this time. Indeed the small country of 7 million residents is surrounded at its borders with the casinos of other countries. Italians have a casino at Campione di Italia, a village enclave completely encircled by the land and water of the Swiss canton of Ticino. The French offer casino gambling at Divonne, Evian, and Annecy, all of which seek patronage of residents of Geneva. The Germans have Casino Lindau and Casino Konstance, while the Austrians have Bregenz, which seeks players from the northeast cantons (regional governments) of Thurgau, St. Gallen, and Appenzell.

The Swiss had historically known casino gambling on their own ground as well. In 1804, a room for wagering was built within a café in Lugano and games of biribisso (a lottery-roulette type game involving drawing numbers from a leather sack), bassetta, (a game involving betting on when a specific valued card will be dealt from a deck), and dice were played. Prior to 1874, matters concerning gambling was subject only to laws of the cantons. There are records, however, of only one full casino operating under the law. It was established in the town of Saxon in the canton of Valais in 1847 and was given a 30-year concession. A casino in Geneva was open without a license between 1857 and 1864.

The Swiss Constitution of 1874 banned casinos, although the term *casino* was not fully defined. Soon halls with the game of boule, a nine-number variation of roulette, were established. Other games also appeared, all operating outside of the law. The matter was elevated on the political agenda and once again, by popular vote, gambling casinos were banned. A vote giving the new law effect found 55 percent of Swiss citizens saying "no" to casinos in 1922. All gaming halls were closed. But not for long.

Boule came back in 1927, as an exception was granted for the game as long as bets did not exceed two Swiss francs and that the federal government received a tax of 25 percent on the profits. In 1959, betting stakes were raised to five Swiss francs. In 1977, slot machines featuring skill factors were permitted to operate beside boule games. In 1990, other slots were authorized by laws of the cantons. The machines soon became a matter of public concern, as they were omnipresent in bars and restaurants and the effects of widespread compulsive gambling were noticed.

In 1993, the Swiss voters amended their constitution. By a vote of nearly 3 to 1 (72.4 percent), they indicated that casinos should be allowed to operate. The size of the vote margin notwithstanding, the referendum vote was not necessarily a rousing show of popular support for wide-open gambling. The amendment included provisions banning all nonskill slot machines outside of casinos and imposed a tax rate on casino profits that could be as high as 80 percent. An additional requirement was that casinos have an active program for controlling problem gambling—called the "Swiss Social Concept." Only the state-run lottery could offer games of chance outside the doors of licensed casinos.

The Swiss public displays suspicion of any social change. The Swiss culture has emphasized personal responsibility, thrift, and hard work. The notion of having full-scale casinos in their midst, as opposed to just having them on their borders, was not a matter to be taken lightly. While entrepreneurial promoters of casinos may have thought they could use the notion of a "Social Concept'" as a ruse to gain votes, the political leadership was not buying into a ruse. They were going to introduce casinos only after much deliberation.

It was not until four years later, in 1997, that a draft of a casino law was compiled by the national parliament. This law was subject to many revisions before being placed in front of the voters for another ratification vote in 2000. After being passed by the voters, regulations were adopted by the government, and licensing of casinos could begin once the total package was put into effect by a presidential decree.

Applications for licenses were received in 2000, recommendations were made by a new seven-member federal gaming commission, and licenses were granted in 2001 by the federal executive council. In late 2002, the first casinos opened.

The law permitted two types of casinos: A casinos, and B casinos. Several guidelines were used to measure the qualifications of the applicants. Among these were experience in casino gambling, location of proposed facilities, and the contents of a proposed plan to deal with problem gambling.

The A casinos are allowed to have an unlimited number of tables and slot machines. The licensing commission felt that each A casino should have a "catchment" area of at least 1 million residents. However, as some casinos served border areas this was not a hard and fast rule. The winning applicants for seven A casinos placed their facilities in Lugano, just north of the Italian border; Basel, on the border of both France and Germany; Baden, near the largest Swiss

city of Zurich; major central cities of Bern (the capital) and Lucerne;the tourist city of Montreaux; and the northeastern city of St. Gallen.

The A casinos pay a basic tax rate of 40 percent of their winnings, but this rate increases 0.5 percent for each 1 million Swiss francs in annual winnings above 20 million Swiss francs. In 2005, the effective tax rate for the seven casinos was 52.1 percent.

In 2005, the A casinos averaged 282 slots and 19 tables each. The largest, Lugano, had 32 tables and 360 slot machines. The A casinos are also allowed to have as many types of table games as they desire. (ESBK 2005a).

The B casinos are permitted to have 150 slot machines each, with a maximum bet of nine Swiss francs per play. Individual machines can have progressive jackpots with prizes as high as 25,000 Swiss francs. The number of tables is subject to a formula related to machine numbers, and maximum and minimum bets are set by law. The 12 B casinos averaged 120 machines each, with five having the maximum of 150 machines while others had from 68 to 125 each. The casinos averaged 10 tables each.

The B casinos are distributed over a wide geographical area. The southern border area near Italy has two casinos, at Mendrisio, just 7 kilometers from the border, and in Locarno, 50 kilometers away. The eastern mountain region has casinos in St. Moritz, Davos, and Bad Ragaz. The northeast has a casino at the German border in Schaffhausen, and another in Pfaffikon near Zurich. Near Basel there is a casino at Courrendlin, and near Geneva there is one in Meyrin. The central western mountain tourist area has B casinos in Fribourg, Interlaken, and Crans-Montana.

Casinos Austria, an international gaming giant operating in more than 60 jurisdictions and on ships, has ownership participation in six of the casinos, which they also manage: St. Gallen, Baden, Lucerne, Bern, Pfaffikon, and St. Moritz.

The Swiss law has a surprising wrinkle in its taxation provisions. The small (B) casinos pay a higher initial taxation rate than the larger (A) casinos. The rate is set at 40 percent for the first 10 million Swiss francs in annual wins, and it increases 1 percent for every million thereafter. There is a philosophy behind this partially regressive tax structure. First of all, the notion that the "rich should pay more with higher tax rates" has no credence with casinos, because in no case anywhere in the world does a poor person own a casino. All owners are either rich, very affluent, or they are corporations or associations of one sort or another—as in Switzerland municipalities own portions of many casinos. (A casinos must have collective ownership, either by corporations or governmental units, while B casinos may find controlling ownership in private hands, as does the large Mendrisio casino) (ESBK 2005b).

Second, there was a recognition that smaller casinos do not have promotional budgets to recruit affluent players who may live further distances from the casino. Smaller casinos are less likely to invest in attractive amenities such as upgraded restaurants or shows. They also rely more on machine gaming, and they have fewer employees for each Swiss Franc or dollar that they take from the customers. In any event, when the rates are all thrown together, the effective tax rate on the gaming wins for the B casinos is 48.5 percent (ESBK 2005a).

The collective tax rates reflect the reality that the B casinos for the most part are small. The 12 facilities average 29.6 million Swiss francs in annual wins. The smallest three—Davos, St. Moritz, and Courrendlin—win less than 10 million Swiss francs. However, given its wonderful location right at the Italian border on a superhighway less than 45 minutes from metropolitan Milan with nearly 7 million residents (an amount equal to all of Switzerland), Casino Admiral in Mendrisio won 121.6 million Swiss francs in 2005. It paid a tax of 80 percent on the top 61.6 million Swiss francs it won.

Reflecting the tax philosophy presented above, the average A casino employees 190 workers, while the B casino hires 78. Switzerland is a land of high wages and this certainly applies to casinos. Waiters and waitresses as well as checkout clerks in small markets earn 20 Swiss francs an hour (US$17), but casino employees do much better. Their wages approach 50 Swiss francs an hour (US$42). The top casino (the A casino in Baden) gave average salaries of 108,838 (US$90,000) in 2005, while the lowest, a B casino at St. Moritz gave Swiss francs 55,000 (US$45,000). Then again, it is not all that bad to be stuck in St. Moritz (ESBK 2005a).

An essential part of the new policy authorizing casinos has come to be known as "The Swiss Social Concept." Casinos are required to have programs that deal with problem gambling and problem gamblers. As a part of the licensing process, the casino applicants have had to show that they would have a specific program for controlling problem gambling and play by troubled gamblers.

The operation of the programs is monitored by the national gambling commission. Casinos keep extensive records of Social Concept activity. Each casino has a Social Concept Committee, which consists of administrators, supervisors, and front line employees such as dealers. The committee has a trained psychologist or psychiatrist as an advisor. All employees are given an extensive training course on the nature of problem gambling and the signs of troubled gambling that they must report to management and ultimately the committee.

Players must show identification at casino doors, where they are given information about problem gambling. Each casino has a brochure listing problem signs, such as the 20 items on the Gamblers Anonymous questionnaire. Employees report signs of troubled gambling to management. The signs are considered either critical or serious. Three critical signs include (1) player verbalization about "suicide"; (2) tantrums—yelling, cursing, throwing objects; (3) a player's "failure" to use a restroom when necessary. Any exhibit of these behaviors results in an immediate report to the committee, and upon verification (the player is given notice and opportunity to respond), the player is banned from all 19 casinos for life.

Less critical but serious signs include things like changing appearances (from a previous clean look to being dirty), acting as if one had not slept in a long time, acting nervous, looking about suspiciously, and changing bets in unusual ways. In these situations, employees make a written report describing the action observed and give it to management. This process can also be initiated by a third party, such as another player or a family member. The report will generate a period of several weeks of observa-tions of the player. Then if the behaviors persist, the matter is referred to the committee where the player may be subject to a mandatory ban for life. Alternatively the player could be given restrictions limiting play to a few times a month.

The players may appeal committee action. After one full year, a player may request that a ban be lifted. The request must indicate that the problem has ended, that the player has a job, a source of income, that all debts have been paid, and that his or her family situation is stable. While the Swiss have very strict banking secrecy laws, they are set aside here. Bank accounts must be revealed or the player may not return. Players must demonstrate that they underwent a treatment program.

Players who are banned from the casinos are referred to counselors for treatment. Several casinos even pay for initial visits to the counselors.

References

ESBK (Eidgenossiche Spielbankenkommission). 2005a. *Tabella Ricapitolativa Casino Svizzevi 2005.*

ESBK. 2005b. *Ordinanza federale-Variente I, and Variente II.*

Thompson, William N. 2007. "Public Integrity In Casino Gambling: The Swiss Social Concept." *Public Integrity* 9, no. 4 (Fall): 377–388.

Thompson, William N. 2007. "Switzerland's Casino Renaissance." *Casino Lawyer* 3, no. 1 (Winter): 13–15.

Thompson, William N. 2008. "Imbedding Social Responsibility." *International Gaming and Wagering Business* 29, no. 7 (July).

Thompson, William N., with Robert Stockard and Peter J. Kulick. 2007. "Exclusionary Policies in Casino Gaming Facilities." *John Marshall Law Review* 40, no. 1 (Summer): 1221–1257.

The United Kingdom

The United Kingdom is rich in millennia of gambling history, stretching from the time of the Roman Empire to today. The most persistent form of gambling has involved horse races.

Roman soldiers conducted horse races for pleasure—and wagering—as early as 200 CE, while government officials in Great Britain gave official recognition to a horse race as early as 1174. The excitement of racing was tied to the Crusades as soldiers brought Arabian racehorses back from their adventures. Henry VIII also imported racehorses for breeding, and later kings kept stables of racehorses for their enjoyment. Charles II was instrumental in setting up racing at Newmarket, and it is suggested that the royal family even moved all official activities to that location during racing season in the reign of William IV. At the end of the 17th century and the beginning of the 18th century, three "Oriental stallians"—the Byerley Turk, the Darley Arabian, and the Godolphin Arabian— were imported from the Middle East to Britain. All thoroughbred horses today can trace their lineage to one of the three. Two types of races have now developed: steeplechases, which involve jumping obstacles, and flat racing, either on straight courses or enclosed oval tracks.

Racing has been governed by the Jockey Club, which was established in 1752, and more recently by the British Horseracing Board, which was set up in 1993. The two now give oversight as the British Horseracing Authority.

Today there are more than 60 tracks in the United Kingdom, and betting is conducted by private agents using fixed odds, as well as by the track authorities who use a pari-mutuel system. While the legal status of gambling ebbed and waned during history, legalized betting on horse races at the site of the races has been a constant. In 2005, there were 8,588 races involving almost 95,000 horses. Nearly 6 million people attended the races. The United Kingdom represents two-thirds of the wagering on horse races in Europe.

While horse race betting has withstood most of the efforts of antigambling reformers, other types of betting were not so lucky. The widespread use of games for wagering greatly disturbed King Richard III, as he felt that able-bodied young men were gambling when they should have been perfecting skills—such as archery—needed for defending the realm. In 1388, he banned betting. With legislation in 1541, Parliament gave its authority to a ban on all games involving money. Gambling continued and so Parliament felt the need to pass a similar law in 1665.

On the other hand, while monarchs and Parliament railed against gambling, they also turned to lotteries as a way of funding activities. Queen Elizabeth I granted permission to hold a lottery in 1566 in order to raise money to improve harbors, and James I chartered a lottery in 1612 to raise funds for support of the new colony at Jamestown, Virginia. Lotteries continued unabated until they were subjected to a general ban in 1826. They did not return until 1994.

Forms of casino gambling flourished during the 17th and 18th centuries. Noblemen were so engaged in gaming with the likes of Beau Nash at the tables of Bath—an old Roman town—as well as in luxurious London houses, that Parliament worried that their estates were being depleted in the activity. In 1710, they passed the Statute of Anne which rendered all gambling debts uncollectible in courts of law. The heights of reckless elite gaming came in the early years of the 19th century during the regency and reign of George IV. Players filled the tables of houses such as William Crockford's casino.

When Queen Victoria ascended to the royal throne in 1837, a new wave of reform came with her. She guided the passage of the Gaming Act of 1845, which effectively closed down the casino gambling activity, at least in any open manner. Casinos remained closed for 115 years. The reform era of Queen Victoria also led to the passage of the Street Betting Act of 1906. At that time many private agents were working the streets taking bets on horse races and other contests. The act made their activity illegal.

Declaring acts illegal and actually stopping them are two different things. Street betting and clandestine casino gaming persisted, so much so that in the 1940s Parliament created the Royal Commission on Betting, Gaming and Lotteries. They made their report in 1952, and it guided policy decisions for a decade. Several recommendations were enacted with the passage of the Betting and Gaming Act of 1960. The emphasis of the act was on the personal liberty of citizens who wished to gamble, and little concern was shown for possible criminal effects of the gambling.

The "problem" of street agents selling wagers was solved with one bold stroke. Successfully solved—if you were not a moralist. The street betting agents were simply allowed to apply for a license to conduct their trade legally and without abatement, if they agreed to move the activity off of the streets and into buildings. They did so, and illegal street betting ended—completely.

The issue of casino gambling was a bit more tricky. Parliament did not want to stop casino gambling. Indeed, they found most voices telling them that the citizens wanted to gamble. Moreover, even religious voices supported gambling, as they had been the recipients of many of the profits from games. Parliament felt that they could do as they did with street gamblers, simply "clean up the act." With the 1960 act and revisions in 1963, they permitted private clubs to run games for private members. The games could be of any type; however, they had to give the player an "even chance." This latter provision was not easy to define. In actually, the casinos ignored the rule, or in a feeble attempt to abide by it, they simply offered individual players the chance to bank all of the action on a table or series of tables. Any player who seriously attempted to do so, would find that his welcome (and membership) had run its course.

As being private clubs, the government took little effort to control who was running the show and how their finances were being directed. Unfortunately for the United Kingdom, the permission to start clubs coincided with Fidel Castro's takeover of the Cuban government, and in turn the Cuban casinos were closed. Most of the Cuban casinos had been run by American mobsters the likes of Meyer Lansky. Lansky and other mobsters quickly set up shop as operators of casinos in London. Within a few years, new "private clubs," dominated the gambling scene in the United Kingdom. Their numbers soared to over 1,200.

Policy leaders quickly learned that they had made a mistake. They reacted with a 1968 Gaming Act that increased control over casinos. The new act created a Gaming Board. In conjunction with local officials, the gaming board qualified new casino owners and granted licenses if the owners could demonstrate that there was an "unstimulated demand for gambling" by the public in their location. To do this, the applicants would have to show that existing casinos were crowded, or that there were still a lot of arrests for illegal gambling in their neighborhoods. The law also decreed that only central (West End) London and selected larger cities and seaside resort towns could have casinos. Membership in the new casino clubs was strictly regulated, as were the premises. Drinking was not allowed on gaming floors. Slot machines were considered devises that would "stimulate" gambling; therefore, each casino was limited to having only two machines. There was fear that the Gaming Board might authorize too many casinos in order to generate tax money, so the law provided that there would be no gaming tax. In 1980, a new law permitted taxes on gaming on a sliding scale up to 33 percent.

Under the act, the number of casino licenses stabilized at 120, with 20 of them being in West End London. However, as the centuries turned, many voices called for new reforms that could allow the casinos, or collectively, the casino industry, to compete with the expanding casinos of Europe. A new Gaming Act of 2005 was passed. The act created a new 10-member Gaming Commission with powers to license casinos as well as bingo clubs and betting shops. They also can revise the rules for licensing and the numbers of permitted games. The gaming tax may be set as high as 50 percent. There are now 144 casinos. They produce a house win of 656 million pounds.

The commission has licensed 4,200 casinos, betting shops, and bingo facilities. Also there are 260,000 arcade machines and pub and restaurant slot machines. The new law also permits remote or online gambling.

While the modern lottery was not developed until the 1990s, a special lottery was created in the wake of the parliamentary report. In 1956, the post office began to issue "premium saving bonds." The bonds paid little or no interest, but their holders were entered into periodic drawings for cash prizes. The holders

Crockford's Casino, London.

could redeem the bonds at any time and receive back the face value they paid for them. This "lottery" is still active.

The National Lottery was authorized in November 1994. It offers the public a 6/49 lotto game in twice weekly draws. Over 30 million players are drawn to 24,000 sales outlets to purchase tickets. Nearly two-thirds of the population plays regularly, making the lottery the number one lottery in the world in terms of gross sales. Annual sales are 5 billion pounds (equivalent to US$10 billion). Half the sales money is returned in prizes, 28 percent goes to good causes, 12 percent to the government, and 10 percent to commissions, overhead, and profits to the operator. The national lottery is unusual in that its operation has been given to a private company, Camelot, which is monitored by the Office of the National Lottery.

References

Clotfelter, Charles, and Philip Cook. 1989. *Selling Hope.* Cambridge, MA: Harvard University Press, 22.

Encyclopaedia Britannica. "Horse." http://www.britannica.com/EBchecked/topic/86993/Byerly-Turk.

Griffiths, Mark D., and Richard T. A. Wood. "Lottery Gambling and Addiction: An Overview of European Research." https://www.european-lotteries.org/data/info_130/Wood.pdf

"The History of Horseracing." http://www.mrmike.com/explore/hrhist.htm.

Miers, David. 1999. "Great Britain." In *International Casino Law*, 3rd ed. Edited by A. Cabot, W. Thompson, A. Tottenham, and C. Braunlich, 383–405. Reno: Institute of Gambling Studies, University of Nevada, Reno.

Thompson, William N. 1988. "Legalized Gambling in British Casinos." *Las Vegas Sun*, March 13.

Latin America

ARGENTINA

Argentina has all major forms of gambling: casinos, slot machine parlors, lotteries, bingo halls, racetracks, and a variety of lotteries. The 41 million citizens occupy a land base about one-third the size of the United States. The country is divided into 28 provinces, plus the national district of Buenos Aires City. Both the provinces and the national government have authorized lotteries, casinos, and other forms of gambling. Until the 1990s, the government operated almost all of the gambling; since then, a privatization drive has brought many new casino organizations to the country, upgrading that form of gambling. Until very recently, no casino gambling was allowed in the national city of Buenos Aires; however, under the guise of being in international waters, dockside ships have been licensed to offer casino gambling at the port. In fact, one is the largest casino in the country.

Casino gaming has been common in Argentina, starting in the colonial days of the 18th and early 19th centuries when viceroys from Spain governed the land. At that time and even after national independence in 1810, casinos were privately owned and locally licensed. This structure of minimal regulation and local control changed drastically in the mid-20th century.

As in most Latin American politics, a chief executive and his appointed council—as opposed to a broad representative legislative chamber—control government. This pattern of executive rule derives from colonial traditions and cultural expectations. Military governments also have been common in the region. Argentina's governmental structures fit these patterns. In 1943, General Edelmiro Farrell assumed the role of "keeper of the national conscience" after deposing the civilian government. His selected council included General Juan Peron, who was the minister of war, the vice president, and the secretary of labor. General Peron succeeded to the presidency as the head of the new Argentine Labor Party in 1946. His election resulted from widespread support from the working classes and the Catholic Church. He remained the leader and virtual dictator until other military officers deposed him in 1955. Many changes occurred under the leadership of Farrell and Peron, including the structure of casino operations. Peron advanced industrialization programs requiring increased national control at the expense of provincial powers. He also fostered public ownership of enterprise.

In 1944, a presidential decree closed all private casinos in Argentina. The national government controlled all casinos from then on. One consequence of this action, remaining to this day, was the closure of land-based casinos in the national capital city of Buenos Aires and its suburbs. This decision influenced the development of South American gaming in other countries. Casinos in Argentina, Uruguay, Chile, Ecuador, Colombia, and Surinam marketed their properties to wealthy Buenos Aires players. The other major target area for marketing is Brazil, which also lacks legal casinos.

The National Lottery Administration (La Lotteria de Beneficial) has operated a national drawing since 1893. It also took charge of oversight of the the publicly owned casinos for the national government. In 1947, the administration created a casino commission to direct operations. The commission consisted of representatives of the Ministries of Finance and Labor and the National Bank.

The first casinos authorized to be part of this organization opened in the beach resorts in the province of Buenos Aires, about 200 miles from the capital city. Casinos operating as private casinos in Mar del Plata, Necochea, and Miromar (December 1944) continued as national government casinos. In 1945, the government nationalized the casino at Termas de Rio Hondo, a hot springs resort in the province of Santiago del Estero. A decree in 1946 reiterated that all casinos were under the jurisdiction of the national government but recognized that provinces could prohibit gaming within their borders.

Casino revenues were to be spent on social work, health, and urban sanitation programs. Later additions to the list of gaming recipients were schools, universities, local governments, tourism programs, medical foundations, and the Eva Peron Foundation. The government set admission charges for players and fees for exchanging checks and purchasing chips. In 1951, the government assessed a fee of 0.5 percent of the value of the chips purchased by players, but later eliminated the fee.

The national casino system expanded by nationalization of a private casino in Mendoza in 1947 and the creation of a casino annex at Mar del Plata in 1949. In 1954, casinos opened at the skiing and lakes resort of Bariloche in Rio Negro Province and at

A view of Mar del Plata, the largest casino in South America, located 200 miles south of Buenos Aires.

Termas de Reyes in Jujuy Province. Another casino opened at Termas de Rosario de la Frontera in Salta Province in 1959.

In 1963, a national casino opened at the edge of the great Iguazu Falls in Misiones Province. Casinos came to Alta Gracia and La Cumbre in Cordoba Province in 1971. The provinces of Corrientes and Chaco and the city of Parana in Entre Rios Province received authorizations for casinos in 1972. In the same year, a new national casino opened in the seaside resort of Piromar in Buenos Aires Province. Later in the decade, the remote coastal cities of Rivadavia and Puerto Madryn in Chubut Province and the interior city of Tandil in Buenos Aires Province established casinos. A seasonal casino in the oceanside resort of Las Grutas in Rio Negro Province also began operations.

After the fall of the final Peron government in the mid-1950s, the interior provinces tried to reassert autonomy over many public policy areas previously dominated by Peron officials. Several provinces wanted their casinos back, and they were able to get them. In 1960, the national casino at Mendoza closed, and the provincial government assumed control of gaming. In 1961, the casino at Termas de Rio Hondo was transferred to the provincial government of Santiago del Estero. In 1962, a presidential decree authorized provincial participation in all revenues from the national casinos. Subsequently, the provinces acquired the casinos in Salta and Jujuy. These and other provincial governments started province-operated casinos. The interior provinces of San Luis, San Juan, La Rioja, Tucuman, Santa Fe, Misiones, and Corrientes established provincially owned casinos. The major difference between national and provincial casinos was that the latter were permitted to have slot machines.

A movement toward privatization on a national level began in the mid-1980s. The public treasuries of the nation faced trouble from Argentina's continuing economic crises. The incentives for generating revenues by sales of casino properties were present.

The central government negotiated with the province of Rio Negro to transfer the national casino at Bariloche. In the early 1980s, the government of Mendoza Province had been anxious for resort developments. Ernesto Lowenstein saw the possibility of developing a world-class ski resort at Las Lenas on the edge of the Andes. In exchange for taking a risk with his development, he asked for a casino concession. The province was happy to comply with his desires. The resort opened in 1985, and two years later, a casino began operations. The Lowenstein Resort Company owns the casino, which Casinos Austria operates under a management contract. In 1989, the provincial government granted a second private casino concession to the developers of the new Ora Verde Hotel in Mendoza City. These two private casinos, the first in more than 40 years in Argentina, were the impetus for the privatization of the existing government casinos at both the national and provincial levels. Other new private casinos were also authorized, and the Mirage organization of Las Vegas was instrumental in starting a major facility at Iguasu Falls at the Brazilian border. In the late 1990s, casino policy was clarified as all authority over casinos was given to provincial governments. Many new licenses were given to private operators. As a consequence there are now more than 70 casinos in Argentina. Most are private but some are still owned by provinces. All permit slot machines.

Among the new casinos, two stand out. The town of Tigre is but a 25 minute drive from downtown Buenos Aires, but it is outside of the capital federal district. The province granted a casino license. The Trilenium Casino de Tigre facility offers gambling on three levels, with nearly 75 tables and more than 1,700 slot machines. The Casino de Buenos Aires is a riverboat with four floors of gambling containing 100 tables and 600 slot machines. It opened its doors in 1999. The casino is owned by the Spanish Cirsa Corporation.

In addition to the slot machines in the casinos, Argentina has allowed the establishment of machines at a racino in Palermo, in more than 400 slot machine halls, and in scores of bingo halls. Nearly 20,000 machines are in operation. The National Lottery Administration also controls and administers other gaming. A major track near Buenos Aires offers horse racing. Three tracks conducted 4,800 races and collected US$133 in bets in 2005. There are also off-track betting facilities. Argentina has 800 horse breeders, who produced 6,600 foals in 2005, the fifth-largest number in the world (following the United States, Australia, Ireland, Japan). The industry employees 100,000. Another form of legal gaming is parlay betting on soccer games. The administration also offers various lottery products. Additionally, the provincial governments run lottery operations.

Coauthored by Andrew Tottenham

References

"Argentina Casinos." Jobmonkey.com, Casinos and Gaming. www.jobmonkey.com/casino/html/argentina_casinos.html

Awwad, Michael. 2007. "Argentina Casinos." Ezine Articles. http://ezinearticles.com. Accessed September 5, 2009.

Casino City's Global Gaming Almanac. 2006. Newtown, MA: Casino City, 78–79.Tottenham, Andrew, and William N. Thompson. 1999. "Argentina." In *International Casino Law*, 3rd ed. Edited by A. Cabot, W. Thompson, A. Tottenham, and C. Braunlich, 277–284. Reno: Institute of Gambling Studies, University of Nevada, Reno.

BOLIVIA

The remote, landlocked, mountainous country of Bolivia is not at all distinguished for its gambling activities. Most of the almost 9 million citizens are of indigenous heritage and do not live prosperous lives. The country has an authorized lottery but that seems to be the extent of legalized gambling.

Although casinos do not operate within the confines of a legal framework, a large portion of the population of the national city of La Paz has nevertheless had occasion to visit local casinos. Casino owners have been operating casinos for years on a quasi-legal (tolerated) basis. In 1993, the president issued an executive order declaring the facilities to be illegal. A 1994 city statute in La Paz permitted lotteries, however, and local entrepreneurs used it as a ruse for opening casinos. After a federal raid had closed down 13 of the country's casinos, the mayor of La Paz authorized the opening of two in the city, holding that the casino games were municipally approved lotteries. The wrangling between the city and national authorities has scared off many potential foreign investors. As a result, pressure has increased for the National Congress to act on a casino bill that was first introduced in 1991, but no action has been taken on the issue. In 2002, the government did allow foreign investors to develop a casino in Santa Cruz under the auspicies of the lottery. The facility has 100 machines as well as "table" bingo. In 2008, a second but smaller casino was permitted to open its doors.

References

"Casinos and Arcades in Santa Cruz." www.boliviabella.com/casinos.html.

Thompson, William N. 1999. "Bolivia." In *International Casino Law*, 3rd ed. Edited by A. Cabot, W. Thompson, A. Tottenham, and C. Braunlich, 286. Reno: Institute of Gambling Studies, University of Nevada, Reno.

BRAZIL

Brazil is by far the largest country in Latin America, with a land mass larger than that of the 48 contiguous states of the United States and a population of 180 million. The country boasts two of the largest cities in the hemisphere: Rio de Janeiro and São Paulo.

Although casino gambling is currently illegal in the country, the population participates in many forms of gambling, including illegal casino-type games. The wealthy, among a population with a wide gulf between the rich and poor, support the casinos of the surrounding countries with a great share of their patronage. They also frequent the casinos of the United States.

Casino gambling thrived in Brazil in the 1930s and 1940s; however, it was prohibited by presidential order in 1946. Remnants of casino-type games remain. Machine gaming of a video variety is prevalent in the country's many bingo halls. Sports betting and football pools are also popular, as are cockfighting, horse racing, and all forms of lottery games. A private and only quasi-legal lottery called jogo do bicho ("the animal game") is played to support the activities of the Mardi Gras celebrations in Rio de Janeiro.

Through the 1990s and up to the present, there have been efforts to legalize casinos in some form. A casino bill was narrowly defeated in the 1991 session of the national legislative body. In 1995, a special committee was set up to study gambling and casino games. The issue remains controversial. Some organizations consider casinos to be a threat to their own financial interests. There is considerable political, economic, and cultural support, however, for the reconsideration of legalizing casinos. However, the government's antigambling posture manifested itself strongly when President Lula de Silva ordered the closure of over a thousand bingo halls in 2004. The next year, the national senate overruled the presidential decree and the halls have opened again.

Today's anticasino lobby is led by church forces advancing moral arguments. Pro-casino legalization arguments include the globalization of casino gaming, the reduction of trade barriers, the opening of markets, and the pressures and opportunities associated with multinational, integrated market groupings, such as MERCOSUL (the Southern Cone Common Market of Brazil, Argentina, Paraguay, and Uruguay). All the other members of MERCOSUL have legalized casino gaming, and Brazilian tourists often visit their gaming facilities, such as Punta del Este, Uruguay, and Mar del Plata, Argentina.

Coauthored by Larry Dandurand

References

Casino City's Global Gaming Almanac. 2006. Newtown, MA: Casino City, 83.

Dandurand, Lawrence, and William N. Thompson. 1999. "Brazil" In *International Casino Law*, 3rd ed. Edited by A. Cabot, W. Thompson, A. Tottenham, and C. Braunlich, 285. Reno: Institute of Gambling Studies, University of Nevada, Reno.

CENTRAL AMERICA

There is legalized gambling activity throughout Central America. However, the activity varies considerably among the several countries.

BELIZE

Belize did not join the world of gambling until the 21st century. Casinos were first permitted with a 2000 law, and regulations adopted in 2004 make Belize an international player in Internet gaming. License holders pay a fee to the government for their site, and while they must have a presence in the country, they may locate their servers anywhere. A gaming control board grants licenses to online companies as well as land-based casinos. There are three casinos. The Las Vegas Hotel and Casino in the Corozal Free Zone has 31 tables and 400 gaming machines, while the Princess Hotel in Belize City also offers 400 machines but only three tables for play. The Palace in Ambergris Caye has but a few tables and 30 machines. The government also conducts a lottery with several games. The casinos do not draw tourists, but they are able to exploit the many Chinese immigrants who have found entry into the Caribbean country.

COSTA RICA

Costa Rica has both lottery games and casino games. The National Lottery is run for the Junta de Protection Social, the country's major welfare charity. Until very recently, the casinos operated on a basis that most charitably would be called "Third World." The casinos purportedly operated under the provisions of a 1922 law that indicated the games that were legal and the games that were illegal. For instance, craps was illegal, but dominos was legal. Blackjack was illegal, but rommy (a variation of the word *rummy*) was legal. Moreover, roulette gambling was illegal, but if a game was not gambling, it was legal. Slot machines were also illegal.

Not too much notice was given to gaming in Costa Rica before the 1960s. Games were played, but both the operators and the players were Costa Ricans, so it was all a local thing. Then residents of the United States discovered the country. It was close to the United States, and it seemed to be quiet and peaceful. It was the perfect place to retire or to run away if your name was Robert Vesco (a fugitive financier of the Nixon era) or you had the Internal Revenue Service chasing after you. Costa Rica refused to extradite fugitives to the United States. A growing population from the United States was accompanied by growing tourist interest in Costa Rica. The casino activity reached out to foreign "visitors." In 1963, an ex-dealer from Las Vegas named Shelby McAdams saw an opportunity. He tied a roulette wheel on top of his Nash Rambler car and headed south on the Pan-American Highway. He introduced a new style of casino gaming. And along with a German expatriate named Max Stern, he offered "first class" gaming. McAdams and Stern were accepted by appreciative local residents, and soon others imitated their operations. Local governments had casinos closed in 1979 and 1980, but they reopened under a system of political tolerance. In the 1980s, casino gaming spread to all the major hotels in San Jose, as well as to outlying resort hotels such as the Herradura, Irazu, Corobici, and Cariari.

Casino operators knew that the patrons wanted blackjack, roulette, and craps games, so they read and reread the 1922 law. Collectively they came up with their solution, and for two decades, they alternatively sought alliances with government officials or fought the efforts of government officials who wanted to read the law another way. The editor of this volume was stunned when he visited most of the area gaming facilities in 1989. One casino was named Dominos. Indeed, in the middle of the gaming floor there was a long table and over it was a sign that said "dominos." Inside the table there was a layout that showed the field, the big six, come, don't come, pass, don't pass, and other familiar-looking dice table configurations. The players held two little cubes with white dots on each of their six sides, and they rolled the cubes into the corner of the table. As they did so, they yelled such things as, "Baby needs some new shoes," "eighter from Decatur," and "seven come eleven." The editor asked the manager just what they were playing. With a straight face, he said, "Dominos." The editor looked at the table, and inside the play area there was indeed a stack of dominos. He said, "What are those for?" The manager said, "Oh, if an investigator or stranger comes in and we think he wants to cause us trouble, we ask the players to put the cubes down and throw the dominos." As play continued at the "craps," also known as "dominos" table, a police officer came in. But he was not there to cause trouble, merely to see the manager, who spoke to an assistant. Momentarily the assistant returned with a carton of cigarettes, and the policeman left (with the cigarettes).

The casinos also offered the game of rommy. Rommy was played with a shoe of six decks. Two cards were dealt to players, and the dealer also took two cards. The players then either "stood" or asked for more cards. If the player's cards added up to a number closer to 21 (without going over 21) than the dealer's cards, then the player won. All payoffs were on an even-money basis. The casino managers insisted that this was not "blackjack" because blackjack was prohibited by the law. This was "rommy." There was no blackjack payoff of 2–1; there were payoffs of 10–1 if the player had three 7s and 3–1 if the player had a 5–6–7 straight in the same suit. Rommy was a legal game.

The editor noticed a small roulette wheel in the back of a casino. He was told that they tried this but the government at the time did not accept it (perhaps they had not given the authorities enough cigarettes?). The roulette game they tried was one called Golden Ten or Observation Roulette in Holland and Germany, where it was popular at the time. The wheel was stationary, with its number slats in the middle of a big metal bowl. The dealer would roll the ball slowly so it would make wide ellipses as it rolled to the center. While the ball was slowly moving downward, the player would observe it closely and predict where it would land. With great skill, the predictions could be correct. Hence, argued the casinos, the game was not a gambling game, but a skill game. The argument worked better in Holland than it did in Costa Rica. The casinos also set up a roulette layout and called the game canasta (a legal game). In this "canasta" game, a single number was drawn out of a basket of Ping-Pong balls (similar to a bingo basket). The number was the winning number for a game played on a roulette layout.

The casino very much wanted to have slot machines, but there was no way they could read them into the 1922 law. In the matter of taxes, the casinos seemed to pay what the government demanded, and that amount was quite flexible and certainly much less than per table fees stipulated in municipal ordinances.

In 1995, the casinos stopped trying to fight the law. The law was changed, clearly permitting casino games of craps, roulette, and blackjack. Slot machines were also authorized. There are also sports books. As of 2000, the number of casinos had been reduced; there are now approximately 30 in the country, with half of them being located in the capital city of San Jose or nearby. They must be in resort hotels, and the hotel must own the casino. Together the casinos have 600 machines and 175 table games. The largest casinos are in the Gran Hotel, and the Irazu, Presidente, and Royal Dutch Hotels.

The main action today in Costa Rica is Internet gambling. Since 1997, more than 220 Internet gambling enterprises have been operating out of the country. They invite play from persons outside of the country's borders, with the United States being the prime market. Sports betting is the main product. The Internet operations employee 10,000 people in Costa Rica. Prior to 2008, there has been no government regulation of the sites. While the United States government has attempted to prosecute operators whenever they can gain jurisdiction over them, several operators have retaliated by bringing a complaint against the United States with the World Trade Organization. They claim that since some Internet operations are permitted in the United States (e.g., under the Interstate Horseracing Act), there is discrimination in not allowing Costa Rica sites to market to the United States.

EL SALVADOR

Legalized gambling is relatively new to El Salvador. A ban on all gambling had been set forth in an 1882 law, which over the years was honored more in the breach. Nonetheless political instablitiy and civil war had made the possibilities of having developments on the casino front rather tenuous. Nonetheless, there were many houses of gambling operating at the beginning of the 21st century. In a fit of morality, national parliament ordered that all these houses be closed down in 2002. The next year the Chamber of Tourism began a campaign to have casino regulations instituted. Instead of a law, a new policy of organized toleration ensued. Today there are several small casinos, with only two of any size. Both are in the capital city of San Salvador. The Crown offers 13 table games and 54 slot machines, while the Siesta has 100 machines and only four tables. A lottery has only recently allowed instant games.

GUATEMALA

Guatemala's penal code of 1880 prohibits all gambling. One exemption to the law is given to the National Lottery organization that conducts a monthly game that benefits poor persons (both as employees of the lottery and as beneficiaries of programs supported by the lottery).

The penal code had also been totally ignored by others running gambling operations. In 1979 the brutal and corrupt regime of General Lucas Garcia authorized the opening of Club Monja Blanca in the penthouse of the Hotel Guatemala Fiesta in Guatemala City. A private group of operators consisted of expatriates from Cuba and Costa Rica. General Garcia's military "henchmen" were quite interested in the daily revenues of the casino, as they took their "share" along with the government's tax share. Very little of the take filtered down to the poverty programs that the casino was ostensibly supporting. The casino remained opened for three years. In 1982, General Rios Montt overthrew the Garcia government. Montt was a Fundamentalist Christian and was morally opposed to casino gambling. Even when he was overthrown by Mejia Victores in 1983, the casino remained closed. Today there is one tolerated casino in the capital

city. The Fantastic Casino offers gaming on 190 machines and at three tables.

In addition to the one casino, there is other authorized gambling that seems also to violate the letter of the penal code. Private charities are permitted to run raffles and lottery games that include weekly drawings and instant tickets. Also, there is a large private bingo hall on the Avenida Reforma just one block from the Hotel Guatemala Fiesta.

HONDURAS

In Honduras the "action" is found in two casinos at night, and in the plaza of the Tegucigalpa Cathedral by day. The poor people visit the marketplace each day. There they buy and sell groceries and lottery tickets. As with many less-developed as well as several forward-looking countries, the lottery operations are of the poor, by the poor, and for the poor. People with no other jobs—and maybe no job possibilities—can sell tickets on consignment. The profits from the lottery are also designated to go to programs for the poor.

Honduras is a very poor country, and Tegucigalpa certainly does not have the airs of a national capital. Its streets are narrow and dusty, and many people seem to wander them without a sense of their destination. Cows graze on garbage that is thrown into a dry riverbed. The most visible commercial sign in the city is the Coca-Cola sign on the side of a mountain just above the central business and government district. It seems to be a reminder to all that their independent sovereign country may not be totally in control of its own affairs—maybe people in Atlanta have as much control over their lives as they do. Although many Third World countries have towns and cities that could be called "quaint," the presence of machine guns on each corner and outside of each major store or office building keeps the word *quaint* from entering the mind.

U.S. commercial interests are in Honduras, selling Coca-Cola and also running large banana plantations. They and their employees, as well as military personnel, provide a marketing base for the casinos. Unfortunately, the poverty of the country as well as the devastation of Hurricane Mitch in 1998 has weakened prospects for strong casino revenues.

Three casinos operate in Honduras. Two are located in cities: one in Tegucigalpa at the Honduras Maya Hotel; another in the country's business capital, San Pedro Sula, near the Hotel Copantl Sula. Private entrepreneurs from the United States operate the two hotels. One of the management teams is also active in the casino industry in Curaçao; the other operator has a history of old ties to Cuban and London casinos. The third casino is a small facility located in the Carribbean beach community of La Ceiba

The two urban casinos have roulette games, blackjack, and slot machines, and the casino at San Pedro Sula also has poker games, *punto banco,* and bingo sessions. The casino tax represents 20 percent of the gaming win.

This editor's visit to Honduras in January 1989 revealed some unique features of the gaming scene. At the entrance to the Maya Hotel casino was a sign that informed players to "check their guns." While this was startling, there was a guard holding his rifle "at the ready" just outside the doors. The manager was asked if the sign was serious, and he gave assurances that it was, and that their "vault" was full at the moment. A listing of casinos for Honduras also indicated for the San Pedro Sula casino that "Guns must be checked at the doors."

The Casino Copan in San Pedro Sula had a feature not encountered in other casinos. In the past the casino had difficulties in granting credit to players. Most of the players were local residents. When they were approached to pay back their loans, they considered it an affront to have an American demanding repayment of a loan to them. Courts were also reluctant to order locals, many of who may have been living on modest means, to pay money to the "rich" American casinos owners. The casino decided to cut off all credit play, but then discovered that their crowds decreased considerably. The operators came up with a solution. They found local agents who would be happy to purchase chips from the casino cage at a discount, and then loan the chips to the players. They would have all responsibility for collection on the loans, and if they made the collection, they of course would realize a good profit—as they purchased chips at a discount and also charged the players a loan fee. The loan agents were local residents in good standing and usually with good connections to judges and other local officials. The patrons borrowing chips from them would be sure to pay them back, as their standing as honorable citizens was at stake with these loans. The casino operators assured me that the loan agents did not use any unacceptable methods to collect loans.

NICARAGUA

Nicaraguan law forbids casinos, yet at the same time imposes fees on slot machines and gaming tables. The national police tolerate the gaming. In 2003, it was reported that there were over 5,000 machines in operation in casinos, bars, pool halls, and slot arcades. Ten casinos are also opened for business, with seven of them in the capital city of Managua. There are 50 slot arcades.

PANAMA

Panama has had a national lottery and casino gambling during most of its history as a nation. The Republic of Panama gained its independent status in 1903 following a separatist revolution from Colombia, which was supported by the United States. The United States then negotiated for rights to dig the Panama Canal and control its operations. A Canal Zone area was put under the American flag, and U.S. military bases were located in the zone. The U.S. presence as well as canal activities has brought people from all over the world to Panama, and the country looked to these people to support casino activities. The lottery, however, has been marketed to local residents, and it has served a social welfare function—first, by giving jobs to many persons who sell tickets and administer operations, and second, by dedicating its profits to programs to help the poor.

The U.S. military left the Canal Zone and invaded the governmental center in Panama City in 1989 in order to capture President Manual Noriega because of his involvement in the drug trade. That invasion involved a major firefight and the loss of hundreds of lives. Along with the invasion, the United States imposed an embargo on Panama. The policies had the effect of killing any tourist-type activity for many years. On January 1, 2000, the United States gave up control over the operations of the Panama Canal and by that time had withdrawn almost all its military from Panama. The withdrawal removed much of the market that had existed for casino gaming in the earlier years. Panama has readjusted with new government initiatives for redeveloping tourism opportunities. Casino gaming has returned to the tourist package, and the government has authorized new casinos with private ownership.

The first casinos in Panama were also under private control. Several gaming rooms were opened in the Old Balboa Gardens region of Panama City. They offered dice, roulette, and blackjack games. In the early 1940s, several gaming establishments came to the Plaza Cinco de Mayo in Panama City and to the city of Colon, where the canal meets the Caribbean Sea. After a government change in 1945, all casinos were placed under central ownership of three Panamanians who won a government concession for the activity. In the early 1950s, the government permitted several casino gaming activities to be held for the benefit of the Red Cross and other charities. The private and charity gaming ventures came to an end in 1956 when the national government took over the casinos.

A national casino administration was established within the Ministry of Finance and Treasury. Its goal was to enhance tourism and to generate greater revenue from tourists as well as from Americans stationed in Panama and other businesspersons coming to the country. The national policy was directed at the placement of casinos in hotels. In the late 1950s, casino activity began in the El Panama, Continental, Granada, and Siesta hotels. In 1965, a new national law reorganized the casinos, allowing them in hotels located in cities over 200,000 in population with a capital value of $1.5 million. The law also authorized slot machine–only casinos in other locations. At the time of the U.S. invasion, the government operated 10 full-scale casinos: six in Panama City hotels, two in Colon hotels, and one each in the city of David and on Contradora Island (which was exempt from the population requirement.) Six Panama City hotels had slot machine–only casinos, as did three shopping centers, three airport locations, a bar, bowling alley, and five smaller cities. The full casinos offered blackjack, roulette, craps, and poker games, as well as slot machines.

According to the editor's 1998 interview with gaming board officials in Panama City, in 1997 the government shifted its policies, realizing that its casino administration did not have the resources to fully develop the industry for tourism. Privatization was authorized. Bids were accepted from 13 prequalified companies to run the casinos. Three companies were granted licenses to run casinos for 20 years. After that time licenses may be renewed. The casino facilities had to be located in new five-star (and old four-star) hotels that have 300 rooms. The casinos had to advertise the tourist aspects of their facilities. In addition to annual licensing fees, the casinos pay a tax equaling 20 percent of their win. Slot machine–only casinos pay a tax of 25 percent.

The regulations have been modified as the number of casinos increased in the 21st century. Today there are more than 30 casinos in addition to 26 slot machine halls. Panama also facilitates internet gaming as an operator can apply for a license by making a $40,000 first-time fee payment and then pay an annual payment of $20,000. There is no tax on any foreign wager received. There are 42 sites in operation.

References

Casino City's Global Gaming Almanac. 2006. Newtown, MA: Casino City, 87–92, 96–97.

"Fantastic Casino." www.casinocity.com/gt/guatemala/fantasti.

Gambling il dado. "Land Casinos El Salvador." http://www.ildado.com/land_casinos_el_salvador.html.

Gambling il dado. "Land Casinos Honduras." www.ildado.com/land_casinos_honduras.html.

Online Casino City. "Panama." http://online.casinocity.com/jurisdictions/jurisdiction.cfm?Id-32.

SLOGOLD, "Belize Gambling License." http://www.slogold.net/belize_gambling_license_get_gambling_license_in_belize.html.

Thompson, William N. 1999. "Guatemala." In *International Casino Law*, 3rd ed. Edited by A. Cabot, W. Thompson, A. Tottenham, and C. Braunlich, 302. Reno: Institute of Gambling Studies, University of Nevada, Reno.

Thompson, William N., and Cecily Hudson. 1999. "Panama." In *International Casino Law*, 3rd ed. Edited by A. Cabot, W. Thompson, A. Tottenham, and C. Braunlich, 303–305. Reno: Institute of Gambling Studies, University of Nevada, Reno.

Thompson, William N., and David Nichols. 1999. "Costa Rica." In *International Casino Law*, 3rd ed. Edited by A. Cabot, W. Thompson, A. Tottenham, and C. Braunlich, 296–299. Reno: Institute of Gambling Studies, University of Nevada, Reno.

CHILE

Chile offers lottery gaming as well as parimutuel betting on horse races and casino gambling. The Loteria de Concepcion began in 1921, and it devotes its profits to several charities, including the Red Cross and the Universidad de Concepcion.

The southernmost country on the South American continent, Chile has a population of 17 million on 292,258 square miles of land. The country is a strip of land 2,650 miles long and no wider than 225 miles. It is nestled between the Pacific Ocean and the high Andes. The variety of climates and terrain appeals to all categories of tourists. Still the isolated geography restricts the country's ability to utilize its gambling facilities as a means of attracting outside revenues.

The struggle for Chilean national independence from Spain, led by Bernardo O'Higgins, lasted for many years during the first decades of the 19th century. When the local forces emerged with political control, they sought to deal severely with the sinful acts that were remnants of the days of Spanish colonial rule. The "sin" of gambling was high on the "hit list." An 1812 law proclaimed all games to be illegal. The law stated that gambling "compromised, demoralized, prostituted, and ruined" civilian members of society by corrupting the innocent. Gaming was a "genuine crime" and a "detestable occupation." An 1818 decree by O'Higgins saw gambling as the "worst scandal." Cafe owners were subject to fines for permitting games in their establishments. Another decree in 1819 labeled gaming "repulsive" and promised to punish violators of the prohibition to "the full severity of the law."

Yet, as the days of independence unfolded, Chilean lawmakers were aware that they could not fully suppress old habits from colonial times. In 1847, the national legislature recognized that "people gambled anyway." They opted for controlled legalization by authorizing municipalities to designate areas for gaming. An 1852 statute provided for local councils to license casinos. Later in the century, however, all gaming was again made illegal after a new wave of morality swept over the lawmakers.

Modern casino gaming in Chile dates back to 1913 and the vision of the city leaders of Vina del Mar. This seaside resort community (now a city of 300,000) successfully drew tourism with its racetrack. Local facilities were inadequate, however, to use tourism to foster growth. Council members debated about creating a lake and reclaiming land from the sea to build a municipal baths center, the *balneario*. From this debate came the idea of casino gaming. Shortly after the opening of the baths, casino plans gained momentum. Vina del Mar is only 80 miles from the capital city of Santiago, and its newly developed baths and beaches attracted many urban dwellers. The Vina politicians turned their attention to the lawmakers in the large capital city.

It took until 1924 before the national government decreed a new policy that would allow selected resort cities to establish casinos. In 1928, new legislation specifically designated the creation of the first nationally recognized casino at Vina del Mar. It authorized a new local government corporation to build a casino at the oceanfront near the balneario. The corporation could also select a private concessionaire to operate the casino. The initial concession agreement would last for 25 years. It has been renewed several times.

Casino gross profits were taxed and the proceeds designated for public works. Taxes are on a scale up to 70 percent of gross gaming win. Of this tax, 30 percent goes for road construction and improvements in the region around Vina del Mar. The remainder goes to the city government to develop tourism facilities. The casino also pays a 7 percent gross win tax directly into the national government's general fund. Entrance fees charged to patrons go directly to the municipal governments.

The original gaming regulations at Vina del Mar and the other locations required the exclusion of certain people from gaming: those under 21, those under the influence of alcohol, those with bad behaviors, and persons known (through previous experiences) not to have sufficient funds. Gaming employees and public employees who deal with public funds also could not gamble. Under the old law, women could not gamble without permission of their husbands. Residents of the casino towns could only gamble if they obtained prior approval from their municipal governments. A provision in the 1924 national law, which was not enforced, required that any unaccompanied women must have the written permission of their husbands, or former husbands, if they wished to enter the casino. Nonetheless, all patrons must still show identification and pay an entrance fee as they come into the casino. Foreigners must show their passports. The Vina del Mar casino has a restaurant and bar facility, but the other casinos do not. Patrons cannot drink in gaming rooms.

The municipality constructed the current buildings at Vina del Mar in 1929 and 1930. On New Year's Eve, December 31, 1930, the wife of the mayor of Vina del Mar cast a ball into a spinning wheel. A croupier called out "Negro y ocho" ("black and eight"), and the casino was open.

The casino now draws as many as 2,000 players a day in the summer season. During the high tourist time, the casino has 28 baccarat and *punto banco* tables, 18 American roulettes (with two zeros), 4 blackjack tables, and 2 craps tables in the main gaming room. The casino gives credit to selected players

known to have sufficient means to gamble. They will also cash checks. Complimentaries are limited to restaurant and bar services available within the casino. There are no hotel facilities or complimentaries for rooms or transportation. The casino arranges group tours, but there are no gambling junkets. During the summer season, many players come from Brazil, Argentina, and the United States. In other seasons, most players come from the Santiago region.

The casino has 500 employees. During the editor's visit to the casino in the early 1990s, all the dealers in the main room were men. Women could work only the lower-stakes games in the other rooms. The casino's entrance fee is 800 pesos (US$2.50), which is waived for persons wishing only to observe the art collections regularly displayed in a gallery and hallways or to attend events in the 700-seat showroom.

National laws designated a casino for Arica in 1965. Arica, 1,100 miles north of Santiago, is a desert city of 150,000 residents located beside the ocean and near the Peruvian border. Its sandy beaches attract many tourists. In 1969, a casino was approved for Puerto Varas, a town of 25,000 that is 600 miles south of Santiago. Puerto Varas is on a beautiful lake and provides tourists access to magnificent glaciers farther to the south. The beach resort of Coquimbo, an oceanside city of 75,000 that is 300 miles north of Santiago, won approval for a casino in 1976. In 1990, casinos were also approved for the cities of Pucon, Puerto Natales, and Iquique.

The municipal governments owned these casinos and contracted with private organizations to operate them. The legal framework changed considerably when the national government passed a new casino law in 2004. The law created a

Federal Gaming Commission and expanded the number of casinos to 24. All are under national control. Each local region with the exception of the city of Santiago was permitted to have casinos. The country's largest casino is now located at Monticello, just 35 miles south of Santiago. The new facility has a 155-room hotel, a retail shopping center, a convention center, a spa, and a bingo hall with 300 seats, in additon to 1,500 slot machines and 80 table games.

Resources

Rutherford, James. 2008. "Chile's Domino Effect." *International Gaming and Wagering Business,* October: 4.

"South American Beat." 2008. *International Gaming and Wagering Business,* July: 14.

COLOMBIA

Tourist magazines boast of Colombia's beaches on the Caribbean, ports on the Pacific, mountain grandeur, and Amazon jungles that yield the world's finest emeralds. Colombia is a beautiful land. Democracy has prevailed in its political institutions since 1957. Free elections for the office of president occur every four years. With a one-term limit on the office, each election has seen a peaceful transition. With its 44 million residents, it could be an ideal country.

But Colombia has its problems. A new agricultural commerce developed around the illegal drug industry, and drug activity has created a level of violence not witnessed since the days of the Spanish conquistadors. The problems of developing tourism based on the casino industry in Colombia are monumental, and perhaps insurmountable.

Bogota, the capital city, has nearly 7 million residents and a feel similar to New York and Paris. Still, the prominence of soldiers guarding street corners with high-powered weapons confirms unrest and uneasiness. Murders of judges and other political officials who battled the drug lords of the Medellin cartel continue to leave doubts as to who controls the country. The very word *Colombian* has become synonymous with negative images that bode no good for a national tourism industry.

Nevertheless, there is a gambling industry. Horse racing is authorized, there is a national lottery and local lotteries, and there are casinos. Somehow they have managed to get customers, but few would expect that high-rolling tourists could be found among their clientele.

Colombia has had many casinos, but until very recently, there was little cohesiveness among their owners and operators. The commercial games were not subject to common rules or regulations. Until 1990, the national law was of little practical significance for the casino industry. There were references to taxes for tourism development, but national taxes were not collected. In a visit with national officials in 1989, the editor of this volume gained the impression that the national government wished to avoid any political controversy that might attend a debate on casino policy. With so many other more troubling problems, casino policy was one "can of worms" that could remain closed.

In 1990, a process of change began. The Colombian government undertook national health care reform and looked to gaming revenues to fund health programs. A private company was begun under the auspices of federal authorities. Called at first ECOSALUD, and now ETESA (Empressa Territorial para la Salud), it holds an exclusive government charter to license and/or to operate directly or through franchising arrangements almost all forms of gaming in Colombia, except for the lottery. Since the creation of federal authority, laws have been passed to specify the rules for blackjack games, machine gaming, and racetrack betting. As of 2008, there are 18 larger casinos operating under the official policies of the national government. Each had about 8 to 10 tables and 100 to 125 slot machines. Bogota has six of the casinos, the largest being Casino Hollywood with 160 machines and 30 tables. Medellin has four casinos, with Casino Caribe leading the group with 400 machines and 16 tables. Cali, Cucuta, and Palmira each have two casinos, while the Casino International still operates on San Andres Island. In addition to the full casinos there are several hundred slot machine halls, which collectively have nearly 40,000 machines.

The rules for casino gambling were confusing until policies clearly put the authority into national hands. The editor interviewed Carlos Marulanda Ramirez, the cabinet minister of economic development, in 1989. Ramirez's ministry was in charge of tourism and casino policy. He admitted that "there is no clear policy as I can see it, and I am the Minister." He

was studying the matter because he felt the country should have some direction for its casinos. Ramirez acknowledged that casinos were low-priority items for a government caught up in the broader issues of economy, violence, and justice. Politicians were wary of gambling, and although they support a national lottery and horse racing establishment, they were hesitant to endorse casino gaming officially. Ramirez believed at the time that casino policy was best developed outside the legislative process.

Casino gaming is legal under legislation passed in 1943 and 1944 and presidential decrees issued in 1977 and 1978. An earlier law, passed in 1927, had prohibited casino gaming. Under the 1977 decree, a national tourism corporation within the Ministry of Economic Development would authorize casinos for a term of 20 years in the cities of Cartagena, Santa Marta, and Cali and within the region of Guajira. The 1978 decree specified that a national tourist investment company would own the Cartagena casinos. All casinos would exist according to agreements between the owners and the *alcalde* (mayor of the city). Fifty percent of the public revenues from the casinos would go to promote tourism. Yet, the laws and decrees did not dictate the types of games played, the rules of the games, the taxation of gaming activity, or the inspection of the gaming halls and their personnel. The laws were simply broad statements saying that there could be casino gaming. Although the laws mention four jurisdictions, casinos existed in locations not specified by the national policy.

A national policy could have emerged before the 1990s, as in earlier years the national government appointed the local government officials. (The alcaldes are now popularly elected.) Still, the development of gaming policy never influenced appointments of local officials. Because of the local nature of casino licensing and control, there was no definitive list of casino properties in Colombia, until the latter years. There were some strange results of divided control over casinos.

The Bogota alcalde would license casinos, but not allow roulette. Yet, the game of roulette is a game of choice among Latin players. Therefore, the local casino operators used their ingenuity to develop *espherodromo,* an alternative game. Eleven billiard balls, 10 with numbers and 1 solid white, are released from a high platform and rolled down a chute. The chute splits into two, and part of the balls go in each direction as their descent follows a path not unlike a path on a meandering water slide. The two chutes then meet and the balls go into a large bowl, hitting each other. They descend until one enters a hole at the bottom of the bowl. This ball has the winning number. The concept is, of course, the same as for roulette. The payoff on the 10 to 1 risk is 9 to 1. The house wins with the white ball, giving it a 10 percent edge over the players. Espherodromo has been taken to its ultimate form in Eugenio Leal Pozo's four Bogota casinos—the Versailles and Gallery 21 in the Tequendama Hotel and the Club Diversiones and Ambassador. He developed an automatic elevator system that returns the balls to their starting platform for the next play. Two dealers work the game. One dealer conducts betting activity, and the other oversees the machine. Eugenio Leal Pozo is a Cuban expatriate who worked in the Gran Casino of Havana and the Colony Club of London. He formerly owned the casino at the Hotel Hispaniola in Santo Domingo. He came to Bogota in 1975 and to the Tequendama in 1985. His two

A most funny looking game: espherodromo, the Bogota variation of roulette.

hotel casinos are small, but very plush, and they offer a few blackjack tables, one baccarat game, one *punto banco* table, four slots, and espherodromo.

Eugene Leal Pozo also owned a casino on San Andres Island. The island is two hours from Bogota by air (one hour from Cartagena). National tourists do not come to gamble; almost all players in the island's two casinos are locals. As in Bogota, Leal has been an innovator on the San Andres casino scene. He has introduced a roulette wheel with 10 numbers and one zero. In his International Casino, the players suffer the same odds disadvantages as they do at espherodromo. Yet, many like the action more than that provided by his two standard wheels with 36 numbers and 2 zeros.

Tourist magazines all consider Cartagena de Indias to be one of the most fascinating cities of the continent. It was founded in 1533 and soon became a walled fortress guarding Spanish shipping that used the harbor as a point of debarkation for wealth of all kinds. The present city has two parts: the walled old city and the new resort beach community called El Laguito.

The two casinos are in the new area. The drug wars of 1990 resulted in the temporary closing of the two casinos; however, they have since reopened. The Casino Turistico de Cartagena was a "down market" property. If it had many customers, it would be a grind joint (*see* Glossary). An outside entranceway on St. Martin's Street was lined with two rows of Bally mechanical slots that were always exposed to the salty sea air. The four roulette and six blackjack tables also showed the effects of being exposed to the elements. At 6:00 p.m. on a Saturday evening in January 1989, only one table was open. The property may

exist today only as a repository for a license that can later be moved or sold for a lucrative profit.

The other casino, the El Caribe, has been the premier gaming property in Colombia. Its licensing status is also confusing. The casino started in the Caribe Hotel. Then, 15 years ago, a major emerald company based in Bogota constructed an office and shopping complex near the hotel. The company also envisioned having a 300-room hotel in the office-shopping complex and planned to build a foundation to support a hotel tower. The company gained control of the casino license and moved the gaming facility to its property. The hotel was never built. Meanwhile, the Ministry of Economic Development supported the construction of a new Hilton Hotel (the government owns 46 percent of the property). The deluxe hotel with 298 rooms and offers full facilities for all tourist activities. During an interview in January 1989, the minister of economic development stated that the hotel would have a casino in the future. But others suggest that such talk has been going on ever since the hotel opened. The managers of the El Caribe casino affirmed that they based their agreement to operate the facility on an understanding that Cartagena would have no more than two licenses. The minister's position is that he is the government, and he can have a license if he decides there should be one. The managers suggest that the local government must approve all licenses, and the local government said "only two" casinos. On the other hand, the Hilton possibly could take the license from the Casino Turistico, or it could negotiate to have the El Caribe operate a Hilton casino under its license.

The El Caribe developed into a major casino property only after a new U.S. management team took charge in 1985. It introduced U.S.-style gaming, retrained dealers, replaced French roulette with the faster U.S. roulette games, remodeled the facility, installed a *prive sala* (private room) with four full games of baccarat, and opened a craps table. A special feature of the casino was a series of cockfights that were held in a special ring just outside of the main gambling area. Players could watch the fights and place private wagers on the birds. A low ceiling over the gambling area permitted the installation of a system of mirrors (affectionately called the Cartagena Catwalk) that permits security personnel to observe action on all tables in a pit simultaneously. There are no security cameras except in the cage area. The U.S. managers also set up a gambling junket program for East Coast high rollers. Yet, as the drug crises deepened, players refused to come from the United States. In 1989, most foreign play came from Canadians.

References

Casino City's Global Gaming Almanac. 2006. Newtown, MA: Casino City, 85–87.

Gambling il dado. "Land Casinos Colombia." http://www.ildado.com/land_casinos_colombia.html.

Thompson, William N. 1999. "Colombia." In *International Casino Law*, 3rd ed. Edited by A. Cabot, W. Thompson, A. Tottenham, and C. Braunlich, 290–294. Reno: Institute of Gambling Studies, University of Nevada, Reno.

ECUADOR

In October 2008, Ecuador offered a new twist for the gambling world. The government determined that its new 21-seat Supreme Court would be selected by a lottery. All former justices were placed into a pool of candidates. The action was to be effective until a permanent court could be selected by more traditional means in 2009. However, many of the justices who "won" the lottery indicated that they would not serve, as they found selection through a gambling process to be demeaning.

South America's small Pacific Coast country of Ecuador, with 14 million people, offers gambling products that include a lottery and 13 casinos. Commercial casino gaming began in Ecuador in 1949. Rules adopted in 1978 govern the 13 casinos. The largest casinos are located in two large cities: Guayaquil by the Pacific, and the capital Quito, high in the Andes Mountains. Smaller casinos are in the coastal cities of Manta, Machala, and Salinas.

Guayaquil has five casinos. These are in the Hilton, Oro Verde, Boulevard, and Uni. Most hotel guests are businessmen attracted to the country's commercial center. In contrast, Quito attracts visitors to its old city and government buildings and monuments. The

The Boulevard Hotel and Casino in Guayaquil, Ecuador.

city serves international visitors traveling to the Galapagos Islands, Equadorian possessions. Quito also has four casinos located at the Hilton, Casino Plaza, Swiss Chalet Hotel, and the Tambo Real Hotel.

In 1978, the Ministry of Industry and Commerce decreed that the national tourism company, now called CETUR, would license casinos. Casinos were classified according to size and whether they were permanent or seasonal. License applicants had to prove their financial ability to be in a gaming venture. They must also have a minimum number of tables and slot machines, depending on their classification. Casinos may have restaurant and bar facilities, or offer those services on a concession basis.

The regulations also govern employees. Dealers and others must register with the government. Dealers must abide by a code of conduct that includes a prohibition on gaming in casinos. Other rules prevent dealers from gambling, drinking on the job, and requesting loans from players. If a casino fires a dealer for violating the rules, the dealer cannot work in any other casino after that.

Besides dealers, certain others cannot gamble in casinos. These include minors (under age 21), public employees, bankrupt persons, parolees, and people certified as mentally ill. The regulations also prohibit players from bringing guns or other arms into the casino. The Minister of Finance sets tax levels.

All the casinos are in hotels that the local governments consider to be first class for their communities. CETUR approves the locations.

Credit play is permitted, but the casino must certify that the credit player has a determined amount of real estate wealth. Casinos limit credit play to a few well-known players because involuntary collection processes are difficult to manage. The casinos do not cash checks. The only complementaries are drinks and light snacks.

References

"Ecuador Chooses New Supreme Court by Lottery." http://www.boston.com.

Thompson, William N. 1999. "Ecuador." In *International Casino Law*, 3rd ed. Edited by A. Cabot, W. Thompson, A. Tottenham, and C. Braunlich, 300–301. Reno: Institute of Gambling Studies, University of Nevada, Reno.

MEXICO

With a population exceeding 110 million and an active tourist industry, Mexico could expect to be a lucrative market for casino gambling. Actually, for many decades in the early 20th century, it was. Casinos performed well in cities bordering the United States, drawing in gamers from their northern neighbor. The casinos were associated with corruption, however, and following the election of reform president Lazaro Cardenas, they were closed down in 1938. In 1947, the national legislature ratified the Cardenas decree by making all slot machines illegal. The casinos of Tijuana (at the Agua Caliente racetrack) and Mexicali had been very popular with Americans, and hopes have remained over the past six decades that they would reopen.

Indeed, discussions for reopening casinos have had the appearance of being quite serious. In the 1990s, the discussions had an increasing measure of urgency, especially as economic troubles in Mexico increased. In 1996, the final draft of legislation for legalization was prepared for the National Congress. The plan called for 10 casinos, one each to be located in a tourist city or border town. Sites selected included Tijuana, Juarez, Mexico City, Acapulco, Cancun, Cabo San Lucas, Cozumel, Monterrey, Puerto Vallarta, and Reynosa. Many U.S. companies rushed their representatives to Mexico City to offer governmental officials their proposals. The Mexican Tourism Agency studied the issue of casino gambling and concluded that gambling would benefit the tourist economy.

As with previous proposals, however, just when action was about to be taken, forces of resistance intervened. Governmental corruption again was exposed, as was an increasing drug trade and the involvement of organized crime operatives close to the government. Fears were expressed by leading politicians that casinos could be dangerous and that they could aid drug dealers with money-laundering services. In 1997, the casino proposal was set aside. The talk continued, as Mexico solidified its position as having a "history of false starts." Nonetheless, at the beginning of the 21st century, some breakthroughs on the casino side were witnessed.

Mexico, while reluctant to embrace casinos, had embraced many other forms of gambling. The lottery has been active throughout the nation's history, even in its colonial era. A national lottery dates back to 1770. There have been dog races and horse races (numbering 22 in 2008), bingo parlors, and sports betting opportunities on international soccer as well as on all major U.S. sports events, both professional and collegiate.

In 2005, the Minister of the Interior opened the door, not a wee bit but widely, for a return of machine gambling. While traditional slots were still banned, bingo games could be conducted on free-standing machines. The minister accepted the logic used for having "class two" machines on Native American lands in the United States— that the machines are "player-banked games." Also there could be other machine "numbers" games, offering either the illusion of skill or a player-banked pool from which prizes were drawn. The minister also indicated that a number of permits would be given for machine arcades, either free standing or in conjunction with bingo parlors, racetracks and sports betting halls. An eager gambling industry has stepped forth to test the luck of the Mexican players. Racinos and mini-casinos have proliferated. American slot manufacturers have swooped over the countryside selling their wares. By 2008, it was estimated that there were as many as 35,000 machines in operation. False starts have turned into a real start toward casino gambling. Yet, live table games are still prohibited. The machine parlors have adjusted to this reality by utilizing electronic roulette, blackjack, craps, and other table games.

The Caliente racetrack in Tijuana has undergone a $40 million renovation and now offers 1,000 machines, live bingo, as well as a race and sports book. Another large racino is at the Hippodrome in Mexico City. It has 400 machines. A racino in Guanajuato may be the country's largest machine parlor, with 1,333 machines in operation. The leading company in Mexican gaming is a Spanish company, Codero, which has more than 100 machine outlets. Another Spanish company, Zitto, controls 6,500 Mexican machines.

While the Mexican government exercises few controls over the machines— beyond licensing—operators have established a strong association that has set forth machine testing requirements as well as integrity controls, which are widely followed. It is hoped that more formal rules can be set forth in legislation that can then lead to more developed casino gambling, which can appeal to visitors from the United States. Thusfar, almost all the gamers are local Mexican residents.

References

Casino City's Global Gaming Almanac. 2006. Newtown, MA: Casino City, 271.

Clearly, Anna. 2006. "In Tijuana, Gambling Makes Noise," *San Diego Union,* August 14.

Lofgren, Paul. 2008. "Mexico, So Little Is Known, So Much to Tell." *International Gaming and Wagering Business* 29, no. 10 (October): 1, 23, 37.

Thompson, William N. 1999. "Mexico." In *International Casino Law*, 3rd ed. Edited by A. Cabot, W. Thompson, A. Tottenham, and C. Braunlich, 217. Reno: Institute of Gambling Studies, University of Nevada, Reno.

"Welcome to Mexico." 2008. World Casino Directory, November 3, http://www.worldcasinodirectory.com/mexico.

PARAGUAY

Paraguay, the most remote country in South America, is landlocked and surrounded by Argentina, Bolivia, and Brazil. It is a founding member of the Southern Cone Common Market (MERCOSUR). The other members of MERCOSUR are Argentina, Brazil, and Uruguay. The four countries of MERCOSUR have eliminated import tariffs and have a free exchange of goods, services, capital, and labor. Paraguay has 6.6 million inhabitants residing in an area of about 157 thousand square miles.

Paraguay permits almost all forms of gambling, including horse racing, lotteries, cockfighting, bingo games, and casinos. Casinos have been located in all the major urban areas of the country: Asunción, Ciudad del Este, and Pedro Juan Caballero. Paraguay also has had small gaming casinos operated by local owners holding government licenses. With the exception of the operations in Asunción, the capital of Paraguay, the casinos are very small. The Ita Enramada was the leading facility prior to the overthrow of President Alfredo Stroessner in 1989. Soon afterward it became overshadowed by the casino at the Asunción Yacht Club.

Casino gambling began under the regulation of the national government in 1943 when a casino opened in a hotel in downtown Asuncion. The casino owner, Senor Valentino, formed a corporation that later developed the Ita Enramada Hotel and Casino resort complex on the Paraguay River in suburban Asunción. The casino relocated to the Ita Enramada facility in 1975.

The Asunción casino operated under a long-term concession granted by the government of President Stroessner. Valentino's wife, Dora Valentino, maintained operations after his death. She also owned the casino at Ciudad Puerto Presidente Stroessner (now Ciudad del Este), the Paraguayan border city near the famous Iguazu Falls, the Brazilian city of Iguazu Falls, and the Argentinian city of Port Iguazu (which has a casino). The Valentino company also held concessions to operate a weekly national lottery game, a quinela game, and bingo in Asunción. The Catholic University has operated the sports pool (PROBE), and horse-race betting has been under the control of other private operators. Small casinos in other communities have been operated by local owners holding government concessions.

The Valentino company's monopoly over major gaming activities received a serious setback after President Stroessner was deposed in February 1989. Dora Valentino's concession for the casino at the Hotel Acaray in Ciudad del Este expired. Unexpectedly, it was not renewed, and the concession was awarded to a group of Brazilian businessmen. They moved the casino to the Club Rio del Este in downtown Ciudad del Este. That casino closed. The Acaray Palace Hotel and Casino reopened and then closed again.

Dora Valentino began constructing a $30 million, 250-room resort hotel just north of the city, near a proposed major international airport. The foundation and shell of what could have become the largest hotel in the nation was built. Intentions were to move the casino to the facility. Construction halted, however, when casino plans stalled. The government had given only one casino concession for each region. Obtaining another concession in Ciudad del Este proved a difficult process. As the new hotel is technically outside the city and within the Hernandez region, Dora Valentino has claimed that the area is eligible for a second casino.

While the Valentino company argued for a second casino in the Ciudad del Este area its competitors won the right to have a second and third casino (besides the Ita Enramada Casino) in Asunción. Another casino is at the Asunción Yacht Club (the Paraguayan Hotel and Casino and Yacht and Golf Club). The Asunción Yacht Club Casino has outclassed the Ita Enramada Casino. The Ita Enramada Casino is eight miles downriver from downtown Asunción on the Paraguyan River. The Asunción Yacht Club Casino is also on the Paraguyan River, about four miles downriver from downtown Asunción. Concessions for the casinos were extended in 1995. However, today the Ita Enramada is closed and only two casinos operate in Asuncion, one being at the Yacht Club and the other in the downtown area at the Hotel Excelsior.

In addition to the casinos at Asunción, one casino operates in Ciudad del Este and another in San Bernardino.

References

Casino City's Global Gaming Almanac. 2006. Newtown, MA: Casino City, 98.

Thompson, William N. 1999. "Paraguay." In *International Casino Law*, 3rd ed. Edited by A. Cabot, W. Thompson, A. Tottenham, and C. Braunlich, 306–312. Reno: Institute of Gambling Studies, University of Nevada, Reno.

PERU

A variety of gambling activities is permitted in Peru, including horse racing, cockfighting, lotteries, and casinos. Casinos were not legalized until 1992. At that time, the country of nearly 29 million persons was in the midst of a violent struggle with revolutionary guerrillas. The economy was on the edge of collapse, with unmanageable inflation. Things have turned around in the past decade and a half. What was once a hostile atmosphere for casino operations is now a good market in a stable political and economic situation. Still the notion that casinos can help build a base for tourism has not been realized.

Peruvian law requires that full casinos must be located in one of 10 tourist zones. They receive 10-year renewable licenses, and they pay taxes of 20 percent on their gross gaming wins. The capital city of Lima has about 80 percent of the casino action in the country. The city has eight full casinos, and another 70 slot machine halls are located there and around the country. Most of them are privately owned, although the government owns some. In all, there are more than 17,000 total machines in Peru.

Whereas overall political and economic stability in Peru helps the gaming industry in general, an ongoing dispute

Children everywhere are drawn to games—these kids are playing on a street in Lima, Peru. Do you think they are gambling?

over whether the national or the local law applies to the slot machine parlors caused much confusion until the highest court of the country ruled in 2007 that the national government had ultimate authority over slot machines as well as casino gambling. The number of slot machine halls was cut in half, with closures of facilities that were operating only with municipal approvals.

Growth of the Peruvian casino industry is unlikely, as the markets are near saturation at the moment. It is estimated that over 90 percent of the play comes from local residents and not from tourists, a situation that does not allow for casinos to contribute to the economic development of a country.

References

Cabot, Anthony N., William N. Thompson, Andrew Tottenham, and Carl Braunlich, eds. 1999. *International Casino Law.* 3rd ed. Reno: Institute for the Study of Gambling, University of Nevada, Reno, 313.

Casino City's Global Gaming Almanac. 2006. Newtown, MA: Casino City, 77, 93–94.

Fonseca Sarmiento, Carlos. 2008. "Peru." In *International Casino Law and Regulation.* Boulder CO: International Masters of Gaming Law.

URUGUAY

Uruguay is a small country with an area of only 63,000 square miles (the size of Missouri) and a population of about 3.5 million. It is between the two largest countries of South America: Argentina and Brazil. These countries with their restrictions on casino gambling (nearby Buenos Aires did not have a casino until recently) provide tourist market customers, especially for Uruguayan facilities along the Atlantic Coast beaches. Uruguay has a free economy, and the flow of foreign currency in and out of the country is unrestricted. There is no discrimination between nationals and foreigners, and for that reason there has been an inflow of casino investment dollars.

Private casinos existed in Uruguay more than 100 years ago. The first gaming law passed in 1856. Legend has it that French immigrants started casinos to conduct their traditional roulette games. The government took over the casinos early in the 20th century, and up until the 1990s, all casinos were government owned. Two municipally owned casinos were in the capital city of Montevideo, and the national government owned a series of small facilities along the ocean and in interior cities bordering Brazil and Argentina. Then the government authorized the building of a private five-star hotel with a casino in Punta del Este. The facility, which opened on January 1, 1997, is operated by Conrad International. It is the nation's largest casino, with annual revenues in excess of US$140 million.

In Montevideo, the earnings of the two municipal casinos—the Parque Hotel and Hotel Casino Carrasco—go to the city government. In the rest of the country, Dirección Nacional de Casinos del Estado (an entity of the central government) owns and operates the casinos. Forty percent of casino earning goes to the municipality in which the casino is established, 20 percent to the Ministry of Tourism, 10 percent to the National Food Institute, and the last 10 percent to a special fund for the preservation of the casinos. In 1995, a national casino was opened in the Hotel Victoria Plaza in Montevideo. All of the government-owned casinos of Uruguay are being offered for sale to private parties as the goal is to have total private ownership in the near future.

Uruguay also has facilities for horse racing and bingo games, and the government also operates a lottery.

References

Delgado, Conrado Huges. 1999. "Uruguay." In *International Casino Law*, 3rd ed. Edited by A. Cabot, W. Thompson, A. Tottenham, and C. Braunlich, 317–319. Reno: Institute of Gambling Studies, University of Nevada, Reno.

"South American Beat." 2008. *International Gaming and Wagering Business*, July: 14.

VENEZUELA AND SURINAME

Venezuela is a country of 27 million people lying at the far north of South America on the Atlantic Ocean. The law establishing legalized casino gambling in Venezeula was passed in 1997. Later regulations set tax rates for casino properties. In addition to casinos, other gambling activity is also legal in Venezuela, including bingo games, horse and dog racing, and government lotteries. Prior to 1997, there were several casinos operating with permission of local governments. All controls and licensing are now at the national level. Today casinos operate on Margarita Island—a tourist resort area—and other locations under the national rules. Under the law, casinos are permitted in five-star hotels with 200 rooms if they are located in tourist zones. Margarita Island is one such zone. The casinos are given 10-year renewable licenses. They are taxed at a rate of 20 percent of their gross gaming wins. Most of the locally permitted casinos closed because they could not meet requirements for licensing. The major casinos include the Gran Casino Margarita, located in the Margarita Hilton Hotel. It is run by CIRSA, a Spanish gaming company. A second Margarita Island casinos is at the Laguna Mar Allegro Resort. Mainland casinos include ones in Guyana, La Urbina, Maracaibo, and Pampatar.

The Republic of Suriname, the former Dutch Guyana, is located on the northeast coast of South America. The country received independence from the Netherlands in 1975. There are 470,000 people, with more than 250,000 of these persons living in the capital city of Paramaribo.

Suriname has bingo games, a lottery and casinos. Casino licenses were first granted by the national government in 1996. There are four major casinos in Paramaribo, located at the Hotel Ambassador, Torarica Hotel, Golden Truly Hotel, and the Princess—which is the largest with nearly 400 machines and 15 table games.

Resources

Gambling il dado. "Land Casinos Venezuela." http://www.ildado.com/land_casinos _venezuela.html.

Maguire, Patricia A., and Sergio C. Buth. 1999. "Suriname." In *International Casino Law*, 3rd ed. Edited by A. Cabot, W. Thompson, A. Tottenham, and C. Braunlich, 314–316. Reno: Institute for the Study of Gambling, University of Nevada, Reno.

"Suriname Gambling." World Gambling Review. http://www.worldgamblingreview .com/gambling/suriname.

Thompson, William N. 1999. "Venezuela." In *International Casino Law*, 3rd ed. Edited by A. Cabot, W. Thompson, A. Tottenham, and C. Braunlich, 320. Reno: Institute of Gambling Studies, University of Nevada, Reno.

Zilzer, Carlos. 2005/2006. "Playing Blackjack in Venezuela." Blackjack Forum, http://www.blackjackforumonline.com/ content/playingblackjackinVenezuela.htm.

Middle East and Asia Minor (Including Israel, Lebanon, and Turkey)

The Middle Eastern and Asia Minor region is dominated by Muslim countries (with one notable exception). These lands have with very few exceptions abided by the word of the Koran which speaks against almost all gambling. Hence we find no legal casinos or public gambling in Afghanistan, Pakistan, Iran, Iraq, Jordan, Syria, Saudi Arabia, the Arab Emirates, Qatar, Yemen, and Oman.

There have been casinos for a time in Turkey and Lebanon as well as in North Africa Muslim venues (which are discussed in the entry covering that region). First our attention will be placed upon the one non-Muslim country of the region, Israel.

Israel is a gambling country. It has had a lottery almost since the inception of the new state. However, allowing casinos has been a heated and controversial issue. With a brief two-year exception—perhaps not an exception at all—there have been no legal casinos. While casino gambling may be an important economic issue, the dominant issue for the nation is defense. Serious efforts for Jews to escape persecution by returning to establish a state began in the 19th century. The state of Israel was declared in 1948, and the neighboring Arab countries immediately declared war. Since then, Israel has fought wars with the surrounding Arab nations in 1956, 1967, 1973, and 1982. In 1993, the Oslo Accords provided for peaceful relations between the Israelis and Palestinians. It proved short lived and gave rise to the Intifada, which targeted civilians in fall 2000. Hostilities persist.

Gambling has deep roots in the life of the Jewish people. Since the Biblical era, drawing lots was a common way to solve social and legal disputes. The first to gamble may have been Joseph's brothers, who drew lots to determine who would tell Jacob about the death of Joseph. In the last century, the goals of lotteries changed and they are now aimed at national targets, such as purchasing land for the good of the State of Israel.

Data reveal that every Israeli (18 years or older) spent an average of US$112 on lotteries. Concerning the annual sale of lottery tickets, Israel is 47th in the world, with 15 billion shekels sold in 2002 (approximately US$670).

Israel is a country with a lot of gambling, both legal and illegal. Kiosks located in every neighborhood sell tickets for the twice-weekly national lottery game, soccer pools, and instant lottery games. The government takes most of the revenues from the games, but player wins are not subject to income taxes. Gambling vessels operating on international waters sail from Haifa and Éclat. Advertisements in Israeli newspapers tout the features of floating casinos, including the provision of kosher food and entertainment. A sizeable number of Israelis travel abroad in order to participate in casino gambling. Illegal casinos operate in various locations and receive only cursory and occasional attention from the police.

Having a legal casino on Israeli soil caused much soul searching. After much debate it was finally agreed that there would be a casino, but it would be in Jericho, on the West Bank in Palestine. (The city was given to the Palestinians as part of an agreement reached in 1994.) At first glance it would seem to be an inspired choice. Jericho is one of the oldest cities in the world. It was the first city captured by the Israelites after their exodus from Egypt. The Palestinians had hopes of making the city a major tourist destination. Their leader, Yasser Arafat, maintained a home there. The Oasis Casino, the name of the casino, was the only legal gambling establishment in the area, and a magnet for Israelis and others in the region. However, the Palestinian population was not permitted to gamble at the facility.

The Jericho casino raised very serious questions for a number of senior members of the Israel Defense Forces. They warned that the Palestinians would not be able to secure the area. There were also concerns that Jericho's profits would be used as a prime funding source for Palestinian terror attacks against Israel. These profits were estimated at more than $1 million per day from the time of the casino's opening in 1998 through September 2000, when the violent Intifada erupted. The Palestinians forces chose to use the casino facility as a military base, and when they did not heed Israelis warnings to stay away from the building, the building was destroyed by Israeli military attacks.

While the Jericho casino had been operating in territory outside the active control of Israel, it operated with tacit if not actual positive approval of Israel. Most

Israeli leaders saw many benefits in the existence of the Jericho casino. First, they realized that there was and is a demand for gambling among Israelis and the casino could help meet that demand, drawing players away from illegal casinos and a casino in nearby Egypt (in the border town of Taba) as well as casinos on boats and in more distant venues (e.g., Hungary, Romania, Greece). Second, the creation of the Palestine casino lessened pressures to establish casinos in Israel, pressures that would involve confrontation with strong moral interests, including religious circles and members of the Labor Party. These interests may have recognized Israeli complicity in the decision to open the Jericho casino, but the fact that the casino was under Palestine Authority jurisdiction muted their opposition.

Third, the existence of the casino allowed Israeli money to move to Palestinians without direct appropriations. These investments helped to lessen hostility of Palestinians toward Israelis, and in turn lessen Israeli hostility toward Palestinians. The many jobs the casino gave to Jericho residents allowed them to build careers that could help develop a more vibrant local community. Strong healthy Palestine communities would be more likely to wish peaceful relations with Israel, as they would have a lot to lose in an atmosphere of hostility— which has turned out to be the case.

On the other hand, the two-year existence of the Jericho casino did present some downsides for Israel. First, there were questions about where the casino profits went. Certainly many of the dollars went to Yasser Arafat of the Palestine Authority—a major owner of the casino. Much money that was intended for the community of Jericho and the Palestinians purportedly went to Arafat instead, and he may have used the money to plan attacks on Israel and also to add to his personal bank accounts. *Forbes* magazine cited Arafat as the sixth wealthiest of "kings, queens, and despots" in the world, having a $300 million account derived in part from the casino. Second, while the casino drew as much as $1 million a day from Israeli players—as many as 97 percent of the casino customers—many Israelis continued to gamble at illegal casinos. They also participated in quasi-illegal and questionable casino activity on the Internet and on boat cruises.

The closure of the Jericho casino siphoned away most of the commercial activity of the community of Jericho. The casino had invigorated a local economy, but the closure cost 1,600 jobs. The closure had collateral damage as well. The casino was being operated by Casinos Austria International, and that company's net profits fell 24 percent in the year following the closure.

While the Jericho casino has now passed into history as but a footnote in the chapter on gambling, there has also been other activity aimed toward establishing casinos in Israel. To date, the activity has not achieved success.

In 1995, there seemed to be considerable interest in having one or more casinos in Israel. Labor MK (Member of the Knesset) Avi Yehezkel thought that several casinos might be on the horizon. He was head of the Knesset Tourism Subcommittee. The mayors of Tiberius, near the Sea of Galilee, and Nahariya, on the Mediterranean, told him that they would like to have casinos in their cities. There was also talk of building one in Yerucham and Mitzpe Ramon, both economically depressed towns. Meanwhile, a bipartisan Knesset bill called for establishing one or more government-sanctioned casinos.

The first candidate was Eilat, a resort city of 36,000, located on the southern tip of the Red Sea. There were plans for both a permanent docked casino ship as well as a land-based casino. Eilat is near Taba, a popular Egyptian town, which has its own casino. Additional locations suggested for casinos have included the Ben Gurion airport between Tel Aviv and Jerusalem, as well as Dead Sea resort areas and the northern cities of Kiryat Shmona and Beit Shean, both near Nazareth.

The demand for gambling in Israel has also been made evident by a proposal to have a casino on an airplane. In May 2002 *Maariv* daily newspaper in Israel indicated that the transport ministry had authorized a Boeing 747 to be operated by Icelandic airlines with a casino aboard. Israel investors were prepared to use as much as $30 million to convert the jumbo jet, which would make four-hour flights with 230 gambling passengers, leaving from Ben Gurion airport out into Mediterranean skies and then back. Even though it received approval of the transport ministry, the plan was rejected due to strong objections of the government's legal advisor and the Israeli Supreme Court.

Even with the operation of the Jericho casino, illegal casinos persisted in Israel, and they continued to operate after the closure of the casino. The *Jerusalem Post* reported that 13 percent of the Israeli adult public continued to gamble at underground casinos in the year following the closure (September 16, 2001). The *Post* indicated in 2003 that illegal casinos were handling bets in excess of US$3 billion dollars per year (June 17, 2003). However, in the 2001 survey that they reported, nearly one-third indicated they would not hesitate to gamble in a legal casino if it were allowed (September 16, 2001).

These casinos are still a sore point for all government officials as they are a venue of individual crime as well as scenes of violence, perpetrated both by terrorists and by those seeking to control the operations. The police investigated a case in which eight people who were residents of Nazareth were murdered in what they described as an "underworld battle" for control of illegal gambling in northern Israel (*Jerusalem Post*, April 11, 2003). The police also accused four Palestinians from east Jerusalem of organizing and assisting a suicide bombing by Hamas (a Palestinian terrorist organization) on a pool hall and illegal gambling den in Rishon LeZion, which killed 15 Israelis on May 7, 2002 (*Agence France Presse*, October 6, 2002).

As with those who oppose casinos on the Arab side of the border, there is also an Israeli opposition, which coalesces around religious interests. The casino interests have been mindful of opposition arguments and they have promoted things such as "Kosher casinos" as well as having casinos furnish funds to fight illegal gambling and the problems of compulsive gambling. To date, all such efforts have been in vain and shall probably remain in vain until the magic allure of peace descends over the region.

The same conclusion may be offered for the success of casino gambling in Lebanon, although there is a casino in place, 15 miles north of Beirut. In the mid-20th century a peaceful Lebanon was known as the garden spot of the eastern Mediterranean. Muslim and Christian populations shared the land in tranquility. It was the vacation destination for the region. Gambling entertainment fit well into the motif. There was an active lottery and a horse track with betting. In 1959, Casino du Liban opened with three major rooms for table gaming catering to the world's top high rollers. The casino was a luxurious facility offering the finest of dining as well as a dazzling dance review. The building was on a hillside overlooking the Bay of Jouniehoff the Mediterranean. For nearly two decades, the casino attracted well over a million visitors a year. Then history intervened. In 1975, a major civil war erupted, pitting the country's Muslims against its Christians. The Muslins were also divided into factions. From 1975 through 1989, war activity impeded the ability of the casino to function, although it kept its doors opened. When the violence was simply too much, the casino closed in 1989. It remained closed until the end of 1996. In 1996, a reconstruction project costing US$50 million was completed and the doors of the casino opened again. Slowly the allure of the former casino began to return. From 1998 to 2005, annual gross gaming revenues climbed from US$80 million to US$130 million. Then the facility hit against the wall of violence once more. A war broke out between Lebanon forces and the Israeli military. In 2006, an air attack found a bomb falling and exploding nearby, leaving a crater on the road to the casino, less than a mile away from the facility. The doors remain open, but hopes of having a world-class casino attracting the world's best players have faded away. The national lotto game also has become a casualty of war, as the game was suspended during hostilities, with over $2 million dollars in unpaid jackpots.

Internal politics—not violence—has closed down casino gambling in Turkey. As part of the Muslim Ottoman Empire until World War I, gambling was totally forbidden in Turkey. Following the war, Kemal Ataturk introduced a republican government, which was not only secular, but actually sought to suppress Islamic traditions and practices. In one of his moves against the former Muslim rulers, he granted a commission for Italian financiers to remodel the Sultan's Palace, the Yildiz Kiosk, into a casino. The gambling facility opened in 1926. Play was restricted to include only persons who were not Turkish nationals. The experiment with casino gambling was short lived, however, as the investors did not pay their bills to local suppliers and a police raid discovered that 80 percent of the players were Turks. In 1927, the facility closed.

In 1939, a national lottery was authorized. It offered passive games until 1989, when instant lottery tickets were sold. A private Dutch firm operates the games. Turkey also has a horse racing track with betting.

In 1969, another brief interlude of casino gambling ensued as an American investor opened a free-standing casino that was later moved to the Istanbul Hilton Hotel. The project was sold to other Italian investors who as those before did not meet all their business obligations. After a few years of operations, the casino was closed until 1983. Then a general law was enacted that was aimed at promoting tourism. By 1987, there were 27 casinos. They were originally divided into two types—table casinos that would allow only foreign players, and slot machine casinos that would permit Turks to play along with foreign guests. However, a major dispute between a player and a casino over a slot machine jackpot led to a government decree in 1988 to the effect that no Turkish nationals could enter any

casino to play slots or table games. Nonetheless, the number of casino continued to grow—until 1997. In that year the Turkish parliament, which had come under more influence from Muslim interests who were also against foreign investment, passed a law requiring all casinos—then 76 in number—to close within six months. The president of Turkey vetoed the action, but parliament overruled the veto, and the national courts upheld the casino ban. In 1998, all casinos were closed and 20,000 Turkish casino employees found themselves without jobs.

References

"Casino du Liban Board Approves Accounts." *Gaming News,* March 30, 2006, www.casinocitytimes.com/news/article.cfm?contentId=157498.

"Casino du Liban, The Legend," www.cdl.com.lb/upper1.htm.

"Down But Not Out." Beirut Nights Radio, August 5, 2006, www.beirutnights.com/forum2/viewtopic.php?=&p=30758.

Thompson, William N. 1988. "Turkish Gaming Policy Makers Perpetuate 'Misunderstanding.'" *Las Vegas Sun,* October 9: 2E.

Thompson, William N., and Jerry Johnson. 1999. "Turkey." In *International Casino Law,* 3rd ed. Edited by A. Cabot, W. Thompson, A. Tottenham, and C. Braunlich, 533–540. Reno: Institute of Gambling Studies, University of Nevada, Reno.

Thompson, William N., and Asher Friedberg. 2003. "Politics of Casino Gambling: Israel and the Palestinian Authority—An Update." *Gaming Law Review* 7, no. 6: 421–426.

Thompson, William N., Asher Friedberg, and Carl Lutrin. 2001. "Gambling in Israel and the Jericho Casino." *Gaming Law Review* 3, no. 1: 25–32.

United States

ALABAMA

Even though Mobile, the first city of Alabama, has had a rich history of pirates, houses of ill repute, Mardi Gras celebrations, and gambling dens of inequity, most sinful activities in the state have been effectively suppressed in modern times. One major exception was the illegal enterprises of Phoenix City, which during and after World War II catered to a clientele made up mostly of soldiers from nearby Fort Benning, Georgia. A major cleanup was instituted in the 1950s by state attorney general John Patterson. Patterson launched the crackdown activity after his father, a candidate for attorney general at the time, was murdered by local mobsters who were running the town. In 1954, John Patterson was elected in place of his father. He was subsequently elected governor of the state.

Gambling activity resurfaced in the 1980s. However, it now operated on a legal basis—for the most part. Charitable games were permitted under the control of local governments, and the state also authorized the establishment of dog race and horse race betting. The largest track in the state opened near Birmingham, and it pioneered an unusual event. The track (actually concentric tracks) featured both dog and horse racing on the same day and on the same card. The experiment with pari-mutuel gambling on races was not overly successful, as it was initiated just a few years before the state of Missis-sippi authorized commercial casino gambling as well as Native American casino gambling. Several of these facilities were near the Alabama border. Also, two other states bordering Alabama—Florida and Georgia—started very active lottery games that drew gambling play from Alabama.

The Alabama Poarch Creek tribe of Native Americans, led by Eddie Tullis, reacted to the new gambling ventures by creating three large bingo halls—one in Atmore near Mobile, and the other two near Montgomery—and by seeking a compact for casino games. State officials refused to negotiate a casino compact, but the tribe began using class two video gambling machines anyway, claiming that they were electronic bingo devices. The casinos have a total of 2,500 machines.

As the 20th century ended, the legislature gave serious consideration to legalizing new forms of gambling, including table games and machine gambling for racetracks. There are now four dog tracks in existence, while Birmingham closed its horse race activities. The legislature was able to authorize a public vote on the question of having a state lottery. In 1998, the governor was actually elected on a platform that included the lottery proposal. In October 1999, however, the voters of the state shocked not only Alabama but also the whole nation when they said "no" to the lottery by a vote of 54.3 percent to

45.7 percent. The lottery proposal was designed to duplicate the Georgia experience in that it designated revenues for free college scholarships for Alabama high school graduates with good records. With the negative vote, Alabama became only the second state (the other being North Dakota) to receive a negative vote on a state-operated lottery proposal.

References

"Bible Belt Suffers Big Losses on Gambling Issue." *Crossfire.* CNN Television, October 15, 1999.

Peck, John. 1999. "Focus Helps CALL Leader Lure Churches to Activism." *Birmingham Times,* 17 October: 1.

Roberson, Roy. 1991. "Loss of Horse Racing May Cost Alabama Millions." www .ag.auburn.edu/aaes/webpress/1991/horse racing.htm.

ALASKA

Native Alaskans and Native Americans in Alaska conduct bingo operations. There are also many bingo games sponsored by charitable organizations. Much of the revenue for the games' sponsors comes from the sale of pull-tab tickets. Alaska permits many raffle-type games for a variety of nonprofit interests. One of the most interesting games allows people to pick the time for the first breakup of ice floes in the spring each year. In recent years there has been interest in developing casino gambling. The proposals for increased gambling have not found support in the legislature, however, or among the general population of 650,000. In 1990, a ballot initiative to permit limited stakes casino games in bars and taverns was soundly defeated by a 60 percent to 40 percent margin.

References

"Alaska Gambling Board Initiative." 1990. www.ballotpedia.org, accessed September 5, 2009.

"Alaska Gaming Commission." 2008. www.ballotpedia.org, accessed September 5, 2009.

Thompson, William N. 1997. *Legalized Gambling: A Reference Handbook.* 2nd ed. Santa Barbara, CA: ABC-CLIO, 163–166, 186.

ARIZONA

In 1908, all gambling activity was banned by the legislative body in the Arizona Territory in an effort to win congressional support for statehood. By mid-century, however, the state of Arizona had legalized pari-mutuel horse race and dog race betting and had also established active charity gambling operations. The state has also had a lottery since 1991. When charitable "Las Vegas Nights" were authorized, commercial gambling suppliers actually took slot machines around to the events. The state also permitted the sale of slot machines, and in the 1980s, several businesses were importing used machines from Nevada and repairing and reselling them throughout the country. The businesses were supplying many of the machines to illegal operators, yet the state took no direct actions to stop the sales.

The many Native American tribes of the state were therefore set back when the state refused to negotiate a compact for casino gambling including machine gaming. After several years of legal maneuvering, the tribes won a federal court order mandating negotiations, and in 1993, the governor made an agreement and tribal bingo halls were converted into tribal casinos with slot machines. Now 15 of the state's 21 tribes operate a total of 22 casinos; the largest ones, in the Phoenix area, are operated by the Fort McDowell, Ak-Chin, and Salt River Pima tribes.

References

"Arizona Tribes with Casinos." Arizona Department of Gaming. http://www.gmstate.az.us/casinos.htm.

Dombrink, John D., and William N. Thompson. 1990. *The Last Resort: Success and Failure in Campaigns for Casinos.* Reno: University of Nevada Press, 158–161.

Thompson, William N. 1997. *Legalized Gambling: A Reference Handbook.* 2nd ed. Santa Barbara, CA: ABC-CLIO, 165.

ARKANSAS

In terms of legal gambling, Arkansas is best known for the Oaklawn Park horse racing track in Hot Springs and also for a dog track in West Memphis. Yet the real story of gambling in Arkansas involves wide-open illegal casinos in Hot Springs (in Garland County) that operated for over a century with connections to many of the leading mobsters in the land. In the mid-1950s, reform governor Orval Faubus sought to close down the gaming. Local Garland County judges overruled his efforts, however, and Faubus dropped the issue. After a staunch antigambling Baptist minister was elected to the legislature, the issue was reopened. He pushed a resolution demanding that the governor shut down the casinos. In 1963, the governor responded. After he did so, the citizens of Hot Springs circulated petitions to legalize casinos. The question was put on the ballot in 1964. The campaign for casinos was led by the local chamber of commerce; however, it was opposed by both Faubus and his 1964 opponent, Winthrop Rockefeller. Arguments that the state could experience a financial windfall from casinos fell on deaf ears, and the voters defeated casinos by a vote of 318,000 to 215,000.

The doors of the casinos have been closed since then, but casino proponents keep trying to win public support. In 1984, another petition was presented to the voters. Again, Garland County residents led the campaign. The state's young governor, Bill Clinton, opposed it. His wife, Hillary, led the campaign against casinos with a statewide speaking tour. Voters said "no" by a 71 percent to 29 percent margin. In 1996, voters again said "no," by the same overwhelming margin. This time, the appeal had been not to produce state revenues but rather to meet the competition from riverboat casinos in surrounding states. The dreams of returning to the glory days of gangsters and excitement in Hot Springs remain, but all the gambling is confined to the short racing season at Oaklawn Park each summer.

A proposal was put forth in the 2000 election that would have allowed six counties to have local option votes on casino gambling. The voters of Arkansas defeated casinos one more time. The voters did approve lotteries in a 2008 vote, which repealed an 1836 constitutional ban on the games.

References

Dombrink, John D., and William N. Thompson. 1990. *The Last Resort: Success and Failure in Campaigns for Casinos.* Reno: University of Nevada Press, 144–151.

Rose, I. Nelson. "2000 Election Results." www.gamblingandthelaw.com.

CALIFORNIA

California, the most populous state in the United States with 38 million people, is one of the leading venues for gaming in the world. The state is home to several of the largest horse racing tracks. It also has one of the world's largest lotteries, hundreds of poker clubs, horse racetracks, and dozens of Native American casinos.

Shortly before California became a state in 1850, gold was discovered at Sutter's Mill on the American River. The news spread quickly, and soon a "rush" of forty-niners here headed West. Between the time gold was discovered and 1860, more than 350,000 immigrants had come to the Golden State. They were miners and prospectors who had free spending habits when they made their personal discoveries—or whenever they got money in their hands. Gambling was pervasive, as San Francisco became a center for a wide variety of "sin" activities. Gambling was also widespread in smaller cities and in the many mining camps of the state. Soon both the state and the local communities were charging fees for operating gambling halls.

The sinful nature of California did not last. Mining opportunities lessened as gold veins were depleted. But California offered many other opportunities—good agricultural lands and ports for commercial activity. Waves of nonmining people—"good" people—came to the state looking for normal business activities and also for opportunities to raise families and build futures for their children. The dominant interests of the state—the mine owners and railroad interests—did not see that their roles in society were incompatible with those of the newer immigrants. The power elite responded to cries of public outrage and demands to clean up the sinful activities prevalent in the state. Actually, the first state constitution had contained a ban on lotteries, but casino gambling had been accepted by local authorities, until the citizens acted. Gamblers in San Francisco were lynched in 1856, and the legislature took notice. In 1860, all banking games were banned, but poker games could continue to be played. (The rule against banking games remained until 2000, when the final effort to win legal status for Native American casinos was successful, and the constitution was changed.) The slot machine was invented in California in the 1890s, and machines operated in the open until state laws specifically made them illegal in 1911.

Wagering on horse races was legalized in 1933. However, the major distinguished form of gambling in California from the 1860s through the 1980s was the poker club. Many debates in court and in the legislature revolved around definitions of different kinds of games that were legal or not and whether certain poker clubs could be considered public nuisances. Courts ruled that the clubs could exist only under the authority of local ordinances. Management of the 90 existing poker and card clubs of California are not allowed to participate as players in the game, nor are they allowed to take a percentage of the money bet by the players. The card club furnishes a dealer and then charges players a participation fee per hand or a fee based upon how long the player sits at the table—the fee is collected each half-hour. There are over 1,500 tables in the clubs of the state. The largest clubs are in southern California. These include the Commerce Club (in Commerce) with 233 tables and the Bicycle Club (in Bell Gardens) with 180 tables. The clubs were, for the most part, unregulated until 1997, when the legislature activated a state gambling control commission. The commission makes decisions on new licenses and rules for the games that may be played and also makes recommendations regarding taxes. The law establishing state regulation also set a moratorium on new or expanded clubs until year 2010.

California also permits charity gambling. There are many bingo halls in the state. The charity gambling and the poker clubs opened the door for Native American casino gambling in the state in the 1980s, precipitating an ongoing controversy that by the year 2000 had been mostly resolved.

There have been continuing efforts to legalize casinos in California since the mid-20th century. In 1950, the voters decisively defeated a plan for creating a state agency that could have authorized all forms of gambling, including casinos. In 1975, a legislative bill for casino gambling in Placer and El Dorado counties, near Lake Tahoe, died in committee. A 1977 plan called for three casinos along highways leading into the state of Nevada. A 1979 proposal to have casinos in Jackson failed, as did a 1982 plan to put casinos in the towns of Adelanto in San Bernardino County and Clear Lake in Lake County. The sponsor of the plan was arrested for holding illegal games to get funds to run his campaign.

The opposition to casinos became an element of the campaign for a state lottery in 1984. Sensing that the public was adverse to the notion of having casinos and that they might fear that a successful lottery vote could strengthen efforts to get casinos, the lottery sponsors put a provision into their constitutional initiative that stated casinos would be banned in California. The measure passed, and this meant the constitution would have to be amended if there were to be any casino gambling—similar to that in Nevada.

The ban did not stop the Native American quest for casinos, but it certainly "muddied the waters." Several tribes set up bingo and poker games, but they did not follow the local rules governing them. This precipitated a series of cases leading to the U.S. Supreme Court's ruling in *Cabazon v. California,* which said that Native Americans could run games according to their own rules as long as the games did not violate the general public policy of the state. Hence, since poker and bingo were allowed, they did not violate the general public policy of the state. The case in turn, caused the U.S. Congress to pass the Indian Gaming Regulatory Act of 1988.

The Native Americans of California are located on more than 100 small reservations, called *rancherias.* The Native Americans wanted casino games, but the governor would not make an agreement with them to allow the games. Nonetheless, the Native Americans installed a variety of slot machines, and they also played nonbanking versions of Nevada casino games. Legal squabbles seemed endless until the tribes sponsored a legislative initiative to mandate that the state give them an agreement to have some casino games. The 1998 campaign for Proposition 5 turned out to be the most expensive initiative campaign in U.S. history, as the Native American interests invested almost $70 million in the effort. Nevada casinos that opposed the Native American casinos invested $26 million in the campaign.

The proposition passed by an overwhelming margin. A court challenge struck it down, however, on the basis that the 1984 amendment to the constitution said casinos were banned. The Native Americans returned to the campaign. In March 2000, they won passage of Proposition 1A, which amended the constitution to allow Native American casino gambling in California. The 2000 passage gave ratifica-tion to compact agreements that were made in 1999. The door was also opened to revise the compacts, and several tribes did so in 2004. There are approximately 60 tribal casinos in the state. Their agreements indicate the numbers of machines each is allowed. The 1999 compacts limited tribes to 2,000 machines. In turn the tribes agreed to contribute money to two different funds, one run by the state and the other distributing money to tribes that did not have casinos. The state fund covered costs of regulations enforced by the California Gaming Commission. In 2004, new agreements with a select number of tribes permitted their casinos to have unlimited numbers of machines, while each agreed to pay the state increased fees. The new compacts also provided for casinos to give the state $100 million a year to support transportation bonds. Collectively the tribes now furnish the state with approximately $300 million a year from casino revenues.

References

Cabot, Anthony. 1999. "California." In *International Casino Law*, 3rd ed. Edited by A. Cabot, W. Thompson, A. Tottenham, and C. Braunlich, 9–16. Reno: Institute of Gambling Studies, University of Nevada, Reno.

Dombrink, John D., and William N. Thompson. 1990. *The Last Resort: Success and Failure in Campaigns for Casinos.* Reno: University of Nevada Press, 162–164.

Dunstan, Roger. 1997. *Gambling in California.* Sacramento: California Research Bureau, California State Library.

Lutrin, Carl, and William N. Thompson. 2000. "A Tale of Two States: Political Cultures Converge around a Divisive Issue: California, Nevada, and Gambling." Paper prepared for the Western Political Science Association, March 26, San Jose, California.

See also Native American Gambling: Contemporary (in General Topics section).

COLORADO

Colorado offers a state lottery, charity games and raffles, pari-mutuel horse race and dog race betting, and casino gambling activities. The modern era of gambling began when the lottery was initiated in 1983 for the purpose of raising funds for parks and environmental projects. As with many other lottery states, the normal legislative funding for these projects was reduced in accordance with the lottery gains, and in effect the lottery money simply went into the general fund of the state. The experience only confirmed that it is very difficult to have lottery funding for any ongoing programs that are normally funded by legislative action. The "modern" situation of using lotteries for regular government programs is contrasted with the experience in colonial times, when lotteries were utilized to fund specific capital projects—college buildings, roads, bridges, military arms.

There was one difference that citizens noticed in Colorado after the lottery was initiated. Many of their state parks now had signs proclaiming that the park was being supported by the lottery, which of course was true—but possibly also false. In some states, the lottery money is added to budgets; however, it is difficult to trace the funds. Often they are merely shifted from one program to another one.

In 1990, the voters were persuaded to approve limited-stakes casino gambling for three mountain towns—Blackhawk, Central City, and Cripple Creek. The gambling rules were patterned after those in South Dakota—$5 maximum bets on blackjack and poker games and on slot machines. One of the motivations for voter approval was the fact that the casinos of Deadwood were marketing their gambling to players from Denver, the largest city within a one-day drive of Deadwood. Even though the governor opposed the proposition, it passed with a 57 percent favorable vote. The number of casinos in existence at one time has fluctuated considerably from more than 80 to fewer than 60—the approximate number as the new century began.

Subsequent to the successful vote, several other towns in Colorado have sought voter approval for casinos, only to have their propositions lose by big margins. Two of the three towns with casino gambling, Blackhawk and Central City, are located on winding mountain roads about one hour west of Denver, and the third town, Cripple Creek, is one hour west of Colorado Springs. How the three towns were picked for the ballot proposition in 1990 is no mystery. In 1989, leaders from a group of about a dozen communities approached the legislature and requested passage of a law permitting casino gambling in their venues. They received very serious consideration; the legislative votes were close, but the proposal was defeated. Afterward, a few of the leaders decided that the only way they could succeed would be to circulate petitions and secure a statewide vote on a constitutional amendment permitting casinos. Since these campaigns are expensive, the leaders of the effort asked the dozen communities to fund the initiative. Most of the towns declined to make a financial contribution to the campaign. Blackhawk, Central City, and Cripple Creek, however, agreed to make the financial commitment necessary for a successful campaign. As a result, leaders decided that the casino proposition would apply only to these three towns.

Casino policies—rules and regulations, taxation, and licensing actions—are determined by a five-member Colorado Limited Gaming Control Commission. The policy enforcement activities are conducted by the Colorado Division of Gaming, an agency within the Colorado Department of Revenue. The amendment approved by the voters permitted the taxation rate to be as high as 40 percent of the casino win. The top rate in a progressive tax structure, however, is 20 percent of the gambling revenue. There are also extensive fees charged by both the state and local governments. For instance, the local governments charge between $750 and $1,500 annually for each gambling device (machine or table). The state requires each employee to go through a licensing process and pay a $200 fee before working in a casino.

The slot machines in the casinos must pay out in prizes at least 80 percent of the money that is played. The state has no fixed limit on the number of machines in a casino. Many have several hundred machines. In 2008, there were over 13,000 machines in the casinos of the state.

The ostensible purpose of the Colorado gambling has been to aid in tourism development. State taxes, however, go to the general fund directly. Moreover, the overwhelming numbers of players—certainly over 90 percent—are from the two metropolitan areas located near the casinos.

In 2008, the voters of Colorado passed an amendment that permits the three casino towns to vote to increase gambling limits from $5 a bet to $100.

In addition to the casinos in the three mountain towns, the state has approved compacts for two Native American casinos in Ignacio and Towac, each located in the southwest corner of the state.

References

Dombrink, John, and William N. Thompson. 1990. *The Last Resort: Success and Failure in Campaigns for Casinos.* Reno: University of Nevada Press, 152.

Nathan, Richard. 1999. "Colorado." In *International Casino Law*, 3rd ed. Edited by A. Cabot, W. Thompson, A. Tottenham, and C. Braunlich, 17–25. Reno: Institute of Gambling Studies, University of Nevada, Reno.

CONNECTICUT

Today Connecticut has two of the largest casinos in the world. However, they have existed for less than two decades. Modern gambling came to Connecticut swiftly and almost completely in 1971. A lottery, off-track betting, and horse race betting all became legal at the same time. In 1972, dog racing and jai alai betting were legalized. (There is a track at Bridgeport today,

Foxwood's Native American casino is the largest casino in the world.

but jai alai action has now ceased.) Only casinos and sports betting remained prohibited, and efforts to bring about their legalization also started in the 1970s. Bills allowing a casino in the depressed community of Bridgeport were introduced in 1981. The measures died in a state legislative committee. Bills were also defeated in 1983 and 1984.

The momentum for casinos seemed to die. But Connecticut permitted casino games for charities, which were allowed to hold "Las Vegas Nights." And Connecticut had Native American tribes. One organized reservation belonged to the Mashantucket Pequots.

They started bingo games and then requested negotiations for casino gaming. After several court battles, the state negotiated to allow the tribe to offer casino table games. In 1992, the tribe asked for slot machines even though they were not permitted in other entities in the state. Without going through the negotiation process, the state agreed to allow the machines if the tribe would give the state 25 percent of the revenues from the machines. The National Indian Gaming Act prohibited state taxation of tribal gaming; therefore, the state and tribe called the fee a contribution exchanged for the right to have a monopoly over machine gaming in the state. When a second Native American casino opened on a new reservation created by the Mohegans, the Pequots renegotiated the amount of money from the machines that they give the state. By 2008, the casino revenues of the two facilities reached nearly $2.5 billion. The state receives almost half a billion as its share of the bounty.

The Pequot casino, called Foxwoods, is located near the town of Ledyard. The casino complex is the largest in the world, with more than 300,000 square feet of gambling space, a bingo hall with 3,200 seats, 7,200 gaming machines, and 380 tables. It produces gambling wins of approximately $1.5 billion a year. The Mohegan Sun casino, which is near Uncasville, is managed by Sun International, a company with gambling experience in South Africa and the Bahamas that had earlier acquired and later sold the Desert Inn Casino in Las Vegas. The casino has a gaming area of 150,000 square feet,

3,000 machines, and 180 tables. An expansion in 2002 added the world's largest planetarium dome, with a 10,000-seat arena, a 300-seat nightclub, and 40 new shops and restaurants. In 2008, the Pequot reservation opened a new MGM casino of more than 50,000 square feet, with 60 table games and 1,400 machines.

References

Dombrink, John D., and William N. Thompson. 1990. *The Last Report: Success and Failure in Campaigns for Casinos.* Reno: University of Nevada Press, 127–129.

"Mashantucket Casino & Gambling Information." World Casino Directory. http://www.worldcasinodirectory.com/connecticut/mashantucket.html, accessed November 20, 2008.

WEFA Group (with ICR Research Group, Henry Lesieur, and William Thompson). 1997. *Study Concerning the Effects of Legalized Gambling on the Citizens of the State of Connecticut.* Eddystone, PA: WEFA Group.

DELAWARE

Delaware instituted its lottery in 1975. Because the state is very small and also surrounded by other jurisdictions with very active lotteries—Pennsylvania, New Jersey, and Maryland—state leaders sought a mechanism to win play from neighboring states. They decided to let players try to pick the winners of professional football games. Rather than incur the expense of professional

consultants to advise them on appropriate point spreads for the games, they tried to develop that expertise in-house. It was the bureaucrats against the wise guys from Philadelphia and "Jersey." The "big guys" (professional gamblers) also bet actively with the illegal bookies who used the Las Vegas line, that is, the line set by Las Vegas casinos (see Glossary). With a few quick phone calls, the true experts could discover which Delaware lines were faulty. The players continuously beat the game, and the state abandoned it before it could put the entire state budget into a deficit. Nonetheless, in 1992, when Congress passed a bill banning sports betting across the United States, Delaware was one of the four states that was given an exemption. There has been an effort to revive the sports betting. The state continues to operate other lottery games, including instant tickets, numbers, and Powerball lotto games.

Delaware has one thoroughbred racetrack and two harness tracks. The state authorized all types of slot machines and other gaming machines for its racetracks in 1995. Delaware Park in Wilmington offered the machines first, but Harrington Raceway and Dover Downs soon followed them, and GTech won a contract to furnish the machines. Each racino facility has up to 3,200 slot machines.

Delaware Park pursued a strategy somewhat different from that in other states, as it sought to make a strong separation between the machine gaming and the track wagering. Track efforts to bring slot players to the track windows were simply unsuccessful. A track manager commented that people got too confused and that clearly they had a dedicated group of slot players who had no interest in racing. An unused 60,000-square-foot section of the grandstand was converted to slots. No racing monitors were placed in the room, and players had to go to another room to make racing wagers.

Reference

Deleware Lottery Games. http://lottery.state.de .us/index.asp.

See also Racino (in General Topics section).

DISTRICT OF COLUMBIA

The District of Columbia was the unlikely site of a major casino in the 1840s and 1850s, which catered to many lawmakers and other public officials of the day. (It is described under the biography entry on Edward Pendleton.) In the modern era, efforts to have riverboat casinos and also gambling on video lottery terminals have been made—and they have been defeated each time they were proposed.

In 1980, the voters of the District defeated a proposal to have a lottery, a feat accomplished in the modern era by only two states—North Dakota and Alabama. The 1980 proposal, however, was burdened by a provision that would also have permitted dog race betting. In 1981, a proposal for a lottery standing by itself was approved. Today the lottery offers most nonmachine games, including two multi-state lottos, Powerball and Hot Lotto.

References

The Washington D.C. Lottery, www .winningwithnumbers.com/lottery/games/ washington-dc.

See also Pendleton, Edward (in Biographies of Leading Figures in Gambling section).

FLORIDA

Florida has one of the nation's most profitable lottery as well as a history of active pari-mutuel enterprise in the United States. The pari-mutuel industry features horse racing, dog racing, and jai alai games. The state has had a long history with underground gambling and with elements of organized crime that ran gambling operations throughout the country and in many other places as well.

Casino-type gaming was part of the early history of the state. In 1879, the state permitted cities to authorize gaming; however, this effort ended with a ban on casinos in 1893. After a major destructive hurricane in 1928, the state turned to gambling once more in an effort to raise revenues. Pari-mutuel wagering on jai alai, dog racing, and horse racing was permitted. Another experiment occurred between 1935 and 1937, as slot machines were temporarily permitted. That effort was destroyed by the intrusion of illegal operators.

Miami had been designated in the 1930s as an "open city" by the Mob. That meant all organized crime families were welcome to live in Miami and to conduct their business operations, whether they involved sex, drugs, or gambling. During the 1940s, illegal casinos flourished in the southern part of Florida. Meyer Lansky made Miami Beach his headquarters for much of his adult life.

From there he guided his activities in Cuba, the Caribbean, and Las Vegas. In 1970, he actually initiated a campaign to legalize casinos in Miami Beach. His contrived arrest on a meaningless drug charge was timed, however, for just before Election Day. The passage failed by a large margin even though some polls showed it ahead a few weeks before the election.

The presence of organized crime figures in Florida also contributed to the defeat of a campaign for casinos in 1978. Before Atlantic City opened its casinos, Floridians initiated a ballot proposition for gambling. Although polls showed this proposition with a chance to pass, an active campaign against the casinos led by Govenor Reubin Askew caused a major defeat of the proposition, which failed to pass by a 73 percent to 27 percent margin. In 1986, another vote defeated a casino proposition by a 67 percent to 33 percent margin. In the same election, the voters approved a lottery for Florida. Casino forces, this time linked to Las Vegas gambling entrepreneurs, tried again in 1994. They spent over $17 million on the campaign, the most money spent on any ballot proposition in U.S. history up to that date. It was expensive, but again they oversold their product, and the measure went down to defeat, with less that 40 percent of the voters favoring casinos. Efforts continued through the rest of the decade to get machine gaming at racetracks or other forms of casino gambling into Florida. The efforts failed until 2005; however, after 1996, the tracks were allowed to have card rooms.

The Florida lottery was very successful from its inception after a 1984 referendum. In the same year, the state saw cruise ships conducting casino gaming with voyages into international waters.

Bingo games at the halls of the Native Americans in Florida were also successful. It was the Seminoles who generated the initial federal lawsuit over Native American gambling. The Seminoles' first facility was in Hollywood, just north of Miami. They built a second hall in Tampa when the city gave them lands, supposedly for the purpose of having a Native American museum. After the land was put into trust status for the tribe, the Seminoles initiated gambling at the site. A third Seminole gambling hall is in Okeechobee. The Miccosukee tribe developed a gambling hall on the Tamiami Trail west of Miami. The tribes installed various video gambling devices in their halls under the pretense that they were lottery devices. The courts did not agree, however. In 1996, the U.S. Supreme Court made a major ruling by holding that the Florida tribes, as well as tribes in other states, could not sue states and force them to negotiate compacts for casinos as the part of the Indian Gaming Regulatory Act. Authorizing tribes to do so violated the Eleventh Amendment of the U.S. Constitution, which prohibits most suits against states in federal courts. The tribe never won an order forcing the state to negotiate a casino agreement, although the state governor later voluntarily negotiated 25-year compacts allowing slot machine gaming. The compacts were approved by the federal government in 2007, but in 2008 they were challenged by the state legislature. Nonetheless, there are now seven casino facilities in the state, the one run by the Miccosukee tribe near Miami and six run by the Seminole tribe—two in Hollywood, one each in Brighton, Coconut Grove, Immokalee, and Tampa.

Florida gave voters in two countries (Dade and Broward) with pari-mutuel dog racing, horse racing, and jai alai facilities the option of choosing to have slot machines at tracks. Only Broward County voters approved the initiative, and now slots are operating at four locations in the county north of Miami. Additionally, the state legislature has failed in efforts to ban cruise ships with casinos from making "cruises to nowhere" from Florida ports. Fourteen cruise ship casinos were operating in 2008.

References

Casino City's Global Gaming Almanac. 2006. Newtown, MA: Casino City, 306–307.

Dombrink, John D. 1981. "Outlaw Businessmen: Organized Crime and the Legalization of Casino Gambling." Ph.D. diss., University of California, Berkeley.

Dombrink, John D., and William N. Thompson. 1990. *The Last Resort: Success and Failure in Campaigns for Casinos.* Reno: University of Nevada Press, 42–82, 132–138, 166–167.

Hayes, Ben, and F. Brooks Cowan. 2008. "Florida Casino Law." *International Casino Law and Regulation.* Boulder, CO: International Masters of Gaming Law, 1–4.

See also Lansky, Meyer (in Biographies of Leading Figures in Gambling section).

GEORGIA

Legal gambling activity in Georgia has generally been confined to lotteries—in the earlier years and in modern times as well. The lotteries of Georgia have been innovators in many respects. Public works were beneficiaries of lotteries in the 1780s, as they funded a hospital for seamen at Savannah, in addition to courthouses, streets, and a fire department for Augusta.

There is an aura of irony surrounding Native American gaming today, as the plight of Native peoples has been tied to their exclusion from lands in the eastern United States. A very sad part of that history is the Cherokee exclusion from Georgia and the forced march of Cherokees to new homes in Oklahoma—a march that became known as "The Trail of Tears." After Native Americans were torn from their lands in Georgia, between 1805 and 1832, the state instituted land lotteries as a means of redistributing Cherokee and Creek Nation lands to white settlers. In 1832, lands in northern Georgia thought to have gold deposits were also given away through lotteries. A case can be made that these lotteries did not involve gambling, as the state did not make any money from the enterprise. People registered for the lottery and were given free tickets. Georgia was the only state to distribute lands through lotteries.

Georgia was the first state in modern times to use a lottery to finance college scholarships. In this regard, the state started a trend followed by other states. In 1992 the voters approved the Lottery for Education Act as they set up the Georgia Lottery Corporation. The lottery sales have been very successful, with the public eagerly purchasing tickets in order to support educational projects. Some of the lottery proceeds go to support pre-kindergarten programs as well as computers in public schools, but the unique project of the lottery is the HOPE scholarship. As a result of lottery profits, every high school graduate in the state with a "B" average or above is given free tuition and other support to attend a public college in the state. By 2006, the lottery had transferred over 10 billion dollars to students in Georgia.

References

"Georgia's Land Lottery." About North Georgia, http://www.ngeorgia.com/history/lotteries.html, accessed December 5, 2008.

"History of Lotteries," Georgia Lottery, http://www.galottery.com/stc/aboutus/history.jsp, accessed December 5, 2008.

HAWAII

Tourism is one of the mainstays of the Hawaiian economy. Therefore, many interests have sought to bring casinos into the state. The efforts go on unabated. The efforts have never won the support of the important decision-makers, however, so Hawaii does not have casinos. Also, Hawaii has avoided having lotteries, charity gambling, or pari-mutuel wagering. There certainly is an underground scene offering gambling products in an illegal form, but leaders fear that bringing gambling into the open air of legality would only encourage bad elements. Hawaii is one of two states (the other is Utah) in which no form of gambling whatsoever is permitted under the law.

Reference

Dombrink, John D., and William N. Thompson. 1990. *The Last Resort: Success and Failure in Campaigns for Casinos.* Reno: University of Nevada Press, 161–162.

IDAHO

Idaho was the next-to-last state (before South Carolina in 2000) to have an existing form of legal gambling made illegal on a statewide basis. In 1947, a statute made slot machines as well as punch boards legal even though the state constitution placed a ban on lotteries. The state supreme court ruled in 1953 that the machines violated this prohibition of lottery games, and they enjoined future use of the machines (*State v. Garden City,* 265 P2d. 328, 1953).

Since then, pari-mutuel gambling for thoroughbred, quarter horse, and dog races has been authorized, as has charitable gambling. There are five tracks in the state. A lottery began operations in 1991. Several tribes in the state offered high-stakes bingo games and began serious negotiations for casino gambling in the early 1990s. The state refused to negotiate, however, using the Eleventh Amendment as a defense (the Eleventh Amendment bans suits against states in federal courts except in certain circumstances). The Coeur d'Alene tribe of northern Idaho decided to try something new. They instituted a nationwide lottery using telephone lines and the Internet. Considerable litigation ensued. However, the game was not sufficiently profitable, and the tribe dropped it. The tribe has installed nearly 500 machines at their gaming facility, claiming that the machines are lottery games. The state has objected to their presence, but there has been no concerted action to remove them. Finally, in 2002 the voters of Idaho passed an initiative that legalized the machines on tribal lands. Six tribal casinos now operate 4,500 machines in their casinos.

References

Idaho Lottery, www.idaholottery.com.

Thompson, William N. 1997. *Legalized Gambling: A Reference Handbook.* Santa Barbara, CA: ABC-CLIO, 163–166, 189.

ILLINOIS

By the time the riverboat casinos of Iowa were in operation in 1991, the state of Illinois had already reacted to the notion that their citizens would be enticed to cross the Mississippi River to gamble in another state. Illinois lawmakers feared that the Iowa boats would simply become parasites upon the Illinois economy, taking both profits and tax money away from Illinois. Illinois knew gambling. Racetracks had been in operation since the days of the Depression. A lottery began selling tickets in 1972. Bingo games were very popular, especially in urban areas. Also, the state had considerable experience with illegal casino-type organizations. These forms of gambling, legal and otherwise, were seen as inadequate to meet the marketing threat from Iowa.

As a result, the Illinois legislature legalized riverboat casinos. They acted quickly, with legislation arriving on the governor's desk in January 1990 and the licensing process starting in February 1990. Ten licenses were authorized for the state, with each license holder being allowed two boats. Each boat would have a maximum capacity of 1,200 passengers. The boats would have to be on navigable waters; however, no boat could be inside of Cook County. This restriction was offered as a concession to the horse racing tracks near Chicago, which is in Cook County. The tracks feared that the boats would have an unfair competitive edge over racing. However, in 1998 the restriction was removed, and a boat was authorized for the community of Rosemont.

Casino operations began in April 1991, just after the Iowa boats began operations. Illinois lawmakers decided to meet the threat of Iowa competition by offering more "liberal" gaming rules. Iowa had limits on casino gaming. Illinois did not share these. There was no $5 bet limit, nor was there a $200 loss limit per cruise. The boats were required

to make cruises, unless there was bad weather. In such a case there would be "mock cruises," with players entering and leaving the dockside boat at set times. The Illinois boats did very well compared to the Iowa boats in their first years of operation. Therefore, Iowa eliminated its $5 betting and $200 loss limits in 1994.

Well before the advent of riverboat casinos, there had been efforts to bring legal casino gambling to Illinois. During the Prohibition and World War II eras, there were several illegal gambling halls in the state; however, their numbers and the openness of their operations declined in the 1950s and 1960s. Instead, an effort grew to legalize casinos.

In the late 1970s Mayor Jane Byrne suggested having casinos to produce extra revenues for snow removal activities in Chicago. The Navy Pier site was selected for casino gambling. The efforts were stymied, however, by Springfield lawmakers. In 1992 Chicago mayor Richard Daley conferred with several Las Vegas operators, and together they proposed a $2 billion mega-resort complex for the city. The project engendered considerable support, but it was ultimately defeated owing to the opposition of Governor James Edgar.

The Illinois riverboat casinos are regulated by a five-member Illinois Gaming Board appointed by the governor. The board issues licenses, collects taxes, and enforces gaming rules with inspections, hearings, and fines as necessary. The board may also revoke licenses. The boats pay license application fees of $50,000 each. After operations begin, they pay an admission tax of $2 per passenger and also pay 20 per-

Iowa and Illinois turned to riverboat casino gambling in the early 1990s when their agriculture business suffered hard times.

cent of their gaming win (players' losses) as a state tax. Half of the admissions tax and one-fourth of the gambling tax are returned by the state to the local city or the county where the boat is docked. Each boat has a single docking site. Over the years, the gaming tax has risen considerably. In 2007, the gaming tax and fees amounted to 52 percent of the gambling revenues. That year, the state received over $1.3 billion in casino taxes, as collective revenues were about $2 billion. After a casino closed in Galena and its owners sought to move its license to Rosemont, the state imposed a sliding scale of tax rates that went as high as 70 percent of the gaming win—if the casino boat's win exceeded $200 million for the year. It was agreed that the highest rate would go back down to 50 percent if a 10th licensee was again operating.

The granting of the 10th license has been a matter of contention for most of a decade. Two times the state offered to auction the license off to the highest bidder. One party bid more than $520 million just to have the license. However legal complications have kept a 10th boat from operating, at least before 2010.

References

Dombrink, John D., and William N. Thompson. 1990. *The Last Resort: Success and Failure in Campaigns for Casinos.* Reno: University of Nevada Press, 129–130.

Ficaro, Michael. 1999. "Illinois." In *International Casino Law*, 3rd ed. Edited by A. Cabot, W. Thompson, A. Tottenham, and C. Braunlich, 26–32. Reno: Institute of Gambling Studies, University of Nevada, Reno.

INDIANA

Before Indiana began a state lottery in 1991, it had been one of only four states in the United States that had no legal gambling. Although the effort to establish the lottery was ongoing, a campaign for casinos was also taking place. Following several years of lobbying efforts and studies of a variety of proposals, the state legislature passed a riverboat gaming law over the veto of Governor Evan Bayh in 1993. The next legislative session also authorized horse race betting within the state. There are now two tracks.

The strongest motivation for approving casino gambling was provided by the fact that several casino boats in Illinois were drawing much of their revenue from Indiana residents. Four Illinois casinos were located in suburban Chicago within 50 miles of the Indiana border, and another license was held by a boat in southern Illinois a short drive from the Evansville metropolitan area.

Indiana's new law authorized licensing of 11 casino boats for counties bordering Lake Michigan waters as well as those on the Ohio River and Patoka Lake. The licenses can be granted only if the residents of the county where the boat operates approve casino gaming in a referendum vote. Most of the gaming-eligible counties held votes; some were positive and some were negative. The Patoka Lake license was not activated, as the United States Army Corps of Engineers was determined to own the rights to control the water of the lake. In 2004, lawmakers authorized that the 11th license be given to interests wishing to establish a casino in the resort community of French Lick in southern Indiana.

In December 1994, the first two licenses were awarded, but there were legal difficulties. The federal Johnson Act prohibited gaming on the Great Lakes. The state had claimed an exemption to the provisions of the act in the riverboat legislation, but the matter had to be clarified in Congress, with the attachment of a rider to the Coast Guard Reauthorization Act of 1996 that exempted Lake Michigan waters from the Johnson Act for purposes of gaming on Indiana-licensed casino boats. Difficulties with the Ohio River arose, as the waters of the river were within Kentucky. This was resolved by requiring boats on the river to cruise within a short distance of the shore.

The 1993 legislation created an Indiana Gaming Commission made up of seven members appointed by the governor. The governor also appointed the executive director of the commission. They accomplished at least some of their original goal as revenues for Illinois boats experienced a small decline while Indiana boats surpassed Illinois revenues.

The commission has a very wide range of powers. It may make any rules necessary for carrying out mandates of the 1993 act. Additionally, it accepts applications for licenses and conducts all investigations of applicants, including investigations into personal character. It selects the licensees and oversees their operations. It takes all disciplinary actions if rules are violated and may revoke licenses, which are granted for a five-year period. The boats must be at least 150 feet in length and have the capacity to carry 500 persons.

The first boat to begin operations was Casino Aztar in Evansville; it opened its doors for gaming on December 8, 1995. Casino Aztar is a 2,700-passenger boat with 35,000 square feet of gaming space.

Two other boats started gaming operations on June 11, 1996. Both are docked in Gary, Indiana. Donald Barden's Majestic Star is a 1,500-passenger vessel with 25,000 square feet of gaming space. Donald Trump's Trump Casino occupies 37,000 square feet of gaming space on a 2,300-passenger boat.

On June 29, 1996, the Empress Casino boat began cruises in Hammond. The 2,500-passenger vessel has a gaming floor of 35,000 square feet. Hyatt's Grand Victoria Casino and Resort started cruises in Rising Sun on October 4, 1996. The boat was the first casino to invade the Cincinnati, Ohio, metropolitan area. It carries 2,700 passengers and has a gaming floor with 45,000 square feet.

The Argosy Casino began operations on the Ohio River at Lawrenceburg, also near Cincinnati, Ohio, on December 13, 1996. The 4,000-passenger yacht has a gaming floor of 74,300 square feet.

The Showboat Mardi Gras Casino started cruises out of East Chicago on April 18, 1997. It has gaming space of 53,000 square feet and carries 3,750 passengers. On August 22, 1997, the fifth Lake Michigan boat license was activated as the Blue Chip Casino opened in Michigan City. The 2,000-passenger vessel has 25,000 square feet of gaming space. The ninth boat to begin operations is at Bridgeport, across from the Louisville, Kentucky, metropolitan area. It is operated by the same company that runs the Caesars Palace casino in Las Vegas. The City of Rome riverboat carries 3,750 passengers and has 93,000 square feet of gaming space. Gaming began in late 1998. The tenth license was for a boat on the Ohio River near Cincinnati.

The casino boats must go out into waters for cruises, although one off Lake Michigan has a special channel for its cruises. An amendment to the original 1993 law clarified conditions when the boats could remain docked. Basically, these include any time that the boat captain feels that safety requires that the boat remain docked. In any case, the boats are required to have two-hour cruises. If the boat is docked, the cruises are mock cruises.

The casino boats pay a gross gaming tax of 20 percent of their win. Of this amount, one-quarter goes to the city where the boat is docked (or county if not in a city), and three-quarters goes to the state's general fund. There is a $3 admission fee, which is also shared among state and local governments.

Coauthored by Carl Braunlich

Reference
Braunlich, Carl. 1999. "Indiana." In *International Casino Law*, 3rd ed. Edited by A. Cabot, W. Thompson, A. Tottenham, and C. Braunlich, 33–38. Reno: Institute of Gambling Studies, University of Nevada, Reno.

See also Gambling Devices Acts (Johnson Act and Amendments) (in General Topics section).

IOWA

Iowa may have the distinction of having more forms of legalized gambling than any other state. The pastoral agricultural land of the *Music Man* has more than pool halls to corrupt its youth. It has a lottery with instant tickets and massive lotto prizes via Lotto America; it has dog racing and horse racing—thoroughbred, harness, and quarter horse racing. It has bingo games and pull-tab tickets for charities, and it has casinos—on land, on rivers, on lakes, and on Native American lands. Although many of these games were already in place by the end of the 1980s, Iowa led the nation in establishing riverboat gaming with legislation that was passed on April 20, 1989.

Even though the Iowa "experiment" led to a massive expansion of gambling throughout the Midwest, in a sense it was supposed to represent only a small, incremental change in gambling offerings—not a major change in the landscape. The proponents of casinos for Iowa were responding to a general downturn in the agribusiness economy of the state. They were quick to say they did not want Iowa to "be like Las Vegas." Indeed, during the legislative campaign for casinos, the words *casino* and *gambling* were not used. The casino gambling was supposedly just a small adjunct to riverboat cruises designed to recreate Huckleberry Finn excursions down the mighty Mississippi. Only 30 percent of the boat areas could be devoted to casino activities. Ostensibly, the operators would offer many activities on the boats in order to satisfy the recreational needs of the entire family. Originally the boats had to have actual cruises, betting was limited to $5 a play, and no player could lose more than $200 on a cruise. These limits have been eliminated, and now boats no longer cruise. Instead, they remain docked while players gamble. The notion that the casinos are a catylst for other recreational activity has been totally abandoned.

In 2005 the state granted a license for a land-based casino in Council Bluffs, across from Omaha, Nebraska. Approval has also been given for slot machines to be placed at racetracks. In 1992, the state negotiated compacts with three tribes for operation of casinos on their Native lands.

References

"Casinos and Gambling, Iowa Casinos," www.jobmonkey.com/casino/html/iowa_casinos.html.

Creighton, Lorenzo. 1999. "Indiana." In *International Casino Law*, 3rd ed. Edited by A. Cabot, W. Thompson, A. Tottenham, and C. Braunlich, 39–41. Reno: Institute of Gambling Studies, University of Nevada, Reno.

KANSAS

Kansas began lottery operations in 1987. It offers instant games, daily numbers games, and lotto, as well as participation in the multistate Powerball game. As a result of the adoption of the lottery, three small Native American reservations—Iowa,

Kickapoo, and Pottawatomie—won the right to offer casino games after a long struggle for a compact with the state of Kansas. The lottery legislation opened the doors for the Native groups as it seemed to permit the state to offer any and all kinds of gaming to the public. This has led the state to launch a unique plan to have its own casinos. Kansas also allows pari-mutuel wagering for both dog and horse races.

It is an unlikely place, being the land of the film *The Wizard of Oz,* but Kansas is in the process of embarking upon a new American (that is U.S.A.) experiment: having "socialist" casinos.

The motivation for legalizing casinos seems to be the same in Kansas as it has been in other venues. First, the state has a fiscal crisis: among other things, the state faces a court mandate to put an extra $900 million be put into public education. Second, nearby venues have established casinos that draw customers from Kansas—there are the Missouri riverboats in the heavily populated Kansas City area and also new Native American casinos in Oklahoma.

The passage of March 2007 legislation (signed by the governor on April 12, 2007) authorized government owned casinos.

The effort to pass the legislation took several years and encountered several hurdles. Commercial and Native American interests in the state very much wanted a casino, or casinos, in the Kansas City, Kansas, area in order to meet the competition from Missouri riverboats. However, the Kansas state constitution seemed to clearly state that private casinos would be illegal. Lotteries (privately run) were "forever prohibited," and the term "lottery" covered casino games. Proponents realized that it would be extremely difficult to win a statewide popular vote changing the constitution.

In 1986, 64 percent of the voters amended the constitution to allow a "state owned and operated" lottery. In 1994, the state courts ruled that the vote permitted the lottery to operate casino games. On the basis of the ruling, and in accordance with the Indian Gaming Regulatory Act of 1988, the state negotiated compacts with three tribes to have Native American casinos. Subsequently, the legislature entertained proposals to permit the establishment of new tribal lands in Kansas City, at a site near a horse and dog track and NASCAR racing facility, amusement center, and shopping area. Competition among the three tribes as well as federal hurdles regarding off-reservation casinos made a winning political compromise impossible to achieve. Still state forces wanted to attract gamers away from the Missouri boats. The "magic bullet" for change flashed into the legislative chambers in 2007: have the state lottery "own and operate casinos." Work toward a solution began in earnest. Proponents needed support, hence they acquiesced in allowing all three racetracks (the one near Kansas City, one in Frontenac at the southeast corner of the state, and one in Wichita) to have government-owned lottery-run slot machine casinos. Each would be allowed up to 800 machines. They also responded to appeals for a second casino in Kansas City, one in the Pittsburg area not far from Neosho and Springfield, Missouri, and a casino in the Wichita area. The "wild west" town of Dodge City, with some claim to being an attraction for tourists, was also authorized to have a lottery-run casino. The non-track casinos could have table games and slot machines. In total, the legislation granted permission for 10,600 gaming machines statewide.

Thus the legislation permitted seven casinos—three at racetracks and four at designated cities. All would be under the "complete control" of the lottery, and hence, as the Kansas lawmakers interpreted the matter, "owned and operated" by the lottery. On paper, the interpretation seemed to be as much a fiction as Frank Baum's Land of Oz. Therefore, the governor, who supported having the casinos, immediately asked the state attorney general to institute a "friendly" lawsuit challenging the law—and hence inviting the courts to wave their "wand of approval." In January 2008, the District Court in Shawnee County ruled that the new law was constitutional.

Before, applications could be taken for casino licenses, the voters of each county designated for a casino had to give their approval. Accordingly, voters of Wyandotte (Kansas City area) said "yes," as did the voters of the southeast counties (Cherokee and Crawford), and Ford County (Dodge City). The voters of Sedgwick County (Wichita) said "no," and therefore there can be no casino at the Wichita racetrack. However, voters in adjacent Sumner county said "yes," meaning the other Wichita-area casino will be in the county 20 miles south of the city.

The application process involves several steps. The owners of the two racetracks were given the exclusive right to bid for licenses at their facilities. Those wanting the other four casinos submitted bids that first had to be approved by the local county governments as well as being endorsed by any city in which they might be located. They had to have at least three years of experience in casino gaming. With that endorsement in hand, they could then go to the state lottery commission and negotiate a contract for the casino. In the contract, the applicant had to commit to investing $225 million into the facility for three of the non-track casinos, and $50 million for the Dodge City casino. The track slot casinos had to agree to pay taxes of 40 percent on the machine wins, while the other casinos had to agree to state taxes of 22 percent on their gaming wins and an additional 5 percent in local taxes.

The casinos will be regulated by the lottery through its concept of "total control." While the private parties would be expected to run the casinos, they would be doing so for the lottery, and the lottery could intervene and control such operations in any manner it wished. Hence the state advanced the idea that the casinos were "lottery owned and operated."

References

Thompson, William N. 2008. "No Socialists in the Land of Oz." *International Gaming and Wagering Business* 29, no. 8 (August): 22.

Thompson, William N. 2008. "Socialist Casinos for the Land of Oz." *Casino Lawyer* 4, no. 3 (Summer): 8–10.

KENTUCKY

Kentucky is the home of horse racing. Tracks operated in Kentucky beginning in 1789, four years before statehood. More racehorses are born and bred in Kentucky than in any other state. The Kentucky Derby is the most famous horse race in

A horse farm in the famous Bluegrass country of Kentucky.

the United States. In 1988, 61 percent of the Kentucky voters said they wanted a lottery, and the next year one was established that offers instant games, lotto games, and numbers games as well as Powerball interstate lottery tickets. Charitable games are also permitted.

The fact that many states bordering or near Kentucky—Indiana, Illinois, Missouri, Mississippi—offer casino gambling pressured state leaders into making plans for casino gambling. In 1999, the governor recommended that as many as 14 casinos be authorized for the state. The notion of casinos in Kentucky is not too far out of bounds for most residents, as Kentuckians remember that the middle decades of the 20th century found many wide-open

but illegal casinos operating along the Ohio border. The seven racetracks of Kentucky have been supporters of the idea of having casinos—that is, as long as they are located at the tracks and operated by the tracks. The idea of casinos has not received much support in the state legislature, however.

References

Casino City. "Kentucky Casinos and Kentucky Gambling." http://kentucky.casinocity.com.

Eaton, David H. 2000. "The Kentucky Lottery." Manuscript, College of Business and Public Affairs, Murray State University, Murray, Kentucky.

Kentucky Lottery, www.kylottery.com.

See also Horse Racing (in General Topics section).

LOUISIANA

Louisiana has both a long historical attachment to gambling enterprise and a recent one as well. Louisiana was a critical part of early gambling history in the United States, as New Orleans was the site of many clandestine dens of games when Andrew Jackson led the national military forces against the British redcoats in the battle named for the Crescent City in 1815. In 1828, John Davis opened what has been considered the first real casino in the United States, at the corner of Bourbon and Orleans Streets in New Orleans. Following the Civil War, a well-bribed state legislature authorized the infamous Louisiana Lottery Company. The company began to sell tickets throughout the United States. It continued operations until 1895, after federal laws prohibited its use of the mail system. In the early 1900s, all gambling was technically illegal, but gambling continued. Slot machines were openly played through the 1930s. Gambling clubs kept operating even as Senator Estes Kefauver's Senate committee on organized crime targeted the state for enforcement activities. In the meantime gambling on horse races had been legalized.

The modern era of legalized Louisiana gambling began in 1990 when the legislature gave the green light for the start of a new state lottery. In 1990, an act was also passed that opened the door for Native American casinos. In 1991, riverboat casino gambling was approved along with video poker machines for truck stops, racecourses, restaurants, and taverns. The next year, authorization was granted for a single land-based casino in New Orleans.

There are now multitudes of gambling sites in the state. Lottery tickets and charitable bingo games are in each parish. Nearly 15,000 video gaming machines are widely dispersed throughout the state in bars and restaurants and at truckstops. Machines are also permitted for three racetracks. In 1996, however, the voters of each parish were empowered to vote on whether there would be machine gaming in their parish—at casinos, tracks, truck stops, or restaurants. About half of the parishes said "take out the machines," although none of the riverboat casino parishes voted against the machines. One parish with a track said "no" to the machines. Machines were removed from the parishes objecting to them in 1999.

Louisiana has three Native American casinos. The largest, at Marksville (Tunica-Biloxi tribe) and Kinder (Alabama-Coushatta tribe), were originally constructed and operated by Grand Casinos. The third casino is near Charenton and is run by the Chitimacha tribe. Fifteen riverboat casino licenses have been granted, as has the license for the New Orleans casino. The New Orleans casino project opened in a temporary facility, however, and failed to generate sufficient revenue flows. The project for a permanent casino was put on hold for three years as the operators sought the protection of the bankruptcy court. The permanent facility was opened at the end of 1999, as the state allowed a special annual fee of $100 million to be cut in half. Several of the riverboats operations have also experienced failure and have seen licenses withdrawn and given to new vessels.

Louisiana has suffered from having considerable competition for its gambling patronage. Louisiana does not exist in a vacuum. Many gaming opportunities are available to residents in adjacent jurisdictions. Texas offers lottery sales and racetrack betting and also has had machine gaming in truck stops—although prizes were awarded in the form of merchandise, not cash. Mississippi has a wide array of casinos. A major Native American casino is in the central part of the state. Several casinos are located in Tunica, a northern Mississippi county near Memphis, Tennessee. Others are located in cities on the Mississippi River. The largest casinos are found on the Gulf Coast within a hundred miles of New Orleans. A considerable portion of the patronage of Mississippi casinos comes from Louisiana.

But patronage and revenue do not constitute the major problem with Louisiana gambling. Patterns of public corruption that seem endemic in the state's history came to the fore once again as licensing of gaming facilities and distribution of gaming equipment began. One governor, Edwin Edwards, was linked to a system of bribery involving several casino license holders. He was convicted and was sentenced to a prison term. Also, an organized crime ring was tied to persons distributing slot machines around the state.

Reference

Buchler, Harold and Conrad. 1999. "Louisiana." In *International Casino Law*, 3rd ed. Edited by A. Cabot, W. Thompson, A. Tottenham, and C. Braunlich, 42–63. Reno: Institute of Gambling Studies, University of Nevada, Reno.

Dombrink, John P., and William N. Thompson. 1990. *The Last Resort: Success and Failure in Campaigns for Casinos.* Reno: University of Nevada Press, 167–170.

LOUISIANA LOTTERY COMPANY

Most lottery activity was banned by law before the advent of the Civil War. All but three states had constitutional or statutory prohibitions on the activity. In the 1860s the federal government began to consider legislation to keep lottery schemes from using the mail system (see Federal Lottery Laws). Amid these efforts to discourage lotteries, Louisiana lawmakers were persuaded in 1868 to charter a private company to run a lottery for 25 years. Other southern states had also established lotteries as a means of creating revenues during a period of governmental impoverishment brought on by the aftermath of war, defeat, and reconstruction. The Louisiana lottery was clearly the largest, and within 10 years the other states ended their lottery experiments, leaving Louisiana's lottery in a monopoly position in the entire country.

The 25-year charter was won for an annual fee of $40,000 that was promised by the promoters—a New York syndicate including John Morris and John Morrissey as well as New Orleans front men. A nationwide promotion campaign popularized drawings, which were conducted with much fanfare by two retired Confederate generals. Tickets cost from $2 to $40. Ninety percent of the sales of tickets were to persons living outside of Louisiana, and they used the mails to purchase tickets. Monthly prizes were as high as $600,000. Annual profits for the lottery company reached as much as $13 million. When the lottery charter was about to end, Morris sought a renewal for a fee of $1 million a year.

Considerable opposition to the lottery arose from many sectors. The lottery's operators were accused of corruption as well as extensive bribery. The federal government passed many acts seeking to stop the sale of tickets outside of Louisiana, but there was little effort to enforce the laws. An 1890 statute seemed to be more effective, and the promoters were cut off from the use of the mail. Efforts to win support for a renewal of the lottery were unsuccessful, and in 1893 the state joined all the others in the country and banned all lotteries. The syndicate that operated the lottery moved its operations to Honduras and shipped tickets into the United States through Florida. Congress plugged the loophole discovered in the law, however, and passed a very definitive prohibition against the importation and interstate transportation of lottery materials. The effective end of the Louisiana Lottery in 1895 marked the end of this form of gambling until New Hampshire began its state-run sweepstakes 69 years later in 1964.

Reference

Commission on the Review of the National Policy toward Gambling. 1976. *Gambling in America: Final Report.* Washington, DC: Government Printing Office, Appendix 1.

MAINE

In 1980, Congress passed the Maine Indian Claims Act, granting a financial settlement of $81.5 million to the Passamaquoddy, Penobscot, and Maliseet tribes. Part of the funds was used to purchase 300,000 acres of land that was put into trust for the tribes. The act specifically gave the state of Maine jurisdiction over civil and criminal law matters on any lands put into trust for the tribes as a result of such purchases from the settlement. After Congress passed the Indian Gaming Regulatory Act of 1988, however, the tribes sought negotiations so that they could have gambling that would be controlled by the federal government or by the provisions of a compact. The Penobscots held bingo games that violated state rules. Subsequent court actions upheld the state's power to control the gaming. Nonetheless, the state has tolerated bingo games that may extend beyond limits approved for other charity games in Maine.

Since 1973, the state has offered several lottery games, including instant tickets, lotto, and a daily numbers game. In the 1980s, Maine was a member of the Tri-State Lotto game with New Hampshire and Vermont. There are also charitable raffles and bingo, and harness racing is conducted on three tracks. In 2003, the voters of Maine approved slot machines for racetracks, and in 2005, machine gaming began at Hollywood Slots beside the racetrack in Bangor. A 36,000-square-foot facility offers 500 machines for play. In 2008, the voters turned down a proposal for a casino in Oxford County in the southeast part of the state.

References

"Maine Casinos and Maine Gambling." Casino City Network, http://maine.casino city.com, accessed November 20, 2008

Maine Lottery, www.mainelottery.com.

Maine's First Racino Opens." Maine Casinos and Gambling Forum, http://www.maine gamblingforum.com/.

MARYLAND

In 1973 Maryland began a state lottery. The state's gambling products include instant games, a lotto, a daily numbers game, and keno. It also participates in the six-state Big Game lotto. In 1974, Maryland authorized an "interest-only" lottery, based upon Great Britain's premium bonds. In Great Britain's system, a player purchases a bond and remains a player in a monthly lottery as long as he or she holds the bond. The bonds draw no interest. Instead, funds equal to part of the interest are put into a prize pool. At any time the player may redeem the bond for the full price paid for it. In other places, such as Cuba and the former Soviet Union, these are called "lottery savings bonds." Many people buy such bonds for a couple when they are married or when a child is born. The former Soviet Union used these bonds in the 1920s, and Castro tried to institute this form of lottery in Cuba to replace the traditional lottery that had been operating before the revolution of 1959. After much planning, Maryland dropped its plans for the "interest-only" lottery, as the game could not promise the flow of revenue the state could gain from the other lottery games.

Maryland has had its share of active casino proponents, but their efforts have have been successful only with regards to slot machine gambling. First, nonprofit service clubs and organizations won the right to have slot machine gaming at locations in counties that border the ocean. Then in 2008 voters approved a proposition placing 15,000 slot machines at five locations in the state, one being in the city of Baltimore.

The state has also had an active horse racing industry for hundreds of years. There are six tracks as well as five off-track betting facilities. Since 1870, the Preakness, the second leg of thoroughbred racing's Triple Crown, has been run at Pimlico race, located on the edge of Baltimore. The track was also the site of one of the most notable match races in U.S. history, when in 1938 Seabiscut defeated Triple Crown winner War Admiral.

Clotfelter, Charles T., and Philip J. Cook. 1989. *Selling Hope: State Lotteries in America.* Cambridge, MA: Harvard University Press.
Thompson, William N. 1997. *Legalized Gambling: A Reference Handbook.* 2nd ed. Santa Barbara, CA: ABC-CLIO.

See also Horse Racing (in General Topics section).

MASSACHUSETTS

Gambling (European-style) came to Massachusetts with the Pilgrims. In fact, gambling activity must have been pervasive, because the leaders of the colony saw fit to ban all gambling in 1621 in the Plymouth settlement's second year. Similar prohibitions were instituted by the Puritan groups that settled the Massachusetts Bay Colony. The political leaders knew at the beginning what they surely know now: that residents of Massachusetts love to gamble. The state lottery, begun in 1972, now has sales of more than $3 billion a year, trailing only New York in sales. The state has instant games, lotto, and daily numbers games and also sells tickets in the multistate Big Game lotto. Massachusetts introduced the first instant lottery game in the United States in 1974. Massachusetts has also had a strong charitable gambling establishment, as well as pari-mutuel gambling for five dog and horse tracks.

Massachusetts has attracted much interest from casino gambling entrepreneurs. In 1978, a major campaign was initiated to win permission to place commercial casinos in the towns of Hull and Adams. The MGM Grand casino company was a major promoter of the idea. Local residents voted in favor of having casinos; however, legislative efforts that lasted more than three years only resulted in rejection. The state has one Native American tribe, the Wampanoags, which has a small reservation on the exclusive resort island of Martha's Vineyard. Residents of the island have adamantly opposed the notion of having a casino near their expensive homes. The tribe agreed and made a deal to purchase land and create a new portion of their reservation near New Bedford, a declining city on the main coast. The governor negotiated the first stages of a compact for a casino. The proposed casino has confronted a series of roadblocks, however, and by 2009, no casino was in operation. Meanwhile, the legislature has continued to reject the idea of placing slot machines at racetracks. In fact, the racing industry faces retrenchment as the voters decided to ban dog racing with a vote in 2008.

References

"Casinos Back on State Agenda." *Boston Globe*, February 3, 2009, www.boston globe.com/news/local/massachusetts/articles/2009/02/03.

Dombrink, John D., and William N. Thompson. 1990. *The Last Resort: Success and Failure in Campaigns for Casinos.* Reno: University of Nevada Press, 108–114.

Thompson, William N. 1997. *Legalized Gambling: A Reference Handbook.* 2nd ed. Santa Barbara, CA: ABC-CLIO, 90, 165.

MICHIGAN

In November 1996, Michigan voters passed Proposition E, which allows Detroit to develop three unlimited stakes, Las Vegas–type casinos. Although the victory for casino proponents was relatively narrow (51.8 percent to 48.2 percent), it was unexpected in most quarters. In the 1996 elections, voters in Ohio and Arkansas rejected casino proposals by wide margins. Detroit voters had rejected casinos in advisory votes in 1976, 1981, 1988, and 1993 before voting yes in advisory votes in 1994 and 1995. The Michigan vote was the first statewide victory for unlimited casino gambling since the 1976 New Jersey vote. Detroit has become the largest city in the Western Hemisphere with casinos located within its boundaries.

Michigan passed supplemental legislation to enable the licensing process to begin. The process involved recommendation from the city government and final action by a new state casino gaming commission. Proposition E actually designated two of the companies that would receive licensing. It was stipulated that preference had to be given for two licenses to organizations that had sponsored the successful Detroit advisory vote in favor of casinos in 1995. Those two companies were the Greektown and Atwater groups. The Greektown Group of investors took on as partners a Chippewa Native American tribe that runs several casinos in Michigan's Upper Peninsula. The Atwater Group teamed with the Circus Circus (now Mandalay Resort) Company for its proposals. These two winning proposals joined a successful proposal for the MGM Grand Company of Las Vegas. As a part of the licensing, the casinos won the right to have temporary facilities. The first temporary facility was opened by the MGM in the summer of 1999, and the other two followed in the fall.

In addition to many fees, the casinos must pay a tax of 18 percent of their gambling winnings. Of this amount, 55 percent goes to the city of Detroit and 45 percent goes to the state government's public education fund. Originally it was estimated that the casinos would have revenues approaching $1.5 billion a year. In the first year, two casinos had more than $700 million.

The voters in Michigan were not strangers to casino gambling and other forms of gambling. In fact, the election victory for Proposition E could be credited to the existence of the Windsor, Ontario, casinos. The first Windsor casino had opened in 1994. A second riverboat casino opened two years later. Approximately 80 percent of the business in the casino came from the United States, and most of those gamblers were from the Detroit region. It was claimed that the Detroit economy was losing around $1 million dollars a day as Detroiters crossed over the Ambassador Bridge and through the Detroit-Windsor tunnel.

The state had its own casinos, which were operated by Native American tribes under agreements made in 1993. A state lottery was established in 1972 after voters removed a ban on this form of gambling. The removal of the ban also enabled the establishment of casino gambling for the Native Americans, as did a 1975 law that authorized charitable gambling, including charitable casino gambling. Pari-mutuel horse race betting began in the state in 1933 in an effort to garner public revenues amid the Depression economy.

The billion-dollar Native American casino industry of Michigan is anchored by the Soaring Eagle Casino in Mount Pleasant on the lands of the Saginaw-Chippewa tribe. The casino is one of the largest Native American casinos in the country, having a gaming floor of 150,000 square feet, more than 100 tables, and 4,000 slot machines. Other large casinos are located in Peshawbestown near Traverse City, in Sault St. Marie, and in Baraga near Marquette. Other casinos are scattered across the state in Brimley, Watersmeet, Wilson, Petoskey, Athens, Manistique, Manistee, St. Ignace, and New Buffalo. Native American casinos had agreed to pay the state 10 percent of their machine revenues (with 2 percent going to local governments) as long as there was no other machine gaming in the state. After Detroit casinos were licensed, the state dropped its 8 percent share of the tax, but the tribes agreed to continue the 2 percent tax to the local governments. However, when new tribes won the right to have casinos, they agreed to the 10 percent tax under the conditions that the state not allow any further expansion of non-Native gaming. When in 2006 the state gave permission for the lottery to place keno games in over 4,000 bars and taverns, these tribes balked at the tax payments and a legal conflict ensued.

References

Dombrink, John D., and William N. Thompson. 1990. *The Last Resort: Success and Failure in Campaigns for Casinos.* Reno: University of Nevada Press, 114–119.

Michigan Lottery. "Michigan Lottery Through the Years." www.michigan.gov/lottery.

Wacker, Fred, and William N. Thompson. 1999. "Michigan." In *International Casino Law*, 3rd ed. Edited by A. Cabot, W. Thompson, A. Tottenham, and C. Braunlich, 64–71. Reno: Institute of Gambling Studies, University of Nevada, Reno.

Wacker, R. F., and W. N. Thompson. 1997. "The Michigan Question: A Legal Quandry." *Gaming Law Review* 1 (Winter): 501–510.

MINNESOTA

Minnesota has been a very active gambling state, as the the editor of these volumes observed during a tour of the state in 1996. Shortly after the state lottery began in 1989, the governor signed agreements allowing Native American tribes to have casino gaming. The agreement (which could only allow such gaming as was permitted others in the sate) was based upon the fact that Minnesota also allowed private social card games and machine games that could give replays as prizes. These were the first state-tribal compacts negotiated in the United States.

The eleven tribes in Minnesota now run 19 gambling halls, with bingo, blackjack, and machine games. The largest casino is Mystic Lake, which is run by a Sioux tribe and located within the Minneapolis metropolitan area. With a monopoly facility serving several million people, the casino grosses several hundred million dollars in net profits each year. Each of the 300 tribal members has received annual per capita bonuses approaching a million dollars because of the casino profits. Other large casinos include the Treasure Island in Red Wing; the two Grand Casinos in Hinckley and Onamia; and casinos in Duluth, Carleton, Granite Falls, Mahnomen, and Morton.

The state also has pari-mutuel racing. Canterbury Downs, the largest track, was closed, however, shortly after the Mystic Lake Casino opened. Since that time there have been repeated efforts to allow the track to have machine gaming as a tool to restore live racing and also to gain revenues for a new stadium in downtown Minneapolis. The efforts have failed. However, racing has begun again as the track has been purchased by the tribe which runs Mystic Lake.

Charitable gaming prospers, as Minnesota sells more pull-tab tickets than any other jurisdiction. Charities win over $200 million a year from the sale of the tickets, ten times as much as they win at bingo games.

Reference
Minnesota State Lottery. 1994. *Gambling in Minnesota.* Roseville: Minnesota State Lottery.

MISSISSIPPI

The state of Mississippi has the third-largest volume of casino gambling of any venue in North America. Approximately 30 casino boats generate nearly $2 billion in gambling wins each year. The state also has one of the largest Native American casinos—the Silver Star, initially run by the Las Vegas Boyd Group on behalf of the Mississippi Choctaw tribe. The casino, near Philadelphia, has almost 100 tables and 3,000 machines. The state has no other legal gambling activity—no lottery gambling or charity games.

Mississippi did not set out a deliberate course for casino gambling. Instead, the state seemed to just let it happen. Casino-style gambling arrived in Mississippi aboard the cruise ship *Europa Star* on December 19, 1987. The 157-foot ship, with a Panamanian registration, docked at Biloxi and began a series of "cruises to nowhere." Gambling activities on the ship included roulette, bingo, and slot machines. Short roundtrip cruises were made three miles offshore of Biloxi but within the boundaries of a series of barrier islands. The ship operators claimed they were in international waters. The state attorney general sought to end the gambling by claiming the ship was in state-controlled waters until it was three miles outside the barrier islands.

Before the matter was resolved in court, the legislature took up the issue. At first legislators sided with the attorney general. In March 1989, however, a law was passed allowing large ships—at least 300 feet long—to conduct gaming in the waters inside the islands. One ship, the *Pride of Mississippi,* operated under provisions of the law for one season; however, it could not operate at a profit. Nonetheless, businesses along the Gulf Coast pleaded to the legislature for more open gambling rules, as the ship had generated significant tourist revenue for them. The legislature now had the Iowa model for riverboat gambling and decided to duplicate it—to an extent.

In March 1990, the governor signed into law an act permitting casino gambling on riverboats. The boats had to be at least 150 feet long and located in navigable tributaries and in oxbow lakes in counties bordering the Mississippi River or on the Gulf Coast. The counties were given the option of having elections banning the boats from their waters. A measure describing a

The Las Vegas Casino boat in Mississippi.

regulatory framework almost identical to that in Nevada was enacted into law in the summer of 1990.

The Mississippi law is distinguished from other riverboat laws in that there was never an expectation that the riverboats would have to leave shore. There was no cruising requirement. Eventually the facilities lost all pretense of being navigable operations. Instead, barges were moved into the permissible waters; gambling structures were constructed on top of the vessels, and hotel and restaurant facilities were constructed around the barges. The barges included flotation mechanisms so they could rise and fall as water levels changed during flood seasons. Most gamblers cannot perceive that they are over water when they are gambling. In addition to fees, the boats pay taxes of 8 percent on their gambling wins to the state; an additional tax equaling 10 percent of the state amount is paid to local governments. The casinos are open 24 hours a day and unlike the situation in other riverboat states, players may enter and leave gambling areas whenever they wish to do so.

Most of the boats are located in several distinct areas of the state. The Gulf Coast (Biloxi and Gulfport) has a dozen casino boats; Tunica County, near Memphis, Tennessee, has about 10 boats; there are 4 boats in the Greenville area and 4 boats in the Vicksburg area. The largest casino is Beau Rivage, which was opened by Steve Wynn (but later sold to MGM Mirage) in Biloxi in 1999, with 1,000 hotel rooms.

Hurricane Katrina devastated the casinos along the Gulf Coast. In an effort to restore the vitality of the casino industry, the state permitted rebuilt casinos to be fixed to the land, although they had to be built within 800 feet of the coast.

Reference

Shepard, Thomas B., and Cheryn L. Netz. 1999. "Mississippi." In *International Casino Law*, 3rd ed. Edited by A. Cabot, W. Thompson, A. Tottenham, and C. Braunlich, 480. Reno: Institute of Gambling Studies, University of Nevada, Reno, 72–91.

MISSOURI

Legalized gambling has a short history in Missouri. The Missouri state lottery began in 1986, while pari-mutuel racing started operations in June 1987. The most noticeable form of gambling in the state is found on 12 riverboats that started operations in the mid-1990s, during a very confusing series of court battles and voter referenda.

The initial vote to approve riverboat gambling came in November 1992. The legislative initiative authorized casino boats for the Mississippi and Missouri rivers. The boats had to take two-hour cruises, and players could not lose more than $500 during the cruise. After the referendum, seven companies applied for licenses. Before the boats could cruise with full-scale casino gambling, however, the state was hit with a lawsuit challenging the right to operate casino games. The state constitution banned lotteries.

The initial court ruling was that most casino games were lottery games. The boats that were operating had to close down their machines, roulette wheels, and baccarat games, as these were considered lotteries. They were permitted to have live poker and blackjack games. A few did for a short time. (The riverboats could not have a "lotteries," as the voters, in 1986, had amended the constitution to permit only a state-run lottery.)

The casinos got together and put a new constitutional initiative on the ballot in April 1994. This time the voters said "no" to the initiative. The casinos immediately started another petition campaign, however, and in November 1994the voters approved the required constitutional amendment. Fourteen casino boats were then approved for the state's waters. Twelve were in operation in 2008. The boats pay fees and a tax of 20 percent on their gambling win, which is shared between the state (18 percent) and the local community (2 percent). The boats have enjoyed a mixed success, as they have faced considerable competition—among themselves and with boats in Iowa, Illinois, and Mississippi. Since the beginning, the boats sought to have the $500 betting loss cap eliminated, but they have failed in these efforts until the voters acquiesced with their wishes in November 2008.

They casinos also sought to remove the requirement that they have to cruise in the rivers and be docked within the channels of the rivers. This ridiculous requirement was revealed for its stupidity when a commercial barge hit one of the boats in its dockside position at a time when there were 2,500 players aboard. A major catastrophe was narrowly avoided. Several companies began to put boats in artificial channels cut into the river. The gaming commission approved this move; however, the state supreme court ruled that this violated the requirement that the boats be in the river. Again the casinos went to the voters, and in 1998, the voters said the boats could be in artificial "moats" and that actual cruises were no longer necessary. In 2007, the gaming revenues from the boats reached almost $1.6 billion. Of this amount, $336 million went to the state as tax revenues and admission charges, while $81 million went to local governments. The total tax and admission fees represented about one-quarter of the collective casino win.

References

Maxwell, Sahar J., Christine J. Egbarts, and Timothy T. Stewart. 1999. "Missouri." In *International Casino Law*, 3rd ed. Edited by A. Cabot, W. Thompson, A. Tottenham, and C. Braunlich, 92–97. Reno: Institute of Gambling Studies, University of Nevada, Reno.

Missouri Gaming Association. "Analysis of Missouri Casino Gaming," http://www.missouricasinos.org/analysis.cfm, accessed December 8, 2008.

MONTANA

Montana has more gambling sites than any other state, with the exception of Nevada. There are well over 1,700 age-restricted locations offering more than 19,000 machine games of poker, keno, and slot simulations. The "casinos," which have 20 machines each, may also allow poker-like games on premise. Additionally the operators may sell raffle and pull-tab tickets. Montana is also one of four states that is permitted to have sports betting. Taverns are allowed to let players participate in "Calcutta" pools on events such as football games and World Series games. Prizes must equal at least 50 percent of the amounts that are bet by players. The state also permits pari-mutuel wagering on quarter horse races and participates in the sale of tickets for Lotto America. The bulk of Montana gaming is at the casino sites, 93 percent of which are places that sell alcoholic beverages. There are small casinos in more than 60 cities and towns of the state.

Gambling operations came to Montana more as a result of legal decisions than of deliberately studied policy. The voters legalized gambling in 1972, and two years later the legislature authorized sports pools, bingo games, raffles, and live card games. In 1976, the state supreme court ruled that video keno games were "live" keno games. Tavern owners across the state began installing not only video keno games but also other machines for gambling. In 1984, the Montana Supreme Court said these did not satisfy the "live games" designation. Therefore, the legislature was called into action by the tavern owners. First they approved the placement of five machines in a tavern. Subsequently, the number of machines was changed, and it now rests at 20 per liquor license. As some taverns hold multiple licenses, they actually operate 40 or 60 machines.

The casinos pay a state tax of 15 percent on their machine winnings, as well as a fee of $250 to $500 for (really) live tables. The state receives approximately $20 million in gaming taxes each year.

Six Native American reservations (Blackfeet, Rocky Boy, Crow, Flathead, Fort Belknap, and Fort Peck) also operate machine and poker gambling casinos. They are permitted to have 100 machines each in their casinos.

References

"Montana Casinos," www.500nations.com/Montana_Casinos.asp, accessed December 8, 2008.

Thompson, William N., and Jerry Johnson. 1999. "Montana." In *International Casino Law*, 3rd ed. Edited by A. Cabot, W. Thompson, A. Tottenham, and C. Braunlich, 98–100. Reno: Institute of Gambling Studies, University of Nevada, Reno.

NEBRASKA

During the time of pioneer settlements of the West, Nebraska—especially Omaha—was a wide-open place where gambling flourished. Omaha was a "jumping off" place for adventurers heading for gold and silver mining camps. Casinos prevailed from 1850 through 1887, legally. But even after they were banned by legislation that year, they kept operating. Only after a general crackdown on vice in the 1950s did gambling, prostitution, and the drug trade abate.

Nebraskans voted for a lottery in 1993. The state has also permitted live keno gaming statewide. As a result of these decisions, the Santee Sioux, Winnebago, and Omaha tribes have won the right to have casino table gambling on their small reservations.

For many generations in the 20th century, Omaha was the site of the successful Ak-Sar-Ben thoroughbred racing track. However competition from a dog track in nearby Council Bluffs, Iowa, as well as from Iowa riverboats destroyed the prospects for profits at the track in the 1990s. Efforts for win legalization for full casino gambling at the track failed (although it has been the site of a keno game). The track is permanently closed.

References

"Nebraska's Gambling History." Nebraska ETV. Transcript cited in www.wikipedia .org/wiki/Gambling_in_Omaha_Nebraska, accessed December 8, 2008.

Thompson, William N. 1997. *Legalized Gambling: A Reference Handbook.* 2nd ed. Santa Barbara, CA: ABC-CLIO, 165.

NEVADA

The state of Nevada is the primary commercial gambling state in the United States. For almost half of the 20th century, it was the only state to permit casino gambling. Even today, nearly 20 percent of the casino gambling activity in the United States occurs in Nevada. The state has more than 300 unrestricted casino license holders offering both table games and machine gaming, and 270 of these have gaming wins in excess of $1 million dollars per year. Another 2,000 restricted locations each have 15 or fewer gaming machines. The casinos are found in each of the 17 counties of the state and in every city of the state except for Boulder City—which was a federal enclave until the 1950s. No other North American jurisdiction allows such widespread locations for casinos; instead, most confine casinos to specific communities. The casinos produce revenues of approximately $12.5 billion per year from gambling and $13 billion more from other sources—rooms, food, and beverage sales. The casinos employ more than 200,000 persons, and with support industry employment they represent one-third of the employment in the state. The taxes from gambling and other aspects of casino enterprises constitute approximately 40 percent of the public revenues of the state and its local governments. No other jurisdiction in the world receives as large a share of its public budget from gambling taxes.

Although casino gambling is found in all but one jurisdiction in the state, there are certain important concentrations of casinos in the state. Of course, the primary gaming center is the Las Vegas Strip, a four-mile-long section of Las Vegas Boulevard, which has many of the largest hotels in the world—all with casinos. Downtown Las Vegas has several large properties located around Fremont Street. The town of Laughlin on the Colorado River at the southern tip of the state has 10 casinos. In the northern part of the state, the traditional gaming city of Reno (and its suburb, Sparks) has 35 major casinos, and the Lake Tahoe resort area has 5 major casinos.

HISTORY OF GAMING IN NEVADA

Nevada became "the" gambling state by a series of historical accidents as well as by deliberate policies. As late as the 1840s, Nevada was basically an unexplored region of barren desert and mountains. Paiute, Washoe, and Shoshone Indian tribes had traversed parts of the state and established some communities, but their numbers were small and their lifestyle was often nomadic, as they would live in the climatically comfortable mountains during the summer and then descend to the desert floor in winter months. The climate and terrain made the area one that most people moving westward sought to avoid or to cross in great haste.

One critical aspect of Nevada's geography that is pertinent to its economic development is its proximity to California. (Even today one-third of the state's gambling customers come from California.) The two states have the longest land border of any two states in the United States. People rushed to California in the late 1840s as gold was discovered. The new state of California was populated by all sorts of prospectors and other independent get-rich-quick entrepreneurs during the 1850s. The area that became Nevada was

made part of the Utah Territory in 1850. The volume of gold strikes in California began to wane in the late 1850s just as the great Comstock Lode was discovered near Virginia City, Nevada, in 1859. A mad silver rush paralleled the earlier California gold rush, except this time the fortune hunters came to Nevada from California. The first waves of population left an indelible mark upon the character and outlook of politics in the state. The influx of the new population was accompanied by desires to cut off political relationships with the Utah Territory and its religiously oriented government. President Buchanan signed a bill on March 2, 1861, just two days before he left office, which established the Nevada Territory out of the western one-third of the Utah Territory. Buchanan had been rather hostile to the nature of Utah society throughout his presidency, and the new status for Nevada was his parting shot against a community that seemed almost diametrically opposite to that found in Nevada.

The issue of gambling was quickly placed on the public agenda of the new state. President Lincoln appointed New Yorker James Nye to be territorial governor. Nye was not a prospector, and Nye did not care for gambling. He recoiled at the prevalence of sin institutions when he settled down in Nevada and persuaded the new legislature to prohibit gambling. A person who operated a game could be charged with a felony; a person who played at a game could be charged with a misdemeanor. In spite of the law, the games continued.

After statehood was achieved in 1864, the legislature reversed its thinking. In the 1867 session, a law was passed legalizing casino games. It was vetoed by the first elected governor, H. G. Blasdel. Two years later, the legislature repeated its action, and when the bill was vetoed again, they overrode the veto. The new law barred local governments from passing ordinances against gambling. Any person was able to get a license to operate a game from the county sheriff for a fee ranging from $1,000 to $1,600 (depending upon the population of the county). The fee was split equally between the state and county treasuries.

By the turn of the century, the Populist movement was gaining strength across the United States and in the Silver State. In concert with temperance organizations, civil leaders attacked the local sin industries. A ballot initiative sponsored by such groups sought to make both gaming and prostitution illegal in Reno. When the voters turned down the measure in 1909, the sponsors approached the state legislature. There they were successful, and gaming ceased to be legal on the last day of September in 1910. Another way of saying the same thing was that illegal gambling began on October 1, 1910.

By 1911, the legislature had second (and third) thoughts. Certain card games were legalized, only to be made illegal again in 1913. In 1915, limited gaming was permitted again. Enforcement of the gaming limits was sporadic at best and nonexistent as a rule. In lieu of fees when gaming was legal, operators now paid bribes to local officials, who pretended that gaming did not take place.

A move to legalize gambling was revived in 1931 when state assemblyman Phil Tobin of Humboldt County introduced the legislative measure. Although opposition was voiced by religious groups, Tobin's bill passed the assembly on a 24–11 vote, and the state senate on a 13–3 vote. On March 19, 1931, Governor Balzar signed both the six-weeks for residence divorce law and the measure to legalize casino gambling. A second law passed later in 1931 permitted local governments to regulate gambling and established fixed fees for gaming statewide. The fees were shared, with 75 percent going to local governments and 25 percent to the state. Licenses were granted by county commissions, and all regulations were enforced by the sheriffs.

In 1945, the state legislature decided that state control was necessary, as several outside operators were planning larger and larger casino projects. The state Tax Commission was given the authority to license casinos, which had previously received licenses from county boards. Subsequently the process became one of dual licensing. The state also imposed a 1 percent tax on the gross gaming wins of the casinos. The Tax Commission was empowered to collect the tax. Two years later, the state attorney general ruled that the Tax Commission could deny a license based upon its assessment of the character of the applicant. In 1949, the requirement that applicants must be of good character was written into the law. The Tax Commission was given a staff for casino regulation for the first time.

GAMING REGULATORY STRUCTURE

During the early 1950s, considerable negative attention was cast upon the casino industry as a result of the U.S. Senate Kefauver Committee hearings on organized crime. To avoid further national scrutiny, the state responded with regulatory reforms. Legislation in 1955 established a specialized three-member full-time Gaming Control Board, which was administratively located with the Tax

Commission. In 1959, the Tax Commission was eliminated from the state's casino regulatory picture. Instead a five-member Nevada Gaming Commission was created. This part-time group still serves as the final voice for the state on gaming matters. In a sense it is the "supreme court" for gaming.

As a result of these changes, Nevada now has a two-tier structure for regulating gambling. The Gaming Control Board acts essentially like a policeman and a tax collector for the casino industry while the Nevada Gaming Commission makes final decisions on licensing casinos and formulating regulations as well as handling disputes that cannot be resolved by actions of the Gaming Control Board.

The three board members are appointed by the governor for four-year terms. One member is designated as chair by the governor. He or she must have five years of experience in public or private administration. A second member must be a certified public accountant or have expertise in finance or economics. The remaining member must have law enforcement experience. Board members may not be engaged in any partisan political activity during their term of service. They may not have any financial ties to casinos, nor may they be employed by any casino for one year following their board service.

The board oversees the work of a staff of more than 430 individuals, who are organized into several divisions. The investigations division checks into the backgrounds of persons who wish to have gambling licenses. The cost of this background check process is paid by the license applicant. An enforcement division works in the casinos to assure that all the games are honest and that all gaming laws and regulations are being obeyed. An audit division checks accounting procedures in the casinos and makes sure that all flows of money are accurately recorded and reported for purposes of taxation. A tax, license, and administration division collects gambling taxes and publishes reports on casino activity in the state. There is also a corporate securities division that monitors the financial condition of casinos that are owned by publicly traded corporations. An electronic laboratory investigates all gaming devices to assure their integrity.

The five members of the Nevada Gaming Commission are also appointed by the governor for four year terms. They, too, must not have an interest in any casinos, nor may they be involved in partisan politics. The commission has no staff. It gives final passage to rules and regulations and makes final decisions regarding disciplinary action against any gaming interest—action that can also include revocation of a license. In 1969, the legislature created a seven-member Gaming Policy Board headed by the governor. The board was charged with making recommendations to the legislature for reforms in the gaming law. It has met only occasionally over the past 40 years.

Although the state's gaming regulatory structure is considered one of the finest arrangements for regulating gaming in the world, local governments (counties or cities) are still involved in the process. They must also license casinos, and they collect fees separately from the state fees and taxes. The state gaming tax has risen to 6.75 percent of the gross gaming win, and casinos must also pay a variety of fees both to the state and to local governments based upon the number of tables and machines in the facility.

References

Cabot, Anthony N. 1999. *Federal Gambling Law.* Las Vegas: Trace.

Cabot, Anthony N., and Marc H. Rubenstein. 1999. "Nevada." In *International Casino Law,* 3rd ed. Edited by Anthony N. Cabot, William N. Thompson, Andrew Tottenham, and Carl Braunlich, 101–120. Reno: Institute for the Study of Gambling, University of Nevada, Reno.

Cabot, Anthony N. 2008. *Nevada Gaming Control Board, Nevada Gaming Abstract 2007.* Carson City: State of Nevada.

Skolnick, James. 1978. *House of Cards: Legalization and Control of Casino Gambling.* Boston: Little, Brown.

See also Boulder City, Nevada: Nongambling Oasis; Kefauver Committee (in General Topics section); Las Vegas; Reno; Laughlin.

BOULDER CITY, NEVADA: NONGAMBLING OASIS

Boulder City, Nevada, is the only community in the state of Nevada where gambling is not permitted in any form. The small city of about 15,000 residents lies 25 miles southeast of Las Vegas and abuts the Colorado River. Boulder City was not part of Wild West mining days of the Silver State. Rather, it was a government creation, established in 1931 as a city to house workers for the building of the Hoover Dam. The Boulder Dam Project had been authorized by an act of Congress in 1928. Almost immediately thereafter, the state of Nevada and the federal government sought to exercise their separate authority over the parcel of land selected for a new workers' community. The federal government, even in the years right before Nevada legalized casinos in 1931, recognized the state as a rogue among the members of the union. Gambling was openly operating in Las Vegas, as were houses of prostitution, which actually were in conformity with the local law. Las Vegas was also considered to be the location where violations of the national prohibition against alcoholic beverages were most apparent. In 1929, some thought was given to making Las Vegas the base camp for the construction workers. After Secretary of the Interior Ray Wilbur visited the "sin city," however, he recoiled at the notion of workers living among saloons and prostitutes and being tempted to spend their salaries in casinos. Wilbur declared that a "model" community be constructed closer to the site of the construction.

Secretary Wilbur invoked the provisions of the Reclamation Act of 1902 and created a 144-square-mile enclave out of unappropriated federal lands surrounding the site of the dam. The enclave included a town site for Boulder City. The city was made a federal reservation much in the same legal form as the Native American reservations of the same era. Federal law dominated city life, and Nevada law was unenforceable. A prohibition against liquor was put firmly into place and remained in place even after the Twenty-first Amendment ended national prohibition in 1933. Prostitution was strictly forbidden, as was gambling, even though it was soon made completely legal by the Nevada legislature.

Boulder City, the first "planned community" of the 20th century, was to be an isolated oasis of morality and "quality life," albeit surrounded by the many diversions of Nevada society. Author Dennis McBride writes that "everything was designed and blueprinted long before the first spadeful of earth was turned at the site. The government decided how many people would live in Boulder City, and which businesses would be allowed to operate" (McBride 1981, 16–17).

The city was built on desolate desert lands. The lands were transformed into a hospitable environment for workers who desperately needed quarters for themselves and their families. The same consortium of companies that was chosen to build the dam built the city. They hired an architect to lay out the streets. He also designated lands for parks and golf courses. The architect incorporated desert landscaping into his plan. The need for quick construction led to modifications, however, and the golf course idea was abandoned. Also, the almost unbearable heat prompted the government to bring in a landscape gardener, aptly named Wilbur Weed, to begin a project that involved planting grasses, shrubbery, and trees everywhere. He selected the correct species of each after much study, and miraculously, his plantings survived to bring a measure of coolness and shade to the streets of the community. The plant-

ings also broke up the wind and dust storms that had otherwise swept through the town as a result of all the construction activity. The autocratic city managers appointed by federal authorities did not let the landscape gardener's work go unnoticed. They decreed that all residents would have to maintain their lawn and garden areas, and if they did not, the city would do so and deduct the cost from the residents' wages at the dam.

The government decided that Boulder City would not be just a place for workers to live temporarily but that it would be a true community. A variety of civic institutions and organizations was sponsored, and churches were invited to join the community. By 1932, four churches were constructed and well attended. Also most of Boulder's principal buildings were finished, and her institutions established. The streets were paved, the boulevards and parks landscaped. There were no more tent neighborhoods; hundreds of houses stood in monotonous rows, each identical to the next. McBride writes:

> Plaster on the new Bureau of Reclamation Administration Building, the dormitory, and the Municipal Building was smooth and white, reflecting the powerful afternoon sun. Fords, Chevys, and other working-class cars lined the streets. New stores in the business district displayed goods behind big polished windows. Arcades with graceful plaster arches shaded the downtown sidewalks.

He continued:

> Where before there had been barren desert, there was now a modern American city. Wives shopped in

clean, well-supplied stores and ate lunch in fine cafes; their husbands worked all week, and brought home a good paycheck. Children went to school taught by bright innovative teachers, and played on green, front lawns and in shady parks. While families in the rest of America went hungry, the people who lived in Boulder City on the federal reservation lived quiet, insulated domestic lives. Boulder today still looks remarkably like it did fifty years ago." (McBride 1981)

A fence surrounded the city, with a gate manned by guards who would only let in workers and residents, who had to carry passes. Eventually more than 5,000 workers lived in the dam-building community. The decision of Secretary Wilbur to create the enclave of "clean living" had several consequences for the development of Las Vegas as a gambling Mecca. First, by banning gambling and other "entertainment" from the vicinity of the dam, Wilbur assured that a large number of federal employees would venture into Las Vegas and support its newly legalized casinos in the 1930s. Further, the restrictions on life in Boulder City—in terms of entrance and exit from the town—precluded a development of hotel accommodations until well into the construction schedule. Only one hotel was available during construction. Accommodations developed in Las Vegas instead. Moreover, as a private center of enterprise, Las Vegas attracted a share of the capital resources that were directed into the construction project. Las Vegas became a major transportation center for materials because enterprise was not allowed to develop in Boulder City.

When the Hoover Dam project was completed, Boulder City declined in population as workers moved away. The town persisted as a government center during the years of World War II, however, as a military force was stationed in the area to guard the dam, considered by authorities to be a target for the Japanese enemy. After the war, the city began to attract workers of the newly developing casino industry of Las Vegas. In the 1950s, the residents moved to have the city removed from federal control. In 1958, for the very first time, residents were permitted to vote for local governing officials. First a commission was elected to write a home rule charter for the city. After a charter was written, it was approved by a vote of the citizens. Then in 1960, Congress passed legislation releasing the land for private sale to the citizens, whose city now came under the jurisdiction of the state of Nevada. The first charter banned both gambling and hard alcoholic beverages, probably in recognition that the charter would not become effective unless ratified in an act of Congress. The state of Nevada had banned prostitution in Clark County (the county including both Las Vegas and Boulder City), so this was no longer an issue. After the city emerged as a home rule town under Nevada law, there were several attempts to legalize both alcohol and gambling. In 1958, the city charter was amended to allow the sale of alcohol both by the bottle and by the glass. In vote after vote, however, the residents have remained firm in the position that they do not want gambling. This adamant standing does not mean that residents do not frequent casinos. The residents, now 15,000 strong, patronize two major casino complexes on their borders: one at the Railroad Pass area on the road to Las Vegas and another on a private enclave of land outside the city limits on the road to the dam and the Arizona state line.

As a resident of nearby Las Vegas, the editor of this volume can attest that Boulder City, the state's only nongambling city, has maintained much of the culture that was imposed upon the city by its federal mentors during the construction of the dam. The city seeks to be a quiet community with good schools and churches, a city that enjoys the very green parks and tree-lined streets cultivated by the federal government in the 1930s. The city adopted antigrowth policies in the 1960s and 1970s and maintains a policy of limited and controlled growth. The latter policies help maintain high values of residential properties. They also maintain a buffer to the urban sprawl prevalent throughout the rest of the Las Vegas metropolitan area. A small-town character prevails. Within this atmosphere there are events such as the autumn art fair that attracts both artists and art patrons from throughout the southwestern United States. The city is also a tourist center, as it is the first motel area near Hoover Dam and the Lake Mead recreational area that was created with the completion of the dam in the 1930s. Visitors to the city who stay in the local motels have access to the many entertainment venues of the Las Vegas area, while at the same time they can enjoy quiet walks through uncrowded green parks beneath trees, much as if they were in a small Midwestern city.

Reference

McBride, Dennis. 1981. "Boulder City: How It Began." Manuscript. Special Collections Library, University of Nevada, Las Vegas.

LAS VEGAS

From its earliest days, Las Vegas catered to travelers. Its springs watered not only the crops grown by local Native Americans but also the meadows (*las vegas* is Spanish for "the meadows") that in the 1830s supported an oasis for whites traveling the Old Spanish Trail between New Mexico and southern California. In 1855, Mormons built a fort and mission there, which also acted as a hostel for those plying the route between Utah and the church's colony in San Bernardino, California. Following the Civil War, several farm-ranches occupied the valley until 1905, when Senator William Clark, principal owner of the newly created San Pedro, Los Angeles, and Salt Lake Railroad, purchased a ranch from local landowner Helen Stewart for $55,000. On this tract he platted his Las Vegas Townsite, a division town complete with yards, roundhouse, and repair shops. In addition, he used the ranch's water rights to supply his town and the thirsty boilers of his steam locomotives.

The little whistle-stop struggled along into the 1930s, experimenting with commercial agriculture and other small industries to supplement its transportation economy, but without success. The first seeds of change came in 1928 when Congress appropriated funds for building

Hoover Dam. Construction began in 1931, the same year that the state legislature re-legalized gambling and liberalized the waiting period for divorce to six weeks. The dam was an immediate tourist attraction, drawing 300,000 tourists a year. But even with these visitors and the 5,000-plus men who toiled on the project, gambling remained a minor part of Las Vegas economy. When construction ended in 1936 and the dam workers left, the city experienced a mild recession. By decade's end, the town's population numbered only 8,400.

The real trigger for casino gambling was World War II. The sprawling Desert Warfare Center south of Nevada's boundary with Arizona and California, along with Twenty-nine Palms, Camp Pendleton, Las Vegas own army gunnery school, and other military bases, provided thousands of weekend visitors who patronized the casinos in Las Vegas. Supplementing these groups were thousands more defense workers from nearby Basic Magnesium and from southern California's defense plants.

This sudden surge in business sparked a furious casino boom, helped by reform mayor Fletcher Bowron's campaign to drive professional gamblers out of Los Angeles. Beginning in 1938, they began fleeing to Las Vegas, bringing their valuable expertise with them. Former vice officer and gambler Guy McAfee opened the Pioneer Club downtown and the Pair-O-Dice on the Los Angeles Highway (later the Strip) before unveiling his classy Golden Nugget (with partners) in 1946. Las Vegas also drew the attention of organized crime figures. Bugsy Siegel and associate Moe Sedway came to town in 1941 at the behest of Eastern gangsters who were anxious to capture control of local race wires, the telephone linking system for taking bets on horse races.

Fremont Street grew, as older establishments bordering its sidewalks yielded to modern-looking successors. But a more significant trend in the 1940s was the Strip's development. The first major resort was the El Rancho Vegas, which revolutionized casino gambling. The brainchild of Thomas Hull, the hotel exemplified the formula he developed for the Strip's success. In 1940, he amazed everyone by rejecting a downtown location for more spacious county lands in the desert just south of the city. In the old West, gambling had always been confined to riverboats and small hotels near some railroad or stagecoach station. With his El Rancho Vegas Hotel, Hull liberated gambling from its historic confines and placed it in a spacious resort hotel, complete with a pool, lush lawns and gardens, a showroom, an arcade of stores, and most important, parking for 400 cars. It was Hull, the southern Californian, who recognized that the highway (with its cars, trucks, and buses) rather than the railroad was the transportation wave of the future and that in the age of electric power, a downtown location was no longer superior to a suburban one.

For the most part, the El Rancho's successors in the 1940s, such as the Hotel Last Frontier, the Flamingo, and Thunderbird, followed Hull's model, although with a larger and more plush format. The Flamingo, built by Bugsy Siegel and the *Hollywood Reporter*'s Billy Wilkerson, freed Las Vegas from the traditional western motif slavishly followed by resorts such as the El Rancho and El Cortez downtown. With its Miami Beach–Monte Carlo ambience, the Flamingo opened a new world of thematic options for future resorts such as Caesars Palace and the Mirage.

The Strip assumed its familiar shape in the 1950s with the addition of 11 new resorts. Several key events contributed to this growth. First, wealthy high rollers and thousands of middle-class gamblers would not have vacationed in the sizzling Mohave Desert in summer had it not been for the invention of air conditioning and the casinos' willingness to equip every new resort with it. Add to this the debut of car air conditioning in the late 1950s—just in time for the arrival of Interstate 15. This multilane highway with its gentle banked turns allowed speeds that cut the trip up from Los Angeles to only 4 hours, and its convenient location just west of the Strip is the main reason why more than half of all Las Vegas visitors still come by car or bus.

While the same was true of convention delegates into the 1960s, that trend began to change following the arrival of jet service in September 1960. Flying twice as fast as its propeller-driven predecessors and able to fly high above turbulent weather, the passenger jet increased Las Vegas visitor totals by several million after the county opened the new McCarran jetport in 1963. Accounting for much of this traffic were ordinary Americans on vacation with their families, but a growing army of trade show visitors and convention delegates contributed increasingly to the town's visitor totals. Abetting the growth of Las Vegas' meeting industry was the liberalization of the nation's tax laws in the 1950s, which allowed substantial deductions for business travel for professional development and for the exhibition of goods. In response, Las Vegas and Clark County officials, anxious to fill their hotel rooms during the

week, formed a convention and visitors board in 1955 and built the Las Vegas Convention Center. They shrewdly located it just behind the Riviera Hotel in close proximity to Interstate 15, the airport and, most importantly, the Strip. By the 1980s, this allowed Las Vegas to host some of the world's largest conventions because the Strip resorts' total room capacity kept pace with each expansion of the convention center—surpassing 120,000 rooms by century's end.

Other initiatives helped Las Vegas parlay these advantages into new rounds of growth. In 1955, the first Lake Mead water reached Las Vegas, liberating it from an unwanted dependence on wells. Then in the 1960s, funding of the Southern Nevada Water Project as part of Lyndon Johnson's "Great Society" awarded the metropolitan area enough Lake Mead water to support a city of more than 2 million people, a vital prerequisite for the city's future growth. In addition, passage of Governor Paul Laxalt's corporate gaming proposal in 1969 promoted the city's future development by ending the traditional requirement that every stockholder be investigated. The new law limiting the licensing procedure to only "key executives" permitted the entry of Hilton, Hyatt, MGM, and other corporate giants into the state. Only these entities, with their access to large pools of capital, could afford the billions necessary to build the megaresorts that characterize Las Vegas today.

In the 1950s and 1960s, a number of new technological advances and social trends reinforced the city's growth, leading to construction of spectacular newcomers such as Caesars Palace. Chief among these trends was the so-called middle-classification of the United States. In the postwar era, with

The opportunity to gamble is everywhere in Las Vegas. Here, slot machines sit adjacent to a baggage carousel in McCarran International Airport.

more Americans graduating from high school and even college and with the postindustrial economy creating more high-paying white-collar jobs, both disposable and discretionary income—crucial to the budgets of gamblers and vacationers—soared. Moreover, income in California increased by more than the national average. Even blue-collar workers enjoyed substantial income gains. Las Vegas also benefited from the growth in automation and generous union contracts that gave workers more vacation and holiday time for leisure pursuits. In addition, the introduction of the credit card by Diner's Club eliminated the need to travel with large amounts of cash. These innovations, along with automated teller machines, debit card, and computers, all made long-distance travel easier, liberating Las Vegas from its dependence upon southern California.

Following a brief recession occasioned by the debut of Atlantic City, which temporarily siphoned off some of Las Vegas' East Coast market, the city rebounded in the 1980s and 1990s. In what has been Las Vegas' most spectacular round of expansion, a new generation of casino executives epitomized by Steve Wynn joined an older group led by Kirk Kerkorian to transform the casino city into a major resort destination. Several factors contributed to the metropolitan area's mercurial growth. First was the construction of several lavish new hotels. The $630 million Mirage set a record for cost when it opened in 1989 and instantly became the state's leading tourist attraction, usurping the title held by Hoover Dam for more than five decades. Quickly eclipsing the Mirage's price tag was Kirk Kerkorian's 1993 MGM Grand Hotel and Theme Park, which at nearly $1 billion was the most expensive hotel ever built.

Casino New York, New York, on the Las Vegas Strip.

The Paris Casino on the Las Vegas Strip: the ultimate themed casino.

Steve Wynn, however, quickly topped this by imploding the Dunes Hotel and replacing it with the $1.6 billion Bellagio. At the same time, former COMDEX Convention mogul Sheldon Adelson took over the venerable Sands Hotel and demolished it to make way for The Venetian, a $1.5 billion Renaissance successor. These and other city-themed resorts such as New York-New York and Paris combined with Luxor, Bellagio, Mandalay Bay, Wynn, and Palazzo to transform the Strip into an even greater tourist Mecca.

The second factor went beyond the money, the new restaurants, and bigger and grander casinos. Wynn helped pioneer a new approach to luring additional visitors to Las Vegas when he introduced the concept of offering special attractions both inside and outside his casino. The Mirage initiated the idea in 1989 with its erupting volcano, white tigers, and bottle-nosed dolphins; Wynn continued the trend with his outdoor pirate battle at Treasure Island and Bellagio's "dancing fountains." MGM's theme park, Paris's Eiffel Tower, Bellagio's "Dancing Waters," and Wynn's 140-foot mountain only added to the fare.

A number of other themes have also characterized Las Vegas efforts to broaden its market, among which has been an appeal to families. This trend actually dates from the 1950s when the Hacienda's Warren and Judy Bayley pursued the niche by offering guests multiple swimming pools and a quarter-midget go-cart track. In the 1970s, new Circus Circus proprietors William Bennett and William Pennington took their casino's clown theme and applied it to families rather than to high rollers as the original owner had tried to do. They added a carnival midway of games, candy stands, and toy shops and later supplemented it with a domed, indoor amusement park packed with thrill rides. Circus Circus repeated this success in the 1990s with its Excalibur Hotel, a dazzling medieval castle priced to attract the low-end family market. But despite these and other efforts to soften Las Vegas image nationally, families have consistently represented no more than 8 percent of the town's visitors.

Another factor reinforcing the casino industry's local development was that in the 1980s and 1990s, Las Vegas gamers acquired a substantial home market as the metropolitan area's population skyrocketed from 273,000 in 1970 to more 1.3 million by century's end. The first major neighborhood casinos catering primarily to locals came in the 1970s when Palace Station (1976) and Sam's Town (1979) began operations. Reinforcing this market was the development of a new sector in the Las Vegas economy: the retirement industry. Following the deaths of gaming figures Del Webb (in 1973) and Howard Hughes (1976), their two companies joined forces to build what eventually became Sun City Summerlin. Since Hughes had purchased most of the outlying lands west of the city in the 1940s and Del Webb possessed the construction expertise to build homes, the companies formed a partnership and began work on Sun City in the mid-1980s. This project, along with its satellite communities, will ultimately contain more than 30,000 homes. Already, thousands of retirees have moved to Sun City and other small projects around the city. Las Vegas is the only place where they can not only "go to the malls" and engage in the traditional forms of leisure offered by Miami and Phoenix but also gamble on horses, sports, and cards.

Beginning in the 1990s, Strip resorts also began to weave shopping into their operations with the addition of high-end retail centers, such as the Forum Shops at Caesars Palace and its clones at The Venetian, Aladdin, and elsewhere. The results have been nothing less than dramatic. As the 21st century dawned, more spectacular resorts, world-class shopping, and special attractions had combined with the growing national and global popularity of casino gambling to make Las Vegas the leading tourist center in the United States—briefly surpassing its nearest rival, Orlando.

Not content with its success, Las Vegas continued to evolve. In the mid-1990s, a new pattern developed on the Strip, first at the Flamingo and Las Vegas Hiltons and then up and down the Strip: the construction of high-rise buildings to house time-share condominiums for vacationers anxious to spend a few weeks in Las Vegas at their favorite resort. By 2000, the next step was to erect entire apartment houses for those wanting to live on or near the Strip all year round or desiring a third or fourth residence. Miami-based Turnberry Associates constructed Turnberry Estates, a complex of four luxury towers behind the old Thunderbird Hotel (the future site of the company's Fountainbleau Hotel) in the early 2000s, while Kirk Kerkorian matched the effort with his MGM Grand Residences, located on land once occupied by that resort's theme park. Other stand-alone condominium towers also sprouted along Interstate 15 and West Sahara Avenue as well as downtown on Fremont Street and on thoroughfares far removed from Glitter Gulch. Kerkorian upped the ante further in 2005 when he announced plans to construct Project City Center, a vertical, sustainable, and iconic-looking community of

TABLE 1. Casinos Listed by Date Opened and Motif

Property	Date	Motif	Comments
El Rancho Vegas	1941	Western	Across from Sahara front entrance; first hotel on the Strip
El Cortez	1941	Mexican	First large hotel downtown
Hotel Last Frontier	1942	Western	Later site of New Frontier, 1955; Frontier, 1966
Golden Nugget	1946	Alaska-Western	Later added hotel rooms; first corporately owned hotel
The Flamingo	1946	Florida-Monte Carlo	Bought by Hilton from Kirk Kerkorian in 1970
Thunderbird	1948	American Indian	Later called the Silverbird, El Rancho
Desert Inn	1950	Arizona Resort-Spa	First hotel with golf course, 1952
Horseshoe	1951	Western	Remodeled version of the 1931 Apache Hotel
Sands	1952	Arizona Resort-Spa	Imploded for Venetian in 1996
Sahara	1952	Africa	
Showboat	1954	Mississippi Riverboat	
Dunes	1955	Sultan-Turkey Mideast	Imploded in 1993 for Bellagio
Riviera	1955	French	First Las Vegas high-rise hotel
Royal Nevada	1955		Just north of the Stardust; demolished in 1970s
Moulin Rouge	1955	Parisian Club	Near the Westside (first interracial hotel)
Hacienda	1956	Mexican	
Fremont	1956	Western	First downtown high-rise
Tropicana	1957	Cuba-Caribbean	
Stardust	1958	Disney-like	Disneyland in Anaheim opened in 1955
Mint	1962		Today the Horseshoe's hotel high-rise
Castaways	1963		Formerly Sans Souci—in today's Mirage Front Driveway

TABLE 1. *(Continued)*

Aladdin	1966	Arabian Nights	Opened as Tally-Ho; high-rise, 1976; imploded, 1998; open 2000
Caesars Palace	1966	Greco-Roman	
Four Queens	1966		
International	1969	Cosmopolitan Cultures	Became Las Vegas Hilton, 1971, after Kirk Kerkorian sold it
Landmark	1969	Cape Canaveral Missile Gantry	Imploded 1995—across from convention center entrance
Plaza	1971	Railroad Station	Formerly Union Plaza on site of old railroad station
Circus Circus	1971	Circus	The casino opened in 1968
First MGM Grand (Ballys)	1973	Hollywood; New Year's Eve	Burned in November 1980 and rebuilt by Kirk Kerkorian
Harrahs	1974	Riverboat, now Carnival	Formerly Holiday Inn–Center Strip until 1992
Marina	1974	Nautical	Today part of new MGM Grand
Palace Station	1976	Railroad	Opened as Bingo Palace
Maxim	1977		Closed 1999
Imperial Palace	1979	Japanese-Chinese	
Sam's Town	1979	Western	
Barbary Coast	1979	San Francisco	
Vegas World-Stratosphere	1979	Outer Space; now World's Fair	Reopened as Stratosphere Tower, 1996
Fitzgeralds	1980	Irish	
Gold Coast	1986	Alaska Gold Rush	
Arizona Charlies	1988	California Gold Rush	
The Mirage	1989	South Seas	
Rio Suites Hotel	1990	Brazil	
Excalibur	1990	Medieval Europe	
Santa Fe	1991	Santa Fe	
Luxor	1993	Ancient Egypt	
Treasure Island	1993	Pirates-Buccaneers	
Second MGM Grand	1993	Wizard of Oz; now City of Entertainment	First hotel with a theme park
Boulder Station	1994	Railroad	
Hard Rock Hotel	1995	Rock 'n' Roll	

(Continued on next page)

TABLE 1. *(Continued)*

Property	Date	Motif	Comments
Texas Station	1995	Texas and Railroad	
Monte Carlo	1996	Monte Carlo	
The Orleans	1996	New Orleans	
New York-New York	1997	New York	
Sunset Station	1997	Spain and Railroad	
Reserve Hotel	1998	African Jungle	
Bellagio	1998	Tuscan Village	Replaced Dunes Hotel
Mandalay Bay	1999	Tropical Paradise	Replaced Hacienda Hotel
Paris	1999	Paris	
The Venetian	1999	Venice	Replaced Sands Hotel
The Regent Las Vegas	1999		First resort in Summerlin
Hyatt Regency-Lake Las Vegas	1999	Mediterranean	First resort at Lake Mead
The (new) Aladdin	2000	Arabian Nights	Replaced old Aladdin; now is Planet Hollywood
Wynn Las Vegas	2005		
Palazzo	2007	Classical Italian	Adjacent to Venetian
Encore	2008		Adjacent to Wynn Las Vegas
M	2009		South of Las Vegas Strip

Source: Prepared by Dr. Eugene Moehring, Department of History, UNLV. Updated and revised from William N. Thompson, *Gambling in America: An Encyclopedia of History, Issues, and Society*. Santa Barbara: ABC-CLIO, 2001, 222–223.

The Las Vegas Strip. Here on one street are 18 of the 20 largest hotels in the world. Note the critical position of McCarran International Airport at the foot of the Strip.

more than 7,000 apartments and hotel rooms, along the Strip south of Bellagio on part of the old Dunes golf course.

All of these enterprises, however, were threatened by the national economic downturn of 2008, which proved that Las Vegas was no longer recession-proof. The spiraling cost of oil and gas, which dramatically raised airline fares and cut flights, along with a real estate bust that not only afflicted Wall Street and the nation but also Las Vegas' growing home market exposed the Strip's new vulnerability to external economic forces. In the 20th century, the "old Las Vegas" had catered primarily to multimillionaire high rollers and business executives whose wealth largely insulated them from the economy's periodic downturns. But the 1990s emphasis on pursuing the low-end family market at resorts like Excalibur and Circus Circus teamed with the growing effort by Steve Wynn and others to make Las Vegas a world destination by supplementing Caesars Palace with must-see resorts like The Venetian, Bellagio, Paris, Wynn, and Mandalay Bay to put the city at the mercy of economic forces that afflicted all tourist markets.

For most Las Vegas leaders, this was a small price to pay for transforming their city from the high-roller playground of the Rat Pack days to a world destination boasting 35 million visitors annually. Once little more than a desert gateway to Hoover Dam, in just 60 years Las Vegas became a city of 2 million and the fastest-growing metropolis in the United States for 20 straight years. External forces, technological innovations, visionary leadership, and a knack for exploiting popular culture all contributed to the phenomenon that Las Vegas became.

Written by Eugene Moehring

References

Elliott, Gary. 1999. *The New Western Frontier: An Illustrated History of Las Vegas.* Carlsbad, CA: Heritage Media Corp.

Findlay, John M. 1986. *People of Chance: Frontiers of Gambling from Jamestown to Las Vegas.* New York: Oxford University Press.

Moehring, Eugene. 2000. *Resort City in the Sunset: Las Vegas 1930–2000.* 2nd ed. Reno: University of Nevada.

RENO

"The Biggest Little City in the World"— Reno, Nevada—was settled in 1868 as a community planned around a railroad center serving the Comstock mining area of Virginia City. The city grew sufficiently during its early years to allow its survival after silver-mining interests waned. Nonetheless, the city had to turn to other activities to remain economically viable. Reno and Nevada accepted certain behaviors and activities not allowed elsewhere. The city did not ban the prostitution that became part of the scene in the early mining years. The city held the Jeffries-Jackson boxing match in 1910, when other states banned the sport. In the early decades of the 20th century, Reno established its reputation as a place where divorces could be easily obtained. Gambling was permitted from the beginning without interruption. (From 1910 to 1931, however, the gambling activity was illegal, even though openly tolerated.)

When Nevada's legislature passed the wide-open casino bill of 1931, Reno became the premier casino city of the United States. It maintained that status until Las Vegas accelerated its development in the 1950s.

The first legal casinos of the 1930s were merely the same bars, taverns, and restaurants that had operated gambling over the previous two decades in their back rooms. The largest was the Bank Club, which had conducted games in its basement. Within a month of the new law, a renovated and enlarged facility was opened on the ground floor. It had the first electric bingo board in a casino. Other facilities proliferated with small-scale gambling.

The operations of Bill Harrah and the Smith family redefined the nature of Reno and of casino gambling generally in the later years of the decade. When they developed their properties, Reno became much more than just an outlaw town offering quickie divorces. It was a destination resort.

The Smiths came from Vermont, where Raymond I. "Pappy" Smith had run carnival games. In the early 1930s, he migrated to a beach location near San Francisco, where he began to take dollars from "suckers." In 1935, California attorney general Earl Warren began an antigambling crusade. "Pappy" and his two sons, Raymond A. and Harold, decided that the legal air of Reno would be better for their health. They started a bingo hall on Virginia Street in the red-lined area where gambling was permitted by the city council. They called their place Harolds Club. The other clubs and casinos acted like carnival operators and tried to take all the players' money as fast as they could, but the Smiths tried a new approach in their facility. They viewed their customers as their ultimate "bread and butter" only if they were nurtured, well respected, and well treated. Every day Pappy Smith would walk the floor, joke with players, and give "donations" to players who lost all their money. Every player always had a meal and enough money for a bus ride home.

The Smiths were also promoters. For a short time, they had a game called mouse roulette. A mouse would be released into a cage having a circular board with numbered holes. The mouse would eventually go into one of the holes, and the number on the hole would be the winning number in the game. Players discovered, however, that they could make noises, causing the mouse to quickly run into the nearest hole. The game had to be taken out as it lost too much money for the casino.

The Smiths launched casino gambling's first national (and world) advertising campaign. They placed 2,300 billboards on major highways throughout the country. The billboards featured a covered wagon and the words "Harolds Club or Bust." The signs soon appeared in countries on every continent. The world knew that there was a Reno and that Reno had casinos. The Smiths also opened their doors to women players by being the first casino to hire women as dealers. In 1970, Harolds Club was sold to Howard Hughes. It was Hughes's only northern Nevada property.

Bill Harrah and his father were also encouraged by authorities to close down their "bingo" games in California. Bill had grown up in luxury, but unfortunately his father's fortune fell apart during the Depression, and he had to leave college to help run his father's remaining business venture, a bingo game at Venice Beach. When Bill visited Reno, he was generally disgusted with the "sawdust" nature of the low-class joints he found. He thought the city could do a lot better. After several tries, he was finally able to set up operations on Virginia Street. He gave his players the feel of luxury—carpets, draperies, good furniture, comfortable restaurants. He was the first Reno operator to bring big-time entertainers to a casino. He also drew customers by creating the largest automobile collection in the world. Harrah is also credited for developing internal casino security by installing the skywalk, also known as the "eye in the sky."

Harrah also developed a casino at South Lake Tahoe, bringing his ideas of luxury surroundings to gambling properties in the area. While developing marketing strategies there, he instituted bus tours for players from the San Francisco area and other parts of California.

Harrah's was the first casino organization with publicly traded stocks. Nevada passed its legislation enabling public stock ownership for casinos in 1969, and Harrah's went public in 1971. In 1973, the stock was traded on the New York Stock Exchange. After Bill Harrah's death in 1978, the company was sold to Holiday Inn. Today it is the giant of the corporate casino industry, having revenues surpassing any other company.

Reno grew with other new properties and with expansions. In the 1950s, the red-line casino district was eliminated, and casinos could be placed in other commercial areas. The 1950s saw gaming grow with the Mapes and Riverside Hotels on lower Virginia Street. John Ascauga started the Nugget in suburban Sparks. Competition from Las Vegas dampened expansion in the 1960s, but the 1970s brought a building revival. Several major properties were opened. The Eldorado started games in 1973, and the Comstock, Sahara (now the Reno Flamingo Hilton), and Circus Circus opened in 1978. The same year, Kirk Kerkorian constructed the MGM Grand with over 1,000 rooms—later expanded to 2,000. The MGM Grand had the largest casino floor in the world when it opened—over 100,000 square feet of gaming space. The MGM Grand was later sold to Bally's and subsequently to Hilton.

Until 1995, there was no more casino construction in Reno. The market essentially went flat. In 1995, however, the Eldorado and Circus Circus combined to build the largest downtown casino—the Silver Legacy. Today Reno seeks to "hold its own" against competition from Native American casinos in California and the aura of Las Vegas to the south. The city has developed marketing around a series of events throughout the year. The National Bowling Center was built downtown, and it features many tournaments. The city also hosts the world-class Reno Hot Air Balloon Races each year. In addition there is a multitude of music, ethnic, and nationalities festivals. Canada Days is especially popular with a key market segment—tours from the country to the north.

The 45 casinos of the Reno-Sparks area (Washoe County), with approximately 15,000 rooms, produce gambling revenues of approximately $1 billion a year, or 12 percent of the state's revenue and 2 percent of the national gambling revenue. The casinos are not as able to appeal to high rollers as are the Las Vegas properties. Las Vegas casinos win about 40 percent of their revenues from table games, whereas Reno properties win less than 30 percent from tables. Next to Las Vegas, Reno will continue to be number two, and they will have to "try harder" just to stay in place.

References

Kling, Dwayne. 2000. *The Rise of the Biggest Little City: An Encyclopedia History of Reno Gaming, 1931–1981.* Reno: University of Nevada Press.

Land, Barbara, and Myrick Land. 1995. *A Short History of Reno.* Reno: University of Nevada Press.

Rowley, William D. 1984. *Reno: Hub of Washoe County.* Woodland Hills, CA: Windsor Publications.

See also Harrah, William F. (in Biographies of Leading Figures in Gambling section).

NEW HAMPSHIRE

New Hampshire has prided itself on being a low-taxation state. It is one of a very few states that has never had a state income tax or sales tax. In the 1950s and 1960s, however, the costs of government were going up, and because the state was familiar with gaming—it had legalized both horse race and dog race wagering decades before, and charitable bingo games were popular—political leaders felt that there was a better way of increasing revenues than raising taxes. In 1963, the legislature came up with a novel idea: sell sweepstakes tickets in the manner used with the Irish Sweepstakes. The state was close to large population concentrations in Massachusetts, Connecticut, and New York. A rationale behind the idea was that the state could gain public revenues from nonresident gamblers. Tickets cost $3 each, and persons purchasing them had to register their names and addresses for drawings. Winners would have horses assigned to them, and the grand prize winners would be those whose horse came in first. There

was considerable interest in the sweepstakes, but ticket sales fell far below expectations. The state was quick to change the lottery format after New York adopted a more direct lottery ticket sales procedure in 1966, and then after New Jersey revolutionized ticket distribution methods as it began its lottery in 1970.

As New Hampshire modernized its lottery in the 1970s, sales picked up, and revenues became an important part of funding for education in the state. New Hampshire formed a partnership with Maine and Vermont to offer the Tri-State Lotto game. Subsequently, they became part of the Powerball consortium. The state had become a winner through a process of imitation.

The legalization of casino gambling for Atlantic City seemed also to call for further imitation in the minds of many. After the momentum for casinos gained speed in the early 1980s, Governor Hugh J. Gallen appointed a Commission for Gambling in 1982. The commission studied jai alai betting, off-track betting, and casinos. The commission came out against all three forms of gambling. Its strongest criticisms were aimed at the casino industry, stating, "for the little promise it holds out as a source of state revenue, [the casino industry] will bring with it serous disadvantages. It will burden the state government and local communities with the cost of policing its operations and providing municipal services for the mass of patrons needed to make it run on a paying basis. It will devastate the existing family-oriented vacation industry" (Dombrink and Thompson 1990, 127). A bill to establish casinos was defeated in the legislature. Since 1982, there have been only futile attempts to expand gambling. Casino bills were again defeated in the legislature in 2005, while simulcast betting was allowed on racetracks in 1991.

References
Dombrink, John D., and William N. Thompson. 1990. *The Last Resort: Success and Failure in Campaigns for Casinos.* Reno: University of Nevada Press, 126–127.

Thompson, William N. 1997. *Legalized Gambling: A Reference Handbook.* 2nd ed. Santa Barbara, CA: ABC-CLIO.

NEW JERSEY AND ATLANTIC CITY

After Nevada, New Jersey is the second leading gambling venue in the United States. The state has one of the nation's premier lottery organizations, it has an active horse racing business, and of course, it has the casinos of Atlantic City.

In 1969, New Jersey became only the third state to institute a government-run lottery. The state's operations were different than those in New Hampshire and New York, the pioneer lottery states. Both of these jurisdictions had fallen short of their desired revenue goals because their games were slow and relatively expensive. New Jersey set its revenue targets, and lottery organizers went after the targets aggressively. They advertised the lottery to wide markets. They reduced the price of tickets to 50 cents each, and they held weekly drawings. Using a new style of ticket distribution, they witnessed unparalleled success. New Jersey became a model for other new lottery states—a model that suggested significant sums of money could be raised through the lottery. The state were widely imitated.

The major reason that New Jersey is a leader in gambling revenues is the fact that the state has authorized land-based casino gambling for Atlantic City. It now has 12 very large casinos, which generate gambling win revenues exceeding $5 billion a year. The casinos of the city draw over 33 million visitors a year to the gambling halls, with more than 1.4 million square feet of gambling space, 43,000 slot machines, and 1,500 tables for games. The hotels also have nearly 16,000 hotel rooms and 700,000 square feet of convention space. More than 46,000 people are employed at the casinos.

For most of a century, New Jersey and urban political corruption seemed to go together like the proverbial horse and carriage, whether it was Jersey City's Boss Frank "I am the law" Hague, or mobsters in control of activities in Newark, or the Republican political machine of Atlantic City. That machine meant Louis Kinley, "Nucky" Johnson, and "Hap" Farley. Scandal surrounded the southern New Jersey beach city that had been known as "the queen of American resorts."

Atlantic City had developed as the premier summer resort after a railroad connected Philadelphia with the seaside in the 1850s. A permanent two-mile-long plank boardwalk along the ocean became a community symbol. Dozens of resort hotels, some being the most luxurious in the country, sprang up near the beach area. A pier was constructed, and carnival rides, pitchmen, and shows featuring palm readers, snake charmers, and freak displays appealed to the masses while other accommodations sought to reach out to the most affluent. By the beginning of the 20th century, more than 700,000 visitors a year were crowding into Atlantic City. The community also attracted the new gangsters who flourished during the Prohibition era, and these individuals had their hand in many illegal activities, including prostitution and gambling. But mainly Atlantic City was known for its entertainment. The Miss America show was created there in 1921, and in 1929 it moved into a new convention center. (In 2003, the show left Atlantic City for Las Vegas.)

The bosses kept illegal activities alive, but the community itself began to undergo a slow death during the Depression years and World War II. Postwar prosperity did not turn the town around, as its infrastructure—its many old hotels—no longer had the amenities that summer visitors demanded. Moreover, better transportation—faster trains and air service—could take vacationers to Florida just as easily as to Atlantic City.

The city fathers had to react, or the community would be totally lost. Kinley and Johnson ended their careers with criminal convictions; Farley looked for a better conclusion for his reign. He was instrumental in winning the Democratic National Convention for the resort in 1964. This exposure, however, only showed the resort for what it was: a decaying relic from the past. Out of that public relations disaster emerged a concerted effort to bring casino gaming to Atlantic City. In 1970, Farley used his political power and his position as a state senator to seek state legislation to authorize a vote on casinos. He was unsuccessful and was soundly defeated for reelection as his political corruption was exposed. Others picked up the casino campaign, however. In 1972, a commission was authorized to study casino gambling. The notion that legalized gambling could help eliminate illegal gambling was voiced, as well as concerns that casinos would bring in more organized crime. The report recommended that the voters of the state decide the question.

A 1974 referendum was placed on the ballot by the legislature. It called for state-owned casinos in communities desiring them. Opposition led by religious groups used the notion that casinos would be in every city—"in your backyard"— and also that the state would be at risk if it were the owner of the casinos. The measure failed by a 60 percent to 40 percent margin.

City fathers were devastated, but in 1976 they reorganized for another battle, making sure the power structure of the state was fully organized on behalf of casinos. Legislative leaders sponsored the bill that put the casino proposition on the ballot. This time the casino proposals called for casinos only in Atlantic City, specified that taxes from casinos would go to aid seniors and the handicapped, and specified that casinos were to be committed to urban redevelopment projects for decaying Atlantic City. The bill also called for casinos that would be private rather than state sponsored. That last provision was important, as the casino advocates had found a company that was operating casinos in the Bahamas—Resorts International Casino of Freeport—that stepped forward to finance most of the campaign. Resorts put more than $1 million into the campaign. The casino proponents included the governor, the legislature, seniors groups, and local leaders throughout the state; opposition was again confined to religious groups. This time the measure passed by a 56 percent to 44 percent margin. Resorts and the other proponents of casinos had spent $1.5 million on the campaign; the church groups opposed to casinos spent $22,000.

The state legislature passed enabling legislation for the regulation of casinos in 1977, and on June 2 of that year Governor Brendan Byrne traveled to Atlantic City to sign the bill into law. Governor Byrne promised that the people of Atlantic City would be helped by the casinos and not hurt by them. To accomplish the goal—revitalizing an economically depressed community with classy casinos run with integrity—the 1977 act created two bodies: the Casino Control Commission (CCC) and the Division

of Gaming Enforcement (DGE). The CCC was an independent body of five full-time members appointed by the governor. It had its own staff. The DGE was part of the state attorney general's office. The DGE investigated license applicants, and also it took initial action against license holders if they violated regulations. Its actions were in the form of nonbinding recommendations to the CCC, however.

The casinos were required to give the state 8 percent of their gambling gross profits to be used for the designated purposes and also additional funds (up to 2.5 percent of gross profits) to be used by a Casino Reinvestment Redevelopment Authority for projects in Atlantic City. Casinos had to be in facilities with 500 hotel rooms each. They would be allowed to have 50,000 square feet of gambling space with 500 rooms, and more space if they had more rooms. There were very strict limits placed over advertising activity. At first the casinos had to close each evening, but after a decade, they were allowed to remain open 24 hours every day. The notion of strict regulation was supported by the placement of state inspectors on the gambling floors at all times, as more than 1,000 regulators were available to monitor the action of the casinos, which eventually numbered 12.

From the onset, it may be suggested that the whole process was compromised. Only one company sought a license at the beginning, and the state was exceedingly interested in gaining revenues from gambling so that it could start fulfilling the many promises made. The first applicant was Resorts International, a company that had developed casinos in the Bahamas. In doing so, the company had developed many ties with questionable characters and had also been involved in giving many gratuities and favors to government officials. The DGE advised that a license not be granted. The CCC after much soul searching agreed to grant a temporary license. In the duration of the temporary license period, the casino realized net profits almost equal to its $75 million capital investment. At the end of the time, it was again investigated by the DGE. The DGE not only reasserted its past reservations about the activity of Resorts International in the Bahamas but also pointed out many violations of New Jersey regulations by the group during the temporary license period. Again the DGE recommended that no license be given. As there were as yet no other casinos in operation, however, the CCC overruled the DGE and a permanent license was granted.

The first casino, Resorts International, started its operations with the temporary license on Memorial Day weekend in 1978. The success of the opening was dramatic, reflecting a strong pent-up demand for legalized gambling on the East Coast. Most players then, as today, came to Atlantic City by roads, with a good share on bus tours. They were not typical tourists in that they stayed only an average of 4 to 6 hours each and spent about $50 each visit.

During the 1980s, many operators rushed into Atlantic City to set up shop. The Golden Nugget, Showboat, Harrah's, and the Tropicana came in from Nevada, and Bally's slot machine company set up its first casino shop in Atlantic City, as did Donald Trump. Some of the casinos experienced substantial success, but for others a reality of flat revenues and slow growth set in. In the early years of casino gambling, the crime rates in the community soared and charges of organized crime involvement

were heard. Yet some researchers claim that the criminal activity was more related to the fact that so many visitors came to town than to the fact that they came to town to visit casinos.

By the time Donald Trump built the largest Atlantic City property, the Taj Mahal, in the late 1980s, the era of growth was put on hold. The casinos were supposed to be a catalyst to cause a rebuilding of the decayed resort city, but this had not happened. Properties near the casinos were boarded up, the city's population declined (although the area population grew), and unemployment levels remained high. The casinos had done their job—they made revenues, and they certainly paid enough in tax revenues to rebuild several Atlantic City–sized cities. There was simply something missing from the political formula. It did not work. On the other hand, casino owners remain optimistic that true success is right around the corner. That optimism received a boost when the Borgata, a joint project of MGM Mirage and the Boyd Gaming Company, opened its casino and its 2,000 luxury hotel rooms.

References

Demaris, Ovid. 1986. *Boardwalk Jungle: How Greed, Corruption and the Mafia Turned Atlantic City into the Boardwalk Jungle.* New York: Bantam Books.

Dombrink, John D., and William N. Thompson. 1990. *The Last Resort: Success and Failure in Campaigns for Casinos.* Reno: University of Nevada Press, 25–41.

Lehne, Richard. 1986. *Casino Policy.* New Brunswick, NJ: Rutgers University Press.

Sternlieb, George, and James W. Hughes. 1983. *The Atlantic City Gamble: A Twentieth Century Fund Report.* Cambridge, MA: Harvard University Press.

NEW MEXICO

New Mexico has many forms of gambling. Horse racing as well as charitable gambling operations have been in existence for many decades. In 1996, a state lottery began operations. Fourteen Native American tribes have been able to negotiate the right to offer casino gambling. They have 19 casinos.

With the expanding gambling establishments, the horse tracks of New Mexico were heavily hit by competition during the 1990s. Over the years the tracks in the state sought relief from the state legislature. Finally, in 1997, the tracks were authorized to have slot machines. The state agreed to let tracks have 300 machines each as long as they could all be tied together in a slot information network. The tracks give 25 percent of the revenue directly to the state and give 20 percent to horsemen through race purses. The tracks keep 55 percent. Machines are permitted to run 12 hours a day, every day—as long as the track offers some racing products.

On May 4, 1999, Ruidoso Downs, less than a half an hour away from the large Native American casino of the Mescalero Apache tribe, was permitted to start operating its machines. The track also has simulcast racing each day of the year so the slot machines are available to players 365 days. Live thoroughbred and quarter horse racing occurs four days a week from Memorial Day to Labor Day. The nation's leading quarter horse race—the All American Futurity—is run on Labor Day. The track is beginning to turn around several years of losses (it never stopped racing), but it would like to be able to stay open longer hours and also have more machines in order to compete more equitably with the Mescalero casino.

Nonprofit clubs are also permitted to have 15 gambling machines each.

References

Casino City. "New Mexico Casinos and New Mexico Gambling." http://newmexico .casinocity.com.

Casino City's Global Gaming Almanac. 2006. Newtown, MA: Casino City, 389.

"New Mexico," http://casinogambling.about .com/od/newmexico/new_Mexico.htm.

New Mexico Lottery, www.nmlottery.com.

New Mexico Racing, www.nmracing.com.

Thompson, William N., and Christopher Stream. 2005. "Casino Taxation and Revenue Sharing: A Budget Game, or a Game for Economic Development." *Thomas M. Cooley Law Review* 22, no. 3 (Michaelmas term): 515—567.

See also Horse Racing; The Racino (in General Topics section).

NEW YORK

New York has been of great historical importance to gambling. With New York being the first state to greet most of immigrants to the United States, New Yorkers saw those immigrants as customers for gambling products. In turn, the immigrants became employees and then the entrepreneurs of gambling. Figures such as Jack Morrissey and Richard Canfield developed casinos that became models for later operators. The first horse racetrack in the New World was on Long Island. Racing has continued to be a major gambling activity throughout the state's history.

When gambling moved westward, it moved with New Yorkers. The Louisiana Lottery was run out of New York City. The early founders of the Las Vegas Strip were from New York; prominent latter-day casino developers in both Las Vegas and Atlantic City have New York roots. New York was the second state to create a lottery (1966), the first state to authorize off-track betting (1971), and the first state to utilize a lotto (progressive jackpot) lottery game (1978).

New York remains an important state for gambling. New York leads the nation in both lottery revenues and revenues from pari-mutuel wagering. The state is the venue supporting several of the nation's major racetracks—Belmont, Aqueduct, and Saratoga. The state receives more public revenue in terms of actual dollars from gambling than any other state. Historically, and in contemporary times, New York has also led the nation in illegal gambling activity.

Given this history, New York officials were very aware of the activity in Atlantic City after May 26, 1978, when the first legal casino gambling began on the boardwalk. Coincidentally, New York was suffering an economic downturn at the time. Not only did the Atlantic City experience look like one New York could duplicate, but New Yorkers feared that competition from Atlantic City could have a drastic effect on hotel trade and other tourism in New York City. It was not long before

there was a concerted effort to get casinos into the Empire State. There were two big barriers to the campaign for casinos, however. First, such gambling authorization would require an amendment to the state constitution. That would take a supermajority in two consecutive legislatures, followed by a vote of the people. Second, interests from around the state wanted casinos in their vicinities. Buffalo and Niagara Falls wanted casinos. The Catskills wanted casinos. So did the Adirondack resort area; and so did several rival locations in the New York City area—the Rockaways, Coney Island, and Manhattan. Legislative representatives could not decide among the communities. Therefore, in 1980, they decided to pass eight different casino amendment bills. Before they could act in 1981, however, Attorney General Robert Abrams wrote a devastating report on Atlantic City, calling it a failure from every possible angle—crime, social consequences, and economic development. The bills did not get out of committees in 1981. Since 1981, bills have been introduced, and there has been lots of talk about casinos and slot machines here and there. Even with the opening of a Niagara Falls, Ontario, casino, which gained over half of its revenues from New York residents, New York officials were slow to build a consensus in favor of any casino proposal. But they kept trying. The Indian Gaming Regulatory Act of 1988 gave lawmakers a vehicle for establishing casinos.

The existence of a wide variety of charity gambling, including "Las Vegas Nights," meant that the state was required to negotiate with Native American tribes for gambling facilities. The Oneida tribe in the central part of the state actually opened a bingo hall in the early 1970s before the Seminoles in Florida did so.

The Seminoles had the resources to take the controversy over Native American gambling through the courts, so they get credit for being the Native gambling pioneers. The Oneidas continued bingo through the 1980s until they negotiated for casino gaming. At first their Turning Stone Casino offered only table games, but now they have over 1,000 machines in the 120,000-square-foot facility. Two other tribes, the Senecas and Mohawks, had bingo games, but there was no other casino until the Mohawks entered into a compact with New York State for a facility in northern New York near the Canadian border. In the early 1990s, the Mohawk site near Massena was the scene of deadly violence as pro- and anti-gambling factions among the tribe contested gambling decisions, and law enforcement officials from Quebec and New York intervened. They have maintained an effective peace since then. Plans to open casinos were in the works there and for other tribes in 2001. When terrorists hit New York on September 11, 2001, the state suffered a financial disaster as well as human losses of life. Lawmakers seized upon the notion of giving multiple tribes the right to have casinos in exchange for up to 25 percent of the slot machine revenues of the facilities. A new law permitted new agreements. Soon the Seneca tribe opened a casino in Niagara Falls, New York, and they set plans for another one in downtown Buffalo. As a result of a land claims lawsuit they and other tribes were given the right to purchase trust lands in Sullivan County, only two hours from New York City. Casino plans for sites there are on the drawing board.

References

Dombrink, John D., and William N. Thompson. 1990. *The Last Resort: Success and Failure in Campaigns for Casinos.* Reno: University of Nevada Press, 98–108.

Thompson, William N., and Christopher Stream. 2005. "Casino Taxation and Revenue Sharing: A Budget Game, or a Game for Economic Development." *Thomas M. Cooley Law Review* 22, no. 3 (Michaelmas term): 515–567.

NORTH CAROLINA

In 1983, North Carolina first permitted limited stakes bingo games offering maximum prizes of $10 per game, as well as raffles. Charities in the state achieve benefits of less than $10 million a year as a result of the games. However, this gaming presented the Eastern Band of Cherokees, who have tribal lands in the western part of the state, to enter a compact with the state in 1994 for machine gaming at their bingo hall. Later the compact was expanded to allow casino table games. The tribe now operates two casinos with a total of 3,300 machines. In the late 1990s, the state authorized up to three video poker machines for bar and restaurant locations. Three thousand locations now have the machines, which are regulated by the State Alcohol Law Enforcement Division.

References
Casino City's Global Gaming Almanac. 2006. Newtown, MA: Casino City, 397.

Report to the Joint Legislative Health Care Oversight Committee on the Effects of the North Carolina Lottery on Incidence of Gambling Addiction. February 1, 2007. http://ncfamilyorg/pdffiles/NCGamblinglegreports07.pdf.

NORTH DAKOTA

The state of North Dakota has perhaps the widest-ranging charity gaming operations based upon casino games in the United States. Residents of the state have played many games of chance ever since statehood was achieved in 1889. Although the games were illegal, authorities were very tolerant of their existence, especially when the beneficiaries of the games were local charities. In the 1970s, the operators of the games began to advertise, and it was clear that they were openly flouting the law.

The attorney general of the state decided to enforce the law. As he did so, he told complaining citizens that if they wanted gambling they should change the state constitution that banned all gambling. The citizens petitioned the legislature to propose an enabling amendment that would permit the legislature to govern gambling. Such an amendment became part of the state constitution with widespread citizen approval in 1976. Then a law was passed legalizing bingo, tip jars (jars filled with a fixed number of pull tabs), pull tabs, and raffles. In 1981, a law was enacted permitting charity blackjack games and poker games. Next the citizens who opposed gambling petitioned to have a vote repealing the law. They got the vote, but not the results they wanted. In 1982, a majority of 63 percent of the voters cast ballots in favor of blackjack.

Blackjack and poker games must be played in sites approved by local governments. The games must be conducted by nonprofit charity organizations certified by the attorney general of the state as qualifying under federal Internal Revenue Service code Section 501c criteria. Individual wagers are limited to $5 per hand. The games are usually held in bars or restaurants, and those enterprises cannot participate in any way in running the games. They must rent their facilities to the charities at a fixed rate that does not depend upon the revenue of the gambling. The establishments may not give any food or beverages to the players, although they may purchase such items. The state imposes a tax ranging from 5 percent to 20 percent (depending upon the amount) on the charities' gambling returns.

Charity gambling provides the most important supporting revenues for major cultural organizations such as public television, the Plains Art Museum in Fargo, and local humanity councils. The leading recipient of funds has been the North Dakota Association of the Disabled.

North Dakota was the only state in the 20th century that experienced voter disapproval of a specific lottery proposal at the ballot box. (Alabama voted against lotteries in 2000.) The voters have defeated lotteries at least three times. The leaders in the campaigns against lotteries have been the officials of the charities running blackjack games. However, the charities took a more relaxed view of a proposition to have the state participate in the multi-state Powerball super lotto games. Such participation was approved by the legislature in 2003 and lotto activity began in 2004.

The state does permit some pari-mutuel gaming; however, there are no major facilities in operation. Under compacts approved in 1994, there are now five major Native American casinos offering machine and table games. They are at Hankinson, Spirit Lake, Fort Yates, New Town, and Belcourt.

References

Cabot, Anthony N., William N. Thompson, Andrew Tottenham, and Carl Braunlich, eds. 1999. *International Casino Law.* 3rd ed. Reno: Institute for the Study of Gambling, University of Nevada, Reno, 135–136.

Casino City's Global Gaming Almanac. 2006. Newtown, MA: Casino City, 398.

OHIO

In 1973, Ohioans voted for legalized lottery gambling with a 64 percent majority vote. The active games generate over $2 billion in sales. Net revenues are dedicated to educational programs. Since the 1930s, most forms of horse racing (thoroughbred, harness, and quarter horse) have had pari-mutuel betting. Telephone wagering and inter-track simulcast race wagering are permitted and are operational; off-track betting has been approved. Ohio also has a very active charitable gaming operation with both bingo games and "Las Vegas Nights."

Ohio citizens have been a strong market for many gambling operations over history. The Ohio River attracted riverboat gamblers during the 19th century, and illegal numbers games and sports betting flourished during the 20th century. Ohio residents have been the primary player base for illegal casinos in Steubenville and also for northern Kentucky locations such as Newport and Covington. The Mayfield Road Gang ran illegal liquor operations during Prohibition and also established gaming outlets for the Cleveland and Toledo populations. Early in his career, gang leader Moe Dalitz operated in the Ohio area before becoming one of the founding fathers of the Las Vegas Strip with the opening of the Desert Inn and Stardust in the 1950s.

In the 1990s Ohio became surrounded by new gaming facilities in nearby states and in Canada. Indiana had riverboat casinos just outside of Cincinnati, Casino Windsor and the new Detroit casinos were but an hour's drive from Toledo, Casino Niagara was within a day's trip of Cleveland, and West Virginia racetracks had machine gaming within miles of the Ohio border. Ohio also provided hundreds of thousands of gamblers for Las Vegas and Atlantic City casinos each year.

The encroaching competition for Ohio gaming dollars generated two concerted campaigns for casinos in the Buckeye State during the 1990s. Both campaigns were led by the Spitzer family, who owned a shipyard in Lorain, just 20 miles outside of Cleveland on the shores of Lake Erie. In 1990, they sponsored a petition drive and statewide election to place a casino boat on their lands. They called the casino a pilot project, suggesting that five years later casinos could be placed in other locations. In the 1990 election, 58 percent of the voters rejected the proposals. In 1996, the Spitzers sponsored a petition drive for five casinos, with two on Lake Erie and three on the Ohio River. That year nearly 52 percent of the Michigan voters said "yes" to Detroit casinos, but in Ohio 62 percent of the voters rejected casinos. As more casinos come to rely on Ohio for gambling patrons in the 21st century, Ohio interests continued to push plans to legalize casinos within their own borders. A 2008 effort followed the opening of slot machine casinos in Pennsylvania. The plan was for a single casino to be located near Wilmington, a town between Columbus and Cincinnati. For the third time since 1990, the voters said "no," this time by a count of 63 percent to 37 percent. Fate changed in 2009. By a margin of 53 percent to 47 percent voters approved four casinos to be located in Cleveland, Colombus, Toledo, and Cincinnati.

References

Ohio Issue 6. 2008. www.ballotpedia.org, accessed September 5, 2009.

Thompson, William N., and Ricardo Gazel. 1995. "The Last Resort Revisited." *Journal of Gambling Studies* 12, no. 3 (Fall): 335–339.

Wacker, R. F., and W. N. Thompson. 1997. "The Michigan Question: A Legal Quandary." *Gaming Law Review* 1 (Winter): 501–510.

See also Dalitz, Morris (in Biographies of Leading Figures in Gambling section).

OKLAHOMA

Legalized gambling has existed in Oklahoma for only a few decades. However, in that time Oklahoma has quietly emerged as a leading gambling venue. Pari-mutuel wagering was authorized by a 58 percent vote of the Oklahoma citizens in 1982. Limited pari-mutuel betting began in 1983. Charitable gambling including bingo games was authorized in 1992. The voters approved a lottery in 2003. Several Native American tribes sought compacts so that they could offer full casino gambling, but the state refused to negotiate (except for off-track betting facilities at bingo halls) until the voters spoke in 2004. They then approved the State-Tribal Gaming Act. The tribes were given the opportunity to sign a model tribal-state compact. By 2009, 33 tribes had done so. They have opened more than 60 casinos. These casinos won in excess of $2 billion for the year. The model compact authorizes the use of gaming machines and also traditional casino table games. Before the compacts, Oklahoma tribes pioneered the establishment of a multistate, multitribal satellite bingo gambling operation that has offered prizes up to a million dollars. The Oklahoma law also provides for machines at tracks. By 2008, there were 45,000 machines in operation in the state.

References

Casino City's Global Gaming Almanac. 2006. Newtown, MA: Casino City, 401–402.

Dombrink, John D., and William N. Thompson. 1990. *The Last Resort: Success and Failure in Campaigns for Casinos.* Reno: University of Nevada Press

McBride, D. Michael, and Susan E. Huntsman. 2007–2008. "Gaming in Oklahoma." In *International Casino Law and Regulation.* Boulder, CO: International Masters of Gaming Law.

OREGON

Oregon has authorized several forms of gambling activities. In 1984, the voters approved a lottery by a margin of 66 percent to 34 percent. The lottery started operations in 1985. The lottery was conducted with traditional lottery games at first. In 1989, the lottery was modified to include betting on sports events through parlay cards, and it was later modified to include making wagers at video lottery terminals. The state of Oregon is one of only four states that is permitted to have sports betting. The lottery runs Sports Action, a program where all bets are made on parlay cards requiring the player to pick winners of at least four games. Point spreads are indicated on the cards for professional football games. The winnings are paid on a pari-mutuel basis, with 50 percent of the bets returned as prizes. Government proceeds from the sports betting are dedicated to university athletic programs. The success of the University of Oregon and Oregon State University varsity teams in recent years attests to the success of the operations.

The state has also permitted card games with financial prizes to be played among players in bars, restaurants, and fraternal clubs (the various establishments may not be participants in the game), and bingo games can be conducted by charitable organizations. Oregon also has had horseracing with pari-mutuel betting for several decades.

These gaming authorizations provided the legal foundation for Native American tribes in Oregon to negotiate agreements with the state in 1992 so that they could offer casino-type games. The authority for Native American gaming is granted in accordance with the Indian Gaming Regulatory Act of 1988. Nine tribal casinos are in operation with machine gaming and bingo in their facilities. The casinos are operated by the Burns Paiute Tribe (Burns), Confederated Tribes of Coos, Lower Umpqua, and Siuslaw (Florence),

Grande Ronde Indian Community (Grande Ronde), Umatilla Indian Reservation (Pendleton), Warm Springs Reservation (Warm Springs), Klamath Tribes (Chiloquin), Coquille Indian Tribe (North Bend), Cow Creek Band of Umpqua Indians (Canyonville), and Siletz Indians (Lincoln City). All the tribes pay the state fees to cover the costs of regulating the games, while several negotiations resulted in revenue sharing arrangements with the state.

References

Casino City's Global Gaming Almanac. 2006. Newtown, MA: Casino City, 410–413.

Oregon Problem Gambling Help Line. "History Highlights: Gambling in Oregon." www.1877mylimit.org/history oforegongambling1.asp.

Thompson, William N. 1997. "Oregon Games: Don't Leave It to Chance." Paper presented to Faculty Forum, School of Urban Studies, Portland State University, November 14.

PENNSYLVANIA

Pennsylvania has had a wide variety of legalized gambling activities for many decades. However, only in the 21st century has Pennsylvania become part of the casino world, as slot machines have been approved for 14 sites across the Keystone State. Continuing controversies over the integrity and political connections of some of the license holders throw a cloud over the new revenues coming into the state as a result of the machine gaming. However, controversy and challenges to the integrity of gambling are not new to the state.

Wagering on harness racing and thoroughbred racing was authorized in the 1930s, but even earlier there was an established illegal network of numbers games and casino games. A state run lottery was established in 1971, and charity bingo was given the stamp of approval by government in 1981. Illegal numbers gambling persisted. This was evidenced by the "666" scandal that touched the state's legal lottery in 1979.

A Pittsburgh television station that announced lottery results controlled the Ping-Pong balls used for the state lottery's numbers game. A "bad" person approached the television announcer and made an offer that should have been refused. But instead the television announcer allowed the person access to the lottery balls and he applied weights (using a paint substance) to all but the "fours" and "sixes." A network of confederates then traversed the state making bets on all three-number combinations of "fours" and "sixes." There were eight such combinations. Unfortunately "666" came up. This is a very popular number for bettors in that it has biblical significance. Not only did the people fixing the contest bet heavily on the number but so too did the general population. With both the population and the illegal gamblers using the state-selected number as their winning number, the state lost more money to winners on that day than they had ever lost before or since that time. The illegal gamblers became suspicious as there were rumors the people were betting heavily on certain numbers in certain locations. In a case of good and evil working together to protect the integrity of the game, the illegal numbers organization launched its own investigation and tracked down people in the network, and then they informed the state police, who in turn were led to the television announcer. He and the others received prison sentences for their involvement. There were two consequences of the "666" scandal that merit consideration. First, there was no state oversight of the rigged game; after all the state ran the game. After cheating was discovered, there was no attempt to close down the game; the numbers game continued without any interruption. Second, the state made no attempt to reimburse the losing players who were cheated in the scandal.

From the moment legal casinos opened in Atlantic City, Pennsylvania could feel the dollars flowing out of their state. Entrepreneurs found it easy to convince many government officials that Pennsylvania had to legalize casinos in order to keep gambling revenues in the state. There have been several campaigns for casinos in the 1980s and 1990s. The first major effort focused upon establishing three casinos in the Pocono Mountains resort area.

Caesars World was a campaign sponsor, as they had purchased four resort properties in the area. Wayne Newton also owned a Pocono property. Several polls and advisory votes were taken in the region, and in all cases the residents rejected the idea. The governor also offered his opposition. Legislative bills for casino failed in 1981, 1982, and 1983. In the early 1990s, following Iowa's lead, there were several bills introduced to permit riverboat casinos. One plan had 20 boats in the state, with from 5 to 10 located in Philadelphia, 5 in Pittsburgh, 2 in Erie, and others in the northeast part of the state. The plan failed to get a floor vote in either house of the legislature. However, in 1999 the boat plan was attached to a plan for slot machines in bars and taverns and at racetracks. The governor said he would approve the bills if they called for a popular referendum. Three bills appeared headed for passage, calling for three separate statewide votes. Opponents, however, maneuvered votes to defeat the measure, and Pennsylvania exited the century with no casinos or machine gaming.

As the 21st century opened, the state faced increasing pressures to fund its many programs. The lottery's revenues were not increasing, and racetrack gambling seemed to be a losing proposition. The governor and track interests seized upon the notion of having racinos provide the answer to the state's budget problems as well as the tracks' economic woes. Several attempts to pass a bill for racinos resulted in ultimate success in July 2004.

In that month, a new state law created the Pennsylvania Gaming Control Board, which was authorized to grant 14 licenses for racinos and slot machine casinos. Together the facilities were permitted to have 60,000 machines. Seven of the licenses were reserved for existing (and one new) racetracks. Seven more were given to new locations. The Philadelphia area was guaranteed four sites, the Pittsburgh area two. Other slot machine sites were designated for Erie, Bethlehem, Chester, Grantville,

Washington, and Bensalem, and also for the Pocono region.

The revenues from the machines were taxed at the rate of 54 percent, with 20 percent going to local governments. Revenues were used for property tax relief as well as aid to the horse owner community through grants and higher purses for horse races. The state had anticipated achieving tax revenues of over $2 billion a year from the gaming activity. Pennsylvania was well on track to meet that goal, as of 2007 with less than one half of the machines in operation, the state's revenue from gaming was $1 billion. Machines were averaging revenues of more than $100,000 each.

References

Collins, Mary D., Michelle Afragola, and Nanette Horner. 2008. "Pennsylvania." In *International Casino Law and Regulation.* Boulder, CO: International Masters of Gaming Law (looseleaf).

Dombrink, John, and William N. Thompson. 1990. *The Last Resort: Success and Failure in Campaigns for Casinos.* Reno: University of Nevada Press, 119–126.

Synder, Brian. 2008. "Maryland's Gamble on Slot Machines." Diamond Back Online, www.diamondbackonline.com/media/storage/papers873/news/2008/04/29/op, accessed October 20, 2008.

Thompson, William N. 1997. *Legalized Gambling: A Reference Handbook*, 2nd ed. Santa Barbara, CA: ABC-CLIO.

RHODE ISLAND

Rhode Island from its inception has been a community marching to its own drummer. In its first era of European settlements, it was a place for persons who rejected the rules of other colonies. In the modern era, immigrants have also left their mark on the character of Rhode Island life. These populations have very willingly become patrons of gambling activity, whether the activities were conducted by illegal mobsters or by a legitimate authority. The state has been only one of four states to permit betting on jai alai games. Parimutuel betting is also authorized for dog and horse tracks. A lottery started in 1974 offers instant games, keno, daily numbers, lotto tickets, and tickets for the Powerball games.

There was an effort to introduce casino gambling into the resort city of Newport in 1980, but an advisory vote showed that 81 percent of the residents did not want casinos. State officials took heed and the effort died. In the late 1990s, the Narragansett Native American tribe won a compact to offer casino-type games; however, no casino was opened by the end of the century.

In 1992, Rhode Island became the second state to have machine gaming at racetracks. The machines were authorized for Lincoln Greyhound Park and a jai alai fronton. The greyhound facility soon dropped "greyhound" from its name and directed most of its advertising toward machine-playing customers. Later the track stopped offering racing altogether. It is now called Twin River Casino. In 2008, there were 4,800 machines opened for play. At first, 33 percent of the machine revenue went to the track and 10 percent went to purses for the dog races. Later the state took 33 percent, the track took 60 percent, and 7 percent went to purses. A second racino—the Newport Grand—has opened with a 50,000 square foot casino that operates 1,070 machines for play.

References

Dombrink, John D., and William N. Thompson. 1990. *The Last Resort: Success and Failure in Campaigns for Casinos.* Reno: University of Nevada Press, 130–131.

"Newport Grand." Casino City. http://casinocity.com/us/rinewpor, accessed November 20, 2008.

"Twin River Casino." Casino City. http://casinocity.com/us/ri/lincoln/lincilnr, accessed November 20, 2008.

See also The Racino (in General Topics section).

SOUTH CAROLINA

The story of South Carolina gambling in modern times has been a fascinating story of video poker machines. In the course of its development, the story led to an unlikely conclusion. South Carolina became only one of two states since 1950 that actually banned a form of casino gambling after it was legally established.

During the 1990s, South Carolina became the land of gambling loopholes. During the 1970s and 1980s, video game machines began to appear in many South Carolina locations. Cash prizes were given to players who accumulated points representing winning scores at the games. No cash was dispensed by the machines; instead, the owners of establishments with the machines paid the players. Although the arrangements seemed on the surface to violate antigambling laws, they survived legal challenges. In 1991, the state supreme court bought into a loophole that the operators offered in their defense.

The operators argued that the machines were not gambling machines as long as the prizes were not given out by the machines directly. The court agreed, and naturally a gaming machine industry began to blossom throughout the state.

Operators "seen their opportunity," as the famous turn-of-the-last-century political philosopher George Washington Plunkitt of Tammany Hall would have said, "and they took 'em." As the gaming revenues flowed in, the operators formed a very strong political lobby to defend their status quo. The legislature addressed the issue of machine gaming, but it could only offer a set of weak rules that have not been rigorously enforced. Legislation provided that gaming payouts for machine wins were supposed to be capped at $125 a day for each player. Advertising was prohibited. There could be no machines where alcoholic beverages were sold, operators could not offer any incentives to get persons to play the machines, and there could be only five machines per establishment. Machines were also licensed and taxed by the state at a rate of $2,000 per year. (Of the tax, $200 is now given to an out-of-state firm to install a linked information system.)

The rules were not followed in their totality. Establishments had linked several rooms, each having five machines. As many as 100 machines appeared under a single roof. Progressive machines offered prizes into the thousands of dollars. Operators claimed they paid each player only $125 of the prize each day. In some cases, they gave the full amount of the prize and had the player sign a "legal" statement affirming that the player will not spend more than $125 of the prize in a single day. Advertisements of machine gaming appeared on large signs by many establishments. Many bars and taverns had machines.

There were thousands of citations against establishments, and fines have been levied. In 1997 and 1998, there were $429,000 in fines in a nine-month period. The practices did not end, however (Palermo 1998, 1, 18).

Several interests in the state did not care for the gambling, and they persuaded the legislature to authorize a statewide vote on banning the machines. According to the legislation authorizing the elections, votes were to be counted by counties. If a majority of the voters in a county said they did not want the machines, the machines would be removed from that county. In 1996, 12 of 46 counties said they did not want the machines. Before they could be removed, however, the operators won a ruling from the state supreme court saying that the vote was unconstitutional. The court reasoned that South Carolina criminal law (banning the machines) could not be enforced unequally across the state. Equal protection under the law ruled supreme in the Palmetto State.

Over the last years of the 1990s, the legislature and state regulators continued to wrestle with issues surrounding machine gaming. One effort to have all the machines declared lotteries and banned in accordance with a state constitutional prohibition on lotteries failed, as the supreme court held by a single-vote majority that the gaming on the machines did not constitute lottery gaming. The 1998 gubernatorial election seemed to turn on gambling issues, as supporters of machine gaming and lotteries gave large donations to the winning candidate. The new governor has sought to win wide support by initiating new "more effective" regulations, but these have not yet won consensus support in the legislature. One new proposed regulation would allow machines to have individual prizes of up to $500 that could be won on a single play. Another proposal would set up a new state regulatory mechanism for machine gaming.

In the meantime, machine gaming flourished. At the beginning of 1999 there were more than 31,000 machines in operation. They attracted over $2.1 billion in wagers, and operators paid out prizes of $1.5 billion. Machine owners and operators realized gross gaming profits of $610 million— approximately $20,000 per machine per year. Almost all of the machines were made outside of the state. Over half were Pot-o-Gold machines made in Norcross, Georgia. These cost $7,500 each. Most of the operators share revenues with owners of slot machine routes. There has been no mandatory auditing of machine performance, although the state authorized the installation of a slot information system.

In 1999 the voters were authorized by the legislature to decide if the machines should stay or be removed. If the voters did not determine the machines could stay, they had to be taken out. But in a surprise decision, the state supreme court ruled the referendum vote unconstitutional. They held that the state's basic law did not provide for the legislature to refer matters to the public for a vote. However, the court also ruled that the remaining part of the legislative bill was intact. Hence, since the voters could not approve the machines, the court ordered that the machines be removed. They were. State leaders, however, were anxious that the tax revenue from the machines not be lost to the state. They urged a petition drive for a lottery. In November 2000, the voters removed a constitutional ban on lotteries. A lottery began operations in 2001.

In addition to a state lottery, South Carolina permits bingo games. One Native American tribe in the state runs a bingo hall, as do charities. The state is also the site of docking for two cruise boats that take players into international waters so that they may participate in casino games.

Coauthored by Frank Quinn

References

Casino City's Global Gaming Almanac. 2006. Newtown, MA: Casino City, 415.

Palermo, David. 1998. "The Secret Slot Market." *International Gaming and Wagering Business* (December): 1, 18–22.

Thompson, William N. 1999. "South Carolina." In *International Casino Law*, 3rd ed. Edited by A. Cabot, W. Thompson, A. Tottenham, and C. Braunlich, 137. Reno: Institute of Gambling Studies, University of Nevada, Reno.

Thompson, William N. 1999. "The South Carolina Battlefield." *Gaming Law Review* 3, no. 1 (February): 5–8

Thompson, William N., and Frank Quinn. 2000. "South Carolina Sage: Death Comes to Video Machine Gambling: An Impact Analysis." Paper presented to National Conference on Problem Gambling, 6 October, Philadelphia, Pennsylvania.

SOUTH DAKOTA

At the ballot box in November 1988, the voters of South Dakota made the state the nation's third commercial casino jurisdiction. The voters amended the state constitution to permit limited stakes gambling, but only in the town of Deadwood. In 1989, the legislature passed an enabling act, and the voters of Deadwood ratified the decision to have casinos in their town. Several casinos opened in November 1989, and there are now 35 in Deadwood. The ostensible purpose of casino gaming was to generate revenues for tourist promotion and for historical preservation projects in Deadwood. Wild Bill Hickok had been shot in the back while playing poker in Deadwood in 1876, but the town was a decaying relic from that time. The town's main block of buildings had burned in the mid-1980s.

Prior to casino gaming, the state had permitted dog race and horse race wagering. The state instituted a lottery in 1987, and in 1989 the lottery began operation of video lottery terminals in age-restricted locations. There are 1,415 locations, with more than 8,200 machines. Each location is allowed to have as many as 20 machines that award, on average, 80 percent of the money played as prizes given back to the players. In the 1990s, nine Native American casinos compacted with the state to operate facilities. There are now 10 tribal casinos. Casinos are located at Sisseton, Hankinson, Watertown, Wagner, Lower Brule, Mobridge, Fort Thompson, Valentine, Pine Ridge, and Flandreau.

The commercial casinos in Deadwood were originally allowed to have 30 games (machines or tables), but as facilities were built together, the state changed the limitation to 90 games each for a single retail location. In addition to machines, which guaranteed prizes equaling 90 percent of the money played, the only games permitted were blackjack and poker. Bets were first limited to $5 per play, but the limit was later raised to $100 by a vote of the people in 2000. In poker games, the casino can rake-off as much as 10 percent of the money wagered. The casinos pay 8 percent of their winnings to the state in taxes; of this, 40 percent goes to tourist promotions, 10 percent to the local government, and 50 percent to the state for regulatory purposes. If regulatory costs fall below this amount, the remaining money is dedicated to historical preservation projects.

In 1989, the lottery began using video machines located in restaurants and bars around the state. Antigambling groups have constantly opposed this machine gambling, viewing it convenience gambling that only hurts local economies. They have been able to place the question of eliminating the lottery machines on the ballot many times, with the same results. They have lost many times. In 1992, 62 percent of the votes said "keep the machines," in 1994, 52.8 percent said "keep them," in 2000, the vote in favor of machines was 53.7 percent, and in 2006, it was 67 percent in favor of machines.

References
Cabot, Anthony N. 1999. "South Dakota." In *International Casino Law*, 3rd ed. Edited by A. Cabot, W. Thompson, A. Tottenham, and C. Braunlich, 138–153. Reno: Institute of Gambling Studies, University of Nevada, Reno.
Casino City. "South Dakota Casinos and South Dakota Gaming." http://southdakota.casinocity.com, accessed December 10, 2008.

TENNESSEE

When Tennessee received statehood in 1796, becoming the 15th state, it was a land on the frontier filled with individualists. Leaders such as Andrew Jackson were very active gamblers, playing many kinds of card games and also wagering on horse races. The heritage of wide-open community life did not last into the 20th century. In the modern era, horse race betting was legalized; however, tracks were not economically viable, and all of them closed before the 1990s. As the 21st century began, Tennessee was one of only three states without any legalized gambling. That changed, however, as a lottery was authorized, and games started in January 2004. The state followed a model initiated in Georgia, which designates that state revenues from lotteries be given to education causes including college scholarships. Following the adoption of the lottery, the state also gave permission to charities to run raffles and bingo games.

References

Thompson, William N. 1997. *Legalized Gambling: A Reference Handbook.* 2nd ed. Santa Barbara, CA: ABC-CLIO, 163–166, 176.

U.S. Casinos: American Gambling Guide & Casino Directory. "Tennessee Casinos and Gambling." www.uscasinolinks.com/index.php?page=141.

Texas

Texas has been the home to gamblers since its inception as a political entity. Whether the Texans were on the frontier in gambling saloons, in illegal Galveston or Dallas casinos, or off in Las Vegas (on in recent years, Shreveport, Louisiana), they have loved the "action." The attorney general of the state, Will Wilson, cracked down on illegal casinos in Galveston in 1957, prompting an effort to legalize the gambling. The efforts were aborted after local voters expressed a dislike for the casinos in advisory votes. Periodically there have been weak attempts to gain support for casinos, but these have all been unsuccessful. In the meantime, charitable gambling operations have been established in the state. Also, "gray" machines offering winners coupons for merchandise have existed openly in truck stops across the state, although their legality has been questioned.

In 1992, the state launched a lottery, which quickly became one of the most successful in the United States, trailing only New York in sales for some years. The lottery offered instant games, lotto, and daily numbers games. Horse racing experienced ups and downs in attempts at legislation over seven decades, but finally in the 1990s licensing for tracks began. There are now six tracks, the biggest being the Lone Star Park near Dallas–Fort Worth. There is also one dog track in La Marque.

The state has three Native American reservations. One—the Alabama-Coushatta—is near Livingston, 70 miles north of Houston. The tribal members once voted against casinos, as they believed that outside gamblers would disturb their quality of life. They are also strongly religious. Another vote in 1999 supported the opening of a casino. Two other tribes, the Kickapoos in Eagle Pass

A lottery ticket machine in a Texas grocery store.

and the Tiguas in El Paso, started gambling operations with bingo games, card games, and machines. The state has refused to negotiate compacts with the two tribes, and legal controversies have surrounded the gambling. Nonetheless, the tribal casinos persisted with their gaming. The state of Texas sued the Tiguas and Alabama-Coushattas, claiming that their tribal lands were given trust status with the understanding that they would not have casinos. In 2001, federal courts upheld the state position and in a rare outcome ordered the two casinos

closed. The Kickapoo casino remained "legally" opened, with 450 slot machines and 22 table games, while the other tribes maintained some gaming activity.

References

Casino City. "Texas Casinos and Texas Gambling." http://texas.casinocity.com, accessed December 10, 2008.

Dombrink, John D., and William N. Thompson. 1990. *The Last Resort: Success and Failure in Campaigns for Casinos.* Reno: University of Nevada Press, 138–144.

UTAH

Utah is one of two states to enter the 21st century with no legally authorized form of gambling (the other is Hawaii).

Efforts to have gambling have consistently failed. In 1992, the voters defeated a proposal to establish pari-mutuel betting on horse racing. Horse races are conducted at fairs, but no betting is permitted. Throughout the state, there are small charity games, but these are operating contrary to the law. Utah residents are not totally adverse to casino betting, however, as Nevada casino entrepreneurs have set up facilities near state lines in order to capture their patronage. Several casinos in Mesquite, Nevada (in Clark County, 30 miles from St. George), and Wendover, Nevada (in White Pine County, 100 miles from Salt Lake City), market their products to Utah gamblers.

Periodically, supporters of casino gambling in Utah try to start campaigns for casinos by pointing out that gambling money is leaving the state. The political leaders of what is probably the most church-oriented state in the union do not, however, give much attention to the advocates of any form of gambling.

Reference

Thompson, William N. 1997. *Legalized Gambling: A Reference Handbook.* 2nd ed. Santa Barbara, CA: ABC-CLIO, 162–167.

VERMONT

Vermont ranks 46th in gambling revenues among the 47 states that have some form of legalized gambling. Only Alaska has less gambling. Vermont began operation of a state lottery in 1978. Of the 38 lottery jurisdictions in the United States (37 states plus the District of Columbia), only Montana sells fewer tickets. Although Vermont is a very small state, it has not joined the Powerball multistate lottery that was designed so that small states could generate sales through offering large jackpot prizes. Previously, the state did join with New Hampshire and Maine in the Tri-State lotto game.

Although horse-race betting is permitted at Vermont tracks, there were no such tracks. There is a short dog racing season at the Green Mountain racetrack.

The closest the state has come to considering casino gambling has been the effort of the Abenaki Native Americans to have lands in the state declared to be reservation lands. It is assumed that if they ever get federal recognition, they will seek also to gain a compact for gambling.

References

Powell, Michael. 2002. "Vermont's Abeniki Fight for Recognition, Heritage." *Washington Post,* December 8, www.washingtonpost.com/ac2/wp-dyn?pagename=article&node=&contentid=A23896-2002Dec7.

Thompson, William N., and Christopher Stream. 2005. "Casino Taxation and Revenue Sharing: A Budget Game, or a Game for Economic Development." *Thomas M. Cooley Law Review* 22, no. 3 (Michaelmas term): 515–567.

Vermont Lottery, www.vt.lottery.com.

VIRGINIA

Virginia established a lottery in 1988 after many false starts over the previous 15 years, with 56 percent of the voters supporting the lottery proposition. Virginia participates in the multistate Big Game lotto, as well as selling its own lotto tickets, numbers games, and instant tickets. The revenues of the lottery are earmarked for educational purposes. Charitable gaming is also permitted, and there are facilities for off-track race betting. There is no casino gambling, as the state has successfully fought off efforts of ocean cruise ships to dock at ports in the state.

Although Virginia has come to gambling authorizations only recently in the modern era, the state certainly has had a history of gambling. Within the first five years of its existence as an English colony, Virginia became the beneficiary of a lottery authorized by King James. In 1620, 20 mares were shipped from England to Virginia Colony, and horse racing with private wagering became a regular activity for the settlers. In later colonial days, lotteries were prevalent. George Washington and Thomas Jefferson participated in most forms of gambling—they played cards, raced horses, and were involved in lotteries. Jefferson conducted a lottery in 1826 in an effort to dispense of his property so that he could pay all his debts prior to his death. Unfortunately, he died before this result could be realized.

Reference

Thompson, William N. 1997. *Legalized Gambling: A Reference Handbook.* 2nd ed. Santa Barbara, CA: ABC-CLIO, 7–9, 89–90.

WASHINGTON

Legalized gambling in the state of Washington was confined to horse tracks until the 1970s ushered in charity gaming. Pari-mutuel horse race betting was established with the opening of the Longacres course in 1933. The state now has five tracks—but not Longacres. The Longacres facility was purchased by Boeing Aircraft Company for plant use, and the track closed in 1992.

In 1973, a gambling commission was created and charities were soon authorized to have bingo games and "casino nights." In 1982, a state lottery was established. The state's tribal reservations won permission to have casino gambling in 1992, albeit machine gaming was confined to player-banked systems known as Class Two machines. Small commercial operations also won the right to have limited machine and house banked table gaming in 1997. Player banked card games had been legal since the early 1970s. There are now about 90 minicasinos.

There are 32 Native American casinos operating under state-negotiated compacts, pursuant to the Indian Gaming Regulatory Act. In 1996, the voters of the state were asked to approve slot machines for the tribes. Only 44 percent were in favor of the machines. The state also authorizes instant video ticket machines (IVTMs) to dispense instant lottery tickets (scratch-off tickets) directly to a buying public that inserts currency into the machine for tickets. These machines can be placed in any location in the state and dispense tickets 24 hours a day, 365 days a year.

The commercial minicasinos are not small facilities, as they offer players up to 15 live casino games that operate almost identically to the casino table games found in Las Vegas. They certainly have the form and appearance of table games in Las Vegas. The minicasinos call themselves casinos.

References

Casino City's Global Gaming Almanac. 2006. Newtown, MA: Casino City, 424–434.

Christiansen, Eugene Martin. 1999. "The 1998 Gross Annual Wager." *International Gaming and Wagering Business* (August): 20*ff*.

Miller, Frank. 2007–2008. "Washington." *International Casino Law and Regulation.* Boulder CO: International Masters of Gaming Law.

"North American Gaming Report 1998." 1998. *International Gaming and Wagering Business* (July): S27–S28.

WEST VIRGINIA

West Virginia launched a state lottery in 1986. By that date, horse race wagering was firmly in place, having won legislative authorization in 1933. Charitable bingo games were also popular. The appearance of the lottery gave the tracks of the state a hook with which they sought to win the right to have machine gambling, which they achieved in the 1990s.

The West Virginia legislature authorized an experimental installation of video gaming machines—keno machines, poker machines, and machines with symbols—at Mountaineer horse racing track beginning on June 9, 1990. At first, only 70 machines were installed. During the experimental time, the number grew to 400 in 1994, most of them being keno machines. The first machines had payouts of 88.6 percent. During a three-year experimental period the lottery agreed not to put machines in other locations. Now machines are at the three other tracks as well: Charles Town, Wheeling Island, and Tri-State—the latter two being dog track facilities. The tracks keeps 70 percent of the revenues, and 30 percent goes to the state. There are now more than 11,000 machines at the tracks. Lottery machines are also permitted in more than a thousand bars and taverns.

The machines are operated by the state lottery. Lottery director Butch Bryan said, "We developed VLTs [video lottery terminals] to save our horse racing industry. We think it is doing what we designed it for. It has been very beneficial to the horse track. It may not cure their problems in the long run, but it will certainly prolong their life. We believe the entertainment aspect of VLTs is good for the horse racing industry" (LaFleur 1992, 65). In 1993, Bryan was convicted of insider trading, bid rigging, and lying to a grand jury in the state's purchase of the machines. He reportedly owned stock in the major company that won the supply contract. His problems, however, have not affected operations and the demand for more gaming. In response to the expansion of gaming in Pennsylvania, in 2007 the state legislature approved a measure allowing casino table games at the four tracks if they receive local voter approval.

References

Casino City's Global Gaming Almanac. 2006. Newtown, MA: Casino City, 436.

La Fleur, Terri. 1992. "Charting the Growth of Video Lottery." *International Gaming and Wagering Business* (August–September): 1, 62, 64–65.

Thompson, William N. 1999. "Racinos and the Public Interest." *Gaming Law Review* 3(5–6): 283–286.

"West Virginia Lawmakers OK Casino Table Games." *Pittsburgh Post Gazette,* March 9, 2007.

WISCONSIN

The state constitution of Wisconsin adopted at the time of statehood in 1848 mandated that the legislature "shall never authorize any lottery." Those words were a death sentence hanging over all gambling for nearly 120 years. In 1965, the voters of the state responded to demands from charities that they be able to have fundraising activities using games. The constitution was changed to allow sweepstakes. The legislature took notice, and in 1973 charitable bingo was permitted. In 1977, raffles became legal. Betting on horse and dog racing was legalized in 1987, as was a new state lottery when voters removed the constitutional ban.

The primary form of gambling in Wisconsin is found in the 24 casinos located on 11 Native American reservations. The casino gambling was legally authorized in compacts between the tribes and the state, first negotiated in 1992, renewed in 1998, and then renewed again five years later in 2003. The 1998 compacts permit machine gaming and blackjack table games as well as bingo, and the tribes agree to pay the state 3 percent of the revenues they win.

The largest gaming complex in the state is on the Oneida reservation near Green Bay. The complex, which includes a full-service Radisson Inn Hotel, a new casino, and a bingo hall as well as satellite gaming areas, has over 4,000 machines and 120 blackjack tables.

The development of casino gambling in Wisconsin fits the general scheme in the United States. It did not happen "on purpose." Using the status of a charity, the Oneidas offered a bingo game in September 1975. Other tribes did the same. For several years, Wisconsin tribes ran games according to the state's legislated rules.

Like other tribes with severe economic needs, however, they took notice when in 1978 a Seminole reservation in Hollywood, Florida, decided to gain an edge on its bingo non–Native American competition. The tribes began offering very large prizes, which violated the state's rules. The large prizes immediately attracted large droves of customers, and profits increased. As with the Seminoles, the Wisconsin tribe's actions were upheld as being legal. During the 1980s, Wisconsin tribes experimented with a variety of games. The Menominees used a Ping-Pong ball device to generate numbers for roulette games and also to indicate cards for blackjack games. But the real casino games came in 1987, following the U.S. Supreme Court's Cabazon ruling.

In March 1987, the Menominees decided to offer regular blackjack games at their gaming facility. In April 1987, just two months after the Cabazon ruling, the voters were asked to amend the state constitution to remove the ban on lotteries. The legislature had put the question on the ballot. The public wanted a lottery to compete with lottery games in Illinois and Michigan and passed the measure by a 70 percent to 30 percent margin.

Based on the lottery amendment, in 1989 the state Department of Justice indicated that the state could negotiate agreements (under provisions of the Indian Gaming Regulatory Act) with the reservations that would permitg them to have casino games. Yet when the state did not follow through on negotiations, the tribes took the matter to federal courts, where they won a ruling forcing the state to negotiate. Soon after, the governor signed compacts. However, these limited the tribal casino games to machines and blackjack.

In 1992, after the governor had concluded casino compacts for the other reser-vations, the Forest County Potawatomis tribe asked the governor if they could have casino games in Milwaukee. The governor and the tribe compromised and reached an agreement allowing 200 machines at the bingo facility. At a later date, they were allowed to have 1,000 machines. As the tribes renewed compacts in 1998 and 2003, they agreed to share revenues with the state, and the state allowed them to have more types of casino games. In 2005 the state received $100 million as their share of the casino winnings. The casinos collectively have 16,000 gaming machines and 300 table games.

In the first decade of the 21st century, the tribes' casinos were winning over a billion dollars a year. Several tribes sought new off-reservation locations for casinos. The four dog tracks of the state were considered to be good casino sites. However three smaller tribes were denied the opportunity to complete a deal for a dog track in Hudson, Wisconsin, because of a decision made by the U.S. secretary of the interior, Bruce Babbitt. A federal special prosecutor then investigated Babbitt, as his political party (the Democrats) had taken large contributions from larger rival tribes that did not want competition from a new casino at the track. He was cleared of any wrong doing, but the tribes were still denied the opportunity for a new casino.

References

Casino City's Global Gaming Almanac. 2006. Newtown, MA: Casino City, 437.

Minash, Linda. 2007–2008. "Wisconsin." In *International Casino Law and Regulation.* Boulder CO: International Masters of Gaming Law.

Thompson, William N., Ricardo Gazel, and Dan Rickman. 1995. *The Economic Impact of Native American Gaming in Wisconsin.* Milwaukee: Wisconsin Policy Research Institute. 50 pp.

Thompson, William N., Ricardo Gazel, and Dan Rickman. 1995. *The Social Costs of Gambling in Wisconsin.* Mequon, WI: Wisconsin Policy Research Institute

WYOMING

Gambling in Wyoming is quite limited. There is a quarter horse racing circuit that draws betting action to tracks at Evanston, Gillette, and Rock Springs. There are also charity bingo games and bingo games operated by the Wind River Reservation. Wyoming residents are within the marketing areas for the casinos of both Colorado and Deadwood, South Dakota. The state also borders Montana, with its many machine gambling halls. For this reason, there have been several attempts by Wyoming business groups and by some political leaders to authorize machine gambling in taverns as well as allowing low-stakes card games. These efforts, however, have never received serious consideration.

References

Casino City. "Wyoming Casinos and Wyoming Gambling." www.casinocity.com/us/wy/cities.html.

"Gambling in the Sate of Wyoming." www.wyominggamblingforum.com.

"Wyoming and Gambling." www.gamblingmagazine.com.

Section Five

ANNOTATED BIBLIOGRAPHY

———————————

Abt, Vicki, James F. Smith, and Eugene Martin Christiansen. 1985. *The Business of Risk: Commercial Gambling in Mainstream America*. Lawrence: University Press of Kansas.

The Business of Risk is perhaps the most comprehensive academic treatment of the gambling industry to be published in the 1980s. The book covers a lot of ground. The authors present a historical development of gaming, followed by a string of evidence detailing the economic power of the industry in the mid-1980s. They present a philosophical analysis of the gambling phenomenon, but more important, they realize that there are crucial differences among the variety of games that are offered for play under the rubric of commercial gambling. They offer a detailed critique of factors that describe state lotteries, casinos, and pari-mutuel betting. Thirteen factors are used for comparisons: (1) the frequency of playing opportunities, (2) prize payout intervals, (3) the range of odds, (4) the range of stakes, (5) the degree of player participation, (6) the degree of skill in the game, (7) willing probabilities, (8) addictive qualities and relationships with other addictions, (9) payout ratios, (10) credit and cash play possibilities, (11) the price of the game, (12) intrinsic interest within the game, and (13) the extent of knowledge needed to play the game.

Abt and her associates also consider the location of the play, the situations surrounding the play, the ownership of the operations, and the bottom-line pub-lic purposes of the gambling activity. A valuable contribution for readers is that the authors treat players as individuals. They do not drift into a common pattern of lumping all players together as deviants or pathological types. Instead, they give a reasoned discussion to many categories of players, including casual players, occasional players, risky (risk-seeking) players, professional gamblers, habitual gamblers, serious gamblers, and—the two categories that receive most treatment elsewhere—obsessive gamblers and compulsive gamblers. The authors clearly see that for the majority of participants, gambling is a normal phenomenon. In this respect the authors proceed to view commercial gambling as a social institution that represents an extension of other legitimate leisure activities. The acceptance of gambling is measured as part of the broader values of the culture.

In the final chapter, Abt, Smith, and Christiansen tried what few before them had tried. They sought to find a model of gambling that could fit "the public interest," noting that "the public good should be the first and overriding consideration of gambling policy" (213). They do not address the topic with precision, nor do they offer the means for accomplishing the goals of achieving the good model. Nonetheless, they advance ideas worthy of consideration even now (more than 20 years later). The public interest must incorporate concerns for player losses as well as for revenues gained for the industry and for government coffers. Jobs gained through gambling enterprise should be considered along with jobs gained or lost in other economic sectors as a result of the gambling activity. Close attention should be given to the relationships of legal and illegal gambling. Does the one drive the other out, or are they complementary activities? The price of legal gambling should be low enough so that players will not seek out illegal gambling competitors. Games must be run honestly, and society must seek to mitigate the harm that arises from excessive gambling by the few. The authors present ample evidence that people do want to gamble, and so the authors support legalization as a freedom of activity issue as well. It is refreshing that three authors who are interested in gambling, who support the existence of legal gambling, also express the viewpoint that gambling can have both good and bad sides and that policymakers should seek out the good side as they consider legalization and regulation.

American Gaming Association (AGA). 1996. *The Responsible Gaming Resource Guide*. Kansas City, MO: AGA.

The American Gaming Association was formed in 1994 as the public relations arm of the commercial casino industry in the United States. From the onset, the organization has expressed concern about problem gambling and the need to have programs to mitigate the negative impacts of irresponsible gambling. The association has found that the industry is positioned vis-à-vis critics much as the tobacco industry and the liquor industry are. Looking at those two industries for models of reaction to criticism, the gambling industry is trying very hard to avoid the posture taken by tobacco, namely a stonewalling posture of denial of problems until there becomes no room for reasonable change. On the other hand, the liquor industry has taken a lead in admitting that drinking causes major problems in society as it seeks to work with other groups in mitigating the problems through general awareness and campaigns such as "the designated driver" program.

The association has sponsored many university research programs, including studies of the prevalence rates of problem gambling and of the effectiveness of public awareness campaigns and treatment programs. They also invited Carl Braunlich of the faculty at Purdue University and Marvin Steinberg, executive director of the Connecticut Council on Compulsive Gambling, to prepare *The Responsible Gaming Resource Guide*. The purpose of the guide is "to disseminate as widely as possible the best programs, approaches and ideas available for dealing with problem and underage gambling" (7). Dealing with problem and underage gambling has been viewed as "good business" by the industry.

The *Guide* offers 16 chapters covering a range of related topics. It leads off with an attempt to find consensus in a definition of problem gambling; it then offers suggestions for mission statements that casinos may utilize as they approach the problem gamblers in their midst. Employee assistance programs are described, as are awareness programs. The authors point to the need for customer awareness as well, and they offer suggestions for signage. Casino credit policies are examined and analyzed as means for mitigating problem gambling. The *Guide* provides a lengthy listing of problem-gambling programs that are available in each of the 50 states plus the District of Columbia. An appendix presents the common measuring devices, such as the Gamblers Anonymous question list, the criteria of the fourth edition of the *Diagnostic and Statistical Manual of Mental Disorders,* and the South Oaks Gambling Screen. There are also bibliographic entries and a wide range of advertising posters that have been utilized by casinos to warn of the problems of gambling and to discourage youth gambling.

The *Responsible Gaming Resource Guide* is a very valuable tool for every gambling enterprise, as it gives helpful hints for this very important arena for public relations. The *Guide* is also valuable for policymakers and students of the gambling phenomenon.

Asbury, Herbert. 1938. *Sucker's Progress: An Informal History of Gambling in America from Colonies to Canfield.* New York: Dodd, Mead.

Asbury's *Sucker's Progress* stands as a classic book on gambling mainly because it offers one of the first comprehensive historical treatments of the subject from the first days of the American nation. Today other books rival and surpass it, however, in intellectual content. Asbury's book seems to just present the topic. It has no introduction, no conclusion, and no theory, and offers little in the way of direction except for part II's chronological order of events that follow part I's chapters concerning specific games—faro, poker, craps, lotteries, and numbers. Reviews have faulted the book for lacking any moral condemnation of gambling and for taking the opposite approach and glamorizing the topic through an admiration of the scoundrels portrayed on the pages.

The many details in the book are not documented, although there is an extensive bibliography. Even though Herbert Asbury does not really show the reader a forest, he more than makes up for that by showing trees, trees, and more trees. The chronology begins with tales of gambling in New Orleans, which he calls the Fountainhead of Gambling in the United States. The story goes back to the days of the first French settlers in the area and carries through to the role played by New Orleans and the Mississippi River during the Mexican War and the later Civil War. The activities of the early gambling pioneers are featured—John Davis, Edmund Pendleton, Canada Bill Jones, George Devol, and Michael Cassius McDonald. Asbury describes gambling on the western frontier, with glimpses of casino games in Kansas City, Denver, San Francisco, El Paso, and Santa Fe, as well as in the mining camps. His book ends up back in the East with major chapters on John Morrissey and Richard Canfield.

One particularly interesting facet of the perspectives offered is that they are made before Nevada emerged as the gambling capital of the world. There are no references to either Las Vegas or Reno, and the book was written in the 1930s.

Barker, Thomas, and Marjie Britz. 2000. *Jokers Wild: Legalized Gambling in the Twenty-First Century.* Westport, CT: Praeger.

This up-to-date volume treats legalized gambling behavior as a given for society, yet as a phenomenon that has both positive and negative consequences. Barker and Britz present cogent descriptions of gambling and various types of gambling activity along with a history of the development of the gambling industry in the United States. Considerable attention is given to Las Vegas and how gambling in that Mecca changed from the Mob days to the corporate megaresort models of today. A full chapter titled "The Dam Bursts" is devoted to the breakthrough in casino legalizations that accompanied the passage of the Indian Gaming Regulatory Act of 1988 and the authorization of riverboat and small-stakes casinos in Iowa, South Dakota, and Colorado.

There is an excellent descriptive chapter on state lotteries as well as an account of the use of the Internet in wagering. The book surveys the issue of compulsive gambling and the relationship of crime and gambling as well as the economic impacts of gambling. A later chapter looks at the work of the National Gambling Impact Study Commission, and an appendix lists all of the commission's recommendations. Another appendix reviews the nature of gambling in 34 separate jurisdictions within the United States.

Barthelme, Frederick, and Steven Barthelme. 1999. *Double Down: Reflections on Gambling and Loss*. Boston: Houghton Mifflin.

The Barthelme brothers are college professors at the University of Southern Mississippi. They teach English, and they write. In this book, the brothers record their trials related to the loss of both of their elderly parents within a short span of time and their increasing losses at the machines and tables of Gulf Coast casinos in Mississippi. Neither had developed his own nuclear family. They record the emotions of family travail that is contemporary as well as part of their psychological past, and they try to relate their gambling problems to the emotions evoked. Their text suggests that gambling activity has provided each of them with a coping mechanism. They have gone through many of the phases of pathological gambling—the big wins, the losses, and chasing behaviors. Yet they indicate that they continued to meet their daily obligations and expectations as college professors, family members, and friends. Their financial gambling losses were supported by a substantial (six figure) but not excessive inheritance. In a sense they say that the money is unearned and undeserved, and hence they give themselves an excuse for throwing much of it away at the casinos—as they are conscious they are doing.

They are saved (perhaps—the final sequence has not been recorded) by a casino that mysteriously overlooks its own self-interest and formally accuses them of engaging in cheating activity. The casino had exploited more than $100,000 from the brothers, yet in a totally misplaced desire for security for security's sake alone, the casino accuses them (while they are losing) of exchanging signals with a blackjack dealer, ostensibly to secure knowledge about the value of the hole card. After the brothers go through the indignity of an arrest and many months of pondering their fate as potential felons, the charges are simply dropped.

In the meantime, the brothers go through a nongambling phase, but then return to another area casino for more affordable action, their basic "fortune" having been dissipated. They go through the entire progression—which at the end does not seem to reveal a "cure"—without benefit of either therapy or Gamblers Anonymous. While they are gambling they exhibit all the emotions and rationales offered by prototypical pathological gamblers, yet at the end they portray themselves as individuals who have returned to rationality. Either they are in a deep denial of their condition, or somehow they illustrate the opportunities for recovery and learning how to gamble more responsibly that are suggested in the work of John Rosecrance (*see* Rosecrance, *Gambling without Guilt*).

Braidwaite, Larry. 1985. *Gambling: A Deadly Game*. Nashville, TN: Broadman Press.

Although *Gambling: A Deadly Game* is presented as if it were a neutral academic study, it is indeed a straightforward attack on gambling. For the person interested in having an overview of the arguments of the opposition to gambling, it does provide a reasonably good starting point. Such a reader would also want to look at the works of Robert Goodman, David Johnston, and Ovid Demaris that are summarized in this annotated bibliography.

Larry Braidwaite's attack on gambling is a broadside. It has a moralistic tone definitely reflecting the deontological view that this "sin" is always "sin," here, there, everywhere, then, now, and forever. Braidwaite sees modern gambling as a force that seduces conservative political leaders as it purports to offer an alternative to increased general taxation. Contemporary state lotteries are denigrated as being sources of regressive taxation. Moreover, lotteries are blamed for

increases in criminal activity. In a twisted logic pattern, Braidwaite decries the expansion of horse race gambling, saying that more racing only means that the race competition will be among second-rate horses—hence depriving racing fans of high value by giving only low-quality racing. One wonders if there is high-quality horse racing at county fair meets that do not have pari-mutuel betting. Braidwaite also finds that tracks are frequented by organized crime characters who do unsavory things to influence races—for example, drugging horses.

The casinos of Atlantic City receive the bulk of his criticism of that form of gambling. There the patron is seen as the elderly day tripper who arrives on a bus only to lose money that he or she cannot afford to lose. But what is worse, that customer is not given a good entertainment value for the money that is spent. The author does not speak to the entertainment values that the typical visitor to Las Vegas can receive outside of the casinos. Braidwaite also attacks widespread illegal sports betting as well as charity gambling—particularly games run by churches. He finds that these games do not further true "Christian" goals.

The information on compulsive gambling in Braidwaite's last chapter is well documented but still somewhat suspect. It is followed by a lengthy discussion of the need for Christian values in a political process encompassing changes in gambling policy. Even though the book is not always based on facts, it nonetheless does make a good presentation of the antigambling case.

Brenner, Reuven, and Gabrielle A. Brenner. 1990. *Gambling and Speculation: A Theory, a History, and a Future of Some Human Decisions*. New York: Cambridge University Press.

The Brenners present a defense of gambling by attacking its opponents. Their general conclusion holds that the opponents are self-interested parties, such as churches, government, and commercial enterprises, who want to be protected from competition from commercial gambling enterprise. Churches and other religious groups have endorsed the use of lots for determining God's will in decision-making situations. They have also used games for social situations and even for raising money for their religious activities. Governments have commanded the time, energy, and finances of the citizenry in times of war and during other situations of public need. Commercial enterprise has also come to rely upon the energies and loyalties of a workforce. Commercial gambling has posed a threat to all three institutions—church, government, and commerce. The church has seen the use of games in order to gain money (but not money for religious activities) as an affront to the supremacy of God as the supreme decision maker. Only God should determine who is worthy and who should be rewarded. Idle chance should not. All three institutions have seen gambling as encouraging idleness and a disregard for duty. Moreover, the gambler through his activity is unable to pass his resources on to the tax collector, the collection plate, or the merchants of society. In more recent years, governments themselves have run games of chance and accordingly have seen commercial gambling as a direct competitive threat.

The arguments in this book are well supported by a multitude of examples and citations to other studies. The authors give an excellent commentary on historical and contemporary distinctions between views toward gambling, speculation, insurance, and investments. Risks are endemic in society, and the insurer and speculator provide opportunities for minimizing the risks one would otherwise have to face. The gambler, on the other hand, pursues risk and seeks to increase risk in his life. Otherwise the activities of all are the same. Risk-provoking gambling activities such as lotteries can add value to lives in terms of renewed hopes for a future that is better than the present. The commentary is valuable.

Nonetheless, the arguments are skewed to support a conclusion that has only partial validity. First of all, religious thought on gambling is very mixed, and a disservice is done when researchers see it as a single unified view. The moral opponents of gambling, whether they be in churches, in government, or in the commercial world, can offer opposition without being self-serving. They can be altruistic and seek a higher good for all society by opposing idleness, drinking, and obsessions with games and by opposing a diversion of societal resources away from other causes. The causes need not be their own pocketbooks. Someone who opposes gambling that leads to pathological behaviors that impose real financial burdens upon all members of society might well take that view because of being truly interested in having a good society—not just because he or she perceives the possibility of having to contribute $100 to public coffers to remedy the harms caused by gambling (this is an approximate amount citizens in the United States might be burdened with because of gambling problems in the nation). Proponents of gambling also need not be financially connected with the industry. They might well be altruistic and truly feel that personal rights and freedoms are best served if gambling choices are given to members of society. Similarly the opponents of gambling can also be purely altruistic in their motivations.

Burbank, Jeff. 2000. *License to Steal: Nevada's Gaming Control System in the Megaresort Age.* Reno: University of Nevada Press.

In *License to Steal,* Jeff Burbank provides readers with valuable material giving insights into the regulation of casinos in Nevada. Burbank knows the Las Vegas casino industry very well. During the 1980s and early 1990s he was a reporter specializing in gambling for both the *Las Vegas Sun* and the *Las Vegas Review Journal.* In *License to Steal,* he ties his knowledgeable perspectives to both a historical record and contemporary case studies of regulatory decision making. He completes the text with seven profiles of recent members of the Nevada Gaming Commission and the Gambling Control Board, members who played key roles in the decisions discussed. Two appendixes present descriptions of the regulatory structures in Nevada and statistical details regarding taxation of gambling and staffing of the agencies.

In his initial chapter, Burbank provides the reader with critical events guiding Nevada gambling in the 19th and early 20th centuries. These events include prohibition, legalization, prohibition, and new legalizations of casino-type gambling. The events provide a cultural backdrop to the legislative decision to legalize casinos in 1931. His treatment of local government regulation in the city of Las Vegas and Clark County during the 1931–1947 period is unique. The book represents the first time an author closely examines the records of the city and county during a time when gambling law first became compromised by Mob influences. The 1931 law gave cities and counties complete control over who would receive a license to conduct games, how many games they could conduct, and the rules they had to follow in the operations. As the purpose of legalization was economic, the local agencies quickly adopted a posture of friendliness toward operators.

Burbank then takes the reader through the era of state predominance in regulation that began with state licensing and taxation in 1945. He shows how the state adjusted to various outside pressures—U.S. Senate investigations in particular—by adjusting its supervision processes. Nevertheless the state never abandoned an attitude of laissez faire and tolerance toward industry actors. This stance comes through in the case studies.

The next seven chapters closely examine seven interesting cases of regulatory law and regulatory politics. The first case involved murder—the hired killing of an employee of American Coin Machine Company. American Coin was exposed for operating gambling machines that were rigged so that large jackpots could not be won. On January 1, 1990, Larry Volk, a computer programmer for the company, was brought down by a bullet outside of his home. He had been cooperating with authorities in a criminal investigation of American Coin. The company had already lost its gambling license and suffered a civil fine of $1 million for its cheating activity. A second case introduces Ron Harris, a technician working for the Gaming Control Board's Electronic Services Division. As a state agent, Harris examined the computer chips for new slot machines and keno game number generators. He discovered some flaws in the programming in the chips. Rather than reporting his discovery, he worked to develop a new understanding of the programs and figured out a way to set the chips on certain machines and then to play the games in order to win big jackpots. He did so many times. Harris was convicted of cheating, served a few years in prison, and was also placed in the state's Book of Excluded Persons. Harris expressed the notion that he was not all that guilty, albeit he knew he was "wrong." Rather he felt after years of observing casinos getting all the breaks from the Nevada Gaming Control Board, he was just an ordinary person turning the tables the other way.

Ron Harris was also involved as a machine tester in the case of Universal Distributing Company, a slot manufacturer. Universal developed a machine that would select winners and losers randomly. If a computer determined, however, that a player was a loser, the machine then was programmed to display a combination of symbols that made it appear to the player that he or she had been very close to having a win. Universal's sales of machines increased considerably in the mid-1980s when the issue of the "near-miss" was brought to the gaming board and commission. After lengthy hearings, the Nevada Gaming Commission ruled that Universal had to reprogram all its machines to remove the near-miss factor.

Burbank also takes a long look at one of the most embarrassing cases in Nevada gaming history. Ralph Englestadt, owner of the Imperial Palace, was "exposed" for having held "Hitler Birthday Parties" in 1988 and before in the private quarters of his casino property. He had World War II memorabilia displayed in ways that seemed to glorify Nazi Germany, at least to many observers. When the matter came to public attention, Nevada's regulators sensed that they had a problem. National news media gave it prominence. Englestadt apologized and removed many of the "offensive" materials from his "war room." Nonetheless, his critics indicated that he had brought disrepute to the state's gaming industry and that he thus violated gaming rules. Some voices suggested that the Imperial Palace should lose its gaming license. While hearings on his license were progressing in front of the Nevada Gaming Commission, a deal was struck with Englestadt. He agreed to pay a fine of $1.5 million and to dispense with several relics, such as touring cars that had belonged to Adolf Hitler.

Two other cases—those of the Royal Nevada Casino and the sport of kings—seemed to have been agonizingly long episodes during which the gaming authorities bent so far over backwards before closing the doors of the operators that one wonders if they were regulatory boards at all. The authorities were certainly seen as a political group of decision makers when the Gaming Control Board recommended that the commission not license a key figure with the Sands—another case. Nevertheless the commission gave the key person a license, and casino owner Sheldon Adelson moved forward with plans that eventually resulted in the creation of the billion-dollar-plus Venetian Casino.

Burke, Michael. 2009. *Never Enough*. Chicago: American Bar Association.

It is appropriate that the American Bar Association chose to publish Mike Burke's story. While the words on the pages do not shout it out explicitly, the implicit message of the book is that lawyers have a special vulnerability regarding gambling addiction. Here a litany of factors that might in turn draw attorneys to this particular addiction as well as other addictions are presented.

Mike Burke's story tells of a journey that has brought him into contact with many problem gamblers, as he has participated in a speaking tour and has served as a counselor on addictions. He relates how the majority of problem gamblers have had experience with other addictions, particularly alcoholism. Mike himself was deeply into alcohol abuse when he began law school. Perhaps law school is as good a place as any to start looking for antecedents for a career of pathological gambling. Law schools may attract persons with certain personality traits and may also reward such individuals. Other studies have reflected on the personality traits of attorneys, leaning toward "Type A" profiles, the need for logic, the need for control, a tendency toward introversion, a liking of competitiveness, and the need to dominate, for instance, by exerting a notion of having superior information or intelligence. Without a doubt these are generalities. Nevertheless, the law school experience demands from most—especially in the first year—an intensity and a focused concentration that may

never be demanded again. Burke tells how he found he could not survive that first year unless he stopped drinking. He substituted an addiction to one substance with an addiction to studies. When the first year ended, his sense of pressure release demanded a replacement, and he returned to alcohol. The values of law school may mesh in quite compatible ways with values of intense gambling activity. After law school Burke returned to alcohol.

Alcoholism may burden many a lawyer beyond his or her capacity to compete successfully at the job. In severe cases, choices must be made. Mike Burke relates that he had to retreat into a recovery program at Brighton Hospital. He stopped drinking entirely and after doing so became a faithful member of Alcoholics Anonymous. But once again, he was faced with a void in his life. Alcohol abuse had served a function for his personality drives. He was waiting for something to replace it. He could have become a compulsive runner, swimmer, musician, or a crossword puzzle addict. He did not. He found gambling. He had enjoyed occasional trips to Reno and Las Vegas, and to a Mount Pleasant, Michigan casino, two hours away from his home. But even that facility was a distance beyond his daily reach. When Casino Windsor opened in 1994, however, Mike was in trouble. He points out that a survey of the National Gambling Impact Study Commission found that when casinos are located close to a community, the rate of compulsive gambling doubles. He is convinced that the survey was accurate. Now a casino was 58 miles and 60 minutes away. Other features of his law practice—and law practices generally—were compatible with the excessive nature of his developing gambling addiction. He was a solo practitioner. He also had a very good reputation in Howell, where he lived. He participated in many positive community activities, several connected with the local public schools. Lawyers do these things.

Mike Burke was trusted. He found that he could, rather easily at first, rearrange his appointment schedules, and even get local judges to schedule court appearances around his gambling activity. He could explain his early morning or late afternoon absences from work with lies about the need to take a deposition in this or that out-of-town location. Time was on his side. The accessibility of the casino was also enhanced by his accessibility to money. As his gambling—and his gambling losses—mounted, he turned to clients for loans that would bail him out. The abundance of friends with expendable money is an attribute of the legal community. This works for a while. Then the source is no longer available. He mortgaged his house—no problem for a respected member of the local legal community. But you can only do this once or twice as well. After he had turned to all the legitimate sources of money that are presented to a good local lawyer, he considered "borrowing" funds from several trusts that he controlled. He made the giant leap to putting his hands onto money that was not his, and doing it in a secretive way that violated legal ethics as well as the law. He told himself the biggest lie of all. When he won, he was going to pay it back. Guess what? He did win. Four times he won slot machine jackpots in excess of $100,000 each. Each time, the jackpot could have gone a long way toward bailing him out. But he did not leave the casino with even part of those winnings. The money just went right back into the machines. He "chased" wins and he "chased" losses.

As he reflects back on his extortion of funds trusted to him by clients, he wonders just why the local bank allowed him to cash checks on the accounts without question. In the last 18 months of his gambling "career," he cashed more than 100 such checks at a local bank. He was never questioned. Why? All he can suggest is that he was a lawyer with integrity—and a pedigree—and that is how he was viewed in the community.

His story became strikingly like that of other compulsive gamblers. As one set of losses chased after another, one set of lies chased after another. The stress affected Mike. He had heart pains and high blood pressure. The idea hit him— he had a cover for a suicide. Inhibitions of shame and family disgrace often lead pathological gamblers to hide their attempts. Las Vegas has a high incidence of fatal crashes involving one car only. Mike lived in a snow belt. He figured that by loading his garbage receptacle with bricks and blocks he could push the receptacle through the heaviest snow in hopes he could activate a fatal heart attack. It all came to an end when he decided to turn himself into the state bar and then the state attorneys general. He bared his soul, and accepted the shame of what he had done. So too did his family accept a shame that they had not anticipated. However, his wife stood by him. Within the next 10 weeks Michael would be arraigned, enter a plea of guilty as charged, and be sentenced in the courtroom where he had practiced law for 25 years. He was sentenced to a term of 3 to 10 years in the state's largest prison. Before his term began he underwent triple bypass heart surgery. While in prison his legal training served him well, as being an "inside lawyer" offered him a veil of physical protection.

Never Enough is a very good read. It moves fast. It is a compelling story. It is not a unique topic, in that many others have written books about their compulsive gambling experiences. However, there is a unique quality about Mike Burke's particular story. It is about a lawyer, and it is about how the practice of law can place a person drawn to gambling squarely in the trigger sites of a very dangerous activity.

Cabot, Anthony N., William N. Thompson, Andrew Tottenham, and Carl Braunlich, eds. 1999. *International Casino Law*. 3rd ed. Reno: Institute for the Study of Gambling, University of Nevada, Reno.

Thompson, William N. ed. 2008–2009. *International Casino Law and Regulation*. 3 vols. Boulder, CO: International Masters of Gaming Law (looseleaf).

Casinos operate in a legalized manner in more than 80 countries of the world. *International Casino Law* presents a descriptive synopsis of the regulatory provisions of the casino laws of these countries as well as many of their subdivisions (e.g., 16 states of the United States and 7 provinces of Canada). In addition there are sections on Native American casinos, gambling on the Internet, and casinos on the high seas. The editors of the book have attempted (and succeeded in about half of the sections) to follow a common outline that is useful for making a comparative analysis of casino law. The common outline includes (1) the history of casinos, (2) their economic impacts, (3) the regulatory bodies of the jurisdic-

tion, (4) authorized games and their rules, (5) licensing provisions, (6) accounting rules, (7) taxation, (8) equipment, and (9) operational guidelines and provisions for disciplinary actions.

More than 35 authors contributed sections to the book. Many of them were native to the jurisdiction they described. The editors have not utilized legal style footnotes as might be found in an ordinary legal textbook, although some bibliographic materials are included. The editors have purposely avoided giving the notion that the book is to be a sole source of legal advice. Only a trained lawyer can provide that, and such advice must be tied to particular facts in particular situations. The editors also realize that their subject matter is a fast-moving (and always expanding) target. For that reason, this book was originally published in three editions over a seven-year period. In 2008 the project of producing the collection was taken over by the International Masters of Gaming Law, and it is being published in looseleaf fashion with new chapters issued as they are written.

The material in the books has been a source for much of the information on various venues of gambling discussed in this encyclopedia.

Campbell, Colin, and John Lowman, eds. 1989. *Gambling in Canada: Golden Goose or Trojan Horse?* Burnaby, BC Simon Fraser University.

Campbell, Colin, ed. 1994. *Gambling in Canada: The Bottomline*. Burnaby, BC: Simon Fraser University.

The Criminology Department of Simon Fraser University conducted two national symposia on gambling in 1988 and 1993. These two volumes contain the papers from these conferences. Collectively, they present a comprehensive picture of gambling operations in Canada as well as a considerable body of other relevant information on public policy and gambling. Each volume presents a province-by-province account of lotteries and casino operations as well as references to horse racing. There are also commentaries on the general Canadian law of gambling and First Nations gambling in Canada (and the United States) as well as pathological gambling, gambling behavior, children and gambling, the ethics of gambling, charitable games, and the economics of gambling.

The articles in the books come from academic scholars, industry operators, and government regulators. Canadian gambling is intrinsically interesting for many reasons. The model of Canadian gambling has elevated the notion of charity games to the style of Las Vegas casinos (in quality if not in quantity). The gaming is quite distinct from patterns found in the United States, yet seems to pursue the same essential goal of bottom-line profits. Many innovations in modern gambling operations have come out of Canada. Moreover, the influence of casinos located near the U.S. border has seriously affected gambling politics to the south (or to the north, in the case of Windsor and Detroit). These two books show the close connections between the two countries that share the longest peaceful border in the world. The books also show the unique qualities of Canadian gambling.

Chafetz, Henry. 1960. *Play the Devil: A History of Gambling in the United States from 1492 to 1955*. New York: Potter Publishers.

Author Henry Chafetz, a New York book dealer, views history as a product of the gambling urge within adventurous people. He presents his story in the form of one interesting character after another, one vignette followed by another vignette. It is an informal history lacking documentation for the many facts and anecdotes presented, but including a bibliography of sources at the end. Among the stories that grab the attention of the reader are ones such as the establishment of a lottery to rebuild Boston's Faneuil Hall after it was destroyed by a fire, the fact that George Washington bought the first ticket for a national lottery in 1793, the wagers on the steamboat race between the *Natchez* and the *Robert E. Lee* in 1870, and the revelation that the Chicago fire of 1874 was not caused by Mrs. O'Leary's cow, but rather by players in a craps game in the O'Leary barn. From stories of more recent years the fact emerges that the discovery of a little black book with gambling records proved to be Al Capone's downfall, as it provided the evidence that he had evaded paying federal income taxes. Chafetz also tells us about the great "Gipper" betting on his own Notre Dame team to win—could Knute Rockne have been asking the players to cover the spread with his "Win one for the Gipper" speech? General Eisenhower apparently also made a bet that U.S. troops would be in Germany by the end of 1944. He lost that one. Chafetz also devotes a chapter to Wall Street, calling the exchange "the Greatest Gamble."

These are all interesting stories, but they are all sidebars. Nonetheless Chafetz tries to draw something out of his fun-packed book that just does not seem to ring true. He thinks all the little stories add up to a grand conclusion that gambling has moved history and that it continues to be a force in the turning of great events. There can be little doubt that leaders have always challenged obstacles with risk-taking behaviors, but to claim that it was the gamble that made the event is a big stretch. The facts in no way build to a substantiated conclusion that gambling is a determining factor in history. Still, gambling is now an important commercial enterprise, and for those who support legalized gambling it is refreshing to know that the notable figures in history did partake of wagers and game-playing activities.

Clark, Thomas L. 1987. *The Dictionary of Gambling and Gaming.* Cold Spring, NY: Lexix House Publishers.

Gambling has its own special language. Names and words are associated with gambling by players and others who are part of "the group" or "fraternity." The proper nouns *Canfield, Lansky, Rothstein, Siegel,* and *Hughes* conjure up notions of power and influence. *Citation* and *Cigar* are linked with winning. *Upset* was also a proper noun. It was the name of the 100–1 longshot that defeated the champion racehorse Man o' War. As a gambler's word, *upset* became associated with any underdog in a contest who won. The word then was taken over as part of the general language. Other gambling words have also come into the common language of the times: *square deal, new deal, no dice,* and *full deck.*

The use of special words that are not in the vocabulary of the ordinary population gives meaning to the lives of those tied to gambling. It lets them know who is in their fraternity and who is not. The use of words is like a secret handshake. The words can be icebreakers for beginning conversations or friendships, for prompting one to inquire about the location of a game, or for asking for information about a race or other event. At the time that almost all gambling was illegal, special words could be used to conceal activities from persons who might not approve. The inside vocabulary can also be used to establish one's esteem and status as a player.

In 1950, David Maurer presented a glossary of terms, "The Argot of the Dice Gambler," in an essay in Morris Ploscowe and Edwin J. Lukas's *Gambling,* a special issue of *The Annals of the American Academy of Political and Social Science.* (See annotation below.) Maurer described many of the facets of gambling terminology. Since then, however, there have been no concerted efforts to document this vocabulary. In modern times, the late Tom Clark's *Dictionary of Gambling and Gaming* stands out as a unique addition to the literature. Clearly it is the best collection of gambling vocabulary available.

Turn card, puppyfoot, snowballing, zuke, blind tiger, super george, dead spot, needle squeeze, twig, king crab. These are only some of the 5,000 or so words and phrases that appear in Clark's volume. Clark was for many years a professor of English and linguistics at the University of Nevada, Las Vegas. He applied his academic training well to the environment in which he found himself, and in doing so he produced a very valuable research resource as well as an intrinsically interesting collection of terminology. He offers the reader 255 pages of terms presented from A to Z. He indicates sources for his definitions (such as *Oxford English Dictionary* or

The Dictionary of American English on Historical Principles), provides selected pronunciation guides, and indicates parts of speech, source languages, variations in spelling, definitions, multiple definitions, synonyms, and explanatory quotations. He also adds an extensive bibliography. The book begins with an introductory section that describes the values of words in gambling and also offers an extensive discussion of the words *gambling* and *gaming* and whether they are the same or not, a topic that is still important to many people in the industry.

Clotfelter, Charles T., and Philip J. Cook. 1989. *Selling Hope: State Lotteries in America*. Cambridge, MA: Harvard University Press.

Where David Weinstein and Lillian Deitch (see *The Impact of Legalized Gambling,* annotation below) assessed the status of lotteries after 10 years of experience in the United States, Clotfelter and Cook present a quarter-century perspective on the phenomenon. Actually they reach farther back before lotteries came to New Hampshire in 1964 to give the reader an overview that is tied to other eras and other societies. The authors present the most comprehensive (called "exhaustive, but never exhausting") treatment of lotteries to date. The two authors, both professors at Duke University, conclude that state lotteries in the United States have all fallen into identical patterns of putting revenue generation ahead of all other values. The public permits this as they do not review policy decisions on lotteries after they acquiesce in their adoption. Actually, the majorities given to lottery referenda by

the public are quite large and often surprising given the fact that key public officials occasionally lead opposition efforts. Up to 1989, when this book was written, only one state had ever had a popular vote against a proposal of a state-operated lottery. In many cases the campaigns are led by lottery suppliers who see adoption of lotteries in new jurisdictions as their source of continued wealth.

A case study of the influence of Scientific Games in the California campaign of 1984 is illustrative. State lottery officials have free rein to pursue the one goal of achieving maximum sales. To achieve more and more sales, they use the most modern applications of marketing principles, identifying customer segments and using the strongest messages possible to influence sales. The consequences of maximizing lottery revenues have led to a very regressive taxation effect. Poorer people and minorities buy tickets in disproportionate amounts, and in turn, lottery organizations direct their advertising efforts at these people. Moreover the advertisements utilized are misleading; they do not tell the truth about odds, and they paint unrealistic pictures of winners while denigrating persons who resist buying tickets.

Clotfelter and Cook lament that all the lotteries have gone in the same direction—they have become revenue lotteries. They ask the public and the political leaders both in lottery states and in states that are considering lotteries to consider two other models of lotteries: one that they call the sumptuary model and another that they call the consumer model. In the sumptuary model, lotteries are offered as a government product designed to meet existing demands of the people for a product that they might seek from illegal sources if there is no legal supplier. In this model the government does not market and merchandise lotteries but rather offers them in a very passive manner—even without advertising at all.

In the consumer model, the government does advertise its gambling products, but it does so in a responsible and, most of all, an honest manner. Odds are accurately presented, and players are given information about play rather than fantasies that cannot be achieved. The authors suggest that those managing lotteries today consider these two alternatives, each of which would be more directed toward the public interest than lotteries under the revenue model.

The National Gambling Impact Study Commission made some rather harsh assessments of lotteries today. Their conclusions were propelled by contracted research conducted by Charles Clotfelder and Philip Cook.

Collins, Peter. 2003. *Gambling and the Public Interest*. Westport, CT: Praeger.

Author Peter Collins is the director of the Centre for the Study of Gambling at the University of Salford in England. He wrote this book while he was an advisor to the government on a new casino law. In these pages, he intellectually wrestles with very basic questions: should governments permit their citizens to engage in gambling? If not, what are the effects of such a prohibition on their lives and liberties? If so, is there a role for government to play in the activity? Should government regulate and tax gambling? In what manner?

Collins reaches back through the centuries to explore and analyze philoso-

phies of morals and ethics to discern if gambling can be considered to be "right" or "wrong." He looks also to economic theory in order to find directions for placing gambling into the flow of commercial enterprise in society.

A focal point for his analysis is found in the philosophies of Immanuel Kant and John Stuart Mill. Try as he may, Collins cannot find any "Categorical Imperative" (ala Kant) regarding gambling. He rejects that gambling is "bad," as it is a natural tendency of man, and it has been pervasive through the ages as an activity in which people desire to participate. There is no universal reason for its prohibition. At the same time, while there are positive qualities attached to gambling activity, there are no universal reasons why it should exist everywhere and always, or why people should be required to gamble. Rather gambling is a phenomenon that must involve free choice both by individuals and by those who would control the activity with governmental authority.

As Collins rejects a Kantian approach to gambling, he also finds the utilitarian approaches such as Mill's "pleasure quest," or his "greatest good for the greatest number," to also be wanting. He simply rejects the notion that we can adequately measure out all "pleasures" and hence quantify the benefits and costs of gambling for a society. His answer to the basic questions comes with the philosophy of Aristotle, who preached for the "golden mean" and "moderation." The good in gambling is something that can make all people happy with its excitement, camaraderie and competition, pursuit of dreams, demonstrations of stamina and strength, and good nature. Yet to find these virtuous qualities in gambling, people and societies must pursue the activity in moderation.

Collins strongly endorses a model of legalization and regulation. The regulators must be mindful that some people will gamble without moderation and this will result in harm. Nonetheless, personal liberty and dignity demand that people be offered a freedom of choice regarding gambling, even if they participate to their own harm. Governments should assist people in making choices about gambling by assuring that all the games are honest, and by helping people become educated about gambling, its rules, its odds, and its potential harms, and they should also encourage support for treatment programs for troubled players. Collins also feels that persons with fewer economic resources may be drawn to gambling that is harmful for them. Therefore he believes that regulations should exist to encourage the hiring of poorer people into gambling jobs, and that taxation benefits from gambling should be specifically directed to projects that will help poorer people and poorer communities.

This is a very well thought out book that demands a close, even intense, reading by persons who may be called upon to make policy decisions regarding gambling operations for governments or for commercial enterprises.

Cooper, Marc. 2004. *The Last Honest Place in America*. New York: Nations Books.

Marc Cooper was an established writer before he penned *The Last Honest Place in America*. He was a war correspondent as well as a contributing columnist for *Playboy, The New Yorker, Harpers,* and *Rolling Stone*. He was offered a chance to cover the war in Iraq, but he declined. He had begun to develop ideas about Las Vegas that he wished to share, which he does in this book. His story starts in 2001, just weeks before terrorists struck the World Trade Center. He discovered that while America was seemingly stunned and subdued, life in Las Vegas went on. However, upon closer examination, it wasn't Las Vegas life, but American life in Las Vegas that went on. Las Vegas was the genuine America, while a dishonest façade of dignity and pretense hung over the rest of the nation. So what was more honest: activity on the roulette wheel at the Mirage or dealings at Enron Corporation? Where was money real? What was more honest: an advertisement saying your social life will change if you put money down for a product, or that you will win or lose if you make a bet at a blackjack table? Las Vegas was honest capitalism, where a billboard proclaimed that if you gave a casino slot machine $1, you could honestly expect to receive 97 cents back. Imagine if a car dealership told you that if you paid $20,000 for a car you would receive back a car worth $19,000—it might be close to the truth, but you never would hear it. Cooper asks if the transplanted residents who came from the rust-belt of the American Midwest feel like they get better opportunities to make a living in Las Vegas. He believes they do.

Cooper takes a closer look at life in Las Vegas to test his theory. He looks at the former mobsters who were present in the casinos, he looks at the new accountants now in control, he examines Mormon interests that have political power, and also the politicians who fell from grace by teaming up with the city's "honest" sex industry. He explores the development of slot machines as the most important element in casino activity, but he also looks at life from both sides of the blackjack table, as well as life as an employee in the back of the casinos. He also looks at suburban life and at homelessness in Las Vegas. He concludes that the "honesty" of the place will continue to make it America's fastest growing city—as people vote for honesty with their feet. It is a compelling story, but it was written in 2004. It cries for a 2009 postscript and a commentary on the question: has the national economy finally caught up with Las Vegas?

Custer, Robert, and Harry Milt. 1985. *When Luck Runs Out: Help for Compulsive Gamblers and Their Families*. New York: Facts on File.

Robert Custer was truly the pioneer of gambling help programs. In 1972, he started the first treatment center for compulsive gamblers at a Veterans Administration hospital in Ohio. In this book, he joins with professional writer Harry Milt to share with his readers the experiences in his extraordinary career. Throughout the book, readers will find case studies of problem gambling that provide real substance for the accompanying textual commentary.

Custer was an important player in the effort that led the American Psychiatric Association to designate compulsive gambling as a disease in 1980. He expands on the medical model in the book. Nonetheless, the authors made a respectable review of other theories of compulsive gambling. Indeed, they put forth their own notions that the manifestation of the disease is tied to need deprivations that may be traced to early childhood experiences. People need affection and approval, recognition and self-confidence. When these are absent,

people seek to cope. One means of coping is "fantasy, illusion, and escape." When gambling opportunities are placed in front of such persons, a pathway to the disease of compulsive gambling is available. But people in such situations (and everyone is exposed to some gambling today) do not just become compulsive gamblers. First they have to play. Then there are phases on the trail to the disease: the winning phase, the losing phase, the bailout, and the desperate phase.

Custer and Milt give consideration to the families of compulsive gamblers, to the female gambler, and also to treatment possibilities. The book is written for a general audience that is interested in gambling phenomena, but most especially for persons who are in trouble or who are exposed to others who are. Custer and Milt offer hope—but the hope comes when people become aware. This book helps those who need a journey to recovery.

Davis-Goff, Annabel, ed. 1996. *The Literary Companion to Gambling*. London: Sinclair-Stevenson.

Davis-Goff presents a classic collection of wisdom and observations on gambling throughout the ages. Her compendium of literary passages on the subject is arranged into three sections: "The Gods," "Man," and "Self." The first section leads off with the Old Testament story of Jonah, followed by entries describing the use of gambling mechanisms to determine divine will and purpose. These examples include words from Tacitus, Shirley Jackson, Bret Harte, Francis Bacon, Charles Dickens, and Robert Louis Stevenson. In these passages, man is powerless in the face of the force of the Almighty. He has no control, no will.

The writings in the second section pit man against man. Here the individual has a choice, free will, about whether to play the game and how to play the game. Many feel (whether realistically or as an illusion) that they can exercise skill and power in the games in order to best their human competitors. Davis-Goff's selections include writings from Sir Walter Scott's *A Legend of Montrose*, Ben Jonson's *The Alchemist*, Herodotus's *The Histories*, and F. Scott Fitzgerald's *The Great Gatsby,* as well as material from the work of Tolstoy, William Thackeray, Plutarch, Damon Runyon, and Mark Twain.

In the final section, gambling is portrayed as a phenomenon that has value in and of itself for the individual. The value may be in the play, which provides a diversion from boredom of life. But also the play can be seen as a lonely pastime, one that may be consumed in personal desperation, although one of excitement for others. Some passages selected are from Lord Byron, Blaise Pascal, James Boswell, Honoré de Balzac, Fyodor Dostoyevsky, and Alexander Pope. The book is replete with many little treasures for the casual or serious student of gambling, or for the casual or serious player of games.

Denton, Sally, and Roger Morris. 2001. *The Money and the Power: The Making of Las Vegas and Its Hold on America.* New York: Knopf.

It is déjà vu one more time, as they say: another exposé of Las Vegas. The theme of Denton and Morris's *The Money and the Power* portrays Las Vegas as even more evil than the Las Vegas found in Reid and Demaris's *The Green Felt Jungle* or Johnston's *Temples of Chance*. The authors are Las Vegas residents, so they should know. Well, perhaps yes, perhaps no. They suggest that the evil force of Las Vegas is not bounded by the geographical isolation of the desert resort city. Rather, the influence of Las Vegas extends far across the nation and indeed around the globe. A big bite to chew. Two subjects are covered here that are not found in earlier broadsides against Las Vegas. The authors suggest (with a few stories) that Las Vegas is the illicit drug center for the nation and even the hemisphere. They also indicate that the gambling industry of Las Vegas has a powerful influence over the politics of the United States.

On the one hand, the stories in the book are fun—a "quick read." On the other hand, the fast-paced shoot-from-the-hip style of the book leads to an assessment that it was also a "quick write." There are several factual errors (mostly but not all of minor importance) to advise the careful reader to hesitate to accept the "forest"—that is, the grand conclusions of the authors. Errors surround their selections and portrayals of certain persons as heroes and others as "devil incarnates." Nonetheless, many of the descriptions of the "trees" do have enough of a ring of truth in them that the book deserves to be read.

The drug stories seem to this editor to be a bit remote. If Las Vegas is infested with drug magnates, it is not noticeable to the city's citizens or to those coming to the city for their vacations and mini-vacations. On the other hand, the stories of recent presidents are fascinating in and of themselves. We knew before that the Kennedys were Las Vegas kind of guys. The depth of Joseph Kennedy's involvement in the casinos seems to be fresh material, however, as do many of the interconnections of the 1960 presidential campaign and Frank Sinatra and his friends. That Lyndon B. Johnson (and Hubert Humphrey) and Richard Nixon were involved makes more good reading. The connections of Ronald Reagan and Virginia Kelly (called Virginia Clinton) and her boy Bill are even more fascinating. The more recent emergence of Las Vegas as the center for national campaign financing deserves the print that it receives. This, however, hardly makes the city a powerful force over national policy decisions.

On the local scene, the machinations of casino finance and the influence of Salt Lake City bankers, both Mormon and gentile, deserve to be explored as the authors have done. Few before them dared to do so. The notion that the local casinos control all important facets of local life in Las Vegas seems a bit overstated. All citizens (who care about it) recognize that the politicians consider the gambling industry to be their most important constituency. That does not mean that people in Las Vegas do not exercise free will over the important activities of their own lives or that they do not have a strong voice in politics on issues of concern to themselves—where the issues do not conflict with those of the casinos. Even where they do, Las Vegas is a two (competing) daily newspaper town, and contrary to the views of the authors, those critical of the casinos and casino moguls do have their say in the press. The casinos do not own all of Las Vegas, and they do not always own the political leaders.

The authors suggest that politics in Las Vegas is corrupt. They suggest further that life in the city is miserable. Yet, something belies their basic theme. Over the past few decades more and more people move to Las Vegas. It has been the fastest-growing community in the nation. Free-thinking American citizens making life choices have been choosing Las Vegas as the community they wish to call their own.

Devol, George H. 1887. *Forty Years a Gambler on the Mississippi*. Cincinnati, OH: Devol and Haynes.

Students of gambling history do not have many firsthand accounts of gambling action in centuries past. Fyodor Dostoyevsky, in *The Gambler,* provides an autobiographical account in a fictionalized format of a bout with gambling fever. George Devol provides another firsthand account of gambling but with a very different tone. Devol does not speak to despair but rather speaks of triumph, for he is the self-proclaimed "best gambler in the world." He cites the Mississippi River in his title, but his escapades extended to the tributaries and also the shores of that great river. He was born in Marietta, Ohio, in 1829, the son of a ship carpenter. Exposed as a child to the crews of river vessels, he got the urge early on to make a life on the river. He often played hooky from school to mix and mingle with the river travelers, and at age 10 he took off. He jumped aboard an Ohio River steamer and was given a job as a cabin boy.

The book is his book, and his stories. The reader must seek always to separate fact from fiction, but the reader is treated to one adventure after another. The stories are presented in chronological order, but in general they appear to be rambling accounts of winners and losers, cheaters of one type or another, and other characters that Devol passed by on his life journey. By the time he was 11 years old he was stealing cards, and he practiced until he could cheat with the best of them. He soon became involved in the games, and the games often involved thousands of dollars. By his account he had won "hundreds of thousands" of dollars while still a teenager, taking advantage of paymasters and soldiers on river jaunts during the Mexican War. George Devol was a good fighter too, as many stories are about the fights he engaged in and often the narrow escapes from mortal danger. Remarkably he survived until he was an old man who could sit and reminisce about the good ol' days.

He became a philosopher in his old age too—a philosopher of gambling. Toward the end of his tome he relates that Thomas Hobbes said that "man is the only animal that laughs." Writes Devol,

> He might have appropriately added, he is the only animal that gambles. To gamble or venture on chance, his own property with the hope of winning the property of another is peculiar to him. Other animals in common with man will fight for meat, drink, and lodging, and will battle for love as fiercely as the old knights of chivalry; but there is no well authenticated account that any of the lower animals ever changed any of their property on "odd or even," or drew lots for choice of pasturage. No master has ever yet taught his dog to play with him at casino, and even the learned pig could never learn what was trumps. Hence gambling is proof of man's intellectual superiority. (296–297)

Dombrink, John, and Daniel Hillyard. 2007. *Sin No More*. New York: New York University Press.

John Dombrink, a professor of criminology at the University of California in Irvine, has been a student of "vice" and "sin" and gambling for more than three decades. His first book (with the editor of this encyclopedia) focused upon political campaigns to legalize gambling. His second book (with co-author Daniel Hillyard) looked at public policy regarding death and dying. This is his third book. Again he collaborates with Daniel Hillyard. Here they examine many activities that have over time been categorized as sinful. These include abortion, homosexuality, and assisted suicide. Their lead chapter is devoted to gambling. They examine recent histories of legalization and phenomena such as Indian casinos, Internet gambling, lotteries, and poker tournaments. They conclude that gambling has become "normalized," and that those who put the label of sin on the activity have been marginalized. People with moral qualms about gambling have effectively been silenced as the activity has swept the nation (being legal to some extent in 48 states).

An analogy to the Civil Rights era follows from their analysis. In the 1950s and 1960s, it seemed that attitudes in some parts of the nation were solidified against the notion of social integration of blacks and whites. Yet national policy required integration at least in public institutions and places of public accommodation. Attitudes remained solid but integration proceeded—sometimes by the force of federal authorities. It was only after substantial integration became a fact of life that attitudes gradually but most certainly shifted toward an acceptance of the new reality. So with gambling, the attitudes of opposition—attitudes that gambling is sin—remained in many sectors after legalized gambling was introduced to communities (for example, in the Bible Belt's rural northern Mississippi). But local people who may have remained opposed to gambling did partake in the activity when it was put in their midst. After engaging in play and trading stories with others who had engaged in play, they came to accept it, and within a short decade (or two) they abandoned their previously held notions that gambling was sin.

Dombrink, John D., and William N. Thompson. 1990. *The Last Resort: Success and Failure in Campaigns for Casinos*. Reno: University of Nevada Press.

The authors make an analysis of factors influencing results of political campaigns to legalize casino gambling in almost 20 states, from 1964 through 1989. They seek to explain an anomaly. During a three-decade period, lottery campaigns had been successful in almost every case where the issue arose, yet only one casino campaign—that in New Jersey in 1976—had been successful. Lottery efforts usually won with large popular majorities, whereas casino propositions were defeated by equally large margins.

After a discussion of the development of the Las Vegas casino industry and its place in the public mind, the authors present case studies of casino campaigns in New Jersey and Florida. Their analysis leads them to discern two policy models at work in gambling legalization campaigns. For the successful lottery campaigns, they find a gravity model at play. Campaign factors are weighed and if a predominance of the issues favors the adoption of a lottery, the lottery proponents are successful. Another model is at work in casino campaigns, however. The authors call it the veto model. Here—if but one major factor in the campaign is negative—the whole campaign falls to defeat. The authors identify several major veto factors: the economic climate, previous experience with gambling in a state (and reputation of gambling in the state), campaign financing and the legitimacy of campaign sponsors, the position of political elites (especially governors and attorneys general), the position of business elites, whether rival gambling interests oppose the proposition, and whether the major issue in the campaign is economics or crime (crime being the veto factor).

Next the book presents case studies from more than a dozen states and nearly 20 campaigns that show the veracity of the model. The governor and the crime issue defeat casinos in several Florida campaigns; the opposition of Governor Clinton brings down a campaign in Arkansas; the lack of credibility of campaign sponsors in Michigan and California dooms campaigns; the attorney general stops a New York campaign cold in 1981.

As the book was going to the publisher, new developments showed casino gambling legalization campaigns to be successful in Iowa and Colorado. Although no veto factor emerged in Iowa, in Colorado the governor offered opposition, albeit passive opposition. Moreover, the year of publication—1990—also witnessed the beginning of an era of Native American casino establishment. Was the veto model falling into disrepute? In a later article ("The Last Resort Revisited." *Journal of Gambling Studies* 11, no. 4 [Winter 1995]: 373–378), coauthor Thompson and Ricardo Gazel suggested that the model has remained viable, although the political process surrounding Native American casino compacts is quite different, and that campaigns for limited stakes gambling ($5 betting limits) are not the same as campaigns for wide-open land-based casinos. Moreover, it was suggested that a governor's opposition to casinos had to be active in order to effectuate a veto. In 1996, the Michigan governor opposed Detroit casinos but did so only mildly and without enthusiasm. The proposition passed on a very narrow vote. The book offers a history of casino campaigns and still provides some valuable guidelines for those wishing to promote or oppose casino legalizations.

Dostoyevsky, Fyodor. 1972. *The Gambler*. Translated from the 1866 Russian edition by Victor Terras. Chicago: University of Chicago Press.

The immortal novelist Dostoyevsky penned the most poignant portrayal of a compulsive gambler and his feelings in this 1866 work. His novel about the tortured gambler Alexis is considered by most observers to be an autobiographical account of a phase of Dostoyevsky's own life. The diary of his wife reveals many episodes when Fyodor would disappear to the gambling tables of Wiesbaden or Bad Homburg only to emerge in a wretched state. Often he would feel compelled to write in order to get the money to gamble or the money to pay back gambling debts.

The account of Alexis became fodder for Sigmund Freud, who read his own psychoanalytical interpretations into the passion of gambling, assigning male and female representations to the equipment of the gambling tables. The book itself is about a few short weeks in the gambling career of Alexis, but it successfully captures the feelings of the moment. It reflects feelings of inferiority and melancholy, as well as heightened arousal that offer many insights into his gambling mania. In this work, contemporary students of compulsive or pathological (or problem) gambling have a universal case study to which they, like Freud, can assign their own theories. Indeed, several reject the Freudian interpretations outright. For instance, other theories are supported by the social notion that Alexis was trying to mimic the behaviors of others (models) to whom he paid deference. His gambling was certainly part of his relationship with his wife. He experienced the spirals that Henry Lesieur addresses in *The Chase*—he chased his losses. Yet, he clung to notions of rationality, albeit the false rationality of the gambler's fallacy that the wheel knows what it has done before and will in the short run even things out. (The law of mathematics only works in the long run—you know, when we are all dead.)

The Gambler is a classic because it is open to interpretation and reinterpretation by all. It is a tabula rasa for gambling scholars. All can see something that supports their own views, and all can join in arguments about what Dostoyevsky is really saying.

Eadington, William R., ed. 1990. *Indian Gaming and the Law*. Reno: Institute for the Study of Gambling, University of Nevada, Reno.

The most rapidly expanding gambling is found on Native American reservations. The rush forward with new casinos, new casino locations, and expanded facilities goes on unabated. Native gambling represents 15 percent of the full gambling market and a third of the casino market. For that reason, it would be expected that the gambling literature would contain volumes on the subject, and gambling journals would have countless articles. Such is not the case. Indeed, in the early 21st century, more than a quarter of a century after Native American gambling began, this book, along with the Kathryn Rand Steven Light book on gaming policy and Native Americans, represent the only comprehensive works on gaming law in this area. William R. Eadington has edited a collection of essays that were initially presented to a special conference in March 1989, just months after the passage of the Indian Gaming Regulatory Act. This of course dates the book. On the other hand, the timing gives the reader perspectives of many important policymakers who were still near the scene of the major decision making surrounding the act.

The panel of writers included U.S. Senator Harry Reid of Nevada, who was happy to take credit for engineering the provision of the act (tribal-state compacts) that was the essential compromise that led to the passage of the act. Former secretary of the interior Stuart Udall also made a presentation, as did several tribal leaders. Academic insights were given by I. Nelson Rose, Jerome Skolnick, and William R. Eadington among others, including myself. Two speakers were Canadian First Nations representatives.

At the time of the conference, the commercial casino industry was feeling very comfortable with the misguided notion that the act had stopped the spread of Native American gambling with an effective set of controls and limits. Native leaders were bristling at the notion that they were being illegally regulated in ways disturbing their sovereignty. They were launching a legal attack upon the constitutionality of the act.

In addition to the political posturing in the presentations, many of the crucial issues facing Native gaming are illuminated. Jerome Skolnick offered the most poignant observation. With the passage of the Indian Gaming Regulatory Act, the federal government for the first time in history had (though the voice of Congress) gone on record as endorsing the use of gambling for positive good in society. This was no small matter.

Editor Eadington provides a very useful service for all gambling researchers by including a full text of the Indian Gaming Regulatory Act and also a full text of the Supreme Court's opinions in the decision of *California* v. *Cabazon Band of Mission Indians* (1987).

Earley, Pete. 2000. *Super Casino: Inside the "New Las Vegas."* New York: Bantam Books.

Pete Earley tells yet another "inside" Las Vegas story. This time it is a story of the 1990s; this time it is a story about the new monster-sized casinos. But what is "inside" is not really new at all. Most of the story has been told before, and it will be told again, and then again. He does provide some new twists, a new writing format (sort of), interesting insights, and a good read. Earley was formerly a reporter with the *Washington Post,* so he knows how to write, but he writes like a reporter, without footnotes and without a list of sources. As is the case with the stories in the daily press, the essential sources are the people that he interviews.

The focus of the book is one casino organization, now called Mandalay Resorts, formerly called Circus Circus. Earley introduces the reader to the founder of Circus Circus—Jay Sarno. He then takes his story through the 1970s when the Circus property is purchased by William Bennett and William Pennington. In the 1980s, the property goes public, with the leadership of Glenn Schaeffer. Then as the 1990s unfold, the company builds its three megacasinos— or supercasinos—the Excalibur, the Luxor, and the Mandalay Bay. With the coming of the 1990s, the organization seeks to change its image as the workingman's "family" casino and become a "high-roller" organization.

Earley's story of life in the modern Las Vegas scene is told thorough several major characters who all seem to find the Luxor to be a place to play out their roles. Some are very peripheral to the casino scene. There are two tourists, a show dancer, and a prostitute. The main players are Chief Executive Schaeffer, General Manager Tony Alamo, and Security Director Keith Uptain. Each actor cycles into and out of the book through a set of vignettes that are sprinkled with sidebars featuring players, room clerks, cab drivers, and others. Not all of the vignettes are at all relevant to the coming of the new casinos. Certainly the many pages devoted to the life of a prostitute and the company she keeps and to the relationships of a show dancer add very little to an understanding of

what has happened since 1990. Their stories have been told for many, many decades, and they did not seem to be any different this time around—well, except for the fact that one prostitute gets AIDS, which is a relatively new wrinkle. The book does offer a good discussion of card counting and also of several cheating scams—but this activity has been around a long time too. Perhaps a major contribution of the volume is found in its discussions of the downfall of William J. Bennett. Earley certainly presents a good case study that could be used in any Principles of Management course.

Eisler, Kim Isaac. 2001. *Revenge of the Pequots: How a Small Native American Tribe Created the World's Most Profitable Casino*. New York: Simon and Schuster.

Eisler presents a well-researched history of Foxwoods casino in Ledyard, Connecticut. The facility grosses almost $1 billion in gambling revenue each year for the benefit of a few hundred Native Americans—the Mashantucket Pequots. The casino came into being as a result of a political miracle that continues. About a dozen members of a state-recognized tribe somehow won federal recognition in the 1980s. Then the tribe established a bingo parlor, Congress intervened by passing the Indian Gaming Regulatory Act of 1988, and the Pequots—whose numbers began to grow as they made money—set their eyes on casino gambling. Through a maze of court cases and strange political decisions by Connecticut politicians, the tribe was given the opportunity to have table games and slot machines. Theirs became the only casino in all of New England, located just seven miles off the major interstate highway between New York and Boston—less than two hours from each of the metropolitan areas. Then the courts intervened again with rulings that effectively stopped efforts to establish Native American casinos in other New England venues.

The story details many of the maneuvers that at times were on the devious side, but at other times seemed consistent with notions of restoring Native American sovereignty in a way that fulfilled the goals of congressional action. The tribe has used its newfound extraordinary wealth in many ways. The 175 members receive a variety of bonuses that assure each will have a lifetime of luxurious living. The tribe supports many good causes; in fact, a significant portion of the revenue—well over $100 million—is given directly to the state of Connecticut. Many Native American cultural causes are supported, and a museum of history has been established. The book emphasizes how English colonists essentially slaughtered tribal members in the 1600s but glosses over the fact that the English had many Native American allies in their conquest of the Pequots, as the Pequots had been a rather fierce tribe themselves and not well liked by any of their neighbors. Be that as it may, there is reason enough for "white guilt" regarding Native American history. The tribe has also showered its dollars on politicians, through lobbying efforts and through direct campaign donations—soft and hard. The political donations have assured that any congressional action to change the Indian Gaming Regulatory Act will effectively be nullified for many years to come.

David versus Goliath. But one wonders just who is David and who is Goliath in the final analysis. Part of Eisler's story has readers cheering for the underdog Pequots, but part should leave the readers wondering if Native America gambling policy has been rationally thought out. Native Americans are the poorest Americans in an economic sense and in the sense of many social indicators. Gambling helps, but does it really move Native Americans closer to the standards of living enjoyed by the majority of Americans? For sure, gaming helps the 175 Pequots. The trouble is that gambling helps only small numbers of Native Americans. There were over 2 million Native Americans in the United States in 1990, according to the census. The majority are not being helped by casinos. Should they be? If tribes are given casinos because Native Americans have collectively been wronged (and they have) and because collectively (but as tribes) they have sovereign rights, then all Native Americans might participate in the enjoyment of gambling revenues coming from casinos that have been established in the name of alleviating the "white man's guilt." To win permanent political favor, gambling tribes might design mechanisms by which their revenues can be shared among all Native Americans—much as tax dollars are taken from all people to provide for the general welfare. The book offers great history lessons and offers great questions for future policymakers—when they get around to wanting to deal with the questions.

Farrell, Ronald A., and Carole Case. 1995. *The Black Book and the Mob: The Untold Story of the Control of Nevada's Casinos*. Madison: University of Wisconsin Press.

Ronald Farrell and Carole Case have produced a volume on what is a side issue in casino regulation in Nevada, the list of excluded persons. Although the so-called black book, which names individuals not permitted to come inside any of the state's unrestricted casinos, is not an important tool in the overall regulation of gambling, it is an item that has received much notoriety since its inception in 1960. The book is linked with what the authors consider to be a notion that the Mafia hovers over the state's casinos ready to move in and take over whenever given the chance.

The authors examine every entry in the black book—45 individuals since 1960. They look at the circumstances surrounding their inclusion. They also examine the processes followed by the Gaming Control Board and the Gaming Commission in the decisions, and they look at the legal challenges and changes in procedures over the years. The authors see the black book as coming out of an era of federal scrutiny over Nevada casinos (the 1950s), but they see it even more as a symbolic rather than a substantive response to accusations that casinos were under Mob control. What is telling for the authors is the "fact" that a preponderance of excluded persons were of Italian heritage, whereas Mob control over casinos was tied most closely to associates of Meyer Lansky: Moe Dalitz, Morris Kleinman, Lincoln Fitzgerald, Bugsy Siegel—not your typical sons of Italy or Sicily. The regulators putting the Italians in the black book all seemed to have names associated with people commonly known as WASPs (white, Anglo-Saxon Protestants). These state regulators were seeking credibility for the casino industry by showing they had control over a group perceived to be "sinful." The authors then argue that the black book is an exercise in stereotyping.

The book is well written and in most cases well documented. The arguments presented certainly carry at least a grain of truth and wisdom. The black book is not an important tool in regulation, and at least 28 of the 45 have "Italian-sounding" names. (The authors used the same criterion in determining they were "Italian"— that their name "sounded" Italian.) On the other hand, the argument has a superficiality that demands somewhat more evidence than is presented in the interesting 286 pages offered.

Findlay, John M. 1986. *People of Chance: Gambling in American Society from Jamestown to Las Vegas*. New York: Oxford University Press.

John Findlay seeks to organize this text around a theme. It is a neat idea, but then, the theme does not quite work. Much is left out of the pages of the book, almost as if it is irrelevant—but perhaps because it just does not fit.

Findlay sees Americans as "People of Chance." They are risk takers descended from risk takers. They are the people who left secure (perhaps) homes in Europe for only a promise of better things (a gamble at best). A postcard currently sold at Ellis Island has this heading: "Gambling on America." The gambling did not stop at Jamestown or at Ellis Island. Americans kept looking westward seeking the same things their European forebears sought— the promise of a better life. And so they headed out to become pioneers on the frontier, gambling with their lives, and along the way gambling at assorted other games. If one is willing to stake one's own life on chance, why not risk money as well? A culture of gambling became pervasive on the trails West and eventually became entrenched in the lives of those who arrived in California. Then the spirit in California moved east into Nevada and Las Vegas, today's Mecca for the "People of Chance."

By concentrating on the West and on Las Vegas, the author seems to neglect the role of gambling in other U.S. cities, particularly those along the East Coast. Bugsy Siegel is mentioned, but he is portrayed as a Californian, and his mentor and financier, Meyer Lansky, is left out of the story. So too are the other Eastern rogues who discovered Las Vegas, not during some silver rush in the 1860s but in the 1950s after Senator Estes Kefauver moved to end Eastern gambling establishments. Kefauver is given a mention in the book as being an agent of snobbish Eastern antigambling forces. In the 1960s, Fidel Castro pushed other gamers toward a safe haven in Las Vegas. Jimmy Hoffa moved Eastern and Midwestern Teamsters union money into Las Vegas. Hoffa was from Michigan, not California. The new visitors to Las Vegas are seen as new frontiersmen, but they are not. They are middle-class and affluent Americans who seek out a place that is different, not a place that reflects the values of their chosen communities. Half of the book is devoted to Las Vegas; an epilogue considers Atlantic City.

This is an interesting fact-filled book. It is a wonderful resource for any gambling library. The author does a great job. Unfortunately he made quite a stretch to find a theme with which to wrap all gambling in the United States. His theme just does not stretch far enough to do the job.

Frey, James H., ed. 1998. *Gambling: Socioeconomic Impacts and Public Policy*. Special volume of *The Annals of the American Academy of Political and Social Science*. Thousand Oaks, CA: Sage.

James Frey took up the task of compiling 13 new essays of gambling with an end-of-the-century perspective. By 1998, the gambling industry had emerged as America's newest growth industry, with casinos—either commercial or Native American—in as many as 30 states and lotteries in 38 states plus the District of Columbia. Sixty percent of Americans gambled each year, and over 80 percent approved of gambling in some form or another. Nonetheless, there were now heightened concerns about the impact gambling was having on the social and economic fabric of the country. As the special issue was being put together, a new National Gambling Impact Study Commission was examining public policy and gambling.

This third volume of *The Annals* that is devoted to gambling starts with William Thompson's essay on gambling throughout the world, suggesting that the Las Vegas pattern of wide-open casinos would dominate thinking in North America but would not be exported to European jurisdictions. Colin Campbell and Garry Smith present an overview of policy issues in Canadian gambling, revealing the paradox of having governments play the roles of both regulator and protector of the public interest at the same time they are operators of gambling establishments. Editor Frey presents an updated survey of federal involvement in gambling regulation. Gene Christiansen explores the role of gambling in the U.S. economy, seeing it as one of the fastest growing sectors and accounting for 10 percent of all leisure expenditures in the society. William Eadington examines different styles of casino gambling, suggesting their varying impacts upon local communities. He is critical of widespread placement of gambling devices in locations accessible to masses of people.

Ricardo Gazel outlines the features of an input-output model of assessing the economic impacts on communities. He concludes that it is essential to look at both the positive and negative impacts of gambling in order to gain a picture of the net value of the enterprise for communities. John Warren Kindt examines the political influence of the gambling industry and its lobbying activities. He traces campaign contributions from the industry and expresses a fear that gambling entrepreneurs could be gaining unhealthy political power in our society. Gary Anders views the very positive contributions of gambling to the development of Native American societies, but he also considers negative influences brought to Native peoples as a result of gambling in their midst. He also laments that Native gambling operations are on smaller urban-area reservations, thereby exacerbating inequalities among tribes throughout the country. Audie Blevins and Katherine Jensen conclude that the introduction of casinos in Colorado mountain towns resulted in substantial economic revival for the towns but at a cost of "cannibalized" retail businesses and extra traffic and law enforcement problems. William Miller and Martin Schwartz found a lack of common ground among studies of casino gambling and street crime. They call for additional research on specific questions tied to more clearly identified theories and hypotheses.

The final three essays of the volume examine pathological gambling. Henry Lesieur explores the costs of treatment as well as the societal costs of pathological gambling. Randy Stinchfield and Ken Winters look at problem gambling among youth. Today's youth are the first generation raised in an atmosphere of pervasive gambling that has been supported by both governments and other institutions including some churches. They call for more research, as findings are incomplete—except for a "robust" finding that young males are much more involved with gambling than are young females and thereby more likely to become problem gamblers. Las Vegas scholars Fred Preston, Bo Bernhard, Robert Hunter, and Shannon Bybee view the changing nature of the stigmas society places upon gambling behavior and consequences for public policy.

Frey, James H., and William R. Eadington, eds. 1984. *Gambling: Views from the Social Sciences*. Special volume of *The Annals of the American Academy of Political and Social Science*. Beverly Hills, CA: Sage.

The second special edition of *The Annals* devoted to gambling examines the many changes that have involved the gambling experience since 1950. The volume offers perceptions into factors that led to the widespread expansion of gambling, most notably in the area of lotteries as well as Atlantic City casinos. Many policy dilemmas are identified as the writers accept the notion that gambling will continue to expand, yet collectively they point to a need for considerable government involvement to control potential negative attributes of gambling. Law professor G. Robert Blakey leads off with a discussion of legal events surrounding gambling since 1950. He discusses the Kefauver Commission, Robert Kennedy's program on organized crime, and the Organized Crime Control Act of 1970 as key milestones for generating federal laws on gambling. He also examines state efforts to control legalized gambling while calling for continued federal efforts to develop coherent policies on illegal gambling in the United States.

William R. Eadington follows with an essay on development of Nevada regulatory law from a time when control was essentially local in the 1940s to the comprehensive state oversight that remains in place today. He suggests that further controls will be necessary as the casino industry continues to expand. These controls may be focused upon credit policy and betting limits in order to protect problem gamblers and also on advertising controls. He offers the strict controls over casinos in England as a model for consideration. Peter Reuter explores difficulties facing law enforcement as a result of the existence of illegal gambling. He sees public opinion as drifting away from support for antigambling laws in light of the need for law enforcement activities in other areas of more concern—mainly in the area of illicit drug trading and use. Jerry Skolnick, author of *House of Cards* (see annotation below), suggests that new casino jurisdictions can achieve the best control atmosphere if the number of licenses is restricted and that potential casino operators should compete openly for the licenses by making proposals that suggest how they will best operate in the public interest. Nigel Kent Lemon offers a capsule description of regulation of

casinos in the United Kingdom and how authorities have dealt with companies that violate rules of operation.

Joseph Rubenstein reviews the campaign to bring casinos to Atlantic City. On the one hand, he establishes that the casinos have accomplished great revenues through their operations. On the other hand, he suggests that there have been difficulties in achieving the urban land development that was a primary purpose of legalization. He points to rampant land speculation along with ineffective government intervention as specific areas of difficulty. Atlantic City is viewed as a unique experiment with casinos but a more typical exercise in a politics whereby dominant concerns of casino revenues outweigh the altruistic goals of urban redevelopment. Dean Macomber's essay examines internal operations of casinos.

H. Roy Kaplan surveys the history of lotteries and their reemergence as a system to generate revenues for governments. He finds that lotteries are regressive taxes and that they have limited value in bringing funds to specific areas selected for political reasons. He is also critical of lottery advertising and concludes that such advertisements promote a no-work ethic in the United States. He finds lotteries to be moral paradoxes, as their increased levels of success are associated with an introduction of greater social problems. Editor Frey offers a cogent review of gambling from a sociological perspective. He laments that sociologists have not applied theories to the gambling phenomenon in a widespread manner, and he suggests that the theories provide a fruitful source of approaches for more understandings of gambling. Igor Kusyszyn concludes that the motives for gambling are quite complex. He suggests that scholars look at gambling as adult play and that psychological theories underlie both problem gambling and normal gambling activities.

Jim Smith and Vicki Abt also look at gambling as play activity and compare gambling games to other games. They suggest that our culture's embracing of many games in youth in effect teaches us how to gamble and play commercial games as adults. Leading scholar of pathology Henry R. Lesieur and treatment innovator Robert Custer present a categorization of pathological gambling, explore the phases of the problem gambling careers, and describe two methods of help—Gamblers Anonymous (GA) and professional counseling. They believed that by the year 2000 the medical model of pathological gambling (that it is a disease) would be fully accepted, the numbers of GA chapters would have increased dramatically, governments would be more involved in treatment, insurance companies would cover treatment that would also have government support, and there would be much more study of problem gambling. It should be noted that these predictions were not fulfilled.

David M. Hayano takes a look at people who experience gambling as their full-time profession. He presents a typology of these gamblers, their background, the games they play, and their rates of success and failure. George Ignatin's excellent essay explores sports betting, starting with the premise that the betting has some attributes of rationality. He further looks at specific games, discusses odds and point spreads, and addresses policy implications for the future.

Goodman, Robert. 1995. *The Luck Business: The Devastating Consequences and Broken Promises of America's Gambling Explosion*. New York: Free Press.

Robert Goodman is a former Boston newspaper reporter who has taken on the cause of fighting gambling in the United States. He became a leading spokesman in opposition to the spread of legalized gambling. In these pages Goodman presents a case buttressed with many documented facts, considerable notes, and an extensive bibliography. It is a point-of-view book, but then he has a strong point of view. He hits all the key points—compulsive gambling, crime and gambling, the economic drain caused by gambling operations that rely on local players, the cannibalization of local consumer dollars when gambling appears on the scene, the regressive nature of gambling taxation, the economic development failure of Atlantic City, and political manipulations by gambling operators.

Goodman expresses a view that governments have taken on attributes of compulsive gamblers as they chase after more and more tax revenues from games even when they realize that the revenue flows are hurting their economies. He also portrays the government as the predator in his discussion of lottery organizations. He concludes that "in considering future policies, it is crucial to understand that gambling expanded not because of a popular movement clamoring for more, but because of aggressive lobbying by the gambling industry" (179–180).

Goodman sees more pressure for expansion and more negative consequences in the future. He calls for a national plan to mitigate such harms. He believes that governments must authorize independent impact statements before there is new legalization and that the impact statements should be shared with the public. He called for a national study of gambling, and the force of his voice was heard by Congress the year after the book was published, as that body authorized the National Gambling Impact Study Commission.

Greenlees, E. Malcolm. 1988. *Casino Accounting and Financial Management*. Reno: University of Nevada Press.

The general literature of casino gambling does not contain many writings on accounting and financial management, yet this is the industry where money is the product. Without the flows of money in and out of gambling establishments (which have no other product), there would be no gambling industry. Amazingly, E. Malcolm Greenlees's volume is the only comprehensive book on the subject. Written in the late 1980s, the book is in need of updating in places, but the concepts discussed are still very relevant.

Greenlees burdens himself with the task of writing for too wide an audience, yet the result should be satisfactory for most. The book is for a general public interested in casino gambling. Therefore there is an initial section examining the environment of casino gambling. The focus is upon Nevada, although Atlantic City information is included. The date of writing precluded a discussion of Native American and riverboat gambling. A chapter on taxation details the state and local obligations of casinos to the degree needed for an actual operator. The author includes a well-written description of revenue flows, and he provides critically needed definitions of basic terminology that is often misunderstood: *win, handle, hold*. The concepts are then applied to the specific operations—first, to slot machines, and second, to a variety of table games.

A very important chapter deals with credit accounting. Credit is the lifeblood of the major Strip casinos and other high-roller facilities, and controls in this area are vital for casino success. An auditing chapter outlines the many reports that are required from a casino accountant. Tax liabilities are also described along with several "tricky" issues, for example, treatment of markers and unpaid debts. The book ends with a general discussion of financial management: internal controls to ensure there are no thefts of assets, controls to ensure full reporting of revenues and revenue transactions, and data necessary for making managerial decisions on operations.

Greenlees's book is well written. It contains many amusing sidelights, and it contains solid documentation. Its value is greatest for the layman interested in casino operations and for the casino accountant who may be assigned to a casino project for the first time. Although the detail of this book might not be sufficient to give an accountant full knowledge to move into all facets of casino work, it certainly would provide that individual with an essential primer.

Grinols, Earl. 2004. *Gambling in America: Costs and Benefits*. Cambridge, UK: Cambridge University Press.

This is a vitally needed book for policy-makers as well as academic scholars.

This is one of a few volumes that comprehensively analyze the most critical questions regarding the legalization of gambling: where does gambling money come from? And where does it go? How does gambling financially impact the social fabric of communities? Who are the ultimate winners and losers when a gambling enterprise locates in a town? Grinols has been a professor of economics at the University of Illinois and Baylor University, and he was formerly a senior advisor to the President's Council of Economic Advisors.

Grinols's book devotes chapters to the notions of personal freedom and its economic value as well as harms that come from gambling. He puts specific dollar figures on matters such as being able to visit a casino without having to leave one's community. He analyzes the economic role of major actors in the gambling equation: the owners of enterprises, the players, lobbyists, government officials, as well as the opponents of gambling. He uses precise economic models to calculate the value of jobs and economic development generated by casinos as well as government revenues. He gives attention to the idea of economic cannibalization that follows a casino coming into a town.

He devotes considerable energy to a review of empirical studies of social costs and benefits associated with casinos. He measures the benefit in not having to travel distances to gamble when casinos are available near one's residence. But he also examines the results of surveys of troubled gamblers and their losses in casinos as well as their participation in borrowing and even stealing funds in order to gamble. He presents a litany of newspaper stories about personal tragedies that come to troubled gamblers and to those who care about them.

Hashimoto, Kathryn, Sheryl Fried Kline, and George G. Fenich, eds. 1998 *Casino Management: Past, Present, Future*. 2nd ed. Dubuque, IA: Kendall-Hunt.

In 1974, Bill Friedman wrote *Casino Management* (Secaucus, NJ: Lyle Stuart), a text describing gambling developments in Nevada along with basic processes of management and regulation. It was revised in 1982. Not until the mid-1990s did new volumes begin to appear on the scene expounding upon managerial aspects of casino gambling. The premier text on casino management, *Casino Management: Past, Present, Future,* is in its second edition. Author-editors Hashimoto, Kline, and Fenich collaborated with each other and also found outside writers to gather materials for a set of chapters that represent the essential topics necessary to an integrated whole.

The first two chapters look at basic information about the casino gambling industry. They include a discussion of terminology, a chronology of events, and the structure of gambling in Las Vegas and Atlantic City, on riverboats, and on Native American reservations. The next set of chapters closely examines the rules of table games and slot games. A third collection of chapters offers commentary on management structures for surveillance, human resources, and financial controls. Following sections deal with marketing, hospitality, and broader social issues: the economic impact of casino gambling, casinos and crime, and children and casinos. A summary chapter looks at the future of gambling. I. Nelson Rose uses his "third wave" model to predict that gambling will be outlawed in the United States in the year 2029.

Accompanying the author-editors' text is a computer disk that explains many casino games. The disk and the text package represent a quantum leap forward from Friedman's 1974 and 1982 editions. The success of the first two editions of Hashimoto, Kline, and Fenich's book suggests that the future will find many more books devoted to the topic of casino management.

Hotaling, Edward. 1995. *They're Off: Horse Racing at Saratoga*. Syracuse, NY: Syracuse University Press.

They're Off takes off with George Washington, the first Saratoga Springs tourist in 1783. Soon there was a resort—the first resort in the United States, then horse racing, and more racing, and more racing. *They're Off* takes off but never really stops. Edward Hotaling has written a long descriptive account of Saratoga, New York, its racing, and many events surrounding the track—boxing matches and training camps, intercollegiate regattas, and casino gambling. The book is set out in chronological fashion, not going anywhere except through time. Within the pages of the meticulously researched effort (with extensive notes and bibliography), however, there are more than mere details of one race after another.

Within the covers of *They're Off* there is evidence, which unfortunately is not highlighted and labeled for the reader, that Saratoga may have truly been the gambling center of the United States from the Revolutionary era through

World War II. The account presented by the author, who is a native of Saratoga, is sprinkled with many inside stories of the American horse racing set. In fact, the horse crowd at Saratoga helped establish the Travers Stakes and gave rise to the development of Belmont and Pimlico tracks and to the notion of an American Triple Crown. Saratoga was the scene of the first major boxing matches, and the first major betting on collegiate sports event took place there.

Four of the nation's leading casino entrepreneurs and gambling giants in history used Saratoga as a venue for their trade. John C. Morrissey won the U.S. boxing championship at Saratoga and later built the grandstands for the track. He also became the leading casino operator in Saratoga as well as in New York City while serving as a congressman and a state senator.

Morrissey was followed by Richard Canfield, who ran the nation's most elegant casino at Saratoga from 1890 to 1905. After Canfield left center stage, Arnold Rothstein came out of the wings. While overseeing the casino games at Saratoga he also manipulated the results of the 1919 World Series in the Black Sox Scandal. Rothstein became the leading bookie in the United States. But he did more while at Saratoga. He mentored Meyer Lansky and Lucky Luciano by giving them the operations of his craps games. In the 1930s, Lansky then came to run the casino games of Saratoga, and he moved his dealers and took his newly developed talents from Saratoga on the road to Hallandale, Florida, and to Havana—and via Bugsy Siegel to Las Vegas. This incredible lineup of "Hall of Fame" level gamblers ended its involvement in Saratoga, as did all other casino operators, only after the Kefauver investigations led illegal operators in the United States to abandon their venues and to go Las Vegas and elsewhere.

The long arduous story of Saratoga racing provides a perfect counterpoint to the notion in John M. Findlay's *People of Chance* that gambling in the United States was intrinsically tied to the nation's westward movement.

Hsu, Cathy H. C., ed. 1999. *Legalized Gambling in the United States: The Economic and Social Impact.* New York: Haworth Hospitality Press.

Hsu, Cathy H. C., ed. 2006. *Casino Industry in Asia Pacific: Development, Operation, and Impact.* New York: Haworth Hospitality Press.

In her initial book Professor Hsu collects 12 essays, each of which analyzes the contemporary casino gambling scene in the United States. The first section addresses historical development of gambling, the second section examines the economic issue of gambling, and the third section analyzes social issues linked to gambling. The four essays in each of the sections take a close look at one major sector of the casino industry—the Las Vegas casinos, the Atlantic City casinos, Native American casinos, and finally riverboat and low stakes (Colorado and South Dakota) casinos. The essays are written by a collection of academic scholars and gambling regulators who bring a variety of perspectives to the subject. Authors include William Thompson, Shannon Bybee, Patricia Stokowski, Denis Rudd, James Wortman, and the editor, Cathy H. C. Hsu.

Although the book presents a neat uniform structure for the topics presented, the individual essays do not parallel one another. For instance, the social impact entry for Las Vegas makes a community comparison of Las Vegas with four other comparably sized communities on factors such as population growth, government expenditures on social welfare, crime rates, and health care indices. The Atlantic City entry focuses upon crime and compulsive gambling in Atlantic City and its environs, and the Native American social impact essay considers tribal divisions and non-Native exploitation of casino developments, as well as traffic and ambient crime. The "other casinos" entry looks at how small towns have been changed with the introduction of casinos and the attitudes of residents toward the new enterprise. Although the original chapters do fly off in several different directions, each stands alone as a valuable contribution, making the book a worthwhile read for a person interested in casinos in the United States and their effects upon life in their midst.

Hsu's second collection of essays look emerging casino type gambling in the Pacific region. The first five articles examine historical and current developments in several venues: Australia, Korea, Macau, Japan, and Southeast Asia. These are followed by discussions of social and economic impacts of casinos in Australia and Korea, the Chinese gambling culture, and licensing and accounting issues in regional gambling. Authors include Hsu, Choong-Ki Lee, Ki-Joon Back, Nerilee Hing, Glenn McCartney, Frederick Gushin, and William Thompson.

Jarvis, Robert M., Shannon L. Bybee, J. Wesley Cochran, I. Nelson Rose, and

Ronald J. Rychlak. 2003. *Casino Law Cases and Materials*. Newark, NJ: Lexis Nexis.

Gambling law had not been a subject taught at law schools to any noticeable extent until the 21st century. While the tentacles of legalized gambling were reaching first into a majority of states and then all but two of the states, the subject was pushed aside as being of either no significance, or of not having the dignity deserving serious legal academic attention. The same factors restrained the development of other academic treatments of the subject. But law schools and the full array of academic disciplines are finally giving notice. More than 20 law schools now have courses devoted solely to gambling. And with this volume they at last, have a legal textbook devoted to the subject. Unlike the earlier works of Professor Rose, this is not a commentary on what is the law and what it should be, but rather a traditional textbook organized around 99 cases as well as passages of legislation and legal commentary. To one browsing the shelves of a law library, this book would fit in well with leading works such as *Prosser on Torts*, or other such volumes on property, procedure, criminal law or other topics.

This law text follows its introduction with comprehensive chapters on state-run lotteries, charitable gaming, pari-mutuel gaming, sports wagering, casino gaming, shipboard gaming, Native American gaming, and Internet gaming. As the law of gaming is rapidly developing, it should be expected that the authors will be constantly working on updates for this essential volume.

Johnston, David. 1992. *Temples of Chance: How America Inc. Bought Out Murder Inc. to Win Control of the Casino Business*. New York: Doubleday.

When Howard Hughes swept into Las Vegas and started buying casino properties from the Mob, the Nevada establishment celebrated. A savior had come to deliver the city from an impending federal crackdown. Nevada suddenly felt legitimate. When Hughes turned out to be a less-than-desirable recluse, worries started up again. But this time (1969) a new state law permitted public corporations to own casinos, and the more reliable Hilton Hotels came to town, followed by other respectable corporate leaders such as Ramada and Holiday Inns.

Starting in the 1970s, casino observers have claimed that the industry had cleaned up its act with major corporations and the federal Securities and Exchange Commission's oversight. Things could not possible go awry. Wrong! The theme of David Johnston's polemical attack on Las Vegas and Atlantic City casinos is precisely that "business as usual" never left, even after the Mob leaders were bought out and left (at least left the management offices of the casinos).

Johnston served as the Atlantic City bureau chief of the *Philadelphia Inquirer* before writing this exposé. He is now on the staff of the *New York Times*. The new casino owners have been not at all reluctant to rub shoulders with mobsters. Worse, they have engaged in a wide array of unsavory practices of their own: cheating stockholders, breaking contracts, laundering money for bad people, falsely advertising their products, and nurturing compulsive gamblers. The writer devotes chapters to specific casinos and their sordid stories. He tells how

Tropicana cheated Mitzy Briggs out of her share of the property, how several casinos were financed with Michael Milken's junk bonds, how Donald Trump engaged in an art of deception with New York politicians and then with New Jersey gambling authorities. The suspicious beginnings of Resorts International are examined, as is the way in which Steve Wynn won advantages for his Las Vegas Strip and downtown properties.

The book makes fascinating reading whether one accepts its tenuous premise or not. Grains of truth certainly suggest that regulators should be more vigilant as they license and oversee operations. The writer can be faulted, however, for not making a conclusion by setting out policies that should be followed by gambling jurisdictions. A similar exposé treatment could probably be directed at electric utilities or automobile giants. But then, Ralph Nader has already done those exposés. Free enterprise makes us what we are, good and bad, and human.

Kaplan, H. Roy. 1978. *Lottery Winners: How They Won and How Winning Changed Their Lives*. New York: Harper and Row.

In his life story, General Colin Powell observes how his father and an aunt won big by betting on a number. As a result his family was able to move out of a troubled neighborhood to a more stable community in Brooklyn. His aunt had had a vision of a certain number in a dream. When she went to church the next day, the first hymn listed above the altar carried the same number. Although, he does not mention it, one might sur-mise that certain family financial pressures were relieved by the win and that Powell could now focus more energy on the academic pursuits that opened up the stairs on the ladder of his success. His story is one story of the consequences of "the big win." Roy Kaplan gathers other stories, but they are not all as happy. The sociologist conceived of a study of winners in conjunction with Dr. Carlos Kruytbosch of the National Science Foundation. Their initial goal was to assess commitment to work in the United States. Kaplan learned much more.

With an incredible tenacity, Kaplan was able to interview 100 big money winners in Illinois, Maryland, New Jersey, New York, and Pennsylvania. He interviewed one-third of all million-dollar winners in the United States as of the mid-1970s. Interviews lasted an average of three hours each. Kaplan sought out all 37 of these winners in New Jersey and was able to interview 33 of them even though most had changed their addresses, phone numbers, and in some cases even their names.

The interviews revealed that many of the big winners had a variety of psychic or religious premonitions prior to their wins; however, the stories were not all that persuasive, as similar premonitions accompanied losing experiences as well. There could be no conclusion but that the winners were not really "chosen" but instead were merely "lucky." Most had purchased multiple tickets over a considerable time before they hit their "big win."

The win was followed by a short period of elation, and then an incredible amount of harassment and feelings of fear. Generally the winner was not psychologically prepared for the onslaught of publicity and then the "nightmarish intrusions" of others into their lives. Many were threatened with physical harm. Telephones rang incessantly with callers begging for money or offering business deals. Winners often felt sympathy for the pathetic situations people portrayed as they asked for money, and as a result felt guilt when they had to turn people down. The calls included attempts to scam the winners. Friendships were strained and even broken. Relationships with coworkers were destroyed. In a period of high unemployment, many of the winners were made to feel guilty that they remained at their jobs—hence depriving others of work. Family life was disrupted as distant relatives expected gifts, and parents fought with children, and spouses with each other. There were some divorces that were a direct result of the win, although those marriages may have been weak ones before the win.

Most of the winners did quit their jobs, although many did not want to. Work relationships changed for the worse in most cases. The study suggested that people work for functional reasons—for survival and out of habit, and not because they derive true satisfaction from their jobs. When the people had a chance to get out of jobs they did not like, they jumped at the chance. The preponderance of winners, however, were people of lower educational attainment and lower income levels. Many lacked marketable skills and could not contemplate moves to better jobs. Moreover, they did not have life skills that permitted them to structure their free time in such a way as to generate satisfaction. Instead they exchanged the "tension and toil of their jobs for boredom and monotony in their expensive new homes" (115). When they wanted to return to work, they found that there were no "good" jobs for them. And psychologically they "could not go home again"; that is, they could not return to their old jobs.

Life transitions were easier for a group of widows that won the big prize. Nonetheless they had fear and confusion thrust into their lives and, cut off from previous personal relationships, felt an added burden of loneliness and isolation they did not have before their winning occurred. This group, however, achieved a greater sense of security and comfort as result of their "godsend" (133).

Kaplan writes, "Of all the bitter pills lottery winners had to take, taxes were the hardest to swallow" (134). Players were often harassed and even prosecuted by the Internal Revenue Service. Many did not anticipate their taxation burdens, and they were also confused by a constant "torrent" of tax advice from friends, relatives, and strangers wishing to be their tax counselors. When some discovered their new high tax brackets, they felt that they had to quit their jobs as they were not keeping much of their wage earnings. Particularly bothersome were inheritance obligations, as the taxes had to be paid on the entire prize amount even though the winners (and winners' estates) were paid annual installments rather than lump sums. To cope with this, many winners felt the necessity to take out special life insurance policies so their estate could meet tax obligations. The promise of instant wealth was not realized by most players, as taxes added to installment payments really only gave them a measure of additional wealth, but nothing close to the amount implied in the announced prizes. Unfortunately, people close to them felt they now had the wealth implied in the total prize.

Kaplan writes that the national study group examining gambling in the mid-1970s recommended that prizes be tax exempt; however, this recommendation was totally ignored by Congress. In contrast, other countries (e.g., Canada) do not tax gambling winnings. A rationale for nontaxation is that all the players' money (the money used to buy lottery tickets) is already after-tax money.

The first purchase the winners went after was a new home, followed by furniture and amenities such as swimming pools. Many became saddled with large mortgage payments before they could assess all their future costs. Although the winning of the big prize introduced many adverse circumstances into their lives, the lucky lottery players did not regret winning, and none wished to give the money back.

Kaplan made his study nearly a quarter-century ago, but there is no evidence that his conclusions would be materially different today. His energy and persistence in tracking down a bit of reality on gambling "winners" produced a text that is valuable for anyone wishing to understand the impact of the gambling industry today.

Karlins, Marvin. 1983. *Psyching Out Vegas: Winning through Psychology in the Casinos of the World*. Secaucus, NJ: Gambling Times of the Carol Publishing Group.

A new employee at Disneyland was starting his job as others do, using a broom and dustpan to pick up litter off the sidewalks. A customer approached him and said, "Excuse me. Could you tell me where Adventureland is?" As she spoke, she was facing a large sign above the employee. The sign said "Adventureland" and had an arrow pointing the direction. The employee, engrossed in picking up candy wrappers, gave her a "Duh"-type look and said, "Can't you read? It's down that way." New employees are closely watched, and a supervisor saw the exchange. He came up to the employee and kindly suggested that it would have been more appropriate to have put the broom and dust pan down, stood up, and said, "Why, yes, it's down the sidewalk this way. Would you like me to walk that way until we can see it?" And, "Enjoy Adventureland; it's one of our most popular attractions." The employee answered, "Okay, sure, but the sign was right in front of her; do we expect our customers to leave their brains in their cars?" "Yes," replied the supervisor, "now you are getting it."

Disneyland expects its customers to leave their brains behind and enter a fantasy land when they pass through the gates. So too do the casinos of Las Vegas. After all, the players are not making investments as if they are at a Wall Street broker. They are coming into a fantasy land, an "Adventureland," where their dreams have no limits. The casinos only ask that the customers leave their brains behind, or at least some of their brains.

Marvin Karlins dissents. He wants the players to use their brains to the fullest and control their emotions so that they can engage in a rational activity he calls "psyching out Vegas." Karlins explores the many psychological ploys casinos use to entice players to gamble and lose—noises, color schemes, floor layouts, lighting, no windows, no clocks, free drinks. He then sets forth his game plan for player victories. He looks at each casino game and presents clues for winning strategies. He explores the odds and gives advice on the best bets. In roulette, the player should only play at a single-zero wheel and make even money bets such as red-black and odd-even. (The trouble is that few Las Vegas casinos offer single-zero wheels.) In craps, the player should only bet the basic pass-don't pass, come-don't come. And the player should bet the maximum odds bet after the first roll out. At baccarat, the player should only make "player" or "banker" bets. In blackjack, the player should use a basic strategy and only play at larger casinos with well-lighted tables in quiet areas. The game played properly demands thinking. The players is advised to stay away from slots, keno, and the big wheel.

Most of the remainder of the text is devoted to money management schemes. The player should always be sober and rested, and he should learn to look like a loser so that the casino will not suspect he is "psyching" them out. For the serious player, Karlins is right on target. He fails, however, to give the most sage advice to his investors—find another broker because the casinos charge too high a commission fee. The casinos have the edge at every game except poker, where it is all between the players. If the player cannot rationalize the notion of playing and paying for the excitement, dreams, and entertainment—the essential Vegas experience will be lost. Of course, players should avoid behaviors that make losing inevitable. Most will lose, however, and most must lose if there is to be a Las Vegas. Still most also do have a lot of fun. When they get fun value for their money, they are not stupid; they are not leaving all their brains at home. Unfortunately a serious reading of Karlins's book may suggest that they

are. The book is for serious gamblers, not for tourists.

Kling, Dwayne. 2000. *The Rise of the Biggest Little City: An Encyclopedic History of Reno Gaming, 1931–1981.* Reno: University of Nevada Press.

Dwayne Kling has penned a thoroughly detailed account of all the properties and the leading personalities (inside and outside the industry) associated with Reno gambling over a 50-year period. Kling was close to his subject. He lived it. Born in Turlock, California, in 1929, Kling started coming to Reno in 1947 and soon played baseball on a Harrah's Club team. After college and military service, Kling came back to Reno to begin a career in gambling. He was a dealer, pit boss, shift manager, casino manager, and owner. He retired in 1995 and began working with the University of Nevada on several history projects.

This volume proceeds from A to Z with minor and major facts—actually appearing almost as if they were the total facts about the Reno gambling scene. That he covers everything is the strength and perhaps also the weakness of the book—the latter because the book does not reveal a sense of what is important and what is not. The book does not attempt to establish a theme or a story line. That being said, this is a document that can be referred to by any serious researcher who wants to know what happened in Reno from the time Nevada gave a new legal status to casinos in 1931 through the next 50 years—a time frame in which the city went from being the leading casino city to being eclipsed by Las Vegas for that title. The book title is somewhat misleading, as Kling does follow several properties into the 1990s. By cutting off much of his story in 1981 (e.g., having no separate entry on the Silver Legacy), however, he leaves the reader without an understanding of the city's most ardent attempts to cope with a new national gambling scene that includes California casinos.

The book's entries are documented by press accounts mostly from the *Nevada State Journal* and the *Reno Gazette Journal*. The book also includes a large collection of interesting photographs as well as street maps with locations of each property described. He also includes a glossary of universal casino gambling terms, which really have no direct connection to Reno for the most part.

Although the book is geographically limited to the direct Reno area, it chronicles many of the major initial events in the modern casino industry. These include the role of customer service and integrity in the industry and also the role of mass marketing and promotions—illustrated most clearly with entries on Bill Harrah and the Smiths (Raymond I. "Pappy" Smith, Harold Sr., and Harold Jr.). Kling also illustrates the beginning of entertainment in casino properties, as well as positive advances in race relations, gender inclusion in the industry, and unionization of resort workers. The entries that should command the reader's closest attention include "Boomtown," "Cal-Neva," "El Dorado," "Fitzgeralds," "Harolds Club," "Harrah's," "Mapes Hotel," "M.G.M. Grand," "Nevada Club," "Primadonna," and "Riverside."

Knapp, Bettina L. 2000. *Gambling, Game, and Psyche*. Albany: State University of New York Press.

Bettina L. Knapp explores the "universal and eternal mysteries" arising out of games of chance. She presents 10 chapters, each of which probes varying types of gambling behavior found in major works of literature. Thus she seeks to bring out pertinent aspects of the gambling personality or the "achiever syndrome." The volume explores works of Blaise Pascal, Honoré Balzac, Edgar Allan Poe, Fyodor Dostoyevsky, Matilde Serao, Sholom Aleichem, Hermann Hesse, Yasunari Kawabata, and Zhang Xinxin. Knapp concludes that gambling is part of society's "mainstream behavior," and only at its extremes does it raise problems for individuals and society. At the same time, players do become victims when habit overtakes reason. Superstitions, signs, omens, and even religious beliefs may serve to hasten the demise of reason and hence make the player vulnerable to the evil side of gambling. The book's brief introduction provides a valuable history of gambling in ancient societies of both the Eastern and Western civilizations. As Knapp begins with a universal discussion of the gambling phenomenon, so too does she develop her essays in a manner that seeks to bring out the universal qualities of gambling.

Lehne, Richard. 1986. *Casino Policy*. New Brunswick, NJ: Rutgers University Press.

Richard Lehne documents decision-making events in New Jersey government and politics from the first statewide campaign for casinos in 1974 until a decade later when nine casinos were in operation in Atlantic City. His focus is on legislative decisions regarding regulatory structures and philosophies, and then the establishment of operational rules by the legislature and the agencies of control. He also seeks to evaluate the effectiveness of the control mechanisms established. Lehne does not try to establish whether or not casinos in New Jersey have been successful, leaving that task to others (he cites the work of George Sternlieb and James Hughes, *The Atlantic City Gamble*; see annotation below). Rather, he concentrates on what the effects of policy have been.

Lehne contrasts New Jersey regulatory styles to those found in Nevada and elsewhere. He expresses admiration for systems that provide multiple agencies for the regulatory process, even when the agencies often must do identical work. He finds that repetition and competition in regulation can produce positive checks and balances resulting in a public good. He leans somewhat toward endorsing the philosophy of Nevada regulation, which establishes strict licensing requirements and then permits casino license holders to self-regulate with a more passive state oversight. New Jersey on the other hand seemed lax in providing strict entrance requirements for licensing, but then sought to provide intensive, constant oversight of all casino activities. The New Jersey system was much more expensive, allowed for considerable bureaucratic growth, was resented by operators, and at the bottom line did not seem to have any better results. In fact, the system in New Jersey invited the operators to be in conflict with the regulators and hence to have to interact with regulators daily in order to resolve disputes. In the course of the constant interaction, the operators pressed their desires for more relaxed operational rules (some rules, such as those on color schemes in the casinos, had been

extreme) and gradually overwhelmed the regulators with their desires for change. Hearing no countervailing voices from a general public, which lost interest in casino regulation soon after the doors of Resorts opened in 1978, the regulators soon began to think like the operators. Lehne uses the model of bureaucratic capture found in the public administration work of Marver Bernstein as a cogent point of reference (*Regulating Business by Independent Commission* [Princeton, NJ: Princeton University Press, 1955]). He then indicates ways in which the agencies in New Jersey could try to loosen the casinos' hold on them.

Lehne seriously suggests that new gambling jurisdictions should reconsider the model of private ownership of casinos. He indicates why New Jersey endorsed the private model and why it probably could not be reversed. On the other hand, he feels that much of the regulatory turmoil that ensued in the Garden State could have been avoided had the casinos been public entities, or perhaps publicly owned with private operators. It would be valuable now with more than a decade of such public/public-private style of ownership and operations in Canada to return to his themes and find out if the country to the north has performed in the superior manner Lehne would envision.

Casino Policy is very well researched and thoroughly documented, with 45 pages of notes and bibliography. It is an academic book, but it can be easily read and understood by nonacademics and policymakers who may face the crucial questions posed by the author.

Lesieur, Henry R. 1984. *The Chase: The Career of the Compulsive Gambler.*

2nd ed. Cambridge, MA: Schenkman Publishing.

The first edition of *The Chase* was written by Henry Lesieur in 1977, at a time when he was a sociologist who rejected the notion that problem gamblers were "sick" people. Over a six-year period and contact with the National Council on Compulsive (now Problem) Gambling as well as with many therapists treating problem gamblers, however, Lesieur accepted a fundamental value in the medical model of problem gambling. Whether or not the troubled gamblers were "sick" in a medical sense, if they could be convinced that they were, they could be put on to the path toward recovery, a path away from family disintegration, away from criminal acts and other social maladies related to their excessive play. Still a sociologist, Henry Lesieur in the second edition of *The Chase* sees no incompatibility between his profession and the psychologists who help the problem gamblers. He sees no problem in considering troubled gambling to be an addiction.

Henry Lesieur's book has received the highest praise from the true pioneers in the treatment field. Dr. Robert L. Custer wrote in the introduction to the second edition:

> *The Chase* is far and away the finest sociological study done on the pathological gambler. It is scientific with a disarming simplicity which gives an informative and impressive body of knowledge for all mental health professionals and laymen. Henry R. Lesieur has written a fundamental study on pathological gambling. His perceptions, insights, and concepts are based on an open-minded scientific approach.

During the compulsive gambler's career, Lesieur sees the player becoming trapped in a chase. The player enters the career with many options, but as he bets and loses, his involvement in gambling action increases, and he finds himself in a spiral with fewer and fewer options available. The options may be expressed as sources of money for gambling: family, friends, job, banks and legitimate lending institutions, loan sharks, and then crime. The gambler is in a career in which the options disappear, with his losses becoming more and more inevitable. Temporary wins help pay off immediate debts, but they do not help the gambler achieve the levels of success desired. Even big wins are not stoppers, because the compulsive gambler needs action. Action is found in playing, and that action exceeds even sexual play in terms of pleasure. And so the chase goes on and on until the gambler either destroys himself—through ruined health, suicide, or legal penalties—or can be rescued by a recovery program with treatment.

The book is a product of a long process of interviewing problem gamblers, their families, friends, and therapists. Lesieur began the research in 1971 and found interviewees wherever he could. He went to Gamblers Anonymous meetings, jails, and state and federal prisons. His hundreds of interviews and his discussions with treatment specialists helped direct him on his chase to gain understanding of compulsive gambling so that we may now share in reading his words.

Light, Steven A., and Kathryn R. L. Rand. 2005. *Indian Gaming and Tribal Sovereignty*. Lawrence: University Press of Kansas.

Rand, Kathryn R. L., and Steven A. Light. 2006. *Indian Gaming Law and Policy*. Durham, NC: Carolina Academic Press.

Steven Light and Kathryn Rand have emerged as the leading academic scholars on Native American gaming. They are both professors at the University of North Dakota in Grand Forks. They offer very balanced views regarding Native American gambling, but it is apparent that they are strong supporters of the rights of tribes to seek economic development through the tools of casino gambling. In this regard, they seem to be quite fortunate that they conduct their research and their direct analysis of tribal gaming deep in the rural Midwest of America, where they are surrounded by large tribal nations that have suffered greatly from poverty for the several centuries they have had to share the continent with immigrants from other continents. Had they done their research from the two coasts and been fed by the political struggles of tribes with often fewer than one hundred members surrounded by lucrative metropolitan markets ripe for offerings of monopoly casinos (such as Foxwoods or Baronas), they might have succumbed to the "myths" that casinos have only made a few Native Americans into undeserving millionaires. Such is not the case in the Dakotas, where even with casinos, tribes struggle with poverty. Also it is much easier to deal with the major concept in their book—sovereignty—when the analysis concerns tens of thousands of Sioux and other tribes than when it is advanced as the political reason why one (a case in California) or two (the surviving members of the Pequots in Connecticut) people should receive all the economic

benefits from a tribal casino. That the Sioux remain a nation is vital for advancing their cause for casinos.

The authors' books are recognized as the most comprehensive analyses of the development of public policy and Native American gaming. The authors' first book devotes an extensive chapter to sovereignty and the struggles to have casinos that involve compromising tribal sovereignty with the sovereignty of state governments and the federal government.

This is followed by a step-by-step political history of Native gaming from the Seminole and California bingo games, to the *Cabazon* Supreme Court case of 1987 and the passage of the Indian Gaming Regulatory Act of 1988, and to challenges and law cases afterwards. Next they present a very precise analysis of the economic and social benefits coming to tribes because of the casinos. This is followed by a tribe by tribe discussion of what casinos have meant for Native American peoples.

The authors' second book is a volume that looks specifically at the development of gaming law for tribes. It describes the federal legislation section by section and takes apart subsequent cases point by point. The two books represent an essential part of the literature of gambling today.

Longstreet, Stephen. 1977. *Win or Lose: A Social History of Gambling in America*. Indianapolis, IN: Bobbs-Merrill.

Stephen Longstreet presents a history that is without a bias—with neither moral condemnation nor romantic illusions about gambling. Longstreet sees gambling as endemic to human nature and pervasive throughout all the layers of the social structure. The author admits to being an amateur gambler, and he enjoys his topic thoroughly. The book starts with a story of a Las Vegas weekend, with portraits of all the appropriate actors on the scene. These include high rollers and ordinary folks, bits of history of this casino and that casino, and descriptions of the games that are played. He then launches his historical journey from the days of the sailors on the *Santa Maria, Pinta,* and *Niña* through the colonial era. Paul Revere, George Washington, Ben Franklin, and Andrew Jackson all had gambling connections. The Mississippi riverboat gambler receives a special chapter, as do those who wagered in Saratoga during the racing season, led, of course by John C. Morrissey and later Richard Canfield.

The author then turns his journey westward to the mining camps of the frontier and to Kansas City, Denver, and San Francisco—the latter being the Mecca for the professional gambler at the midpoint of the 19th century. He ventures north to Alaska and the Yukon with Soapy Smith, and he wanders the West with Wild Bill Hickok, Calamity Jane (Martha Jane Burk), and Canada Bill Jones. Longstreet brings the reader into the 20th century with stories of the Black Sox scandals and the emergence of Reno and then Las Vegas as the world cities of gambling. Additional chapters focus on pit bull fights, horse racing, bingo, numbers, and Chinese gamblers. The last chapter seems to be just thrown on. It takes a look at several compulsive gamblers. The book ends with a discussion of gambling terminology and a solid bibliography and index. Like the other panoramas of history, however, the book lacks documentary footnotes. Be that as it may, the book presents materials in a confident manner suggesting authority.

Mahon, Gigi. 1980. *The Company That Bought the Boardwalk*. New York: Random House.

This is the story of the casino company Resorts International from its unlikely origins as Mary Carter Paint Company to its triumphant entrance on the Atlantic City scene as the first licensed casino on the Boardwalk. The story as told by Gigi Mahon is one of Mob connections and illicit political operations in the Bahamas and of compromise and sellouts in New Jersey.

When Fidel Castro took over Cuba in 1959, he (eventually) closed all of the Mob-infested casinos on the island. The operators of the crime-ridden facilities quickly sought other outlets for their talents. Many of the dealers and employees were "clean," so they could gravitate to Las Vegas and Reno. But most of the owners and managers could not meet the scrutiny of the Silver State's new regulatory and licensing bodies. They went elsewhere, finding havens in England (until 1968) and on many other islands, including the Bahamas.

The author was a reporter with *Barron's* magazine assigned to discover the roots of Resorts International. She looks at one set of Cuban casino exiles and traces their steps through the Bahamas and on to Atlantic City, where they gained new respectability, or at least a lot of windfall profits. The characters in her book include Bahamian politicos Wallace Graves, Ralph Grey, Lyndell Pindling, and Huntington Hartford; a cast of wheeler dealers the likes of Bebe Rebozo, Robert Peloquin, and Eddie

Cellini; a full array of New Jersey politicians and regulators on the make; and Resorts officials James Crosby and Jack Davis.

The story traces the influence of the characters in the New Jersey casino legalization campaign and in the implementation process afterwards. The experience documented by Mahon provides a solid prelude for the Abscam scandals that followed in 1980. The stage was set well for a federal sting operation. The state's leaders had been openly compromised; all the feds had to do was catch them at their game behind closed doors. When the New Jersey regulators willingly overlooked the obvious ethical problems of the Resorts operations in the Bahamas as well as in Atlantic City under a temporary license, they gave the signal that Atlantic City was open for the taking. The state had so bought into the rhetoric of the casino promoters that general economic prosperity would follow when the casinos opened their doors, that state regulators seemed not to care who was behind the doors running the games. The end justified the means, but unfortunately, in the eyes of the author, the ends were never realized.

McMillen, Jan. 1996. *Gambling Cultures: Studies in History and Interpretation.* London: Routledge.

Professor Jan McMillen has organized 15 original essays around concepts that place gambling into a wide context of societal development. The essays look at the social and cultural environment of gambling in national and cross-national milieus. In the initial essay, the editor sets forth explaining why societies permit gambling. She emphasizes dominant values: for instance, pluralism in the United States and concentration of economic and state power in Canada and Great Britain. McMillen finds unique historical qualities determinant in most societies. Other authors include John Dombrink, David Dixon, David Miers, William Eadington, Vicki Abt, James Smith, Mark Dickerson, and Michael Walker. The essays look at gambling in Australia, The Netherlands, Great Britain, Cameroon, Senegal, and the United States.

Millman, Chad. 2001. *The Odds: One Season, Three Gamblers, and the Death of Their Las Vegas.* New York: Public Affairs.

Chad Millman has been a writer with *Sports Illustrated* and ESPN. In *The Odds* he looks at the lonely lives of three individuals and their gambling activity during the National Collegiate Athletic Association basketball tournament in 2000. In doing so he provides extensive background information on sports betting in the United States. He looks at history and at scandals associated with the activity. Millman offers his considerable knowledge about the processes of taking bets and setting lines and odds on games. His book is contemporary, and it gives attention to the two leading political issues on the subject: the proposal in Congress to ban betting on college sports and proposals to stop Internet betting.

The political force of the college sports betting ban and the meteoric rise of Internet gambling opportunities have had a major impact upon Las Vegas sports betting in casinos. The "good ol' boys" who used to be walking encyclopedias of knowledge on games are becoming passé as the sports betting exercise is made more democratic with information flowing on the Internet. Casinos are losing action to Internet competitors (400 sites take sports bets) as organizations have tied together various Web sites into quasi-legitimate operations that can be trusted by players. Although only 2 percent of the Las Vegas gambling revenues come from the sports books, the sports betting activity is important, as it draws gamblers onto the casino floors. It offers the casinos opportunities to promote their other activities.

The three characters of the book include one young man who dropped out of Indiana University to seek his fame and fortune with the "big boys" in Las Vegas. He had been very successful running a sports bookie operation in Bloomington. A second young man leads a two-coast life, alternating between running harness race horses in New England in the summer and living in Las Vegas in the winter in order to make basketball bets in the casino. Both lead lives of isolated desperation on the margins of survival, losing much more often than winning. A third character presents a similarly dismal picture from inside the casino's operations. He works for the sports book manager at the Stardust. He participates in setting and adjusting the lines and sweating out each big game day. Over his shoulder stand Federal Bureau of Investigation agents who finally make a bust, as many players are laundering ill-gained money through their sports bets. His life is also a life of stress and isolation.

All the characters started their sports betting games in Las Vegas with optimism and excitement, and all ended on the margins of society. The book paints a gloomy picture of the future of sports betting in the casinos, with federal legislation seen as cutting out much of the activity, and the Internet making the rest of the activity largely unnecessary for the serious gambler.

Mirkovich, Thomas R., and Allison A. Cowgill. 1996. *Casino Gambling in the United States*. Lanham, MD: Scarecrow Press.

This 432-page volume is a gold mine for gambling researchers. It includes nearly a thousand annotated entries for writings on gambling between 1985 and 1994. Besides the mere listings, the authors give the readers a social and historical context for the gambling industry. Especially helpful is the section on casinos gambling. It is arranged into categories such as Indian gaming, riverboat gaming, casinos and crime, casinos and society, casino law and regulation, and casinos and development. The book also lists gambling regulatory agencies throughout the United States, as well as private associations, organizations, and gambling consultants. Although admittedly limited in a geographic sense and a chronological sense, the book is an essential resource for the student of the gambling phenomenon.

Ploscowe, Morris, and Edwin J. Lukas, eds. 1950. *Gambling*. Special volume of *The Annals of the American Academy of Political and Social Science*. Philadelphia: The American Academy of Political and Social Science.

Morris Ploscowe and Edwin Lukas draw together articles that examine the subject of gambling at a time when public attention associated the activity with crime and just as the Kefauver Committee of the U.S. Senate was beginning its inquiry into the role of organized crime in the United States. This volume represents the first comprehensive collection of studies on the issue of gambling. It is the first of three special issues of *The Annals of the American Academy of Political and Social Science* devoted to gambling over the second half of the 20th century. It is organized under four headings: "Legal Status of Gambling," "Various Forms of Gambling," "The Gambler," and "Gambling in Foreign Countries."

Five essential questions were asked by the editors as they assembled the articles: (1) Does gambling undermine public morals? (2) Is most gambling activity controlled by organized criminals? (3) Do profits from illegal gambling support other illicit activities? (4) Is legalization a tool that can be used to control illegal gambling? and (5) Can laws against gambling be enforced if it is not legalized? The thrust of most of the studies is to portray gambling in a negative light and argue against legalization.

Ploscowe, a New York judge, takes an overview of the law on gambling reaching back into English history and coming forward to discuss bookmaking, pinball (a "menace to the public health" [7]) and slots, and lotteries. Virgil Peterson of the Chicago Crime Commission explains why it is difficult to enforce antigambling laws, mostly in a Chicago context. Paul Deland sees that legalization leads to increased gambling "with all its attendant criminal evils" (23), and Joseph McDonald gives a good early description of casino gambling in Nevada, "a parasite here to stay" (33).

Oswald Jacoby provides more descriptions of games such as punchboards, numbers, and cards—including canasta. Several entries focus on race betting and bookies, and Ernest Blanche presents a good historical overview of lotteries, followed by an essay titled "Gambling Odds Are Gimmicked!" There is also a solid presentation of traditional Native American gambling along with a description of terms used by professional gamblers (also described in a separate article) and descriptive accounts of gambling in Latin America and Sweden. The volume contains an essay by Robert Lindner on the "Psychodynamics of Gambling." His work laments the fact that so little attention has been devoted to the psychology of "the gambler"— meaning the troubled gambler—as he references the work of Ernst Simmel, Sigmund Freud, and Edmund Bergler. He recognizes gambling problems as a disease and also a behavior pattern tied to genetic sources. He sees the gambler as an "obsessional neurotic engaged in what might be called the making of magic" (106). The core of the essay is a case study that is analyzed in a Freudian framework.

Reid, Ed, and Ovid Demaris. 1963. *The Green Felt Jungle*. New York: Trident Press. Reprint, 1994. New York: Pocket Books.

Demaris, Ovid. 1986. *Boardwalk Jungle: How Greed, Corruption, and the Mafia Turned Atlantic City into the Boardwalk Jungle*. New York: Bantam Books.

In the modern era of gambling, Reid and Demaris stand out as the first two authors who leveled a wholesale attack on the legitimacy of "legalized" casino gambling. A consistency runs through these two volumes. The first title, *The Green Felt Jungle*, views Las Vegas in the early 1960s, a dozen years after the Kefauver hearings, and still under the thumb of organized crime families and politicians who willingly did their bidding. The book looks at each major Strip facility and records how the mobsters essentially called the shots. The authors tie Las Vegas to the Lansky mobsters through Meyer Lansky's brother Jake, who was a secret owner of the Thunderbird Casino and in their opinion a partner with the lieutenant governor of the state of Nevada. The many stories and the many charges may be shocking to readers who are not familiar with the Las Vegas scene but they are not exactly earthshaking to people who have followed the news reports of all the events revealed. Reid and Demaris prove to be good collectors of stories, good writers who can turn a phrase and make an event interesting. They do not document their information, however, nor is it presented as new insights that could lead to any action. Nonetheless, coupled with Wallace Turner's *Gambler's Easy Money*, published two years later, the state of Nevada knew it was in trouble, and perhaps state authorities were quite willing to invite Howard Hughes to bring his fortune to the state in order to "clean things up" or, more appropriately, help "clean up" the state's image and the image of its leading industry.

In *Boardwalk Jungle,* Demaris picks up the tale of Las Vegas casinos and the Mob twenty-five years later in Atlantic City. Actually, he presents considerable background information suggesting that the Mob was in Atlantic City a long time before the casinos came in 1978. Demaris looks at the campaigns for casinos in 1974 and 1976 and at the 1977 legislation providing for the casino regulatory framework. He looks at the promises about the differences casinos would make: jobs, urban renewal, prosperity for the poor and elderly, a revitalization of tourism. And the promise that there would be no Mob. Governor Brendan Byrne said these words on June 2, 1977, the day he signed the legislation setting up the rules the casinos would live by: "I've said it before and I will repeat it again to organized crime: keep your filthy hands off Atlantic City. Keep the hell out of our state" (Brendan Byrne archive, www.governors .rutgers.edu/BTB%20Atlantic%20City/ BTB-ACtimeline.htm). No such luck. The theme of this sequel is that the chickens were given to the foxes. The casinos were handed to the Mob.

After providing background material, the author looks at the first casino and how it got its temporary license. Because the state was so committed to starting the economic miracle, a temporary license was given to Resorts International even though the state knew of many past wrongs and bad associations of the company's executives. Even after the company engaged in many practices considered to be against the interests of integrity after the casino opened, nonetheless the state gave it a permanent license because to do otherwise would destroy "the dream."

And so the pattern was set for licensing eight other casinos before Demaris's book was written. But the dream was not realized. Not by 1986 in any regard. Atlantic City was still a slum. The poor were still poor. Unemployment had not ended. Tourism had not returned. Gamers came in droves, but they were the poor and elderly who could not afford the 23 trips they made each year (on average). The state's treasury was not blessed by gambling taxes. The taxes were much less than the take from the state lottery. Crime had increased. Atlantic City had become the Boardwalk Jungle.

The books are written to be sensational. They are not written for researchers, as neither uses notes, cites authority in the text, or provides bibliographies. The very skewed anticasino point of view in each makes the lack of sources a critical shortfall.

Rose, I. Nelson. 1986. *Gambling and the Law*. Hollywood, CA: Gambling Times Press.

Over the past three decades, I. Nelson Rose has emerged as the leading academic authority on the law of gambling. He teaches gambling law, torts, property, and other legal topics at Whittier Law School in Costa Mesa, California. *Gambling and the Law* is the first volume that has been especially devoted to gambling law. Unfortunately, it was not organized as a legal textbook but rather as a set of chapters on seemingly random topics, albeit they do have in many cases very good value separately. Rose did not want to advise the reader on his or her legal problems—lawyers, not books, give advice. Rather he wished to prepare a legal guide to educate the player as a player, the player as a taxpayer, the player as a debtor; the casino as a license holder, a lender, an entrepreneurial organization, a taxpayer, and accountant; and also the academic or the general publican interested in gaming of one sort or another.

The book offers a good discussion on the common law of gambling, on the right to advertise gambling products, on gambling taxation, and on gambling debts. Some chapters are limited in value to people in specific geographical areas—chapters on California poker rules, on Nevada casino licensing. And some chapters stray far from the subject at hand (which is gambling). There are chapters on how to hire a lawyer and how to find legal citations in a library. The book is well documented, with notes both in the form of sources and in the form of commentary.

Rose, I. Nelson, and Martin D. Owens. 2005. *Internet Gaming Law*. Larchmont, NY: Mary Ann Liebert, Inc.

Is Internet gambling legal? This is the main question posed by the authors of this book. The answer is one we already know: "Yes." "Well, maybe yes." "No." "Well, maybe no." "Yes—if, and, yes—but. No—if, and but, except for, and considering whether." And so it goes. In the pages of *Internet Gaming Law*, I. Nelson Rose and Martin D. Owens offer answers—all of the above answers, with critical commentary, and their perceived observations and wit. In addition, there are thorough discussions of many of the 233 law cases cited and scores of pieces of relevant legislation.

Books are fun, if they can be. The reader might think that no task could be as boring as plodding through a law text on the vagaries of Internet gaming. But this editor found the Rose-Owens volume to be an enjoyable read, and even at times fun too.

The book's chapters include a discussion of the basic question above, with a comprehensive review of the legal elements involved in the definition of "gambling." Also included is a chapter reviewing specific postures by federal, state, and local venues on the regulation of online gambling, and another on the philosophical question: Is there a "right" to gamble? One chapter focuses on state laws, another on federal laws, and yet another on Native American gaming laws. The latter offers a comprehensive review of the Indian Gaming Regulatory Act. There is also a consideration of the means for transferring funds back and forth between players and operators. One chapter looks at the roles of mediating persons including bankers, servers, and advertisers. The final chapter looks at the future, with a discussion of technological advances that may preclude any prohibition of online gambling. However, the authors do point to advances that may allow venues to track Internet gaming within their geographical limits. They write "that technology will make Internet gambling quicker, more appealing, and allow easier access from smaller platforms and devices."

They pose prospects that physical gambling may face an inevitable demise. At least land-based casinos themselves will be consumed internally with virtual technologies appealing to their patrons. Their prediction has already become reality, for the Nevada legislature recently gave authorization for casinos to allow patrons to carry around hand-held betting computers as they wander the public areas of the casino.

Rose and Owens eventually see every personal computer worldwide being a "slot machine." Cable television connections will put a potential slot machine into every living room. Betting exchanges, trivia games, skill games, or fantasy leagues will challenge authorities, as these operations dodge the central elements found in the legal definition of the term *gambling*.

Rosecrance, John. 1988. *Gambling without Guilt: The Legitimation of an American Pastime*. Pacific Grove, CA: Brooks-Cole.

John Rosecrance presents an overview of the development of gambling in the United States. He offers chapters on games in the 19th and 20th centuries, taking a look at race betting, lotteries, and casinos during each era. The value of these chapters is that he has taken material utilized before and condensed it into a quick read. The value of the book overall, however, is in his later chapters. Here he focuses upon problem gamblers, the strategies such gamblers use to cope with losses, and treatment opportunities for those who abuse gambling activity. Rosecrance expands upon themes he first expressed in his 1985 book, *The Degenerates of Lake Tahoe*. In that work he described gamblers (who played at Tahoe casino race books) as a fraternity of normal individuals who at various times hit losing streaks or succumbed to bad information and gambled and lost excessively. These gamblers (among whom Rosecrance lists himself) were living in a parallel world. They were not deviant, nor were they psychotic. They were normal. After all, all of us have subcultures into which we retreat at times.

Rosecrance provides a strong argument against the notion that excessive gambling is in and of itself a disease to be fitted into some medical model. Treatment need not require total abstinence, for the essential behaviors are normal. Rather the excessive gambler must be counseled with information, educated, reeducated, and given strategies for coping. In a sense the cure involves behavior modification. The excessive gambler's train has become derailed, fallen from the tracks. But the train can be righted and placed back on the track, and the journey can proceed with the gambler on board. Many other scholars (e.g., see Michael Walker's *The Psychology of Gambling*) have followed a lead provided in Rosecrance's work as they have pursued explanations of problem gambling within the context of acceptable social behaviors, rather than seeing it as a disease or an impulse control disorder. The value of Rosecrance's two major books is in the influence and guidance they have provided for those in the academic professions who look at gambling as their object of study.

Ross, Gary. 1987. *No Limit: The Incredible Obsession of Brian Molony.* New York: William Morrow. (Published in Canada in 1987 as *Stung: The Incredible Obsession of Brian Molony.* Toronto: Stoddard Publishers.)

Gary Ross's excellent description of the case history of Brian Molony penetrates the gambling industry in a way that suggests reforms are long overdue. In *No Limit,* Ross gives a detailed account of Molony's life as a gambler. As a child of 10, Molony was drawn to racetracks near Toronto. Soon he was a bookie for his schoolmates. In college, his early gambling successes turned to failure. He learned how to deceive his friends and family and how to conceal his gambling activity. He was bright and industrious,

and extra work efforts could always give him funds to pay off his losses.

His outstanding record as a student won him a position with Canada's second largest bank—the Canadian Imperial Bank of Commerce (CIBC). He was put on the fast track; at age twenty-five he was promoted to be assistant manager of one of the bank's largest branches in Toronto. There he was placed in charge of loan accounts. His work habits were exemplary, and he earned the admiration of all those about him. He was hooked on gambling, however, and he was a loser. After one disastrous weekend, Molony discovered that his bookie-creditors were demanding an immediate payment of $22,000, "or else." Actually, he was not in physical danger; the creditors would have gladly accepted smaller payments over time. The "or else" was a more psychologically devastating threat: "Pay up, or else we will take no more bets from you." But he had to bet. How else was he to "catch up"?

Molony could not be cut off from the action. As some criminology theorists might view it, he had a motive, he had a desire, and he had an opportunity. He seized the opportunity. To a pattern of excessive gambling he now attached a history of embezzlements of money from loan accounts he controlled (or created) at the CIBC branch. Within 19 months, he had "borrowed" C$10,395,800 and US$5,081,000. Often Molony would borrow from one account to repay another, so the bottom-line embezzlement figure totaled US$10.2 million.

Molony's first $22,000 "loan" was just the initial step in a campaign of chasing losses with more gambling—a campaign that led Molony from local racetracks to the casinos of Las Vegas and Atlantic City. Brian Molony's banking activities constituted the "largest single-handed bank fraud in Canadian history," according to the cover of *No Limit*. Yet the story told inside the cover suggests that the frauds were anything but single-handed. Although unassisted, Molony was constantly aided by very lax standards and shoddy internal procedures at his bank. Gary Ross presents us not only with a true story that reads like a novel but also with a treatise on gambling behavior and the structure of two financial industries—casino gaming and banking.

Ross presents a summary of causes of compulsive gambling—from Freudian analyses to biochemical hypotheses. He examines processes of treatment and describes the program Molony joined after being "discovered." But even when Molony agreed to join a program, he insisted that his problem was not a "gambling problem" but a "financial problem." Molony was "discovered" because some hard-working vice squad policemen listened to months of telephone conversations of known bookies. At one off-guard moment, Molony used his real name, and the police began to track down this big-time gambler, convinced that he must be a drug dealer. When they found that he worked at CIBC, they knew that the game was embezzlement. But for the bank the game was embarrassment. Not only had the bank been "stung" (to the tune of US$10.2 million), but they were "stung" by their own structural incompetencies that prevented an internal discovery of 93 cases of fraud extending over a 19-month period. Now they would be "stung" by publicity.

Readers can almost sense that Molony would still be out there gambling today if the bank had caught him first. Certainly the bank would not have desired to have a public prosecution. He would have resigned, Lloyd's would have covered the loss (which they—the biggest of those "stung"—did), and it would have been business as usual. After all, had the bank not lost much more with poorly secured loans to Third World countries? Instead, the bank was exposed by outsiders. So it went through a ritual of hand-wringing, firing several employees whose actions were unrelated to Molony's, and permitting a graceful early retirement for Molony's immediate supervisor, a man who should have been much more vigilant. Molony's early mentor, a man who engineered his early promotion, was banned to a branch bank in western Canada. His disgrace was followed by a suicide. Pressures of adverse publicity caused some structural changes regarding responsibility and lines of authority in handling loans.

From the book we can sense that some executives at the now closed Marina Casino in Las Vegas might feel that they too were "stung." A low-level credit officer at the Marina refused to give Molony complimentary services because his financial transactions were not in accordance with detailed house rules. The casino lost his business while he was still gambling in the tens of thousands. The rejection by the Marina propelled Molony to higher ground. Soon he was the most prized customer of Caesars Boardwalk Casino in Atlantic City. Caesars sent its Lear jet to Toronto to bring Molony in for gaming weekends. The casino offered him fine meals and female friendships, but Molony wanted only ribs (without gravy), a big Coke, and lady luck. He thought of gaming, never personal pleasure. At home he drove an old car, dressed in untailored suits, skimped on his share of the rent for the apartment he shared with his girlfriend, and embezzled millions. Caesars had to know something was wrong. But they wanted his money so much that they actually sent casino officials to Toronto to open up the casino cage there in order to handle his financial transactions. They helped Molony dodge international money transfer rules as well as New Jersey gaming regulations.

As a punishment from New Jersey authorities, the casino was closed for one day, incurring a million-dollar business loss (to compare with over $3 million won from Molony). No major executives were disciplined. Ross's book has become the basis for a movie titled *Owning Mahowny* (2003).

Rothman, Hal, and Mike Davis, eds. 2002. *The Grit Beneath the Glitter*. Berkeley: University of California Press.

It has been said that behind the false, glitzy, neon façade of Las Vegas, there is a genuine façade. Hal Rothman and Mike Davis have collected a set of 22 essays (14 written by people living in Nevada) which seek to describe the real Las Vegas that lies beneath that "genuine" façade. As a student of gambling, it is important that one seeks to find the reality of life in this community, as the basic industry of Las Vegas has become the model for all casino gambling throughout the world. All eyes of casino developers—be they Asian, European, or American—focus upon Las Vegas as they seek to establish their identities. This has been the case since the 1940s. This is especially the case since 1993, when Nevada regulators permitted

Nevada casino license holders to freely and openly (and without their advance permission) pursue licenses in other venues. (An essay in the book by this editior describes the history of the "Foreign Gaming Rule.") As the industry is a model, so too perhaps the community can be seen as a model for other communities who would wish to have casinos also dominate their social and economic life.

The truth seems, however, that the qualities of Las Vegas life do reflect some unique characteristics that could not be easily duplicated elsewhere. Hal Rothman's shortened career (he tragically died at 48 after a valiant fight against Lou Gehrig's disease) established him as the premier historian of the new American West. He called Las Vegas the first new metropolis of the 21st century and the first postmodern city.

His and Davis's collection of essays may be divided into the "academic" and those called "personal commentaries." The academic articles look at phenomena such as taxes and services in the Las Vegas economy, water policy, power policy, the effects of urban sprawl in the fastest growing city of the land, race relations, and the history of capital movement into and out of the casinos. There is also an excellent piece on the history of the leading employees' union of the community.

Personal stories deal with matters such as growing up in a rapidly expanding Las Vegas, moving to Las Vegas and meeting members of the Mob—who ran the little league. Other essays examine views on gender from a female professor exploring a male-driven community, the community of prison inmates, making movies in Las Vegas, and life as a worker in the casinos.

The title uses the term "Grit"; however, the "grit" is really just the toughness of day to day living by ordinary people. The title should not imply that Rothman and Davis were the first to discover that there is a dark underside of Las Vegas. Writers discovered that even before Reid and DeMaris wrote *The Greenfelt Jungle*.

Rubin, Max. 1994. *Comp City: A Guide to Free Las Vegas Vacations*. Las Vegas: Huntington Press.

Max Rubin is a self-proclaimed Comp Wizard. He plays a different kind of game in Las Vegas. He takes the reader through excruciating detail after detail in an exploration of everything that a player could get "free" from a casino—from parking validations, a drink, buffets, gourmet meals, to a show, boxing match, suite of rooms, or an airline ticket. This is a studied effort that must be designed for the student of casino gambling or the casino executive in training. Rubin explains the processes that casinos utilize in determining which players or nonplayers receive each kind of "comp," or free item. He demonstrates that the system is flawed and that players and others can take advantage of the casinos. Some players who place the notion of getting some item or service as a gratuity above almost everything else will find the book valuable. They will learn they must sit at a gambling table and play very slowly and that they must always get a pit boss to see them as they are sitting down. They must lead with large bets and later lower their bet amounts after the pit boss has recorded them as high rollers. They should buy large amounts of chips in a noticeable manner, but then secretly slip them into their pockets so they do not have to risk them in bets. It is a game—a stupid game. The game is predicated on the notion that many of the tourists who come to Las Vegas are cheap pigs who do not place any value on their time. In this editor's opinion, the point of coming to Las Vegas is having fun and being entertained—hopefully winning some money, or at least not losing too much in the process. It is not being able to pig out on things a person would not otherwise want—such as excess fatty foods and desserts, or drink after drink. So although Rubin's book is fun to read and educational for one wanting to know how casinos think, let's hope it is not used as a guide book for tourists. It really tells a person how to ruin what could otherwise be a very good vacation experience.

Scarne, John. 1986. *Scarne's New Complete Guide to Gambling*. Fireside Edition. New York: Simon and Schuster.

John Scarne has been recognized as being among the leading authorities on gambling in modern times. He has been called America's Hoyle by many people. His knowledge was commanded by the Kefauver Committee and by the Department of War, which called upon Scarne to go among the wartime troops to tell them about the nature of games and the structures of odds, as well as the many scams that crooked players could use. One source claimed that he saved GIs millions and millions of dollars. Legitimate casinos in Las Vegas and Reno also have used his help. Scarne has penned many thick volumes on games: *Scarne's Encyclopedia of Games*, *Scarne—25 New Kinds of*

Skill Games, Scarne on Card Tricks, and *Scarne on Cards*, among many others. *Scarne's New Complete Guide to Gambling* has been his best-selling book. It was originally published in 1961, issued in a second edition in 1974, and then reprinted in a paperback version by Simon and Schuster in 1986. But even with the updated paperback version, much material on the environment of games is very dated. For instance, he neglects the entire wave of government-run lotteries that has swept over North America since 1964. On the other hand, the detailed description given to the mathematics of games and the discussion of luck, chance, skill, odds, payoffs, and gambling systems are enduring. After his general introduction, Scarne presents 30 chapters on the major forms of gambling—horse racing, sports betting, lotteries (prior to the modern United States), the numbers game, bingo, and the many precomputerized table and machine games found in casinos. He also examines games not usually associated with heavy gambling—bridge, backgammon, and gin rummy. He gives extensive treatment to carnival games as well, in addition to punchboards, chain letters, and pyramid schemes. About the only games he neglects to discuss are chess, checkers, and the games they play on Wall Street. The book is capped off with a valuable glossary containing more than 400 items. For the reader who wants a single volume on games, this has to be it.

Schwartz, David G. 2006. *Roll the Bones: The History of Gambling*. New York: Gotham Books.

Schwartz, David G. 2003. *Suburban Xanadu*. New York: Routledge Press.

David Schwartz is the director of the Director of the Center for Gaming Research at the University of Nevada, Las Vegas. His love of gambling has been lifelong. He grew up in Atlantic City, and attended the University of Pennsylvania as an undergraduate. His doctorate work was in history at the University of California, Los Angeles.

Suburban Xanadu is his first book. It is essentially an extension of his doctoral dissertation. It is a great achievement when a newly credentialed scholar is able to have his dissertation accepted by a major publisher, who then distributes it for consideration by the general public. *Suburban Xanadu* offers the reader a history-packed volume on casino gambling in Las Vegas and other American venues. The book presents the material in an orderly manner (chronologically, that is), covering many topics that have been presented in many other volumes as well. Some very good material is new. *Suburban Xanadu* seeks to establish that casino gambling is a normal (e.g., healthy) American pursuit, and that casino operators and regulators have been able to keep the casino industry honest and aboveboard in almost all cases. In this sense, it is a "point of view" analysis; however, it is presented as if it were a factual analysis. The book is very well documented, but the overall tone is not always convincing. "Suburban" is not a proper descriptive term for Las Vegas at all. First, Las Vegas is a city, not a suburb. Second, the Las Vegas Strip—which is technically under political control of the Clark County government—is not now, nor ever was a "suburb." The Strip was developed on open land—the term "rural" might be appropriate—but it was in fact deserted (more accurately: never previously occupied) desert land. Before casinos, no one ever lived by the Strip, and even afterwards no suburbanites lived by the Strip. There have never been single family (stand alone) houses near the Strip. Indeed, numerous apartments accompanied the development of Strip casinos, but they housed dealers, room attendants, and cocktail waitresses, not suburban families. No Las Vegas school is located within walking distance of the Strip.

The use of the word "suburb" also becomes a device for declaring that Atlantic City has been a rousing success. Schwartz concedes that the city of Atlantic City has remained a dismal decaying center of urban blight, but he dismisses the fact that the main purpose of having casinos was to bring urban development to Atlantic City, not to suburbs. The growth of suburban economies around Atlantic City simply has not been the goal, and it has not done the trick. It is not a good basis for declaring the "success" of Atlantic City, any more than one could say that the three casinos of Detroit have given the Motor City economic development, because life is good in Bloomfield Hills.

The other title concept of "Xanadu" comes from a poem by Samuel Taylor Coleridge. "Xanadu" was the pleasure-dome for royalty in some fictional Mideast land. It may work to call the big resort casinos of Las Vegas "Xanadus," but it is unclear why that is important to the intended message (if there is a central one) of the book. The author points out that the typical Las Vegas Strip resort is actually bigger than the Coleridge' fictional "Xanadu," but what does it mean to say Las Vegas is "big"? The Luxor pyramid casino on the Strip is bigger that the Luxor pyramid in Egypt, the Monte

Carlo Casino on the Strip could house all the casinos of Monaco under its roof, and the entire village of Bellagio in the Italian Alps could fit inside the casino of that name on the Strip.

The idea that the Mob, which did dominate early Strip development, was somehow internally honest and professional is advanced and this notion is also unconvincing. Schwartz contends that integrity was present in the Mob-run casinos. Overall, it can be suggested that the casinos were happy to simply have the odds in their favor in honest games (when the players were losing). However, there are ample stories of casinos confronting high roller players who are enjoying fabulous runs of good luck. The stories find the casinos changing honest dealers (for dishonest "mechanics") or changing decks of cards or dice, and then deliberately cheating the players.

The value of the book is not in the opinions of the author but in meticulous well documented scholarship used in drawing out a multitude of stories about activities tied to the emergence of Las Vegas as the leading resort city of the world. It is not a quick read, but it is a good read.

Roll the Bones presents another story—a worldwide story that reads much faster and is not clouded by conclusions that can be challenged. Schwartz traces gambling phenomena from knucklebones of sheep found in caves that are discerned to be gambling devices for our cave man ancestors. He ends with modern day computerized slot machines and automatic card shuffling devices. In between are the stories of critical figures such as mathematicians who expounded upon theories of probability and early casino operators who seized upon new knowledge of odds to develop facilities that could be attractive for the masses. His stories go to all the corners of the earth as he treats the creation of casinos and other forms of gambling on all continents. It all ends in Las Vegas, where the volcanoes and pirate ships and pyramids seem to bring the wide-ranging history all together in one place and at one time. There is no theme other than that gambling has always been with us and probably always will be with us. Holding it all together is a good read between two covers.

Sifakis, Carl. 1990. *The Encyclopedia of Gambling*. New York: Facts on File.

Carl Sifakis has been a crime reporter for United Press International and the *Buffalo Evening News*. He has also been a freelance writer. His writings have gravitated toward the roles of criminal groups in the United States. In addition to this encyclopedia, he wrote *The Mafia Encyclopedia* and *The Encyclopedia of American Crime*. This encyclopedia does give many pages to the underworld connections of gambling. The book covers the subject of world wide gambling from A to Z. Concentrated attention is given to games, their odds, their rules, and ways in which they have been compromised by shady characters. His detailed attention to games finds him offering dozens of items on various games of poker, 10 entries on gin games, and 7 on games of rummy. The detail that is presented on games must be the book's greatest asset. Sifakis also presents a description of gaming in almost every national and subnational jurisdiction in the world. Many of the offerings reflect personal travel experiences. They seem to be dated in many cases, however, and appear to be collections of observations that may or may not have been verified. He does sprinkle the book with many interesting stories about famous gamblers—both nice people and rogues. On almost every page there is an entry that will be of interest to any reader who would relish knowing more about gambling. Did you know that archaeologists digging in Egypt found dice inside pyramids that dated back 4,000 years? And the dice were crooked! Did you know that the Earl of Sandwich—noted for the obvious—was a compulsive gambler? Fun reading. Unfortunately, the writer did not document his entries, so we must either trust him as "the source" or wonder. On the other hand, Sifakis does provide a bibliography that includes many of his sources. These limitations being noted, the material in the book is comprehensive and should have value to all interested readers. The editor of these volumes turned to Sifakis over and over again when refining the entries in this encyclopedia.

Skolnick, Jerome H. 1978. *House of Cards: Legalization and Control of Casino Gambling*. Boston: Little, Brown.

House of Cards receives this editor's nomination for the best book on casino gambling in the 1970s. Author Jerome H. Skolnick, a criminology professor at the University of California–Berkeley, made long on-site inspections of Las Vegas casinos and the regulatory processes in Nevada over a three-year period before putting pen to paper. He collected historical data, and he interviewed hundreds of participants in the Las Vegas scene. He went on inspection tours with gaming agents, and he rode in metropolitan police cars. He came to know his subject very well.

Skolnick wanted to know how an industry so tied to what was considered "sin" and "vice" could be controlled in the public interest. He starts by examining the broad subject of gambling and considering whether casino "action" is "play or pathology." He concludes that the exercise of gambling can have useful meaning for very normal people. A second chapter looks at the legalization of "sin" behavior in the United States—alcoholic drinking, drug use, sexual relationships. He then turns to the casino, first focusing on the people who form this peculiar social institution: players, dealers, hookers. Then he looks at the games that are played in the casino. Internal management and control are considered essential for maintaining the "house edge" with the odds. He examines surveillance and accounting procedures.

Three chapters written by Skolnick's graduate assistant—now professor—John Dombrink trace the rise of the casino industry in Nevada, its search for respectability through legitimate capital investment, and the emergence of corporate gambling. Skolnick then describes the development of the governmental structures for regulation—the Gaming Control Board, the Nevada Gaming Commission, and their subunits. Four chapters are devoted to issues concerned with licensing and the Nevada model of difficult entry and self-regulation with state monitoring. The final chapters consider this monitoring activity: patrolling the casino floor, discretion in enforcement, auditing, and finding hidden interests. In his concluding chapter, the author contrasts Nevada with a widely different model of regulation, that found in Great Britain.

The book is thoroughly documented and well written. It concludes with the dilemma faced by all regulatory agencies. How can a business be promoted for the general economic good of the community and still be held to strict regulatory standards to ensure ethical operations? The question remains unanswered today, more than 30 years after it was posed by Jerome Skolnick.

Sternlieb, George, and James W. Hughes. 1983. *The Atlantic City Gamble: A Twentieth Century Fund Report*. Cambridge, MA: Harvard University Press.

In this editor's coauthored book *The Last Resort* (John D. Dombrink and William N. Thompson, 1990, annotation above), a tale is told of the successful 1976 campaign for casinos in New Jersey. The success and the opening of the first Atlantic City casino halls led to much speculation that large commercial casinos would soon be in more than half of the states. Then like dominos, new campaigns for casinos in state after state fell to defeat. Of course, after that book was published, a movement for Native American casinos and riverboat and limited-stakes casinos changed the pattern of results. It was concluded in 1990, however, that negative reaction to casinos manifested in the many defeats of propositions in the early 1980s was somehow tied to very negative experiences that followed the opening of casinos in Atlantic City.

George Sternlieb and James Hughes document many of those negative experiences in their book *The Atlantic City Gamble*. They provide a well-researched and thoroughly documented account of the New Jersey campaign leading up to the successful 1976 vote. They describe the struggle in the legislature for implementing legislation in 1977, and they chronicle the first signs of realism that came with the licensing process that was followed so that the doors of Resorts International could open on Memorial Day weekend in 1978 (a story told in much more sordid detail by Gigi Mahon in *The Company That Bought the Boardwalk,* annotated above). Soon there were more casinos and soon there was an ABSCAM (a Federal Bureau of Investigation code name based on *Arab* and *scam*)—a bribery scandal that unseated a U.S. senator and exposed the licensing authorities as politicians not always operating above the tables. Political favors flourished in all directions.

Still there were hopes, for there had been many promises. Casinos meant jobs, and by the time Sternlieb and Hughes's book was written there were nine casinos, with 30,000 employees. But not all was rosy on this front, either. The casinos drove existing businesses out of town, as local restaurants and shops could not compete with casino facilities. Also many of their local customers had lost their homes in the mass urban redevelopment called casino construction. It was another case of urban renewal becoming urban removal. It was estimated that 2,000 local residents lost jobs in businesses outside of the casinos. Unfortunately, the jobs inside the casinos did not all go to local residents. Typically the casino employee commuted from the suburbs or from even farther away. City unemployment rates did not diminish. City taxes were supposed to tumble, but they did not. Land was assessed at a

higher value, and taxes went up to pay for additional city services—not for the residents but for the casinos and their many customers. Housing supplies decreased, and housing stock deteriorated as landlords refrained from upkeep in hopes of selling out to casino developers. Crime rates increased.

The authors identified an essential problem in the fact that the visitors to the casinos were not resort tourists like those Atlantic City had attracted 50 years earlier. Now the casinos attracted day trippers on buses. And the day trippers did not spend money outside of the casinos. In chapter after chapter one fact is piled upon another, all leading the authors to conclude in the final paragraph of the book that the costs of casinos development in Atlantic City outweighed the virtues.

Tanioka, Ichiro. 2000. *Pachinko and the Japanese Society.* English ed. Osaka, Japan: Institute of Amusement Industries, Osaka University of Commerce.

Dr. Ichiro Tanioka is the leading gambling scholar in Japan, having authored many books on the subject. This is the first of his books that has appeared in English. In this well-illustrated volume, he brings together many perspectives on the most prevalent type of gambling in Japan, play at the pachinko machine. Although gambling per se is illegal in Japan, pachinko is permitted by legal authorities, who maintain a fiction that the game is not gambling. They assert (and Professor Tanioka concurs) that it is basically a "skill" game, hence lacking the crucial gambling element of chance. They also indicate that the machines are not gambling devices, because prizes are awarded not in cash but rather in merchandise. The authorities pretend not to notice that the merchandise is quickly exchanged for cash by the players outside of the pachinko parlors.

This facet of Japanese gambling law and other parts of the law are explored. So too is the subject of pachinko and pathological gambling. Tanioka examines many types of games, and he ranks the elements of the games such as excitement, expectations, speed of action, money limitations, and rules of play. He then concludes that pachinko is the leading game in terms of its allure for habitual players. He looks at the allure as it impacts various demographic groups in Japan—gender groups, age groups, and social classes. A wealth of statistics reveals the business implications of the pachinko parlors in Japan. Professor Tanioka, who holds his doctorate in sociology from the University of Southern California, ends the volume with a series of proposals aimed mostly at making the game more responsible by eliminating several of its aspects that attract pathological gamblers. This is the definitive English language book on gambling in Japan.

Thompson, William N. 1997. *Legalized Gambling: A Reference Handbook.* 2nd ed. Santa Barbara, CA: ABC-CLIO.

This book is part of the ABC-CLIO World Issues series. The book treats the issue of gambling in the context of U.S. and Canadian developments. An initial chapter introduces gambling by exploring its history and political issues. There are discussions of forms of government regulation of gambling, the rationale for gambling behaviors, and social and religious perspectives on gambling activity. There is also a discussion of the positive and negative aspects of gambling that focuses upon economic impacts and the issue of problem gambling. The book also includes chapters offering a chronology of events, a selection of short biographies of leading figures in gambling history, a review of legislation of gambling, major court cases, several quotations on the subject, a glossary, and a directory of private and public gambling organizations. The book also reviews a wide selection of books and films that have a gambling focus.

Thompson, William N., and Michele Comeau. 1992. *Casino Customer Service = The WIN WIN Game.* New York: Gaming and Wagering Business.

Casinos face a major dilemma: how to take money from customers and send them away empty handed yet still desiring to return. The answer is to give them entertainment value and good experiences. Make them feel good through delivery of top customer service. This is the first volume to be written on the topic of customer service in the casino environment. The book takes a close look at the roles played by executives, supervisors, and frontline employees in the casino. Attention is given to defining just who the customer is, telling how to ascertain customers' wants and desires, and developing a customer service mission statement and objectives that can be measured. Supervisory skills and motivation techniques are examined, as are topics such as dealing with the angry customer, recovery from bad situations, communication, and stress reduction for dealers. The book concludes with several case studies of both successful and unsuccessful efforts at customer satisfaction in casinos.

Thorpe, Edward O. 1962. *Beat the Dealer: A Winning Strategy for the Game of Twenty One*. New York: Random House.

When Edward Thorpe wrote this classic on gambling strategy, he was an assistant professor of mathematics at New York State University. He had received a PhD from the University of California, Los Angeles (UCLA), with research focused upon probability theory. *Beat the Dealer* has to be the most popular application of probability theory ever written. Before this book was written, craps was the most popular casino game. Before craps it was faro. After the book came out, all players who felt they had a brain that could function within a casino environment rushed to the blackjack tables. The casino could be beaten! And they did not have to cheat to beat the house.

Thorpe discusses the many rules of blackjack, and then he explains his winning system. The system is based upon counting cards that have already been played (dealt) and thereby assessing which cards remain to be dealt. If the remaining supply of cards includes an unusually large number of aces and 10-value (face cards and 10s) cards, the probability of having a "natural blackjack" dealt is much higher than otherwise. The natural blackjack consists of two cards—an ace and a 10-value card. The player is more likely to receive a blackjack and so is the dealer. If the dealer gets a blackjack and the player

gets less than a 21 or goes bust (over 21), the player loses his bet—say, for instance, $2. If the player gets the blackjack, the player keeps his $2 and wins $3 from the dealer. This advantage gives the player an odds advantage over the house.

Other advantages may also follow from being aware of the flow of the deck. These are discussed in detail, as are many intricacies of strategies depending on what the player is dealt and what card the dealer shows. Thorpe also exposes flaws in other gambling systems, and he discusses strategies that casinos may use to keep their advantage—or to try to keep their advantage.

Thorpe was not a gambler when as a UCLA student he drove to Las Vegas for a short vacation over the Christmas break. He thought he would find sunshine and cheap accommodations in the gambling city. A fellow professor clued him into a blackjack strategy and urged him to try it out. He went to the tables, but he did not win with the system. But what he did do was discover the game, and he became fascinated with its possibilities. He returned to the university, and he gained access to the high-speed computer of the day. He played hand after hand—hundreds of hands. Soon he had his system, the material for a book, and a new career—and Las Vegas had a lot more blackjack players.

Las Vegas also found that some of these Thorpe system players were winning. So Las Vegas started to ban "counters" from playing blackjack. Players known as "counters" began to use disguises, and cat-and-mouse games ensued for four decades—they are still going on. As a matter of law, the Nevada courts allowed the casinos to expel the "counters," but the Atlantic City casinos were not able to ban them from the games. Instead, Atlantic City operators adjusted by adding decks of cards to the supply that could be dealt for a game, and they began to shuffle cards more often.

Thorpe stands today as a genius who in his quest to beat the house probably did more good for the casino gaming industry that could be imagined.

Turner, Wallace. 1965. *Gambler's Money: The New Force in American Life.* Boston: Houghton Mifflin.

Wallace Turner was a Pulitzer Prize–winning journalist with the *New York Times.* In his 1965 book *Gambler's Money,* he thoroughly attacks the integrity of Nevada casino gambling. He reserves favorable comments for only one operator in the state, Bill Harrah. He strongly suggests that the records of the others justified closing casino gambling down altogether in the state. He regretted that this would not be politically possible.

Turner presents detail after detail about crooked characters and crooked deals, skimming, laundering money, and that infamous Teamsters union fund of Jimmy Hoffa's. A major theme of the book is that illegal gambling profits (either skimmed by the registered owners or funds given to illegal hidden owners) migrate toward other legitimate business. There the money is used to infect the corporate sector with illicit practices that somehow harm the good name of commerce. Turner laments that the southern bloc of U.S. senators is tightly linked to the notion of states' rights (because of the integration challenge), precluding wholesale federal action against the Nevada casino actions that are supported by the state government. Powerful senators such as Pat McCarran, Alan Bible, and Howard Cannon were influential in defending the state's interests. Turner applauded the efforts of the Kefauver Committee, the McClelland Committees, and the work of Robert Kennedy. Somehow he totally missed the connection between John F. Kennedy and his father, the Rat Pack, and their kindred Mafioso clan.

Turner's story is so skewed in one direction that it takes on a total appearance of overkill:

> By the social and ethical rules of American culture, gambling is immoral business, tainting those who operate it. . . . This is a *fact* of sociology, that when gamblers are given a foothold in legality, they rapidly expand it into a permanent bridgehead . . . working their changes on the pattern of American life. (283)

Reading his words, which came into print only shortly after Ed Reid and Ovid Demaris wrote *The Green Felt Jungle* (1963, annotated above), we can understand the elation the good people must have felt in 1966 when Howard Hughes began to buy out the Mob. The book is interesting, fun to read, but the stories are old hat. Society has survived the expansion of casino gambling as a legal commodity into a majority of the states, lotteries into three-quarters of the states, and some form of betting into 48 states. Maybe we have all "gone to hell in a handbasket." If so, we seem to have enjoyed the journey.

Venturi, Robert, Denise Scott Brown, and Steven Izenour. 1993. *Learning from Las Vegas: The Forgotten Symbolism of*

Architectural Form. 2nd ed. (paperback). Cambridge: MIT Press. (First edition, 1972.)

The three authors of *Learning from Las Vegas* are all members of a Philadelphia architectural firm. They joined forces with a class of Yale architectural students and ventured off on a 10-day excursion into the southern Nevada desert and the Las Vegas Strip. The trip took place in 1968. The authors present a defense of the ordinary, the gaudy, even the ugly (or what has been perceived by other architects to be ugly). They see art in the commercial business strip, and its epitome is represented by the casino Strip, otherwise known as Las Vegas Boulevard South. Pop art triumphs in their well-illustrated and diagrammed pages. Las Vegas is presented as a "model" for the commercial strip and supermarket parking lots everywhere.

Venturi, Brown, and Izenour examine the billboards and the large neon signs; the wedding chapels and the shape of the casino buildings, à la 1968; the traffic patterns; and the style of life within the casinos. In their later chapters, they seek connections between what they find in Las Vegas and the rest of the United States. As they do so, they seek out the roots of Las Vegas architecture in the buildings and the utilization of space found in the ancient Roman Empire.

The authors are clearly seeking to shock by their iconoclastic rejection of what had been passing for conventional wisdom in the architectural fraternity of the 1960s. They clearly see buildings and structures as a response to people's needs, but also to their desires and to the patterns of their daily lives. The book represents a precursor to the central notion expressed in *Time* magazine's

1994 article, "All American City" (10 January)—that all of the United States is becoming like Las Vegas. And that, the authors claim, would not be all that bad, for to learn from popular culture would not deprive the architect of his or her status in high-culture society. But then it just may alter the high-culture society enough to make it more sympathetic to current desires.

The shorter 1993 revised edition in paperback offers a short preface and a bibliography of sources that incorporate criticisms and evaluations of the original book.

Walker, Douglas. 2007. *The Economics of Gambling.* New York: Springer.

Douglas Walker is a professor of economics at the University of Charleston in South Carolina. He has devoted his academic career to the study of the costs and benefits of gambling to society. This thorough and well-reasoned volume brings his many years of thoughtful examination of gambling together in a single volume. In this book, he directs his analysis of economics to politicians and decision makers who must wrestle with the questions of legalization and regulation of gambling.

Walker points to the very real difficulties—certainly known by this editor—in putting together dollar figures for costs and benefits of gambling. A first difficulty comes with defining just what a "cost" is, and just who it is that bears this cost. He correctly sees the limits in using questionnaires to measure the costs. Can the researchers get a true sampling of troubled gamblers? This is another problem. How can researchers define just who is a troubled gambler? And then will—or even *can*—the gambler give an accurate accounting of how much money he or she has wagered? And then how much money has he or she borrowed or stolen in order to gamble?

Walker poses a broader question for policy makers. In the absence of a casino, can we be assured that there will be no social costs from troubled gamblers? Good questions all. While Walker offers the questions as vital criticisms of social cost surveys, the reader is left wondering if the costs can be measured at all. And so too, we ask can the benefits be measured?

Nonetheless Walker offers a good analysis of attempts to measure the value of jobs produced in the gambling industry, asking if the jobs are being created or merely shifted from other economic sectors. The chapters of the book provide a good review of economic history and gambling, the economic growth that has come with gambling enterprise, money flows within the industry, and relationships among many industries and the gambling industry. His final chapters review the state of gambling research as he emphasizes the need for transparency in gambling research as well as the issue of conflicts of interest and research. Walker's thorough effort is well displayed in a very complete bibliography found at the end of the volume.

Walker, Michael B. 1992. *The Psychology of Gambling*. Oxford, UK: Pergamon Press.

Michael Walker offers perhaps the best single volume of information on gambling behavior—normal and otherwise. The book is comprehensive in that it gives credence to all the major approaches to gambling phenomena. Nonetheless it is not without a decided point of view. Walker, as distinguished from many writers on gambling behavior that have preceded him, believes that gambling is a very normal activity, albeit subject to abuses. He starts with the premise that gamblers are normal and that they are thinking as they make decisions to play.

Walker's initial discussion focuses upon what he calls "everyday gambling." He looks at the context of play in major forms of games—horse racing, poker, blackjack, and bridge. He sees gamblers starting from a rational position but falling into several categories—part-time players, serious players, bustouts, and professionals. He considers the players' perceptions of luck and skill and their use of thinking strategies—for the most part faulty ones, but thinking ones nonetheless. Walker offers the notion that players are consciously trying to be rational while they play. He then considers games of "pure chance"—numbers, lottos, bingo, and slot machines.

After reviewing many of the theories of gambling (and providing very good descriptions of the theories), he presents the essential message of his book, his sociocognitive theory of gambling involvement. For many people—indeed most—gambling presents a challenge that can be conquered by knowledge and skill. In luck games, players feel that they have a chance, often expressing the notion that "someone has to win." As play progresses, however, the gambler can fall into a trap—not unlike that of any businessperson who has invested in a bad enterprise. Think of the entrepreneur who was losing $1 on each widget he produced and sold. His solution was simple—he had to work harder and increase sales. This line of thought leads to heavy gambling by the gambler—and the business person—and may progress to compulsive gambling.

Walker takes a close look at the measurements utilized to determine who is a problem gambler, including the South Oaks Gambling Screen, the Gamblers Anonymous (GA) scale, and the American Psychiatric Association's *Diagnostic and Statistical Manual of Mental Disorders* (DSM) III, and DSM IV, and he looks at the consequences of heavy gambling on the players as well as on the families of the players. He then rejects the disease model of problem gambling, and he rejects the notion that there is evidence to suggest that gambling is an addiction related to arousal disorders. He also examines a very wide range of treatment strategies for heavy gamblers—from GA steps to psychoanalysis and behavior modification. He concludes with a finding that money is the primary reason for gambling problems. The downfall of the heavy gambler is found in the debts incurred as the player forfeits rationality for irrational thoughts. The most effective treatment for most heavy problem gamblers, then, is to get them to return to rational thought processes. Only then can they correct their misguided behaviors. And then, with rationality restored, they may return to normal gambling behaviors.

Weinstein, David, and Lillian Deitch. 1974. *The Impact of Legalized Gambling: The Socioeconomic Consequences of Lotteries and Off-Track Betting*. New York: Praeger.

Within five years of the first mass-market U.S. lotteries, Weinstein and

Deitch tackled the social and economic questions about gambling that are still being studied. What is the effect of legalized gambling on government revenues, on taxpayers, on family life, and on illegal gambling?

The authors cover a wide range in this short book. They look at the origins of the lottery, lottery administration and marketing, sales experience of the lotteries, operating expenses, and net revenues and their distribution. They seek to measure the impact of lotteries on state finances, concluding that it is quite small. They also find that earmarking funds for programs is not effective unless the legal provisions are very specific. They find that lotteries do not deflect taxes that would otherwise come through sales of other goods. The authors examine the notion of the regressivity of lottery taxes. They are inconclusive in their results, although they see that lottery participation is about equal across all income classes.

Chapters are devoted to foreign lotteries and also to off-track betting in New York State. In a consideration of the social consequences of lotteries, the authors ask, "Is gambling rational?" They conclude that a lottery offers a chance for a big prize that would otherwise be out of reach of a player. For this chance the player need only offer a small consideration that will not affect lifestyle. Moreover, they see lotteries as offering a release from socially induced tensions. Lotteries may operate as safety valves for society. For the most part, they do not think that lottery play will lead to addictive behaviors and the negative social impacts that result—family disintegration, poor work habits, crime. The authors are uncertain about the effects that legal gambling has on illegal gambling enterprise.

The book also poses policy questions about the regulatory format for gambling games—whether they should be run by the government or by private groups. An appendix lists all the states with lotteries (as of 1974) and provides extensive information about the administration of the games. A very thorough bibliography of the early years of state lotteries is included.

David Weinstein's and Lillian Deitch's book is now more than three decades old. The questions asked then by the authors were the right questions. The nature of lotteries and other gambling has changed considerably since 1974, however. All games are faster, and gambling is more pervasive in society. It can be expected that the answers to the questions have changed as well. But then, that is why studies like theirs must continue.

Section Six

LEADING LAW CASES ON GAMBLING

Many policy issues about gambling have not been decided by voters, policy executives, or legislative bodies. Rather, they have come from the judiciary as resolutions between parties in dispute over what the law means. In this section, one of the world's leading authorities on gambling law, Professor I. Nelson Rose, of the Whittier Law School in California (*see* I. Nelson Rose, Biographies), has compiled a synopsis of what he believes to be the 30 leading law cases (or series of cases) on gambling. The cases are arranged chronologically using the date of the first case in the series if there are multiple cases described.

Stone v. Mississippi, 101 U.S. 814, 25 L.Ed. 1079, 1080 (1880), quoting *Phalen v. Virginia*, 8 How. 163, 12 L.Ed. 1030 (1849). The perception of gambling as something akin to disease is illustrated by the U.S. Supreme Court's definition of a lottery. *Phalen* lays out the test for whether a form of gambling is a lottery under federal law: whether the scheme is a "widespread pestilence," meaning, can a player go somewhere, get a ticket and await the outcome without having to play a game:

> Experience has shown that the common forms of gambling are comparatively innocuous when placed in contrast with the widespread pestilence of lotteries. The former are confined to a few persons and places, but the latter infests the whole community; it

enters every dwelling; it reaches every class; it preys upon the hard earnings of the poor; and it plunders the ignorant and simple.

Yellow-Stone Kit v. State, 88 Ala. 196, 7 So. 338 (1890). In this landmark case, the Alabama Supreme Court held that a drawing was not a lottery under its state law when ticket holders were not required to purchase anything or pay an admission fee. This is the first major case to set the precedent that neither benefit to the promoter nor time and effort expended by the customers is consideration; to be a lottery the customer has to pay money for the chance to win. "No purchase necessary" sweepstakes and similar schemes are therefore not gambling.

"The Lottery Case," official name *Champion v. Ames,* 188 U.S. 321, 23 S.Ct. 321, 47 L.Ed. 492 (1903). This is one of the most important decisions ever handed down by the U.S. Supreme Court, not just for legal gambling, but for the country. States were being swamped by Louisiana Lottery tickets, and they asked the federal government for help. Congress responded by passing a statute, still on the books, making it a federal crime to send lottery tickets across state lines. For the first time, the High Court held that the federal government had power over a legal product, simply because it was involved in interstate commerce. This created the modern, massively powerful federal government, since virtually everything involves interstate commerce.

Fauntleroy v. Lum, 210 U.S. 230, 28 S.Ct. 641, 52 L.Ed. 1039 (1908). The U.S. Supreme Court held that the courts of one state must enforce a judgment of a sister state, even if the judgment is on an illegal gambling debt. Again, there is an important factor of timing. States and federal courts must give full faith and credit to the final judgments of all other courts in the American system. However, courts do not have to open their doors to lawsuits involving foreign laws that offend their public policy. The overwhelming majority of courts have held that gambling, even legal gambling, violates local public policy. But the explosion of legal gambling is forcing some courts to reexamine prior decisions. In *Caribe Hilton Hotel v. Toland,* 63 N.J. 301, 307 A.2d 85, 71 ALR 3d 171 (1973), the Supreme Court of New Jersey found the public policy of the state had changed, with the introduction of a state lottery, even before casinos were legalized in Atlantic City. So, a Puerto Rican casino could file suit in New Jersey to collect a valid casino debt.

Federal Communications Commission v. American Broadcasting Co., 347 U.S. 284, 74 S.Ct. 593, 98 L.Ed. 699 (1954). The leading U.S. Supreme Court case on the anti-lottery statutes, 18 U.S.C. §§1301-1307, and what is "consideration" under federal law. The statutes were originally part of the U.S. postal laws, but have been expanded significantly to include radio, television, and federally insured financial institutions, such as banks. The Federal Communications Commission ("FCC") went after television game shows. The Supreme Court held that the statutes, being penal in nature, must be construed strictly. Although the Court defined lottery as being anything with consideration, chance and prize, the Court requires players to expend cash, not just time and effort, for there to be "consideration."

Martin v. United States, 389 F.2d 895 (5th Cir. 1968); *United States v. Fabrizio,* 385 U.S. 263, 87 S.Ct. 457, 17 L.Ed.2d 351 (1966). Two cases demonstrating the law's traditional antipathy toward legal gambling, and creating a problem for advocates of Internet gambling. The defendants in *Martin* were a group of entrepreneurs: Some took sports bets in Texas, made phone calls to their partners in Las Vegas, who then placed the bets with licensed bookies. The Court upheld convictions under the Wire Act, 18 U.S.C. §1084, for using interstate wires for gambling, ruling Congress has the power to prevent all interstate wagers, even to Nevada where the bet would be legal. The federal statute was originally passed to help the states' enforce their antigambling policies. Today Nevada has to enforce special regulations to prevent out-of-state phone bets that would violate federal law. In *United States v. Fabrizio,* the U.S. Supreme Court affirmed the defendant's conviction. His crime: he carried legal New Hampshire Sweepstakes acknowledgments across a state line into New York. There was no accusation that he was helping New Yorkers place bets on this other state's lottery. But the Court ruled the 1961 federal Wagering Paraphernalia Act and other federal anti-lottery laws apply to legal as well as illegal lotteries.

Marchetti v. United States, 390 U.S. 39, 88 S.Ct. 697, 19 L.Ed.2d 889 (1968). The U.S. Supreme Court overturned a conviction for failure to obtain the federal occupational tax stamp to operate as a bookmaker because the requirement that an illegal gambler file tax returns, which could then be used against him, violated the Fifth Amendment protection against self-incrimination. Companion case is *Grosso v. United States.*

Skill versus Luck. The question of skill versus luck has come up in hundreds of cases. Unless a game is a game of chance, it does not fall under the antigambling laws. Examples of how states test for skill: *Morrow v. State,* 511 P.2d 127 (Alaska 1973). In this particular case the question involved tickets for a football pool. The Supreme Court of Alaska understood that there are two lines of cases: Older cases sometimes required that there be no skill at all, an impossibility. New cases look to see if chance is a deciding factor in determining the outcome. The Court decided that Alaska should go with the more modern dominant factor test; and that the burden is on the prosecution to prove at trial the factual question that chance, rather than skill, predominates. *In Re Allen,* 59 Cal.2d 5, 27 Cal.Rptr. 168, 377 P.2d 280 (1962). The California Supreme Court ruled that the card game bridge is legal despite a Los Angeles city ordinance outlawing "games of chance" because bridge was held to be predominantly a game of skill and not luck. The Court used the interesting test of looking at how many books had been published on bridge.

Brown v. Hotel Employees, 468 U.S. 491, 104 S.Ct. 3179, 82 L.Ed.2d 373 (1974). The U.S. Supreme Court upheld the right of New Jersey regulators to disqualify union officials involved in the casino service industry. Local 54 of the Hotel and Restaurant Employees and Bartenders International Union tried to get the regulators' actions under New Jersey Casino Control Act thrown out on the ground that federal law had preempted the field of labor law. The Supreme Court rejected that argument, but remanded the case to the district court to see whether the casino regulators can sanction the union for refusing to get rid of its disqualified officials.

Modern Lottery cases. Legal gambling, including state lotteries, are merely exceptions to the general public policy against gambling. Therefore gambling contracts and regulations are strictly construed.

This is best illustrated in cases involving players filing claims against state lotteries. *Karafa v. New Jersey State Lottery Commission,* 129 N.J. Super. 499, 324 A.2d 97 (1974). An important case in the developing body of lottery law. John Karafa had purchased a lottery ticket that won a $50,000 drawing. Unfortunately, after showing the ticket around after the drawing, he gave the ticket to his mother for safe-keeping—she accidentally threw it out! No one disputed that Karafa had the winning ticket, but the Superior Court of New Jersey dismissed Karafa's suit. The case stands for two important things: (1) Lottery laws must be stringently enforced; and, (2) Unlike other writings, a lottery ticket is not merely evidence of an underlying obligation but the winning ticket is the obligation itself; it is a bearer instrument, like a dollar bill. *Coleman v. State,* 77 Mich.App. 349, 258 N.W.2d 84 (1977). Poor Mrs. Coleman was awarded, wrongly, a $200,000 grand prize by the Michigan Bureau of State Lottery. The Lottery then tried to take back the prize. The Michigan Court of Appeals held that the terms of the Lottery's contract with the purchaser of a lottery ticket were clear and that there was no unilateral mistake or remission. Mrs. Coleman did not win despite the mistake of the Lottery. *Madara v. Commonwealth,* 13 Pa.C. 433, 323 A.2d 401 (1974). Another heartbreaking case in the developing law of lotteries. William Madara lost his wallet, containing a winning lottery ticket, in a flood. He found the wallet and turned in the ticket one year and two days after the drawing. The majority of the Commonwealth Court of Pennsylvania held the lottery rules put a 1-year deadline on redeeming winning tickets; since the prize money was turned over to the state there was no money to pay Madara's claim. Another example of the courts requiring strict compliance with lottery rules. *Molina v. Games Management Services,* 58 N.Y.2d 523, 462 N.Y.S.2d 615, 449 N.E.2d 395 (1983). An important case in lottery law. Mary Molina claimed she won $166,950 in the lottery, but the sales agent failed to keep a record of the purchase as required by the state lottery rules. She sued the sales agent. The highest court of New York threw her claim out, stating that the State and the sales agents were immune from liability under the law, and that the lottery rules had to be strictly complied to prevent cheating.

Olk v. United States, 536 F.2d 876 (9th Cir. 1976), reversing 388 F.Supp. 1108 (D.Nev. 1975). The higher court held tips for dealers, "tokes," are taxable income and not gifts. Dealers argued that tips are merely nontaxable gifts, because they were not allowed under the casino's rules to help players.

Barry v. Barchi, 443 U.S. 55, 99 S.Ct. 2642, 61 L.Ed.2d 365 (1979). A gambling license is a privilege, not a right. There is an important factor of timing. There is no property right in a mere application for a casino license, *Rosenthal v. Nevada,* 514 F.Supp. 907 (D.Nev. 1981). However, once a license has been issued, it cannot be taken away without first giving the licensee due process notice and hearings required by the U.S. Constitution.

Flamingo Resort, Inc. v. United States, 485 F.Supp. 926 (D.C.Nev. 1980), affirmed 664 F.2d 1387 (9th Cir. 1982). Casinos lend money by having players sign written markers, which look like counterchecks and can be cashed at a player's bank. The United States District Court in Nevada ruled that a casino on an accrual basis accounting system had to pay taxes on its outstanding markers, even though gambling debts were not collectible under Nevada law. The casinos reacted by having the Nevada legislature change the law on gambling debts, but not for everyone. In Nevada today, a casino can sue a player if the player signs a written marker which bounces. However, players cannot sue casinos. Players can only file complaints with the state's administrative agency, the Gaming Control Board. Nevada even uses its criminal justice system as a collection agency for casinos: a player who has insufficient funds in his bank when he writes a marker can be charged with the crime of passing bad and checks and extradited from other states. *Nguyen v. State,* 116 Nev. 1171, 14 P.3d 515 (2000). The criminal charges are dropped when the player pays off the casino, with the district attorney getting 10 percent.

Bally Mfg. Corp. v. N.J. Casino Control Com'n., 85 N.J. 325, 426 A.2d 1000 (1981). The Supreme Court of New Jersey upheld regulation prohibiting a casino from acquiring more than 50 percent of its slot machines from any one manufacturer. Bally, which then made 80 percent of slot machines used in the United States, was forced to buy from its competitors for its casino, a victim of its own success. The case shows the vast powers states have even over business decisions of legal gaming operators.

Uston v. Resorts International Hotel, Inc., 179 N.J.Super. 223, 431 A.2d 173 (N.J. Super. A.D. 1981), affirmed 89 N.J. 163, 445 A.2d 370 (1982). Ken Uston, the famous and successful blackjack card counter, won the right to play in Atlantic City casinos. Commercial casinos, like other businesses, have the right to excluded customers for any reason, or for no reason at all, except to the extent a legislature has declared there will be no discrimination on the basis of race, religion, and the like. But, the Supreme Court of New Jersey held the state had so thoroughly regulated casinos, to the point where an operator could not even use a different color felt on a blackjack table, that only the state Casino Control Commission has the authority to set rules for licensed card games. Because the Commission had not promulgated a rule about card counters, casinos could not on their own decide that these skillful players could be excluding from play. Nevada has taken exactly the opposite position, allowing casinos to kick out winning gamblers. See also *Brooks v. Chicago Downs Assoc., Inc.,* 791 F.2d. 512 (7th Cir. 1986), which held a racetrack could keep out winning horse bettors. Although they cannot kick out the card counters, the state Supreme Court up held countermeasures adopted by the New Jersey Casino Control Commission that discriminate against these skillful players. Such rules allow using extra decks of cards in the game, and also allowing frequent shuffling of cards. *Campione v. Adamar of N.J., Inc.,* 155 N.J. 245, 714 A.2d 299 (1998).

In re Boardwalk Regency Corp. Casino License, 180 N.J.Super. 324, 434 A.2d 1111 (1981), modified, 90 N.J. 361, 447 A.2d 1335 (1982). The New Jersey Casino Control Commission found a corporation was qualified to run a casino, except for the presence of two corporate executives/principal stockowners, so it issued a license, subject to the company buying out the President and C.E.O. The lower Court upheld this idea of corporate banishment, but said the two tainted individuals could stay with the company, so long as they had no control over New Jersey subsidiaries. The New Jersey Supreme Court reinstated the original conditions requiring a cleansing of the corporation. The lower Court decision contains a complete discussion of the standards a court uses in reviewing decisions by administrative agencies. The decision set a precedent that a company

could be licensed, so long as it got rid of any individuals who were not licensable.

State v. Glusman, 98 Nev. 412, 651 P.2d 639 (1982). The Nevada Supreme Court held state regulators could require anyone who does business on casino grounds, including clothing stores, to undergo licensing process. The Court did say it was unconstitutional to require the clothing store to pay the $100,000 required to investigate itself. *Flamingo Resort, Inc. v. United States,* discussed below.

Spilotro v. State, ex rel. Nevada Gaming Commission, 99 Nev. 187, 661 P.2d 467 (1983). The Nevada Supreme Court upheld the state's black book, which lists individuals who may not enter casinos in the state. The case involved Anthony John ("Tony the Ant") Spilotro, reported to be in charge of organized crime in Las Vegas, another figure from the movie *Casino.* In *Marshall v. Sawyer,* 365 F.2d 105 (9th Cir. 1966) the federal Court of Appeals agreed and held Nevada's black book exclusion of undesirables was constitutional.

Cases involving compulsive gambling. In 1980, the American Psychiatric Association added "pathological gambling" to its list of official mental diseases and disorders, in the third edition of its *Diagnostic and Statistical Manual of Mental Disorders* (DSM-III). The recognition by the medical community that some individuals cannot control their gambling has created conflicts in every area of law where an individual has gotten into trouble from gambling too much. Many of the early fights involved defendants trying to be declared not guilty by reason of insanity. These attempts failed, when courts found that a compulsion to gamble did not necessarily mean a compulsion to commit fraud. *United States v. Carmel,* 801 F.2d 997, 999 (7th Cir. 1986). Criminal defendants have been luckier with some courts, though not others, when it comes to sentencing. In *State v. Jones,* 197 N.J. Super. 604, 485 A.2d 1063 (1984), the trial court had sentenced an embezzler to less than a year in jail and to make restitution, at $150 per month. The appellate court reversed, clearly thinking that the punishment was not enough, given that it would take 400 years to pay back the embezzled $720,600.22. The gaming industry is now often sued by compulsive gamblers who blame the casinos for their problems. Courts in the U.S. appear to unanimously hold that a casino does not owe a duty to protect compulsive gamblers from themselves, as long as the gaming company follows all laws and regulations. *Brown v. Argosy Gaming Co., L.P.,* 384 F.3d 413 (7th Cir. 2004); *Taveras v. Resorts International Hotel, Inc.,* 2008 WL 4372791 (D.N.J. Sep 19, 2008) (NO. CIV. 07-4555(RMB)).

Com'r. of Internal Revenue v. Groetzinger, 480 U.S. 23, 107 S.Ct. 980, 94 L.Ed.2d 25 (1987). Most lawyers and commentators

overlook *Groetzinger,* seeing it only as a tax case. But this is the first time the U.S. Supreme Court held that a player could be in the trade or business of gambling. Lower courts had tried to distinguish gamblers from "investors," including speculators who trade solely for their own accounts. Because gambling was seen as a morally suspect industry, courts invented legal fictions, such as reasoning that a speculator is involved in buying and selling stocks or commodities with other people while a gambler in not involved in any business relationships, unless he accepts bets as well as makes them. The U.S. Supreme Court implicitly accepted the legitimacy of legal gambling by ruling that a player could declare himself in the trade or business of gambling without having to hold himself out to the public as a bookie. The implications of the decision are much greater than mere tax law. Here was a case argued before the highest court of the land, where a 7 to 2 majority had no trouble accepting a full-time gambler, who did nothing else but handicap horses for his own bets, as being in a respectable trade or business. Interestingly, the professional gambler in this case, Groetzinger, ended up the year losing more money than he won.

California v. Cabazon Band of Mission Indians, 480 U.S. 202, 94 L.Ed.2d 244, 107 S.Ct. 1083 (1987). The U.S. Supreme Court reaffirmed the right of tribes to offer any form of gambling permitted by the state where their lands are located. Congress responded by enacting the Indian Gaming Regulatory Act ("IGRA"). Congress may have thought it was legalizing high-stakes bingo. But, what it got was coast-to-coast casinos.

Petition of Soto, 236 N.J. Super. 303, 565 A.2d 1088 (A.D. 1989), certification denied 121 N.J. 608, 583 A.2d 310, cert. denied 496 U.S. 937 (1990) and *State v. Rosenthal,* 93 Nev. 36, 559 P.2d 830 (1977), appeal dismissed, 434 U.S. 803 (1977). Regulators have tremendous power under the state's "police power," the power to protect the health, safety and welfare of its citizens. In *Soto,* New Jersey courts held that a person involved in the state's licensed casino business has given up her right to free speech, including the right to be involved in political campaigns. In *Rosenthal* the Nevada Supreme Court issued the amazing ruling that the regulation of legal gambling is purely a state legislative issue, with no room for federal or state constitutional rights. Theoretically, the state could discriminate on the basis of race. The case involved the state's denial of a license to Frank "Lefty" Rosenthal, one of the main characters in the movie *Casino,* a fictionalized account of events that actually happened, as told in the nonfiction book *Casino: Love and Honor in Las Vegas* (by Nicholas Pileggi, published by Simon & Schuster, New York, 1995). *Rosenthal's* assertion that there are no federal civil rights with legal gambling has been rejected by other courts, for example, a federal court in Michigan in *United States v. Goldfarb,* 464 F.Supp. 565 (E.D.Mich. 1979). Even the Nevada Supreme Court has held that state regulators must follow their own rules and procedures and that a licensee does have a constitutionally property right, once a license has been issued.

Knight v. Moore, 576 So.2d 662 (Miss. 1990); *Harris v. Missouri Gaming Com'n.,* 869 S.W.2d 58 (Mo. 1994); *Ex Parte Pierotti,* 43 Nev. 243, 184 P. 209 (1919). In the 1820s and 1830s great lottery scandals swept the United States. The result is that most state constitutions forbid only lotteries, not gambling. Times change. To bring in a state lottery obviously involves amending the state constitutional prohibition on lotteries. But is the same true if the state legislature wants to legalize pari-mutuel wagering on horse races, or bingo or casinos? States vary widely in their definition of what is a lottery, or even who decides the question. In *Knight,* the Mississippi Supreme Court ruled the test is what would people consider a lottery today. Because no one would think of bingo as a lottery, the legislature could legalize charity bingo, without having to have an election to amend the constitution. The next year, the legislature brought in casinos. In *Harris,* the Missouri Supreme Court came out with a completely different test, ruling that under Missouri state law a lottery is a game of pure chance. A game with some skill may still be gambling, but it is not a lottery. Therefore, the legislature could legalize blackjack but not slot machines. Even Nevada has a constitutional prohibition on lotteries, but in *Pierotti* the state Supreme Court held slot machines were not lotteries, because players had to go to a location to participate in a game. State supreme courts have reached different conclusion on whether bingo is a lottery under their state constitutions. Compare *Secretary of State v. St. Augustine Church*, 766 S.W.2d 499 (Tenn. 1989) with *Greater Loretta Imp. Ass'n. v. State ex rel. Boone*, 234 So.2d 665 (Fla. 1970).

Connecticut National Bank of Hartford v. Kommit, 31 Mass.App.Ct. 348, 577 N.E.2d 639 (1991); *Sea Air Support, Inc. v. Herrmann*, 96 Nev. 574, 613 P.2d 413 (1980). For centuries, gambling has been against the public policy of every part of the English speaking world, including Nevada. Legalized gambling is simply an exception to the general rule: a license is seen as more a legal protection from being arrested than as a right to engage in a legitimate business. *Kommit* involved a Massachusetts resident using a credit card from a Connecticut bank to get a cash advance to gamble in a New Jersey casino. The Court held that he did not have to pay the credit card bill, because gambling debts are not collectable under the laws of all three states. In 1980, the Nevada Supreme Court ruled, as it has consistently ruled for almost 150 years, that gambling debts are not legally enforceable even in Nevada

and the court will leave the parties as it finds them. The *Sea Air Support* case is significant, because the Supreme Court told the state legislature to change the law, which it did.

Seminole Tribe of Florida v. Florida, 517 U.S. 44, 116 S.Ct. 1114, 134 L.Ed.2d 252 (1996). The Indian Gaming Regulatory Act (IGRA) allows tribes to operate what the IGRA calls "Class III" gaming, the most dangerous forms of gambling, including casinos, slot machines, and lotteries, but only if the state and tribe enter into a compact. The U.S. Supreme Court declared states cannot be sued in federal court without their consent, throwing out the provision in the IGRA that allowed tribes to sue states that did not negotiate in good faith. The High Court refused to say what is left: Is the rest of IGRA unconstitutional? Do tribes have a right without a remedy if the state refuses to cooperate, as the Ninth Circuit has indicated? See, *Spokane Tribe of Indians v. Washington State*, 28 F.3d 991, 997 (9th Cir. 1994), cert. granted and judgment vacated on different grounds 517 U.S. 1129 (1996), dismissed 91 F.3d 1350 (9th Cir. 1996). Or does IGRA allow the Secretary of the Interior to make casino regulations over the opposition of the state, as the Eleventh Circuit has held? *Seminole Tribe of Florida v. Florida*, 11 F.3d 1016 (11th Cir. 1994), cert. denied 517 U.S. 1133 (1996). Following the Supreme Court's decision, Congress voted a one-year moratorium, to prohibit the Secretary from approving compacts which had not been approved by a state. But when the year was up, the Secretary issued regulations allowing tribes to have casinos whenever a state refused to negotiate. As would be expected, this has led more lawsuits, with courts declaring the Secretary's regulations invalid. *Texas v. United States,* 497 F.3d 491, 507 (5th Cir. 2007), cert. denied by *Kickapoo Traditional Tribe of Texas v. Texas,* 129 S.Ct. 32, 172 L.Ed.2d 18 (2008).

Hotel Employees and Restaurant Employees Intern. Union v. Davis, 21 Cal.4th 585, 981 P.2d 990, 88 Cal.Rptr.2d 56 (1999); *Florida House of Representatives v. Crist,* 990 So.2d 1035 (Fla. 2008). Cases have been fought all over the country over new legal questions created by the Indian Gaming Regulatory Act. The *Crist* case is typical: does the governor of Florida have the power to enter into a tribal/state compact, and, what forms of gambling can the tribes insist upon? Courts have held overwhelming that a governor can negotiate the compact, but either he has to be given the power by the state legislature or the legislature has to then ratify the agreement. Courts are more split on what is called the scope of gaming, meaning what forms of gambling can tribes demand. But all agree that if no one in the state is permitted to operate a game, then the state's tribes have no right to demand that game in their compact. So, the Florida Supreme Court ruled that Governor Crist did not have the power to agree to casinos with banking card games, like blackjack, since those games were absolutely prohibited in Florida. The California Supreme Court in *Davis* had to decide questions of what is a casino and what is a lottery.

Greater New Orleans Broadcasting Assoc. v. United States, 527 U.S. 173, 119 S.Ct.1923, 144 L.Ed.2d 161 (1999). The U.S. Supreme Court held federal restrictions on broadcasting of casino commercials were unconstitutional, at least in states that had licensed those very same legal casinos. The Court felt the law had too many loopholes, for example allowing tribal casinos to advertise, and made an irrational distinction based on who happened to own a casino. The federal Department of Justice announced that it will not enforce the federal law against any casino commercial. However, the Supreme Court did not overturn its earlier decision in *Edge Broadcasting,* 509 U.S. 418, 113 S.Ct. 2696, 125 L.Ed.2d 345 (1993), in which it held the same federal law was constitutional in denying state lotteries the right to broadcast commercials from radio and television stations in states which do not have state lotteries; the Court held that this distinction based on geographic location is valid. The case rejected the standard the Court had laid down in *Posadas de Puerto Rico Assoc. v. Tourism Co.,* 478 U.S. 328, 92 L.Ed.2d 266, 106 S.Ct. 2968 (1986), which had given state and federal governments *carte blanche* in regulating casinos. It is unclear what impact the *Greater New Orleans* decision will have on state laws which prohibit advertising of legal gambling.

In re Mastercard Int'l Internet Gambling Litigation, 132 F.Supp. 468 (E.D.La, 2001), affirmed 313 F.3d 257, 261 (5th Cir. 2002). The question about what to do about Internet gambling, including whether current laws already make it illegal, is being discussed on all levels of government, from cities and counties, through states and nations, in courts and legislatures, and even in the World Trade Organization. The major problem for prosecutors is that is it not clear that the ancient antigambling laws on the books apply. For example, the most important federal statute is the Wire Act, 18 U.S.C. §1084, which was designed to prevent illegal bookies from using telegraph wires to receive the results of out-of-state horse races. In the *Mastercard* cases, federal courts ruled that the Wire Act might apply to online bets on races and sports events, but that it does not prohibit Internet casinos and lotteries.

Midwestern Enterprises, Inc. v. Stenehjem, 625 N.W.2d 234 (N.D., 2001); *Barber v. Jefferson County Racing Ass'n, Inc.,* 960 So.2d 599 (Ala., 2006); *Face Trading Inc. v. Department of Consumer and Industry Services,* 270 Mich.App. 653, 717 N.W.2d 377 (2006). Nothing makes as much money per square foot as a slot machine. So, inventors and entrepreneurs are continuously trying to find ways around the prohibitions on gambling. Fairly common are operators who say they are running no-purchase-necessary sweepstakes, but the results are displayed on machines that look suspiciously like conventional slot machines. Sometimes these are disguised as vending machines, such as phone card dispensers, that sell two minutes for $1. But a gambling scheme will not work if the court decides, usually based on the testimony of expert witnesses, that the supposed sweepstakes is merely a sham.

Fitzgerald v. Racing Association of Central Iowa, 539 U.S. 103, 123 S.Ct. 2156, 156 L.Ed.2d 97 (2003). The U.S. Supreme Court upheld the right of the state legislature of Iowa to impose a much higher tax on slot machines at racetracks, up to 36 percent, while the maximum tax on identical slot machines was only 20 percent at riverboat casinos. The High Court held that as long as the lawmakers had some possible, rational reasons for their actions, they were free to regulate legal gambling as they wished. See also *Ah Sin v. Wittman,* 198 U.S. 500, 25 S.Ct. 756, 49 L.Ed. 1142 (1905), where the U.S. Supreme Court held a state's power to suppress gambling is practically unrestrained. It upheld a California statute increasing the penalty from a misdemeanor to a felony for gambling conducted in "barred or barricaded" room as a constitutional classification.

Compiled by I. Nelson Rose

Section Seven

A GLOSSARY OF GAMBLING TERMS

Bank or house (casino): The organization that conducts gambling activity (gaming or wagering). In a house-banked game, the player is gambling against the house; that is, the house is a player in the game. In a player-banked game, the players make wagers against one another, and the bank or house is a neutral observer, usually receiving a set fee regardless of which player wins the game.

Book, bookie: The taking of bets on races or sports events or on the drawing of numbers. A person who makes book, or takes the bets, is called a bookie, although that term is usually reserved for one who takes bets where gambling is illegal.

Chance: An outcome that is determined by a randomly occurring risk that can be calculated. The odds—the probabilities—of a game of chance are known, and a person makes wagers with the knowledge that a random event will determine the outcome. In pure chance games the player cannot affect the outcome with the use of any skill he or she may possess.

Drop: The amount of money that the players put into action with their play. This is the money the player brings to the game and puts at risk. For a casino, it can be measured by the sale of chips from the cage and tables and also by counting cash bets made. For instance, if a gambler brings $100 with him to a blackjack table and plays for several hours (winning and losing), the drop is $100. On the other hand, the handle (q.v.) may be several multiples of $100, as the player could accumulate large wins and then keep playing them until he or she decides to leave the table.

Exotic bets: These are combination bets at horse tracks, dog tracks, and jai alai games. They include the daily double, exacta, trifecta, and quinella. In the daily double betting combination, the bettor makes a wager on which two horses (or dogs) will win two designated races. Both must win for the wager to be successful. The exacta is a combination bet in a specific horse or dog race in which the bettor seeks to predict the first- and second-place finishers in the race in exact order. In a trifecta, the bettor makes a wager on the first three finishers in order. Another combination bet is the quinella. Here the bettor picks the first two finishers, and if they are first and second or second and first, the bettor wins.

Gambling: An all-encompassing term covering activities in which a player places something of value at risk in order to win a prize of greater value should a chance (or an event determined at least in part by chance) occur. The chance events are usually determined by the outcomes of card or dice games, roulette or big wheels, contests, or the drawing of lots or raffle tickets. The legal definition of gambling contains three main elements: consideration, chance, and prize.

Gaming: Gambling activity at games in which a player (gambler) is a participant, as opposed to bets on the outcomes of contests involving other people (sports or racing) or bets on the drawing of lots or raffle tickets. The term *gaming* is the preferred term used by casino executives to describe the activities taking place in the facilities.

Grind joint: A casino or gambling facility that seeks to gain revenues from smaller gamblers by having maximum levels of play. This type of casino is the prevalent form in riverboat and Native American jurisdictions. This kind of play is found in Nevada in casinos that cater to local residents. Also, most of the play in Atlantic City is a grind-type play. The grind casino is contrasted with high-roller, tourist-oriented casinos such as Caesars Palace and the Venetian, found on the Las Vegas Strip, as well as finer European facilities such as Baden-Baden and casinos in Monaco.

Handle: The total amount of money that is gambled (played) on games or contests over a period of time. For lotteries and horse races, it would include all the bets made; for machines, it would include all the coins placed into the machine, regardless of the number that came out as a result of player wins. For a casino table game, the handle is difficult to determine, as it consists of all the bets made in every game, whether by chip or by cash play.

Hit: There are various uses for the term *hit*. It indicates a player's desire to have another play or, in the game of blackjack, to have another card dealt to him or her. The term is also used to designate a one-time bet of a player against another player or against the house (casino). Casinos operate on the principle known as the law of large numbers. Using this principle, they may allow high rollers to make very large bets with the understanding that such a player will continue to make the large bets over a period of time. A one-time hit is very risky for a casino, as the casino cannot use its long-term-odds advantage over the player to make up for occasions when the player will win the hit. Therefore most casinos will limit the size of single bets they allow a player to make.

Hold: The amount of money that the house wins from the player over a period of time. If the player drops $100, plays for a period of time, and then leaves the table with $80, losing the rest, the casino has held $20.

Junket: A junket is an excursion that is organized to bring a large number of players to a casino so that they will gamble, in most cases, a large amount of money. Quite often the casino will pay much if not all of the travel expenses of the players (such as transportation, room, food, beverage, as well as entertainment) in

addition to giving a fee to a junket organizer. In exchange for the discounts or free gifts, the player will agree to gamble a certain amount of money over a specified period of time. Although mid-market and low-market casinos (often called grind joints, as they wish to grind their profits out of players) will have bus tours for daytime or weekend players, the term *junket* is usually applied to tours arranged for wealthy players by the more upscale casinos. The junkets are closely supervised by gambling regulators as well as by the casinos. Junket players are very often playing on credit lines. Junkets have been used to skim (take money illegally) from casinos. Sometimes players will use false credentials (sometimes false identities) to establish their large credit lines, and they will not play all the money advanced to them. Unscrupulous junket operators may extract fees from casinos as payoffs for illegal (unlicensed) ownership of the casino. Also junket operators may be loan sharks operating on behalf of the casinos. Where used properly, however, the junket is a very important element for marketing casino products.

Las Vegas Line: The betting odds or point spreads that are offered for sports betting in Las Vegas casinos. These odds and point spreads are listed in the larger casinos first and then they are imitated by smaller casinos and also by illegal betting operations that operate throughout the country (and the world) and through the Internet.

Luck: The experience of success following a randomly occurring event. Games of luck are tied essentially to randomness, and the risks of the successful random events are subject to laws of probability. The player cannot affect the results by his or her efforts on a single play, but the odds of attaining success are subject to calculation. (Synonymous with chance, q.v.)

Odds: The advantage that one side of a wager has over the other. In house-banked games, the casino will have an odds advantage in an actual game, or it will have an advantage in the payoff structure used in the game.

Player: The person making the bet, wager, or gamble. Other terms for players include *bettor, gambler, gamer, punter,* or *plunger.*

Rake: A part of the pool of funds that the casino (or house) takes from a game such as poker, in which the players are competing against one another. It is essentially the same as the portion of the bets that a race-track takes from all bets on a race.

Skill: The ability of a player to affect the outcome of a game by utilizing a talent either as the result of personal qualities or training or study. Where skill may be a major factor in determining the outcome of the game, the game is called a skill game. For game players, most athletic contests are considered skill games—that is, a skilled football team will defeat a less-skilled team a large proportion of the time if they meet in games repeatedly. Games such as dart games are skill games. In casinos, card counters have the ability to use skills at blackjack games.

Wagering: The betting or staking of money on the outcome of an event such as a sports contest, a horse race, or a dog race.

Win (casino), or gross gaming win: The amount of money the casino (house) holds over a period of time. The gross gaming win is actually the amount bet minus the prizes given back to the players. This is also referred to as the casino's gaming revenue.

References

Clark, Thomas L. 1987. *The Dictionary of Gambling and Gaming.* Cold Spring, NY: Lexik House Publishers.

Fenich, George G., and Kathryn Hashimoto. 1996. *Casino Gaming Dictionary: Terms and Language for Managers.* Dubuque, IA: Kendall-Hunt.

Thompson, William N. 1977. *Legalized Gambling: A Reference Handbook.* 2nd ed. Santa Barbara, CA: ABC-CLIO, 273–281.

Section Eight

SELECTED ESSAYS
ON GAMBLING

THE "BEST" GAMBLERS IN THE WORLD

Almost all of Asia is closed to casino gambling, yet from my study of gambling, ironically enough I have found that Asians are the world's "best" gamblers. They gamble more, they are high rollers, and they enjoy gambling more than others. Casinos around the world rely upon the patronage they receive from Asian players. Over half of the money gambled in Britain's 120 casinos comes from Chinese players. Las Vegas markets its high-stakes products to Japan, Taiwan, and Hong Kong. The card rooms in California are filled with Asian Americans.

Asians gamble the most, but why? In my travels to gaming establishments in Asia, Europe, North America, Central America, and South America, I have found some explanations that seem plausible.

I have not seen many Asians among the "homeless" or "street people" of the large cities. Poor Asians do not have to live on the streets. Asians have strong families, they have family businesses, and they work very hard. Asian people are active, their heads are raised upward, and they exude self-confidence. I even saw these qualities when I visited mainland China. Fifty years of Communist efforts to change human nature did not stymie energy inside the people. This may have relevance for gambling behavior.

You cannot be a "good gambler" unless you have a bankroll. You cannot afford to win unless you can afford to lose. A player needs staying power. When a player knows he or she can lose, he or she can play, and play to the limit. Many an Asian knows that if he or she loses enough to no longer own a house, there will still be a roof over his or her head. The extended family will take the gambler in and provide food and a job in a family business—perhaps a laboring job, but one he or she will be willing to do. The gambler knows that by working hard he or she can get ahead. Quite likely, the wealthy gambler was once a poor person, and through personal effort worked to the top. That can be done again, and the gambler's confidence is not broken by gambling losses.

The manager of a London casino told me the story of a Chinese player who saw his fortune disappear with heavy gambling. Being totally broke, he was soon working in the kitchen of a cousin's restaurant. A year later, he was managing the restaurant, and the next year he owned two restaurants. And he was back in the casino gambling high stakes. The downside of the equation is that the safety-net formula of family and self-confidence provides no inhibitions to stop forces that lead players into compulsive gambling.

Asians often gamble in groups, and they exude excitement in play. They believe the best thing is to win. The second best thing is to lose. The worst thing is not playing. Often at a roulette table they will shout loudly when one of the group wins. They will also shout loudly when the ball falls on a number that is next to the one played. Coming close is cause for cheering.

The players will come and leave in groups, and casino managers must be aware of this. The lesson was learned by one British casino manager confronted with a loud Asian player one night. After seeing that the player was annoying more staid "European" players, the manager tried to gently tell the player to be a little less excited during play. He noticed that the player was young and had had too much to drink. He told the bartender to serve him no more. After several increasingly less subtle warnings, the manager gave up and asked the bouncer to escort the player out of the premises. No sooner had this happened than a crowd of 20 players at six tables gathered their chips and went to the cage, cashed in, and left. Many were regulars, who were not seen for over a month. When the manager threw one of their group out, he threw the entire group out. The next time an incident occurred, the manager found an older gentleman among the group and told him that the casino would like the "loud" player to come back another evening to play, but in the meantime would like to buy the young man and his immediate party (of four) dinner in the adjacent restaurant. The older gentleman made all the arrangements and laughingly accompanied the young man to a very private corner booth in the restaurant. All were happy, and the Asian entourage continued their gambling merriment for several more hours—that night and the next.

Casino managers have offered additional explanations. The players may work in family businesses that operate until late hours. Because these businesses operate on a cash basis, the owner has cash receipts that can easily be brought to the casinos. Also, the owners and the employees have no other place to go (if they do not want to go straight home) at the hour they close their shops. They are like the dealers of Las Vegas with tip money in their pockets when the shift changes at 2 a.m. These people can meet their friends and enjoy camaraderie in the late hour (or 24 hour) gambling establishments.

Asian players are drawn to luck games. Eastern cultures emphasize the luck of certain numbers; persons born in certain years have lifetime luck. One who has luck is urged to act upon the luck. Numerology and horoscopes are well respected. The players gravitate to games that depend on luck. Most Asians are not found at poker tables; they are not blackjack card counters, nor do they frequent craps tables that demand detailed concentration on various combinations of odds. Their calculation is a calculation to find one's lucky number, not a calculation to minimize the house odds. Asians dominate the baccarat tables of Las Vegas. They favor pai gow and pai gow poker games and simple dice games such as sic bo.

I was astounded to find no fortune cookies during travels to central China. Most of the Chinese people with me had never heard of fortune cookies. But an older gentleman had. He told me that Chairman Mao had banned them. The people were supposed to get ahead by hard work, not by luck. The cookies were a bad influence. Mao did not want people to gamble. Everywhere I went, however, I saw people playing games. I never saw money being wagered, but I sensed the spirit was still there. Certainly their relatives around the world have the spirit.

References

Adapted from William N. Thompson. 1994. "The World's Best Gamblers." *You Bet: Canada's Gaming Report* (November): 8–9; also based on author's visits to casinos and on author's classroom lectures in Public Administration 736 ("The Social Impacts of the Gambling Industry"), University of Nevada, Las Vegas, Spring 2001.

THE FAMILY THAT GAMBLES TOGETHER

We're just here to have fun, we create excitement, it's a family experience. It pays off for Las Vegas.

—Mike Hartsell, director of entertainment, Luxor Casino (*48 Hours,* CBS television, March 30, 1995)

The Las Vegas market is an adult destination that people can easily bring kids to.

—Alan Feldman, general manager, Treasure Island Casino, quoted in *Las Vegas Review Journal*, September 7, 1993

If there's a twelve year old in my casino, he'd better be shooting craps.

—Burton Cohen, president, Desert Inn Country Club and Casino, in talk given to International Gaming Exposition, Las Vegas, March 21, 1995.

In 1989 casinos opened in South Dakota, signaling a nationalization of the casino industry. In Las Vegas, a megaresort called the Mirage opened. That opening was followed by a new Circus Circus property, the Excalibur.

Las Vegas was getting ready for competition. Las Vegas was going after family markets. The idea of appealing to younger nongaming family members was not new. Circus Circus had had carnival games for kids since 1974. But the idea it incorporated—providing entertainment for children while parents engaged in gambling—was not made part of general marketing until the Mirage and Excalibur.

A Checklist

Is this effort to capture family vacationers going to work for Las Vegas? Is the marketing approach good for Las Vegas business enterprises? Is it good for families? For society? Let us make some checklists.

One group of considerations applies to the business dimensions. We look at business advantages, then we examine the downside. The second major grouping involves social issues. We look at societal advantages arising from marketing casinos this way; then we explore negative consequences for society.

Business Factors—The Positive

1. *Increase the Size of the Potential Market*. Since families constitute one of the largest vacation markets, the potential associated with this target is substantial. This "family" market is difficult to ignore in an increasingly competitive market.

2. *Fill Hotel Rooms*. In 1994, the hotel room occupancy for Las Vegas was 89 percent. With more hotel rooms scheduled to be completed in the next few years, the challenge to maintain high occupancy rates will be intense. Family vacationers are an obvious target to fill these rooms.

3. *Long-term Customer Pool*. In 1991, the median age of the Las Vegas visitor was 50, with 44 percent of the tourists over the age of 60. A 60-year-old provides a potential 10- to 15-year income stream. A parent, age 40, provides a potential 30- to 40-year income stream. A 40-year-old repeat visitor is worth

A Native American casino in Louisiana caters to families with children.

3 times as much as a 60-year-old. It makes good business sense to go after a younger market.

4. *Atmosphere.* There is a benefit of having a casino full of people. It makes the whole experience more enjoyable. This is true even if many of the patrons are not actually gambling.

5. *Total Revenue Dollars.* Every tourist who visits Las Vegas spends money. Those who choose not to gamble will still spend money on shopping, shows, transportation, hotel rooms, food, and other entertainment.

Negative Business Implications

1. *More Nongamblers.* As the number of families vacationing in Las Vegas increases, the number of nongamblers also increases. With visitors not gambling, the management of Las Vegas properties will change dramatically.

2. *Low Rollers.* Vacationers, especially families, are likely to spend less money gambling. Families will spend less money, and the money they do spend will be targeted toward family-related activities.

3. *Change in Way Business Is Done.* To make a less gambling oriented market profitable, casinos need a change of philosophy from generating the bulk of the property's income from gambling to finding ways to generate revenues from family activities such as entertainment, meals, amusements, shopping, and lodging. In addition, those activities considered as offensive for families may have to be eliminated.

The days of losing money on rooms and making it up in the casino will end. While it is true that not all properties will attract equal percentages of families, the impact will be felt everywhere, since families will search out room, meal, and entertainment values in all properties.

Even though most casinos do not like creating activities that reduce the number of hours that a gambler spends in the casino, the family market will demand that they do so.

4. *Changing the Experience for Current Visitors.* When firms go after new markets, they often ignore what brought them their original success. In the case of Las Vegas this is crucial. The allure of Las Vegas has always been the gambling, nightlife, and glitz. It has not been white tigers and theme parks. As Las Vegas becomes less gambling oriented, it starts to look like other resort destinations. The danger is that potential gamblers will go to other gaming locations, rather than deal with the family crowds in Las Vegas.

5. *New Costs and Liabilities.* Security problems generated by doubling the number of children in casinos is overwhelming. In addition, what will properties do when a minor is caught gambling? The altercation can only have a negative impact on the satisfaction of the family involved. The parents will either blame the casino, the child, or the town. Additional problems can arise from a large number of unescorted children roaming around in a mega-resort. Abductions and accidents are examples.

Social Issues—The Positive Side of the Equation

1. *Promotes Family Solidarity.* The new marketing approach in Las Vegas supports the notion of family values, a theme that is now receiving much attention from national policy makers. Las Vegas is promoting the family vacation by offering accommodations, transportation packages, and various entertainment events at reasonable costs. Family vacations promote solidarity within a threatened institution.

2. *Marketing for All Age Groups.* The appeal of the Las Vegas excitement is one that can grip all age groups, whereas other destinations that are offered as "family" vacation spots typically appeal to separate generations or at least separate age groups.

3. *Accommodations at Reasonable Costs.* The family marketing emphasis has led to a major expansion in the number of hotel rooms in Las Vegas. This volume will act as a damper on efforts to greatly increase room prices. The average room rates in Las Vegas are now considerably lower than those at alternative family vacation destinations.

4. *Makes Children Look at Gambling with More Realism.* The new marketing approach exposes children to the reality of gambling, which is now legal in 48 states. Gambling has become an ordinary part of American life, yet many cling to Victorian notions that it is not only "sinful," but that anyone under the age of adulthood must be shielded from it. This total

prohibition attitude can foster pent-up frustrations and desires that may not be easily discarded at a later time.

5. *Teaches Moderation and Management of Money.* Children can learn the value of money by observing the exposure of money to risk factors.

Social Issues—Downside Factors

1. *Casinos Are Attractive Nuisances.* Children are kept out of bars not just to keep kids from drinking. They are excluded because the people who go to the bars may reach a condition where their language or physical behavior may be offensive to other adults but would be traumatic to children. The bar is a venue where children could be easily hurt. Casinos are no different.

2. *Children Are Drawn into the Gambling Environment.* The placement of rides and attractions makes it impossible for children to avoid gaming areas of casinos.

3. *Children Imitate Other Children.* Young people drawn to Las Vegas can be expected to emulate the behaviors of young people living in Las Vegas. The emphasis on families in casinos has led many local kids to believe this is a place for them as well. A newspaper survey of 769 Las Vegas high school students found that over 47 percent had gambled at local casinos, even though the gambling age was 21.

4. *The Seeds of a Later Compulsive Gambling Problem.* Early expo-

sure to gambling is associated with later compulsive gambling.

5. *Invites Family Discord.* Gambling activity offered in a family vacation setting may not add to family solidarity. Families budget expenses very closely on their travels so that they may experience a variety of activities. There is no room for risks of gambling.

Conclusion

Although Las Vegans might disagree, for most Americans, gambling and children do not belong together. Even though the approach has certain advantages, the family resort destination strategy appears also to have many irrational and perhaps even financially dangerous sides to it.

Reference

Adapted with permission from William N. Thompson, J. Kent Pinney, and Jack Schibrowsky. 1996. "The Family that Gambles Together: Business and Social Concerns." *Journal of Travel Research* 34, no. 3 (Winter): 70–75.

A SOVEREIGNTY CHECKLIST FOR GAMBLING

The Indian Gaming Regulatory Act of 1988 was passed to promote tribal "economic development, self-sufficiency, and strong tribal governments." The Act was passed to enhance a renewal of sovereignty for Native American tribes. Has the Act been successful? The following sovereignty checklist serves as a guide to answer that question.

Consider the positive:

1. Gambling money means tribal survival. If the people of a nation cannot survive, they cannot be sovereign. Survival means food, housing, and medical care. Money from gambling activities has been placed into programs meeting basic needs. Survival is threatened by substance abuse—drugs, alcohol. Gambling revenues are used for treatment and prevention programs.

2. Gambling money means economic opportunity. Without jobs in their homelands, peoples gave up their nationalism by leaving. Gambling has brought jobs to Native lands. Jobs have given members of Nations an incentive to return home and renew native nationalism.

3. Gambling revenue is invested in other enterprises to gain a diversity of employment and secure a stable economic basis for the future.

4. Revenue allows tribes to choose the direction of economic development. Before gambling, many felt pressured to accept any economic opportunity. They allowed lands to be strip-mined, grazed, or timbered in nonecological ways, polluted with garbage and industrial wastes. One tribe explored the prospects of having a brothel.

5. Gambling money gives educational opportunities. Tribes use funds for books, computers, new desks, new roofs, remodeled halls, and plumbing for schools. Schools serve tribes with both cultural and vocational education.

6. Revenues allow tribes to make efforts to reestablish original land bases. They hire archaeologists to identify traditional lands. Lost lands must be the most vital symbol of lost sovereignty, and now through gambling, a measure of sovereignty is being returned.

7. Reservation gambling focuses upon cultural restoration activities. Money is spent on museum buildings that chronicle Native history. Tribes are turning funds to educational programs to reestablish their languages.

8. Sovereignty is political. The money of gambling allows tribes to assert all manner of legal issues in courts and in front of other policy makers. Gambling has also provided a catalyst for the creation of the National Indian Gaming Association in 1983. The Association has participated as a serious lobbying group within the American political system.

9. Economic power is directed at state and local government treasuries. Tribes bring several economic benefits to local and state governments. Gambling employment has resulted in reduced welfare rolls. Gambling tribes give state and local governments payments in lieu of taxes for services they would otherwise receive at no cost. This money is important, and the payments give the tribes a new measure of influence in relationships with these governments.

10. The Indian Gaming Regulatory Act has lent itself to an expansion

of Native American sovereignty by requiring American state governments to deal one-on-one with tribes on an equal footing basis.

In gambling, however, there is a danger to the renewal of Native sovereignty. Consider these items:

1. Native gambling presents opportunities for exploitation of tribes. If nonnative peoples are not closely watched, they can become a force that will seize the gaming opportunity for sovereignty right out of the hands of Native peoples. There have been several accounts of "White Man's greed" in Native gambling enterprise.

2. Native Americans must also be critically aware that any gambling enterprise can be a magnet for scam artists and thieves of all sorts. Although the overall record of Native gambling is good, there is some evidence that thievery has occurred at gaming facilities.

3. Gambling operations can mean less sovereignty if tribes in quest of economic resources willingly yield authority to nonnative governments.

4. Gambling has torn some tribes apart. It can be a divisive issue, as many Native Americans oppose gambling for a variety of reasons—economic, social, cultural. One tribe found that members who lived in an area close to major highway access points tried to separate and form a new reservations because they could reap a greater share of the casino benefits. The collective good was being set aside, because gambling had placed a dollar sign in front of them.

5. Internal divisiveness regarding tribal gambling comes over the issue of how to distribute the gaming profits. Where tribes neglect collective concerns—education, health, housing, substance abuse—and instead direct the bulk of the revenues to per capita distribution programs, they may not be building sovereignty.

6. Gambling can tear apart Native cultures. Several tribes resisted having gaming operations because gambling itself violates religious beliefs, and operations would be seen as desecrations of lands. Others share those attitudes but allow the gambling because they desire economic rewards. Gambling opens up lands to outsiders. They come in buses and automobiles that cause congestion and pollution. They bring drinking and drug abuse behaviors. They engage in gambling. These behaviors serve as model behaviors for members of tribes, especially the young.

7. Gambling jobs may not be the best building blocks for sovereignty. Many of the jobs do not require intensive training—which may be good; however, the skills may not be transferable. Unless revenues are utilized to develop a diversified economic base, the concentration on gambling jobs may only create trained incapacities.

8. Sovereignty for tribes is diminished if the definition of what is

a Native American can be so inclusive as to remove the unique qualities of the tribes' political position. The quest for gambling opportunities has brought many strange folks out of the woodwork, claiming that they constitute a Native nation.

9. Native gambling can invite a backlash. Nonnatives have a five-century track record of taking any benefit they see in the hands of Native Americans away from them.

10. Sovereignty comes with international recognition and open diplomatic relationships. Gambling presents an ultimate danger to sovereignty if gambling Native nations see in their new economic power a weapon for dominating their neighbors rather than a new opportunity to build cooperative relations on an international basis.

Reference

Adapted from William N. Thompson and Diana Dever. 1994. "A Sovereignty Checklist for Indian Gaming." Parts 1 and 2. *Indian Gaming* 4 (April): 5–7; 4 (May): 8–9.

SUPERMARKET CASINOS

There are questions surrounding how the products of the gaming industry should be marketed. Which products should be legal? Where should gaming product distribution places be located?

The Nevada Gaming Commission is focusing upon locations of restricted license locations. These are places permitted to have 15 or fewer gaming machines. The Commission should seek to analyze policy for restricted licenses guided by an overriding concern for the public interest of the citizens of Nevada.

Some gambling operations should be encouraged by state policy; others should be strongly discouraged; still others should be outright banned.

Both opponents and proponents should agree that some gaming can be in the interest of some communities and society—even if individuals find the activity to be offensive in all its forms. Both opponents and proponents should agree that some forms of gambling are offensive to the community and to society. The opponents should not waste energy condemning all gaming, but rather should seek out the most offensive forms and concentrate attacks on those forms. The proponents should not take the position that all gambling no matter the form is good for society. Instead, the proponents should seek out forms that offer benefits to society and make their defense around those forms.

I endorse the religious theology that accepts some gambling. If the game is honest, if the players are not habitual, if the players can meet their other social obligations, and if the bottom line helps the community in pursuit of good things, the activity may be permissible. An occasional game is played at low stakes, honestly, and the beneficiary is the local parish, school, hospital, etc. Permissible. The same can be said of other charity gambling, some Native American gaming, and maybe also of the Las Vegas Strip. Gamblers are recreational tourists, games are honest, and the end result is a growing economy that provides lots of entry-level jobs for

Slot machines are found throughout Nevada in bars, taverns, restaurants, convenience stores, and grocery stores.

persons who otherwise would not be employed.

There are better targets than the casinos of the Las Vegas Strip. My target—the slot machines of the grocery stores of the Las Vegas Valley. The machines of the grocery stores, while honest, attract habitual players whose activity reduces their ability to meet obligations to family and community, and in doing so the machines hurt the community. There is no redeeming value achieved to offset the harm.

The appropriate policy is obvious: take the machines out of the grocery stores. Consider these questions:

1. Who plays these machines? Is the money being played being brought into Las Vegas? Are the players tourists? How many are tourists? I think the percentage would be somewhere near zero. Are the players young or old, male or female? I think we would find most are upper-age females. What is their economic situation? Are they lower-income persons? How many purchase their food with food stamps, before (at least I hope) they play?

2. How many of the patrons of supermarket video slot machines are compulsive gamblers? How many of the players at 3 a.m. are compulsives? How many of the players who stay at the machines for 10 hours in a row are compulsives? I think many.

3. Who is exposed to gambling in the supermarkets of Las Vegas? Everyone. Everyone is not exposed to the Strip gambling. We do not have to go

to casinos. But we have to eat; we do not have a choice about going to the market. Children are exposed to this gambling. Teenagers, too, whereas Strip casinos throw out the teenagers. Recovering addicted gamblers have to have this gambling thrown into their faces when they shop for food. People who want absolutely nothing to do with gambling must be exposed. People are not forced to witness drinking and intoxicated people; they are forced to witness gambling and gambling-crazed people—in grocery stores.

4. Do I receive a better price for food, because of the gambling in grocery stores? When I go to a casino, I can enjoy a low-cost meal, because the casino forfeits profits on the meal in order to get me into the facility, because I might just drop a roll of quarters into a machine. Is my grocery bill less because of the slot machines in the grocery store? After all, my supermarket is sucking out anywhere from $300,000 to $900,000 a year from my neighbors with the machines. The reality is that our grocery store prices are not lower than those in surrounding states.

5. How much money do the machines make? Are the 15 machines (the limit for grocery stores) making an average $30,000 a year (the average for the Strip), or maybe $40,000, or as is the case of one bar, $60,000 per machine? Are the machines taxed (they pay a flat fee) an amount more or less than paid by casinos for their slot machines? There is a $2,000 annual flat tax for grocery store machines, and a $1,000 annual flat tax plus 6.75 percent winnings tax for casino machines.

6. Where does the money go from the profits on the grocery store machines? To employees? Some. To local slot route companies? Some. Most goes to outside corporations that own the grocery stores. Each owner is an out-of-state company.

7. Would the Commission support putting slot machines in bank lobbies? That would be ridiculous. Guess what, each Las Vegas supermarket chain has an over-the-counter branch bank in its lobby along with the gambling machines. Not only do we have the issue about ATMs nearby (also in every lobby), but banks. My ATM will only give me $500 a day—the bank that owns the ATM wants to make sure I spend my money responsibly. But here I am with my bank account; the cash is only a few steps away—junior's college fund.

8. Machine play in restricted locations is supposed to be "incidental" to other business. Can the markets say that from 12 midnight to 6 a.m. the machines are incidental? Would it be more accurate to say that the sole purpose of keeping the grocery stores open at those hours is to serve the cravings of habitual gamblers?

Reference

Thompson, William N. 1998. Comments made in presentation to Special Hearing on Restricted Gambling Licenses, Nevada Gaming Commission, Carson City, Nevada, February 22.

CASINOS WITHOUT CRIME: IS IT POSSIBLE?

Any criminological theory that emphasizes the factor of "opportunity" would have to assess the casino industry—an industry where the essential product is money itself—as one which by its nature is a magnet for criminal activity.

Other studies establish that casinos in the United States have attracted criminal activity. There may be limits to the generalization offered, however. There may be casinos that do not manifest an aura of criminality. In my study tour of 140 European casinos, in 1986 and 1987, I gathered a distinct impression that these casinos were not magnets for crime.

The reaction of the casino industry and its regulators to crime is varied on the European side of the Atlantic. American regulators are defensive about crime. The American reactive posture can be contrasted with the massive roundup of public officials and casino operators following a simultaneous raid by the central Italian government on the country's four casinos in 1983. The casinos were closed and only reopened with a supervisor from Rome placed in each. In 1958, Bavarian officials discovered skimming in the private casinos of the region; they were all closed. Subsequently, the state took over both ownership and control of the casinos. The Golden Horseshoe casino of London won a license over the objections of its neighbors on Queensway Road. The casino agreed, however, that its patrons would not drive on nearby streets. In the first year of operation, the casino permanently banned 167 players, many of them good customers, because they parked cars on adjacent streets. Such a ban can be contrasted with the difficul-

ties the American casinos have in excluding the most notorious criminals from their premises, the legal challenges to the Nevada black book being a case in point. Why the difference? Let us look at a mix of factors distinguishing European casino environments from American environments.

In the United States, most casinos are concentrated in a few locations. There are megacasino groupings in Atlantic City, on the Las Vegas Strip, and in downtown Las Vegas and Reno. European casinos, on the other hand, can be found throughout the continent. In all, there are nearly 300 casinos in Europe.

The European casinos are not concentrated in any immediate location. This pattern of dispersal yields very much of a local clientele for each casino. Typically the player is a regular who goes to only one or two casinos and is personally known to casino managers. Managers are aware when new players come to gamble. With the presence of strangers, they are alerted to the need for greater surveillance.

The monopolistic position of each casino relieves competitive drives that cause American casinos to use psychological traps to entice the maximum play from each gamer. American casinos traditionally have been red, loud, and action filled. European casinos come in every color, but a calming blue is typical. Art objects purposely draw players away from games in order to break action and emphasize an ambience of relaxation. Windows present vistas—forests, sunsets, seashores, valleys, mountains—and also inform the player that time is passing and that time must be enjoyed. Drinks are not allowed on the gaming floors. The free drink is reserved for the special player only, and it is given to the player when he or she desires to take a break.

The American casino seeks to attract the best players—the biggest losers. This leads to policies of granting credit. European casinos do not have credit gaming. The registration desk is a major attribute of the European casino that distinguishes it from the American counterpart. Every player must register before being allowed to enter. The player must identify himself or herself and show a passport if from another country. The player must show his or her age and often occupation as well. The players are required to pay an admission fee. Great Britain's casinos require membership.

The registration desk weeds out non-gamers and hangers-on. Such people who wander through Las Vegas houses pose a constant threat as purse snatchers, pickpockets, and petty thieves. Prostitutes, once identified, can be permanently banned from the European casinos.

The traditions of European gaming are very definitely rural, and most casinos are still in rural communities. Additionally, the casinos of Europe are small in comparison to American casinos. A typical European casino might have 10 tables and a separate slot machine room with 50 low-denomination machines. The average casino would attract 300 gamers per night during the week and 500 on weekend evenings. By contrast, the open entrance, big crowds, and multiple game offerings in the United States make it difficult to spot much criminal activity—gaming cheats, machine manipulators, gamers trying to launder money at tables, and gamers perpetrating scams upon one another. It is also more

difficult to spot dealers who cheat. Being outside of strong bottom-line competitive pressures, the European casinos do not really want compulsive gamblers. These gamers are especially persona non grata if there is reason to believe that they might be gambling with other's money. The casinos honor requests by family members to exclude relatives who might have gambling problems. The casinos observe the occupational status of players, and they can inquire about the nature of the player's job. Belgium excludes lawyers, bankers, and civil servant from casinos. It is felt that these professionals are trusted to handle other people's moneys, and the trust could be broken if they gambled heavily or were observed gambling at all.

The governments of Europe do not have a high financial stake in the casino gaining, yet they make their presence felt at the casinos. Inspectors are always present in most European casinos. They open tables, close tables, and participate in counts. In many they collect taxes on the spot each evening. Gaming tax rates are extremely high, as high as 80 percent of gross win. Yet even with the very high rates, the governmental units do not receive a large share of their revenues from casinos. It is typical for casino taxes to be less than one-tenth of 1 percent of tax revenues. The government—except at the local town level—has almost no stake in casino operations. Therefore, the government exhibits little reluctance in closing casinos if they engage in improper practices.

Another factor that limits criminality in European casinos is the career nature of gaming employment. Dealers are not salaried. Rather they are paid from a collective tip pool. They can more easily accept the notion that they benefit by giving service rather than just working for a check. They know that their success is tied to the success of the casino. Hence they have a greater loyalty to the casino. The loyalty is enhanced by the knowledge that all position promotions are from within and that they have only rare opportunities to gain employment with other casinos. Dealers think in terms of having long-range careers. The bottom line is that it is a good job, it is a career, and it must be pursued in one casino only. Most European casino dealers have a lot to lose if they participate in scams. Skimming and cheating are not worth the risk.

Reference

Adapted from William N. Thompson. 1998. "Criminal Enterprise in American and European Casinos: A Comparative Analysis." Paper presented to the Western Society of Criminology, Annual Meeting, February 23, Monterey, California.

WORD-OF-MOUTH ADVERTISING: THE WIN WIN GAME IN LAS VEGAS

I had lived in Las Vegas only six months, and we were entertaining our first guests from our old home town—Kalamazoo. It was Joe's first trip to Vegas and he was anxious to get to the Strip and "get it on," as he said. "Where should I go? Which casino?" he pleaded. I asked, "What do you want to do?" "Play some slots and maybe some blackjack," he offered. "Ok," I replied, "you should go to the Holiday Inn Center Strip casino (it is now Harrah's), and play the one dollar, stand-alone, slots. Put in the maximum of three coins—three dollars—on each pull of the handle." I told him to stay away from the progressive machines that offer very enormous jackpots, but very bad odds. I was only repeating the local wisdom that a new resident quickly picks up upon moving to Las Vegas. The stand-alone dollar machines at this one casino purportedly offered the best payback odds—over 97 percent—of any place in town. Joe told me he had a bankroll of $200. I emphasized to him that he must leave all his credit cards in his suitcase when he went to the Strip. "If you lose it, just quit!" I told him.

Joe went to the Strip at 8 p.m. He returned to my door at midnight. He looked "high." He was "high." His eyes were glazed over, and he was almost jumping up and down. He said (that is, he yelled), "How can you stay at home at night; why aren't you down on the Strip? This is the greatest place on Earth." I offered that I had a job, I had classes to teach in the morning, and I enjoyed reading and watching the news and Carson on television at night. He shouted," My God, get your coat on, let's go back to the Strip right now." I offered that I was thinking more about going to sleep. Then he yelled out, "$1,200, this is the greatest place on Earth. I won two jackpots, $1,200." Again he begged me to go to the Strip. Then he ran to the telephone and began dialing. He said, "Don't worry, I got my telephone card. I gotta call Jack." I asked, "Jack back in Kalamazoo, Joe! It's 3 a.m. in Michigan." Joe said that did not matter. I heard him say, "Jack, I'm in Vegas, this is the greatest place on Earth, I hit two jackpots, $1,200. You gotta come to Vegas. Oh? Ok. Bye." Joe hung up the phone. "Well?" I asked. Joe said Jack was a little upset being called at 3 a.m. Then he added, "He'll thank me for telling him about Las Vegas." Again he begged me to go down to the Strip. I said, "O.K., tomorrow we'll go to the Strip, and by the way, why don't you treat us to a show while we're there." (Shows were only $20 back in the early 1980s.)

He paused in silence for the first time. He asked, "Why do you think I should take you to a show?" "Well, you do have $1,200." He was silent. "Don't you?" I asked. "Oh, well, I put it all back in." "What about your $200 bankroll?" "Oh, well, I put that in too."

Joe's behavior is one of the primary reasons that Las Vegas has grown to be the number one overnight tourist destination in the world. In 2000, Las Vegas had 35.8 million visitors, more than even Mecca. Mecca gets 35 million visitors each year, because a Muslim must (if he or she possibly can) make at least one pilgrimage to Mecca in a lifetime, if he or she wishes to get to heaven. Many of the visitors to Las Vegas make repeat visits, and I do not think they are making the visits in order to get to a religious heaven.

Las Vegas has succeeded in selling its gambling products through word-of-mouth advertising. As we say in Las Vegas "winners talk and losers walk." With almost any other product—automobiles, appliances, clothing, restaurant meals—those who believe they have received bad results talk. Bad customer stories are repeated to many people; one survey found that 1 in 5 people will repeat a bad results story to 20 people or more. Good stories are repeated to 3 to 5 others (Thompson and Comeau 1992, 26). This is not the case with gambling stories. Winners spread the word, and losers stay quiet. It goes even so far as Joe's story. Losers tell stories about their winning experiences and neglect to balance then with stories of the negative bottom line. A winner in Las Vegas is exhilarated and desires congratulations and admiration from others. Others see them as worthy and brave. But if a person would tell another that he lost money gambling, the reaction would be quite different. From a spouse: "You lost that much gambling! How could you, we need that money for (a) our retirement, (b) our car repairs, (c) the kids' summer camp, (d) the kids' college educations" (pick the poison). A friend might shake his or her head and mumble something about the loser being stupid. A boss might shift his eyes to the cash register and enter a mental note to watch the loser closely. A client or customer might think, "Hmm! So that's why the costs are so high." From a macho to a zero. Just one word difference, "I won"; "I lost." Losers may indeed be stupid, but they are not so stupid that they let the world know about it.

In our customer service book, Michele Comeau and I emphasize the need to keep what we call the Win Win game. Casinos will lose this edge on all other businesses if they ever let customers feel that the games are somehow dishonest (the customers know the odds favor the house, but they expect an honest game). The customer edge is lost through exploitation—for instance, if casinos aggressively pursue compulsive players or young players. And the edge is lost when the casino does not offer good customer service to players.

There is a reason gambling is the fastest-growing industry.

Reference

Thompson, William N., and Michele Comeau. 1992. *Casino Customer Service = The WIN WIN Game.* New York: Gaming and Wagering Business; also based on author's classroom lectures in Public Administration 736 ("The Social Impacts of the Gambling Industry"), University of Nevada, Las Vegas, Spring 2001.

WILL NEVADA BECOME ANOTHER DETROIT? PROBABLY NOT

The automotive industry came to Detroit by accident. The industry could have been located elsewhere. But Henry Ford set up shop in Detroit. There he applied ideas of mass assembly and economies of large scale to the construction and distribution of automobiles. Detroit was centrally located with railroad lines and Great Lakes transportation. It attracted the best labor from populations swelling with European immigrants. Ford's successes attracted other industry innovators and leaders. With his leadership, Detroit came to hold undisputed leadership in the auto industry that lasted into the 1960s.

Today when we think of quality, however, we do not think of the American automakers. We look to the Japanese, who have cornered a third of our domestic market. Although just 20 years ago Detroit was on a roll, that ended. Similarly, for 60 years, when people thought of casinos, they thought of Nevada. Now there is competition. Will Nevada share the same fate as Detroit?

In 1931 Nevada legalized casino gambling. In the 1940s gaming personalities such as Bugsy Siegel, Meyer Lansky, and Moe Dalitz played roles similar to those played by Henry Ford: they made their product accessible to ordinary people. In the world market, at the same time, the effects of war kept other countries from embracing mass-produced gambling. Now, however, there is casino gambling in many areas of the North

American continent and in a preponderance of countries of the world.

Let us look at the factors that led to the downfall of Detroit and ask if they will have the same impact upon Nevada.

1. Groupthink. Detroit was "blindsided" as the forces of groupthink led automakers to believe that their success would last forever.

   Is groupthink present in Nevada? Casino managers may feel they "know it all." Yet in order to maintain a dominant market position, they must accept new ideas whatever their source. Yet this is the case. Nevada's larger and more fluid casino leadership group reaches out for new knowledge. Casino projects need new financing, and the financing necessarily comes from the outside. With the outside money comes new ideas.

2. Innovations in marketing. Henry Ford achieved profits by marketing a basic product to the masses. The notion of making a few models to realize economies of scale became part of management thinking. Year-to-year model changes were essentially cosmetic. When customers wanted real variety, Detroit did not give it. Japan did. The Japanese manufacturers demonstrated an ability to introduce new models by taking only three years to produce a new product. Detroit took five years.

   In the gaming field, Nevada may view production as a mass operation allowing for cosmetic changes only. The new operators on the rivers and on the reservations, however, many of whom are Nevadans, are showing that they can put new approaches into place quickly, aimed at completely different markets.

3. Customer demand. Detroit would not listen to the customer. The "Big Three"—General Motors, Ford, and Chrysler—kept making big cars. They were the last to hear the cry for quality. "Recall" became the industry byword. Competitors came to understand that problems with cars were customer problems.

Customers coming to Las Vegas have many demands, and sometimes Nevada has been slow to listen. Customers want more than just a gambling table. One group of foreign casino tourists asked for a tour of Death Valley. Management balked. They were a gambling house. They refused to help find a means to take the group to Death Valley, hoping, of course, that the group would decide to remain in Las Vegas. The group located a bus company that would transport them. They were given a very complete tour, and they returned to Las Vegas with one thought on their minds—sleep. If the casino had catered to these guests, they could have organized a more relaxing four-hour tour of Death Valley that included slot play beforehand and afterwards, a dinner show, linking gambling and tourism together.

Casino management must capitalize on the tourism value of Nevada by working closely with customers. Managers need to work a lot more on listening skills if they hope to avoid a Detroit-like fate in the future.

4. An easily replicated industry? The automobile industry symbolized America's world economic dominance. Dominance continued as long as other nations lacked capital resources to duplicate factories. As soon as others found resources to invest in manufacturing, they replicated our auto industries. They realized that they could make cars as efficiently as we did and that they could meet the needs of American consumers as well.

Although a car factory can be rather easily replicated, a gaming environment such as Nevada's cannot. Its industry is built upon an infrastructure of variety, entertainment choice, inexpensive hotel accommodations, an ambience of good weather, and constant offerings of many special events.

5. Multiplier factors. Automobile manufacturing is desirable because the factory jobs involved have a high multiplier effect. As many as six residents can be supported from the activity of one autoworker. As autoworkers are laid off, other jobs are also lost. The demise of the Detroit auto industry has been quickened by this negative multiplier.

The multiplier effect in the casino industry is less pervasive. It is greatly influenced by the residence of its gamers. In Nevada, most are outsiders. In new gaming jurisdictions, most players are local residents. If these jurisdictions cannot offer gaming to patrons who come from outside the region, economic growth will be elusive. As future experiences are analyzed, there will be less pressure on other jurisdictions to seek to replicate the Nevada gaming scene.

6. Expertise. Japanese car manufacturers demonstrated an ability to quickly learn the American market and to deliver products that met demands of Americans. They were good competitors. The same cannot be said for several non-Nevada gaming operators. Las Vegas has witnessed the experiences of four Japanese-owned casino operations. Only one was successful.

Also, in foreign arenas, casino gaining is not conducted in a manner that will lure Nevada customers away. Nevada need not fear foreign operators, either within or outside the United States, The experts are in Nevada.

7. Economic incentives. Labor costs and other provisions provided disincentives for automobile manufacturers to remain in Michigan.

The Nevada casino scene is quite different. Gaming employees are not unionized, and wages are standardized at lower levels. Most other casino jurisdictions have higher wages, and dealers are organized.

8. Taxation. Government taxation—both national and local—has driven the cost of automobile production to uncompetitive levels for Detroit automakers. The taxation situation has been a major incentive for auto plants to relocate.

Gaming operations will not relocate outside Nevada for taxation reasons. Nevada casino taxation is the lowest of any jurisdiction—just over 6 percent. New Jersey has a gross tax approaching 12 percent, and most European casinos assess taxes of 50 percent or more on gambling wins.

Conclusion

The factors that brought decay to the Detroit automobile industry appear not to be major concerns for the Nevada gambling industry.

Reference

Adapted with permission from William N. Thompson. 1992. "Is Las Vegas Doomed to Become Another Detroit." *Las Vegas Metropolitan Economic Indicators* 5 (Spring): 1–4; previously presented as a speech to the Governor's Conference on Tourism, December 9, 1991, South Lake Tahoe, Nevada.

THE LAS VEGAS BRAND— A CASE STUDY OF MISMARKETING

In their collective wisdom, the voters of Nevada have used the occasion of the 2008 elections to tell their legislators that they desire to have more public revenues devoted to public education. And they know just where to get the revenue—from tourists occupying the 150,000 hotel rooms in Las Vegas and the other 50,000 or so rooms around the state. Sounds familiar. There is a great public need so let's have some more taxes. But "don't tax you, don't tax me, let's tax the fellow behind the tree." It sort of fits the theme of the national election—everyone gets a tax break, but that fellow over there—you know the one that makes too much money—you know the one. In this case, tourists will expect to find room costs increasing 4 percent more due to an increased room tax. The trouble with the thinking is that there are consequences if such actions are taken. Las Vegas (and Nevada) has thrived in the past by offering its brand of gambling entertainment to the masses, and they have done so by offering their entertainment products at very low prices, relatively speaking.

Indeed, room rates have been given without thought of achieving profits. After all, the patron wished to be in the casino not the room. So what if the room was small and had few amenities—ergo, no little chocolates on the pillow or perfumed soaps in a jar? The room was cheap—that's what counted. This attitude was brought home to me 20 years ago as I was trying to sell in-room security safes for the hotels. Casino and hotel managers emphasized to me that they did not want patrons leaving their rooms and leaving their money behind in safes.

The casinos' restaurants had a single purpose—keep the gamblers from being too hungry to play. Feed them a lot and feed them fast, so they can return to play. And keep the price so low that they do not dare think of leaving the facility for a restaurant somewhere else. Las Vegas became famous for perfecting the "buffet." Again, the processed food was sold at cost—or even at a loss.

Many shows were set up on stages on or adjacent to the casino floor. People could enjoy the shows while they were still playing at the tables or machines. They could even play while circus performers were flying above their heads. Even in show rooms the experience of a 70–80 minute show was $20 or maybe a bit more. In 1980, I saw Siegfried and Roy for $25 at the Frontier. The show got me to the Frontier, but the price did not bring the Frontier its profits. Moreover, there were no nightclubs with cover charges.

Casino gift shops sold souvenirs. The big items were clocks that had dice sprinkled around where the hour numbers were supposed to be. Other hot commodities included used decks of cards.

The branding of Las Vegas yelled out—"inexpensive fun." All that has changed. The room, the restaurant, the show, and the shops have all become profit centers in and of themselves. The profit mix of the large Las Vegas Strip tells the story. The Nevada Gaming Abstract reports the percentage of facility revenues from gambling. In 1970 gambling brought in 59.5 percent of the revenue, in 1975, 58.3 percent. Gambling accounted for 57.4 percent of revenues in 1980, and 57.9 percent in 1985. The year 1990 saw gambling bringing 56.9 percent of the revenues, and then things began to change.

The change came probably with the Mirage, but even at the same time Excalibur—still in the hands of the original Circus Circus organization—was telling guests that they could stay for $29—no matter how many were in their party. The irony was that the Mirage was faulted for one thing—its rooms were not up to the standard of its casino and its public areas. The first major renovation at the Mirage involved major upgrades for rooms. The Mirage also introduced fine dining, and fine shops, and they made the Ziegfried and Roy show a major production performance. Ticket prices soared to over $100. A look at the percentage of revenues from gambling for the large Las Vegas Strip casinos demonstrates the effects of these changes and others that followed.

TABLE 1. Revenue Percentages

1989	59.0%
1990	56.9%
1991	57.7%
1992	56.5%
1993	56.5%
1994	54.9%
1995	53.6%
1996	52.6%
1997	51.3%
1998	50.2%
1999	47.8%
2000	45.8%
2001	43.4%
2002	42.2%
2003	42.4%
2004	41.4%
2005	40.5%
2006	40.4%
2007	40.8%

A consultant for MGM Grand recently informed me that only 38 percent of that company's Las Vegas revenues were now derived from gambling activities. Over the past 15 years the large Strip companies have embraced a new marketing model that has given a new image to the tourist customer. In the mind of America, Las Vegas has changed from "bargain" town to "expensive" town. Examples of steps taken in this evolution are several. One of the critical moments in the change came with the build up to celebrations for the millennium. The costs of rooms during the New Year's season of 1999–2000 became atrocious, as some marketing genius came up with the notion that a person would pay "anything" to be in Vegas for the chiming in of the new century. So they charged accordingly. A friend asked me to inquire about something "reasonable," as they could not believe quoted prices they had seen. I told them to consider a non-gaming property. They agreed, and I went to the Mardi Gras Best Western on Paradise Road—two long blocks off the Strip—for a quote. Standard room, three night minimum, $450 a night. My friend stayed at home in New Jersey. The new image of Las Vegas: "gouging."

Even after the holiday "disaster," which found almost half the rooms empty, room rates remained high. In the new casinos of Las Vegas, the tourist was being sold "a room," not just a place to go to sleep. The room included the special chocolates, perfumes and perfumed soap and shampoo, 500 thread count cotton sheets, three sheets on each bed, a wall sized flat screen plasma television with 400 channels and first run movies. Bath robes and Jacuzzis. The rooms were also large enough to hold a business meeting, with desk and tables and chairs to accommodate, along with three hook-ups for computers, printers, and fax machines, and just down the hall a full business service center. The Venetian and Caesars led the way in the latter category. People got a high-class facility, and they were expected to pay for it.

The restaurants of Las Vegas imitated as well as led all the restaurant offerings of the United States, and the world too. Las Vegas was rated as the number two town in the United States for restaurant sales. When Steve Wynn opened the Bellagio he bragged about his chefs. He pointed out that all San Francisco—certainly one of American's leading venues for cuisine—had five chefs who held the very special destination of being "James Beard Chefs." Five. His Bellagio restaurants had seven Beard chefs. Those dining at the Bellagio and the other top Strip properties were not just into a quick "pig out" session between interludes of gambling. They were purchasing a dining experience, and they did not expect to be rushed. Not with entrees at $100 or more, with bottles of wine in the same neighborhood—at a minimum.

Show prices escalated, as a new commodity joined Siegfried and Roy as the sight to see. "Mystere," "Ka," "Zoomanity," "Oh," and "Angell," made Las Vegas show central for Cirque du Soliel, the Quebec troop of avante garde acrobats and musicians. Caesars and Luxor spent over $100 million dollars setting up stages for their shows. With Celine Dion receiving a salary comparable to the staging cost, ticket prices had to go up. They did—to $150, $200, or more for a show. But the casinos gave customers even more for their money—or for more money. They offered new nightclubs— Christian Audigier, Rain, the Ghost Bar, Risque, LAX, Tao, Pure, and The Bank. Standard fare included a $60 door charge, and a required bottle purchase of $475 per table—and this was just the start. The guests are certainly not rushed to return to the casino tables.

Who pays for all this? Well, my informant tells me that many of the free spending guests referred to the high prices and laughed, saying it was only "funny money" they were bringing to Las Vegas. Bonus money from their businesses, credit card advances, corporation expense account money.

Guess what is drying up?—Funny money. The trouble is Las Vegas has moved away from its sure thing—the middle-class fun seeker and grind gambler. The budget tourist has been scared away, and thus far, Las Vegas gaming resorts have done little to bring back this player. They have done little to bring back the old marketing message. "What Happens in Vegas Stays in Vegas." This is a fun slogan, but not a slogan to regain an over-50 couple worried about their retirement plan.

Visitor volumes are down 5 percent or more for 2008; gaming revenues are down 10 percent to 15 percent. And these factors are built into stock prices.

The stock market tells the story, Wynn Resorts saw its 52-week high of $140 a share fall to $28 before a small rebound. MGM stock values went from highs over $93 to lows under $9; the Las Vegas Sands fell from $122 to less than $5 a share.

To be sure, the new marketing image of Las Vegas "paid off" for the major properties before the national economic crunch hit in 2008. But guess what, the cover story in *Time* magazine in 1994 said that America was becoming more and more like Las Vegas. The message was "We are all in it together." Las Vegas better return to the image it successfully created in the pre-1990 years, and let the high-end properties fade a bit into the background. Part of the excitement of the old Vegas was the opportunity middle American had to perhaps observe the super rich in action. But then the observations were made without having to sit at the $1000 minimum tables with the super rich. Maybe Las Vegas resorts can downgrade some of their rooms a bit. Eliminate the expensive sheets and robes. Maybe some basic review shows can come back with price tags below $100. Here's an idea—maybe a stage show in a casino can be set up for less than $100 million. And maybe sit down dining doesn't require $100 entries. And just maybe the citizens of Nevada would be wise to refrain from their favorite song—"need public funds—sock it to the tourists." Just some ideas—that have been tried before.

Reference

Thompson, William N. 2009. "Branding Las Vegas." *Casino Lawyer* 5, no. 1 (Winter): 13–15.

MACHISMO AND THE LATIN AMERICAN CASINO

The casino is a social institution encompassing an array of interactions that focus upon patterned financial risk taking-gambling. Gambling is an activity that reflects the cultural values of a society. Indeed, the casino may be a microcosm of all society, sometimes an institution for social escape, sometimes an alternative social support system, sometimes an extension of a society. Accordingly we can find that the Latin American casinos reflect a dominant value in society—*machismo.*

In 1989, I witnessed casino managers setting up a cockfighting ring in the casino showroom of Casino del Caribe in Cartagena, Colombia. Locals were invited to bring in their prize birds for matched fights to the death. Actually the casino did not participate in betting on the fights, but it did permit its patrons to do so. The holding of a cockfight in a Latin American casino is doubly symbolic of the main cultural value extant in the society.

Anthropologist Clifford Gertz, in his "Deep Play: Notes on the Balinese Cockfight," offers the arena of the cockfight as a metaphor for life on a South Seas island. He writes, "As much of America surfaces in a ball park, on a golf links, at a race track, or around a poker table, much of Bali surfaces in a cock ring . . . only apparently cocks that are fighting there. Actually, it is men" (Gertz 1972, 5). He continues, "In the cockfight, man and beast, good and evil, ego and id, the creative power of aroused masculinity and the destructive power of loosened animality fuse in a bloody drama of hatred, cruelty, violence, and death" (5). Gertz related that the owner of the winning cock takes the losing bird home to eat, but in doing so engenders feelings of embarrassment mixed with "moral satisfaction, aesthetic disgust, and cannibal joy" (7).

Actually, as a legally recognized event, the cockfight is usually confined to Latin American countries. It is in these countries that the set of ideas called machismo is most blatantly recognized and accepted as a guiding course of conduct for many members of society.

What is machismo? What does it mean, and where does it come from? Machismo has been called a "system of ideas," a "world view," an "attitude," a "style," and a "personality constellation."

Macho is a term dating back to at least the 13th century. The central value among the qualities of macho is maleness. Webster's *New World Dictionary* (1975) defines *macho* as "strong or assertive masculinity," and Webster's *New Collegiate Dictionary* (1984) defines *macho* as "aggressively virile." One achieves the ideal of maleness by displaying fearless courage and valor, welcoming challenges of danger and even death with daring. Positive values of pride, courage, honor, charisma, and loyalty are accompanied with negative values of recklessness and aggressiveness carried to extremes of violence. The macho man is quick to take insult, and he refuses to back away from fights. In sexual relations machismo is associated with chauvinistic behaviors. The woman is in all ways a subordinate partner in relationships.

Economic theories focus on the lack of employment, poverty, and the need of the male to migrate to other locations for economic sustenance—for opportunities to support his family. These are seen as forces taking the male away from the home and placing the young male child under the yoke of his mother. The child aggressively seeks to assert a male role in behavior designed to show an independence from his mother.

The ideas of machismo also are derived from a societal need for hero worship. El Cid, Don Juan, Pancho Villa—these and others stand up to the forces that subjugate the males of the society. They are revered for their charismatic appeal. The macho society becomes a society willing to follow, and the strongman ruler is idealized.

Machismo is manifested in myriad ways in the Latin American casino.

Charismatic Authority Structures

The forces of machismo have left a heavy measure of charismatic authority upon Latin American political entities. The *caudillo*—or "man on horseback"—gains power through battles where mystical leadership traits may be displayed. As a ruler, these traits allow him to win support for his decisions. Respect is only diluted if he relinquishes authority to subordinates. He certainly is very reluctant to permit alternative authority structures such as legislative assemblies to share real power with him.

The Latin casino industry is too often dependent upon the whims of leaders, and it often suffers dislocations when leadership changes hands. Many jurisdictions operate according to presidential decrees rather than deliberative legislative policy.

Violence: Suppressed but Ever Present

The machismo syndrome includes a glorification of violence and a measure of reverence for tools of violence. As sug-

gested above, the macho man believes that the knife and gun, phallic symbols as they are, nevertheless are integral to feelings of manliness. The beliefs would be quite compatible with those of the board of directors of the National Rifle Association.

I asked the manager of the Royal Casino in Tegucigalpa, Honduras, if the sign was serious. He assured me that it was. The sign greeted visitors as they entered the casino door. It read (in both Spanish and English): "For everyone's security, no weapons are permitted in the casino. Thank you." When the casino first opened, the management installed 12 lockers to hold patrons' guns. On the first day the lockers were completely full. Quickly the casino ordered an additional dozen lockers. These are now regularly full of weapons.

The casino managers interviewed in this study denied that violence ever erupted in their casinos. Several establishments, however, most notably those operated by governments, kept medical doctors on premises at all times when the gaming rooms were open. The casinos were certainly mindful of the stress associated with gaming wins and losses and were in a state of readiness in case of strokes or heart attacks.

Creditors, Debtors, and the Sense of Honor

A manifestation of machismo is witnessed in the ability to gain access to money. The macho can successfully borrow money. The true machismo finds ways not to pay it back. This kind of attitude can be dangerous for a casino organization.

Casinos in Latin America, especially ones managed by Americans, have been "stung" by local machos. They learned that it is easy to make loans to local players, but it is very difficult to get repayment. When they tried to collect, they found they were "insulting" the borrower by suggesting that he was indebted to them. Some casinos will make loans only through local agents or if guaranteed by a local businessperson.

National Integrity

The sign on the side of the mountain hovers over the national capital. It is brightly illuminated in the evening, seeming to almost be the symbol of Tegucigalpa, capital city for a "sovereign" nation. The sign simply reads, Coca-Cola. One of the driving forces of machismo is the notion that the male must personally compensate for feelings of inferiority derived from the subjugation of local populations by foreign interests, colonial masters from Europe, or economic masters from north of the Rio Grande. For this reason, most of the countries with casinos insist that gaming work forces consist of local citizens only.

Gender Roles in the Casinos

The casinos of Latin America exhibit employment discrimination against women. Several casinos do have women dealers. These invariably are gaming halls controlled by Americans or foreign nationals and those in Puerto Rico. In Vina del Mar, Chile, women are permitted to work only on low-stakes games or games not considered to be games for serious players.

Discrimination against women is defended with phrases such as "We would like to have women dealers someday. But we are not ready for that now." In one casino I was told that it would not be good. "It is the Latin blood, you know." Part of the message was that male players did not feel comfortable having women controlling their fate by turning cards or spinning the wheels. The casinos felt that the male players would harass the women dealers and seek to compromise their integrity at the games. The casino operators know that the macho man is just too much; the women inevitably submit.

The Games Machos Play

The macho man is favored by supernatural forces. If he is brave, he will keep the favor of his gods. Bravery is really more important than cleverness or rationality. Games such as craps and blackjack offer very good odds to the player, but the good odds can be exploited only by educated play, which involves a long-term commitment to the gaming activity. The machos favor casino games of roulette and baccarat, games based upon the luck factor. In roulette the macho challenges fate by going for the single number.

When playing blackjack, strategy play is rarely seen, and card counters are almost nonexistent. Players would often split 10s, and then they hit 18s and 19s. It seemed that a successful hit on a 19 was evidence of daring and a display of manliness.

References

Adapted with permission from William N. Thompson. 1991. "Machismo: Manifestations of a Cultural Value in the Latin American Casino." *Journal of Gambling Studies* 7, no. 2 (Summer): 143–164

Gertz, Clifford. 1972. "Deep Play: Notes on the Balinese Cockfight." *Daedalus* 10: 1–37.

THERE'S A REASON WE ONLY LOOK FORWARD IN LAS VEGAS

Las Vegas, Nevada, is a very unlikely place to find American history. After all, in this city people worship the future as they always look to the next pull of the handle, roll of the dice, or turn of the card. Also, they make a point out of forgetting that last loss. Just as a gambler would choose to "blow up" (figuratively) all past failures in the casinos, local entrepreneurs choose to "blow-up" (literally) the evidence of the city's seamy past. Las Vegas implodes casinos. The city blows-up its history.

First, the Dunes fell in 1993, then the Landmark was imploded in 1995, and in 1996, the Sands bit the desert dust. The Dunes was pushed aside to make way for the new Bellagio Resort, the Landmark made way for a convention center parking lot, and the Sands (once the building was removed) became the site of the $2 billion Venetian Casino Hotel. Two of the implosions were used as footage for Hollywood movies. So there were economic and commercial reasons for taking these three icons away from our sight. But perhaps there were other motives in getting these venerable locations out of our minds. We do not have even a single plaque to recognize the significance of the locations, but if we did? Maybe one would simply say "Hoffa," another might say "Watergate," and the third just possibly might say "Prelude to Dallas, 1963."

The Landmark was where Watergate began, because it was the reason behind Howard Hughes's loan to President Richard Nixon—and it is generally believed that it was not a loan, it was a bribe given so that when Nixon was elected, he would remove an antitrust action so that Hughes could buy the Landmark. Democratic Party chairman Larry O'Brien was working for Howard Hughes when the bribe went thorough, and it was information about that bribe that Nixon's people were trying to get out of O'Brien's Watergate office. I personally talked to Howard Hughes's guy Robert Maheu, and Maheu said absolutely, the Watergate break-in was to get information about the bribe on the Landmark (Drosnin 1985, 434–447).

The Dunes just may have provided the motivation for the murder of Jimmy Hoffa. It was money from the International Brotherhood of Teamsters (the Teamsters union) that went to finance the Dunes—and Teamsters' money was spread around Las Vegas—but the Dunes was the main place. The Teamsters' loans had all sorts of crooked things around them. There were invitations to skim, and Hoffa got kickbacks on the loans. Hoffa's successor Frank Fitzsimmons kept the loans going after Hoffa was in prison and then he kept them going after Hoffa was pardoned, but Hoffa could not run for union office.

Hoffa wanted to ingratiate himself with the Nixon administration. The federal government passed a new law in 1974 called the Employee Retirement Income Security Act, giving the Department of Labor and the Federal Bureau of Investigation special powers to investigate and prosecute union pension funds that were being misused. I worked for the new pension administration in 1976 and 1977, and the story was still in the rumor mill. In 1974, Hoffa starts singing to the government in exchange for a change in his pardon so he could run for union office, and he was murdered. And what was he singing about before he was murdered? The Dunes. He was telling the government how Fitzsimmons was skimming money out at the Dunes much as he had done. Hoffa told about the Teamsters loan structure for constructing the property.

Ah! But the historical possibilities that lurked in the hallways of the Sands, at one time the most famous of all the resorts on the Las Vegas Strip. Denton and Morris (2001) tell many of the seedy stories that came out of the Sands. This was the home of Frank Sinatra and his Rat Pack. This is where he held a secret ownership and where he solidified his alliances with Chicago mobster Sam Giancana. I always pointed to the Sands and said, well, in my mind it's as good as the theory that Lee Harvey Osward acted alone. The theory that there was a plot to assassinate the president. If there was, it may have started at the Sands. It was not just the Rat Pack. The Sands was John F. Kennedy's casino; that is where he met Judy Campbell Exner, through Peter Lawford (Rat Pack member and Kennedy brother-in-law) and Frank Sinatra. She was also the girlfriend of Sam Giancana, who was working with Santo Trafficante to kill Fidel Castro. One scenario was that killing Kennedy was Castro's revenge, because Kennedy was going with the girlfriend and must have known about the Mob plot to kill Castro. Another scenario was that the Mob was compromising Kennedy and that they had the fix in that Kennedy would back off of Mob activities, but his brother, Bobby Kennedy, was a wild card and would not stop, and sort of screwed everything up, and the assassination was to get at Bobby

Kennedy. But where did it start? The Sands (see Davis 1989).

I think it's beautiful—the triple. Of course, I am happy to repeat the myths. It is a lot of history. Maybe now we will be more sterilized, part of the "we're-a-clean-wonderful-town" thing. But it takes a little bit of the glamour away from Las Vegas.

Source: Unpublished lecture/essay by
William N. Thompson

References

Brill, Steven. 1978. *The Teamsters.* New York: Simon and Schuster.

Burbank, Jeff. 1996. "Vegas History Shifts with the Sands." *International Gaming and Wagering Business* (August): 63.

Davis, John. 1988. *Mafia Kingfish: Carlos Marceloo and the Assassination of John F. Kennedy.* New York: McGraw Hill.

Denton, Sally, and Roger Morris. 2001. *The Money and the Power: The Making of Las Vegas and Its Hold on America.* New York: Knopf.

Drosnin, Michael. *Citizen Hughes: In His Own Words—How Howard Hughes Tried to Buy America.* New York: Holt, Rinehart, and Winston.

IF GAMBLING ENTREPRENEURS TOOK THEIR PRODUCT TO THE FOOD AND DRUG ADMINISTRATION

On December 10, 1984, Thomas R. O'Brien, director of the New Jersey Division of Gaming Enforcement, spoke to a meeting of the Sixth National Conference on Gambling and Risk Taking at Bally's Casino Hotel in Atlantic City. He commented:

It seems to some of us, such a long time ago, that New Jersey undertook to establish this new industry as a "unique tool of urban redevelopment," the success of which is based upon how successfully that industry marketed its only product. That product is not entertainment or recreation or leisure—it's really Adrenalin—a biological substance capable of producing excitement—highs and generated usually by anticipation or expectation of a future event especially when the outcome of that event is in doubt.

I think most of us here today who have had experience with gambling will agree that no form of risk taking or risk acceptance generates the intensity or can produce the amount of Adrenalin in the shortest period of time than a roll of the dice, spin of the wheel or turning of a card, and interestingly enough, the level of excitement is not in proportion to the amount of money riding on the event but depends to a large extent upon the subjective psychological approach to the game by the player. (O'Brien 1985)

Thus the product of legalized gambling, according to a top regulator, was an internally generated chemical substance that moved to the brain and could thereby affect mental activity, that is, produce excitement.

Let us ask if we would really legalize gambling or new forms of gambling if all policymakers accepted this view. If government officials accepted that gambling was in essence a mind-altering drug—as Thomas O'Brien clearly suggested it was—would it be legalized? Consider that legislators might have a hard time making such a decision. After all, how many legislators are biochemists? How many are pharmacologists? How many are medical researchers? None—or at least very, very few. As collective bodies, Congress and state legislatures simply lack the required expertise to make good decisions in the area of legalizing new

Do casinos sell drugs? A sign advertising the Motor City casino in Detroit.

drugs. Rather than flying blind, or simply refusing to make any legalizations of new drugs, Congress has established another procedure. Congress delegates decision-making authority in this realm to the Food and Drug Administration (FDA). The FDA has the required expertise.

So now we can ask: If the FDA were given the mind-altering "gambling drug" to analyze, would it legalize the drug? The answer is not easy. But the process the agency would follow in making a decision is clear. They would first authorize extensive tests—initially on animals (perhaps Canadian mice), but then on selected human beings. What would the tests tell them? The results might be similar to those in our Wisconsin survey (Thompson, Gazel, and Rickman 1996) in which we asked questions about serious problem gambling symptoms (the criteria in the *Diagnostic and Statistical Manual of Mental Disorders*, IV). In that survey, 12.9 percent of all persons questioned—but 19.8 percent of the gamblers—answered yes to any of the symptoms. Perhaps the gambling drug is completely safe for 80.2 percent of those taking it. But 19.8 percent show one or more side effects that suggest the use of the "drug" might possibly be troublesome under the wrong conditions. Almost 1 percent of the population and 1.4 percent of the users (in the Wisconsin study) exhibited serious side effects. These side effects could potentially be life threatening, as this drug leads to widespread urges to commit suicide and to perform socially unacceptable activities—stealing, writing bad checks, cheating on insurance matters, missing work regularly. Nonetheless, many of the 80.2 percent might believe (accurately) that the drug helps them relax,

allows them to get away from daily work or home problems, and gives them a measure of excitement lacking in other phases of their lives. They believe the drug (gambling) improves their lives, and it may. Moreover, there may be economic advantages for promoting the commerce entailed in merchandising the drug. Drug manufacturers (casinos, lotteries, racetracks, and so on) provide jobs to society, and drug sales people pay good taxes. There is also evidence that some people will use the drug (gamble) even if it is not legalized, and if they do, the government will not receive any taxes, nor will the government have the opportunity to control facets of how the drug is used.

So should such a drug be legalized? Perhaps. But before certifying a drug as safe enough to be legalized, the FDA would insist that certain controls alluded to be exercised over its use. First, the FDA might recognize the drug as an adult drug. They could stipulate that the drug could not be taken by children. It would be sold only in select locations, and the dosages sold would be regulated. The buyers, moreover, would have to receive the prior approval of an outside expert (a doctor, perhaps, or a financial adviser) before they could make a purchase. And experts (again, doctors, or financial advisers) would have to monitor the drug use and certify that the individual taking the drug was not having serious side effects. When the side effects became noticeable, the person would be weaned off the drug or in serious cases taken off the drug immediately and completely, lest the drug become addictive.

The FDA has established elaborate controls for the dispensing of drugs. Government policymakers might be wise to follow FDA-type procedures as they establish additional controls over gambling in order to assure that serious problem gamblers do not succumb to the bad side effects of what might otherwise be a good drug for many people.

References

Adapted from William N. Thompson, Ricardo Gazel, and Dan Rickman. 1996. *The Social Costs of Gambling in Wisconsin.* Mequon, WI: Wisconsin Policy Research Institute, 26–27.

O'Brien, Thomas. 1985. "Perspectives on the Regulation of Casino Gaming in Atlantic City, New Jersey." In *The Gambling Studies,* edited by William R. Eadington, vol. 1, 121–127. Reno: Bureau of Business and Economic Research, University of Nevada, Reno.

IT'S THIS SIMPLE: CASINO TAXES STIFLE DEVELOPMENT

This article offers a simple test to a simple proposition that casino taxation rates impact economic development. Quite simply we seek to find if lower casino taxes are associated with greater development activity related to tourism. We look at 11 American states which authorize full-scale commercial casino gambling. Their gambling tax rates are compared with specific casino amenities—hotel rooms, convention space, restaurants, and entertainment venues.

Taxes have been referred to as the price we pay for liberty, but the impacts of taxes are also reflected in statements such as the one offered by Chief Justice John Marshall in the case of *McCulloch v. Maryland* (17 U.S. 316, 1819), the "power to tax involves, necessarily, a power to destroy." Money doesn't grow on trees. The money government takes in taxation is money that could be used to create jobs and economic opportunity if it remained in private hands. Taxes extract money from people and organizations that might otherwise be devoted to generating economic development.

An often quoted passage from premier gaming financial expert Eugene Christiansen outlines our proposition:

> In deciding on tax rates, lawmakers should ask themselves this question:

TABLE 2. Commercial Casinos—Revenue and Tax Collections

	Gambling Revenue	Casino Tax Revenue (CTR)	Casino Tax Rate	2003 Actual Tax Rate
Colorado	$ 698,200,000	$ 95,600,000	20.00%	13.69%
Illinois	$1,709,000,000	$779,900,000	42.50%	45.63%
Indiana	$2,299,000,000	$702,000,000	25.00%	30.54%
Iowa	$1,024,000,000	$209,700,000	20.00%	20.48%
Louisiana	$2,017,000,000	$448,900,000	21.50%	22.26%
Michigan	$1,130,000,000	$ 91,547,195	8.10%	8.10%
Mississippi	$2,700,000,000	$325,000,000	8.00%	12.04%
Missouri	$1,330,000,000	$369,000,000	20.00%	27.74%
Nevada	$9,625,000,000	$776,500,000	6.75%	8.07%
New Jersey	$4,490,000,000	$414,500,000	8.00%	9.23%
South Dakota	$ 70,400,000	$ 5,450,000	8.00%	7.74%
	$27,092,600,000	$4,218,097,195	17.08%	15.57%

what kind of gambling industry do the people . . . want? Tax rates north of 50% mean . . . straight machine gaming undiluted with entertainment. . . . Tax rates this high mean minimal capital investment and minimal job creation. Lawmakers . . . are trading jobs for government revenues. They are also imposing maximum social costs on the communities hosting machines. Tax rates in the 20% range shift the policy emphasis away from revenue generation and toward economic development. . . . Rates below 20% . . . maximize job creation and capital investment. . . . Single digit tax rates . . . make the development of labor-intensive diversified entertainment properties possible. . . . Lawmakers . . . are putting economic development . . . first and government revenue second. They are saying their communities want a new Bellagio . . . not storefront video poker.

When a person or organization is taxed, money shifts from the person to the government. The person loses the money (minus $100), and the government gains the money (plus $100). The total is zero. As a tax burden is shifted from one person to another, one wins (gets to keep $100), while the other loses (has to spend $100). The total is zero. This zero-sum game is encompassed in the following phrase: "Don't tax you, don't tax me; tax that fellow behind the tree." (Quotation attributed to the late Senator Russell Long of Louisiana). For each winner in the tax game, there is a loser.

But do the words of Eugene Christiansen really ring true? The tax rates of the 11 casino states were examined for 2003 along with the real rates from tax revenue collections in 2003, and their total gaming revenues.

Casino City's *Worldwide Casino Guide* (2004 edition) provides a complete listing of the commercial casinos in the 11 states along with the number of hotel rooms, the number of restaurants and entertainment facilities, and the area of convention space at each casino. To the figures listed we have added the space in the convention centers of Las Vegas, Reno, and Atlantic City, as these facilities are directly supported by the casinos.

In order to test our simple proposition, we examine the following four ratios: (1) casino revenue to hotel rooms; (2) casino revenue to convention space in casinos (or supported by casinos); (3) casino revenue to number of restaurants at casinos; (4) casino revenue to number of entertainment venues at casinos.

We have arranged the states according to a blending of their given tax rate (2003) for casino gambling revenue and the actual rate—that being the state revenue collected divided by casino gambling revenue. Table 2 indicates these values. However, the Michigan values have been adjusted, as the state collects an additional 9.9 percent, which they rebate to local governments. Moreover, in 2004 the combined state and local rate was increased to 24 percent. Therefore we count Michigan as one of the "higher" tax states.

The arrangement of the states from lowest to highest taxes therefore is considered to be South Dakota, New Jersey, Nevada, Mississippi, and Colorado, followed by Iowa, Louisiana, Michigan, Indiana, and Illinois. For a simplified analysis, we compare low tax states (South Dakota, New Jersey, Nevada, Mississippi, and Colorado) to high tax states (Iowa, Missouri, Louisiana, Michigan, Indiana, and Illinois).

Hotel Rooms and Casino Taxation

As we begin to examine the amenities that go with casino gambling, the veracity of the Christiansen remarks comes into focus. In the low tax states, we find that $389,567.94 in casino revenue will produce one hotel room, whereas in the high tax states, it takes $2,123,606.00 to have a single hotel room at a casino. When Nevada is taken away from the low tax states, the revenue required for a hotel room still pales in comparison to the high tax states: $470,829.54.

The individual profiles generally follow the supposition that higher taxes stifle development of amenities, with Michigan being an outlier. Their three casinos lacked hotel rooms, with minor exceptions.

Conventions and Casinos

Data show that the small tax states offer one square foot of convention space for each $14,394.51 of gambling revenue, while the large tax states exhibit one square foot of convention space only when they have $94,748.79 in casino gambling revenues. The ratio differentials hold even when Nevada, a major convention state, is removed—the remaining four small tax states have a convention square foot for each $17,645.02 in revenues

Looking at the states individually, we see convention space falling slightly with the increase in taxation; again Michigan is an outlier.

Restaurants and Casinos

We did not consider the size of restaurants in casinos but simply the number of restaurants reported. Nonetheless, the expected differences following from the proposition tested hold. The five low tax states find one casino restaurant for every $18,328,846.12 lost by players. If Nevada is excluded, the amount is $20,465,681.64. The six high tax state casinos require about twice as much in revenues to produce one restaurant: $40,872,147.98.

The trend line follows taxation when we look at the states individually, with the exception of New Jersey, where it can be assumed that their fewer restaurants probably have larger capacities than elsewhere.

Entertainment and Casinos

As with restaurants, the Casino City reports did not consider the size and seating capacity of entertainment facilities, but rather simply the number of entertainment facilities with each casino. The same differentiations persist. The five small tax states find a casino entertainment facility for each $51,433,499.11 in casino revenues ($57,942,929.29 for the four small tax states without Nevada), while the six high tax states require $101,668,665.70 in gaming losses for each entertainment facility at a casino.

The general ratio differences are witnessed as we examine individual states—the higher the taxes, the more revenue needed to support entertainment, New Jersey again being an exception having fewer facilities per casino dollars.

Conclusions

The proposition advanced is found to be valid. Lower casino taxes are associated with greater tourism development. The conclusion follows an examination of actual data, not sample statistics. To be sure, other factors may be present that would influence the amount of economic development—for example, the extent of competition among casinos. Nonetheless policy makers must heed the wisdom of financial experts who tell them clearly the simple truth that they have a choice: they can institute a policy of low casino taxes and aim to have Bellagios, or they can think of government revenues only, institute high taxes and get storefront gaming halls.

References

Christiansen, Eugene Martin. 2003. *Taxes and Regret: A Review of 2002 US Casino Results in a Discussion of the Tax Rates Behind the Fiscal and Economic Policies of Various US Regulatory Jurisdictions* 12, at http://www.ateonling.co.uk/library14/taxes.pdf.

Thompson, William N., and Nathan Myers. 2006. "It's This Simple: Casino Taxes Stifle Development." *Casino Enterprise Management*, November 2006, 92–95.

THEFT IS A SOCIAL COST—BIGGER THAN WE MAY HAVE THOUGHT

Several studies of cost impacts of gambling have been criticized for including the value of stolen property by pathological gamblers as a negative social cost. The studies have considered the worth of the property as a social cost while the critics have indicated that the cost is merely a transfer of wealth from one person (legitimate owner) to another (new illegitimate owner). I dissent from that criticism.

I would offer the following caveat regarding the use of these figures in overall cost impacts per pathological gambler. The costs are not exact, and the costs do involve some transfer values—that is some of the value of the stolen property may indeed remain in the community, and hence, should not be considered in assessing the overall loss of value (wealth) for a community (society). But that is not the full story.

Let us look directly at the value of the items stolen by pathological gamblers. The items may be cash, instruments representing cash value, or tangible items of property. Let's look at a tangible item of property. For instance, a new television in a person's home. Why a new television? Simply, because the thief has been drawn to the item because he has "cased" out a neighborhood, and he has seen a television box in the discarded trash by a home—ergo, he reasons the home must include the valuable item. The store cost of the television was $500. But any understanding of microeconomics would say to Buyer Bob it is worth more, otherwise he would not have made the purchase. We will say the television has a value of $600 to Bob, the legal owner.

What is it worth after it has been stolen? Consider how much it is worth to the thief. Not $600. Not $500. If it had that worth the thief would have gone to the store and purchased a similar type television set. No. It is worth—well, the time necessary to case the neighborhood (two hours), the time to wait for the owner to leave the house (two hours), the time to purchase burglar tools (one hour), the value of the use of the tools ($20—they can be used again). The cost of the use of a vehicle and gasoline ($10)—perhaps a total of $75. Now these are also social costs, because in the absence of the theft by the pathological gambler, they would not have been expended. The thief also incurs a risk cost of detection and police action, but to the thief it is very low because he would not attempt the theft if he thought it was a large cost. So in the first instance, we can see that the television has decreased in value by perhaps $500. Now consider the many transactions needed to get the television back into active use. The thief did not steal it in order to watch it. He sells it to a Fence Frank for $100, taking his profit and running back to the casino (or paying off his debt to Vinnie). The fence rents his space at the flea market and sells the set to Dealseeking Dan for $150. Is it worth $600 again? Hardly, when it breaks down Dan has no guarantee. Moreover, he has to worry that the repairman will see Buyer Bob's ID mark on the set and report it to the police (the police have a report describing the set, and they distribute the description to repair people). He may also lose sleep over the thought. He may come to think it is worth much less than he paid for it. The social cost of the transaction, the time and energy necessary for both Dan and Frank to go to the flea market, is a loss to society.

By now the social costs are close to the cost of the set as it was originally sold. But there are more social costs. Buyer Bob is now afraid to go home sometimes, and afraid to leave at other times. He has lost security and freedom. Social costs. His doctor has also decided that he needs medicine and therapy—more social costs. He buys a new set of locks and window alarms for his house. Social costs. He buys an expensive Doberman Pinscher—more social costs. He convinces the city to assign extra police to his neighborhood. More costs.

Of course, not all these costs would attend a robbery of negotiable cash or checks, but many of the costs would, as some instruments cannot be easily sold, and if there is a home invasion or a personal robbery, the fear factor—which carries costs—has been imposed on the entire society.

References

Lesieur, H., and C. Anderson. 1995. *Results of a Survey of Gamblers Anonymous Members.*

Thompson, Gazel, and Rickman. 1996. (see above); WEFA (Thompson and Lesieur) (see above).

Thompson, W. N., and F. Quinn. 2000. *The Social Costs of Machine Gambling In South Carolina.*

Walker, D. M., and A. H. Barnet. 1999. "The Social Costs of Gambling: An Economic Perspective," *Journal of Gambling Studies* 15.

Walker, Michael. 1992. *The Psychology of Gambling.*

Westphal, J., L. J. Johnson, and L. Stevens. 1999. *Estimating Social Costs of Gambling In Louisiana for 1998.*

Source: This article, by William N. Thompson, appeared in the *Report on Problem Gambling* (December/January 2001): 44–46.

COMORBIDITY AND THE COSTS OF COMPULSIVE GAMBLING

Stories about troubled gamblers losing all their wealth spread by word-of-mouth and also they are spread in sensationalized media accounts. As these stories of losses grow they are embellished with images of embezzlements at work places or offices of charities, or families broken apart and put in distress, and, of course, of suicides. It is in the vital interest of casinos that these stories not spread, it is in the vital interest of casinos that these stories not exist, and that the cases of problem gambling and the effects of problem gambling be mitigated and reduced as much as possible.

Before 2003, the state of Nevada had appropriated exactly zero dollars for programs to deal with problem gambling. Then they had an epiphany, and $250,000 was earmarked for the cause (one-thirtieth of one percent of the money the state gains from casino taxes). All of the money went toward a research project which determined the prevalence of pathological and problem gambling among the Nevada population. So one more study was added to the hundred or so already published telling us that 0.6 percent, or 0.9 percent, or 1.3 percent, or 2.2 percent of adults were current or sometime in their lifetime pathological or problem gamblers. Actually Nevadans were found to have more than double the prevalence rates found elsewhere. End of research. Good research to be sure. Peer reviewed, academically sound. But while the researchers were "the best" in the field, we can still ask "So what?" So what should we do about problem gambling? So what should we do to reduce the problem?

After the study was published, the industry could justifiably say, "Well, it appears that problem gamblers are a very small portion of those who come to enjoy the gambling opportunities we provide." On the other hand, industry critics could point out that the small percentage still adds up to a lot of people (thousands) among the general population. The legislative response was a mandate that casino put brochures and signs around warning players that gambling can lead to problems for some, and indicating that they may call an 800 number for help if they think they have a problem. No real action was taken on reducing the number of problem gamblers or reducing the impacts of their maladies.

Our research led us in another direction. We wanted to know what the dollar costs of problem gambling represented to other people (nongamblers) and to the general economy. Hence we went to the pathological gamblers for answers, or at least to those who would self-define themselves as "compulsive gamblers." In 2002, we interviewed, in an anonymous fashion, 99 members of Gamblers Anonymous groups in southern Nevada.

The average respondent began gambling when 26.82 years old, weekly (or more) gambling began at age 31.84 years, first borrowing at 33.43 years. They identified problems starting at age 34.12 years. They had been in GA for an average of 2.31 years. Their losses on average were $112,400. Before joining GA they had average debts (because of gambling) of $60,714, with 45.4 percent having incurred personal bankruptcies, while 15.1 percent had been sued in court over debts. A majority (63.3 percent) had stolen property because of gambling, with the average thefts (spread over all the respondents) amounting to $13,517. Nine had been arrested, with the average respondent serving 0.16 months in jail or prison, and 0.10 months on probation.

The average gambler lost work time amounting to 8.69 hours a month, while 22.9 percent quit work thus losing 4.2 months of employment due to gambling; 24.2 percent were fired, losing 2.4 months of labor. Only 3.4 percent accepted welfare because of gambling, whereas 5.8 percent accepted food stamps; 14.9 percent were hospitalized because of health problems related to gambling, while 23 percent had outpatient treatments. Nearly two-thirds (65.9 pecent) planned suicide, while 27.7 percent attempted suicide. We calculated an annual cost figure for one pathological gambler to be $19,711 per year. (See the Pathological Gambling entry).

We define the costs as the disamenities borne by persons other than the gambler. However, we acquiesce with critics who indicate that these are not all "deadweight" costs that subtract wealth for the entire economy, but instead many are costs that are merely transferred from one person to another. Critics can also look at this data and say we are only giving numbers, we are not giving meaning. They can say about our numbers what we say about other numbers, "So what?" But there is meaning.

One level of meaning derived from the numbers is simply that the costs are major ones. If we have 20,000 compulsive gamblers in southern Nevada, the economy is losing perhaps $120 million or more per year, and governments are losing over $28 million. The numbers justify appropriations from government of more than $250,000 if we are to make a serious effort to lessen problem gambling.

Another level of criticisms (often from the industry) is that studies such as ours neglect the fact that compulsive gamblers have other addictions as well, and that these other addictions may contribute to or account for the costs identified. Good point. Accordingly we asked about other addictions. Table 3 shows the responses.

TABLE 3. Percent of GA Respondents Reporting Additional Addictions

Alcohol Addiction	22%
Tobacco Addiction	16%
Drug Addiction	9%
Food Addiction	28%
Shopping Addiction	9%

We went back to our numbers and sought to find if those with other addictions exhibited higher costs. For our analysis of the effects (or associations) of comorbidities, we eliminated some individuals who did not fully report on other addictions. Therefore for the analysis of associations we used a base figure of $19,585 annual costs per pathological gambler. To place the figures below in context, we must note that some respondents exhibited few or even no costs on their profiles. This made the average for others much higher.

Only alcohol and drug addiction showed statistically significant relationships regarding the costs. The findings suggest a pattern of complementary and substitute comorbidities as it relates to problem gambling. Alcohol addiction *adds* to the severity of problem gambling.

For the alcoholics in the survey, we found that the extra addiction added $14,460 to their cost profile (holding all other factors constant). However, we also found a quite contrary result from respondents who indicated that they were addicted to drugs. Their gambling cost profile was reduced an average of $19,156, other things being constant. Accordingly a person with gambling, alcohol, *and* drug addiction, would have a cost profile $4,696 below the average ($19,156 minus $14,460).

The results from the analysis of shopping addiction, food addiction, and tobacco addiction were not significant. Nonetheless, they are worthy of note. The "shopoholics" found costs being $4,234 below average. Food addictions added $10,887 to the profiles, while tobacco addictions added $456.

We can surmise that alcohol use complements gambling as the two activities are expected to go together, at the same time and in the same place. Casinos tacitly acquiesce to alcohol addiction, and to be sure some would say that many casinos promote the comorbidity as drinks are often served to gamblers at the gambling site. In Las Vegas, drinks are considered a "free" amenity for gamblers. Certainly a person who is in a "drunk" state would be denied free drinks in a casino as a person who outwardly appears to be intoxicated might create a liability situation. (It can be noted, however, that Nevada does not have a "dram" law assigning tort liability to those distributing alcoholic beverages when the person drinking does harm to another). Thus, other than for individuals who have passed an insobriety threshold, gambling and drinking are accepted, if not at least tacitly encouraged.

On the other hand, one is not likely to see a casino acquiescing to drug activity. Indeed, drug activity is not permitted, nor tolerated on casino floors, either by customers or employees. In can be added that drug use also is more expensive than alcohol use, and that a person high on drugs would probably be considered disruptive to casinos.

The decrease in costs of gambling among compulsive shoppers has two possible explanations. A shopper cannot gambler while shopping, also shopping (like drug use) demands financial resources that may divert one from gambling activity. Shopping and drug use are substitutes for gambling, not complementary activities.

Food addictions do not cause significant increases in the cost profiles, but the increases are large ones. While the dynamic is quite different, casino are certainly associated with food. The casinos of Las Vegas and elsewhere use food—mostly in the form of low cost specials or buffets—as specific advertised attractions to bring players into the gambling atmosphere. Also as free drinks are given to players in Las Vegas, so too we find that meals are probably the second or third most prevalent kind of "free" gift given to players. Tobacco has traditionally been associated with casinos as well, and players were given packs of cigarettes. Like

drinking, smoking is something one can do while engaged in gambling. While the cost increase for tobacco addicts was not significant, it could be expected. The increase was not large, perhaps because a quest for tobacco use may lead players to take breaks in their play in order to "lite up" or to go and procure cigarettes.

Other factors were also related to the cost profiles. Income unquestionably adds to the severity of the economic dimension of pathological gambling, as one might expect. Players with higher household income have a slightly, but statistically significant, higher cost profile. So too do players with credit from bookies. Those with credit lines at casinos have especially higher profiles—and significantly so—with added costs of $25,051 per player. Those who steal from work have costs $14,522 higher than average, a significantly higher amount. This would be expected analytically as the amount stolen is figured into the cost profile. Higher education is also a factor adding to costs, but not in a significant manner. Contrary to expectations, those who play mostly in casinos exhibited a significant lessening of cost profiles, while a lessening of costs for those playing at neighborhood casinos was not significant. Players in bars or stores had a significant increase in the cost profile, adding $1,971 to their cost profiles. We might speculate that the casinos offer greater human interaction and also much noise and light that may distract one from episodes of binge playing. On the other hand, disassociated activity more easily accompanies gambling in isolation in places such as bars and grocery stores where machine play occurs.

These findings from our cost study point to the critical role of policies relating to alcohol use at gambling venues, suggesting that credible programs to address problem gambling call for reevaluation of current alcohol practices.

We now know that comorbidity of alcohol and gambling addiction magnify the economic dimension of problem gambling. What we may not fully understand is how each element of current alcohol availability in gambling venues contributes to addictive behavior. Questions may arise as to the variation in costs with differing availabilities of gambling and alcohol. For example, does the wide distribution of gambling machines in local bars and taverns compared with a more limited gaming district significantly impact the incidence and the magnitude of costs? The suggestions in our research would tend to make us support actions of casinos to reduce alcohol consumption, or if alcohol is not currently present, to support a continuation of such prohibitions. Recently a Native American casino in Iowa did precisely that. On the other hand gaming policy makers in the United Kingdom enacted new rules permitting drinking away from bars and on the gaming floors of casinos.

Reference

Thompson, William N., and R. Keith Schwer. 2007. "Compulsive Gamblers and Alcohol." *Casino Lawyer* 3, no. 3 (summer): 16–18.

A RANDOM THOUGHT OF A LUCKY LAS VEGAS RESIDENT

The cub scout troops of Eberbach Elementary School held their annual carnival on the playground one April Saturday afternoon. As I recall I was about nine years old. I lived four blocks away. That afternoon I was riding my bicycle around with little to do. I had 15 or 20 cents in my pocket. I rode by the school and saw the carnival and I decided to walk around the playground. As I went down the midway, I discovered a game I had never played before. People were pitching pennies onto an oil cloth that was marked in a grid with 100 squares. Each square had a number or an "x". The numbers were 1, 5, 10, and 25. If a penny landed on a square the person pitching the penny won the amount of pennies designated— but the penny could not be on a line, it had to land fully within the square.

I remember making several pitches and winning 5 or 10 cents. I eagerly waited my turn to throw one penny after another. Soon I was out of pennies, but I was quite charged up. I looked all about for another penny, on the ground, in my pockets. I turned each pocket inside out. Then I ran to my bicycle and pedaled home as fast as I could. I ran about the house looking for loose change. I found another 10 cents in a dresser drawer and quickly rode my bicycle back to the carnival. I ran to the penny pitch booth. I started throwing pennies again, and again they missed the mark and my pockets were emptied. I thought about riding home again, but I knew it would be too late, the carnival was already beginning to close down. I saw a friend and begged him to loan me money. He just laughed at me. I was very very dejected as I rode home. All night long I woke up thinking of the penny pitch game.

Thirty-one years later I moved to Las Vegas. Here I have been much luckier than when I was nine years old. Here, in my very first gambling experience, I lost. Although I only gamble on semi-rare occasions, I almost always lose. After I return home, I feel no rush to gamble. I felt it once, and I think I could have the feeling again, but I have been very very lucky, almost every time I gamble now, I lose. And I know I am a loser. Sometimes I think that is the only way one can really survive in Las Vegas.

Reference

Thompson, William N. 2003. *Parables from (a not quite) Paradise, NV 89154.* Bloomingtom, IN: First Books, 118–119. Copyright held by William Thompson.

ANOTHER RANDOM THOUGHT

BY WILLIAM N. THOMPSON

Pick a card, any card
The choice is yours to make
A one eyed jack, seven or nine
Ace, King, Queen, or eight

Pick a card, you select
Heart, Diamond, Club, or Spade
Together for now or if you wish
Feelings that never will fade

Pick a card, if you don't like it
Go ahead and draw again
The card will be your link to me
Your real ace, your heart, your ten

Let's both pick cards together
We will make a winning hand
All faces, diamonds and aces
I'll be the king at your command

Pick a card, then make a bid
And play a no trump lead
We'll convert on all the tricks
Answering each others needs

But existence is not a card game
Not tea leaves, stars or lucky charms
Our lifeline is not upon our hands
But within each others arms

So pick a card, any card
If it's an ace or a lowly two
The cards all really mean the same
They say I'm dreaming, just waiting
for you

Reference

Thompson, William N., and Anthony Juliano, 2004. *Heartlines and Lyrics.* Bloomington IN: First Books Library, 11. Copyright held by William Thompson.

Casino Niagara advises pathological gamblers to "walk away."

Thematic Index

Index

Note: Index page numbers immediately followed by a t or an f refer to a table or figure, respectively.

Gambling, positive case for, 164–167
Gambling systems
  cancellation system, 82
  flat betting and, 81
  history, 79
  horse racing and, 80
  luck games and, 80–81
  Martingale progressive system,
    81–82
  setting limits, 82
  skill and, 79
  sports and, 79–80
Gambling taxes
  and earmarking, 235–236
  equity in, 233–234
  federal excise, 236
  rates, 232–233
  and volume of gambling, 234–235
Games. *See also individual games*
  house-banked, 6, 251
  player-banked, 6, 265
  skill versus luck, 671
Gaming devices. *See individual devices;*
  Johnson Act and Amendments
Gaming Management and Development
  Center, 84
Gaming Research and Review Journal
  (IGI), 83
Gaming Studies Research Collection
  (Library, University of Nevada,
  Las Vegas), 84–85
Gaming versus gambling, xvii–xviii
Gates, John W., 314
Gaughan, Jackie, 315–317
Gaughan, Michael, 315–317
Georgia, 530–531
Germany, 439–442
  Kurhaus (Wiesbaden), 63
Gibraltar, 442–444
Goa. *See* Indian subcontinent (including
  Bhutan, Goa, Nepal, Sri Lanka,
  and Sikkim)
Great Britain. *See* United Kingdom
*Greater New Orleans Broadcasting
  Assoc. v. United States,* 678, 679

Greece, 444–445
Grey, Thomas A., 88–89, 317
Grosso v. United States, 671
Guatemala, 494

Haiti, 416–419
Harrah, William F., 318–319
Harris v. Missouri Gaming Com'n., 676
Hawaii, 531
High seas, laws of gambling on, 77
Hispanic Americans, casino
  employment, 39
Hispaniola. *See* Dominican Republic;
  Haiti
History of gambling, chronology,
  xxiii–xxxviii
Ho, Stanley, 319
Hoffa, Jimmy, 320–321
Holland. *See* Netherlands
Honduras, 494–495
  Casino Copsanti (San Pedro Sula),
  24
Horse racing, 91
  in Canada, 95–96
  cheating and, 18
  colors (jockey and mount), 123
  economic impact of betting, 54
  famous horses, 103–108
  gambling and, 92–93
  gambling systems and, 80
  Hall of Fame and museum, 102–103
  history of, 91–92, 93–98
  Islamic exception for betting on, 54
  Jockey Club of New York, 96
  jockeys, 108–112
  and leading thoroughbred horses,
    103–108
  and leading thoroughbred jockeys,
    108–112
  officials of, 101–102
  owners, 120–123
  participants in, 100–101
  tracks and track organizations, 115–120
  and trainers, 112–115
  types of, 98–100

About the Author

William N. Thompson, a native of Ann Arbor, Michigan, received his BA and MA degrees from Michigan State University and his PhD from the University of Missouri in Columbia. All degrees are in the field of political science. He is a professor of public administration at the University of Nevada, Las Vegas. Previously he has been on the faculties of Southeast Missouri State, Western Michigan, and Troy State (Europe) universities. He was also a research associate with the National Association of Attorneys General, a research advisor for the Pension and Welfare Benefit Programs in the U.S. Department of Labor, and the elected supervisor of Kalamazoo Charter Township in Michigan.

Since coming to the University of Nevada, Las Vegas, in 1980, his research has focused upon developments in the casino industry. He and John Dombrink of the University of California–Irvine were gaming consultants to the President's Commission on Organized Crime. Together they wrote *The Last Resort: Success and Failure of Campaigns for Casinos*. Thompson also coedited and coauthored three editions of *International Casino Law* (with Anthony Cabot, Andrew Tottenham, and Carl Braunlich). He also coauthored *Casino Customer Service with Michele Comeau*. He wrote the ABC-CLIO books *Legalized Gambling: A Reference Handbook, Native American Issues: A Reference Handbook,* and *Gambling in America: An Encyclopedia of History, Issues, and Society*. His most recent book is *Ethics in City Hall*, coauthored with James Leidlein.

William Thompson has appeared as a gambling authority on many major media outlets, presenting commentary on the *Today Show, World News Tonight, Nightline,* CNN's *Crossfire,* PBS's *Frontline* and the *NewsHour with Jim Lehrer,* as well as *The O'Reilly Factor* on Fox News. He has been quoted in major press outlets, including the *Washington Post, New York Times, Christian Science Monitor, Newsweek, The Economist, Readers Digest,* and *Forbes.* He has also been a consultant both to gambling entities, including Native American groups in eleven states, as well as government groups, including the National Gambling Impact Study Commission.

About the Contributors

BO BERNHARD

Bo Bernhard, a Las Vegas native, received his BA from Harvard and his MA and PhD from the University of Nevada, Las Vegas, in the field of sociology. Bernhard serves as the director of the International Gaming Institute and is a professor of sociology at the University of Nevada, Las Vegas.

CARL BRAUNLICH

Carl Braunlich is an associate professor in hospitality and tourism at University of Nevada, Las Vegas. He was formerly in casino management in New Jersey, the Bahamas, and Las Vegas. He is a coeditor of *International Casino Law*.

ANTHONY CABOT

Anthony Cabot is a partner in the law firm of Lewis and Roca in Las Vegas. His many books include *The Internet Gambling Report, Federal Gambling Law,* and *Casino Gaming: Public Policy, Economics and Regulation.* He is a coeditor of *International Casino Law.*

FELICIA CAMPBELL

Felicia Campbell is a professor of English at the University of Nevada, Las Vegas. She received her BA and MA from the University of Wisconsin and her PhD from United States International University. She is the editor of *Popular Culture Review.*

MICHELE COMEAU

Michele Comeau is a gaming consultant and former instructor of communications and marketing at the University of Nevada, Las Vegas.

JAMES DALLAS

James Dallas is a retired United Methodist minister, having served congregations in Nevada and California. He received his BA from Occidental College and his PhD in theology from Claremont University. He teaches at Victor Valley College.

LARRY DANDURAND

Larry Dandurand is professor emeritus of marketing at the University of Nevada, Las Vegas. He received his BA from the University of Minnesota and his PhD from the University of Missouri in Columbia. He served in the Peace Corps in Panama and also taught in several countries as a Fulbright Scholar.

DIANA DEVER

Diana Dever is a professor of social sciences at Mohave College in Arizona. She received her BA from Wayne State University, her MA from Michigan, and her PhD in history from the University of Nevada, Las Vegas.

JOHN DOMBRINK

John Dombrink is a professor of criminology at the University of California, Irvine. His undergraduate education was at the University of San Francisco, and he received his PhD from the University of California, Berkeley. He is coauthor of *The Last Resort: Success and Failure in Campaigns for Casinos.*

ROBERT FAISS

Robert Faiss is a senior partner with Lionel, Sawyer, and Collins law firm in Las Vegas. He has been recognized as the "premier gaming attorney" in the United States and one of "the 100 most influential lawyers in America" by the *National Law Journal.* He received his undergraduate education at the University of Nevada, Reno, and his legal education at American University in Washington, D.C.

BONNIE GALLOWAY

Bonnie Galloway works as a private investment consultant. She has taught business and sociology as an adjunct professor at Rider University, Mercer County Community College, Coker College, and Francis Marion University. She received her BA from

Hillsdale College, her MBA from Wayne State, and her PhD from Western Michigan University.

RICARDO GAZEL

Ricardo Gazel is a research economist with the Inter-American Bank. He was formerly on the staff of the Federal Reserve Bank in Kansas City and the Center for Business and Economic Research at the University of Nevada, Las Vegas. His PhD in economics was awarded by the University of Illinois at Urbana-Champaign.

CARL LUTRIN

Carl Lutrin is professor emeritus of political science at California Polytechnic State University. He is coauthor of American Public Administration. His BA is from Adelphi, his MA is from University of Wisconsin, and his PhD is from the University of Missouri, Columbia.

CHRISTIAN MARFELS

Christian Marfels is professor emeritus of economics at Dalhousie University in Halifax, Nova Scotia. He received his doctorate from the Free University of Berlin, and he specializes in industrial and antitrust economics, with a focus on the gambling industry.

EUGENE MOEHRING

Eugene Moehring is a professor of history at the University of Nevada, Las Vegas. He received his undergraduate education at Queens College, where he also received an MA degree. His PhD is from the City University of New York. Moehring is the author of *Resort City in the Sunbelt.*

NATHAN MYERS

Nathan Myers received his PhD in Public Administration from the University of Nevada, Las Vegas. He teaches at a state college in Evansville, Indiana.

TIMOTHY OTTEMAN

Timothy Otteman received his doctorate degree in Educational Leadership from Central Michigan University in 2008. He now teaches recreational studies at Central Michigan in Mount Pleasant, Michigan.

J. KENT PINNEY

J. Kent Pinney is professor emeritus of marketing at the University of Nevada, Las Vegas.

DAN RICKMAN

Dan Rickman is a professor of economics at Oklahoma State University. He received his BA, MS, and PhD degrees from the University of Wyoming.

I. NELSON ROSE

I. Nelson Rose received his undergraduate degree from the University of California, Los Angeles, and his law degree from Harvard University. He is a professor of law at the Whittier College of Law in Costa Mesa, California, and is the author of *Gambling and the Law* and *Blackjack and the Law*.

JACK SCHIBROWSKY

Jack Schibrowsky is professor of marketing at the University of Nevada, Las Vegas.

ROBERT SCHMIDT

Robert Schmidt is an independent researcher. He received his undergraduate degree from the University of Chicago and his PhD in sociology from the University of Nevada, Las Vegas.

R. KEITH SCHWER

R. Keith Schwer is the director for the Center for Business and Economic Research and professor of economics at the University of Nevada, Las Vegas. He received his BA from the University of Oklahoma and his PhD from the University of Maryland.

GARRY SMITH

Garry Smith is professor emeritus of physical education and sports studies at the University of Alberta in Edmonton. He currently works with the Institute for Business

Development at the university and also is a gambling research associate with the Canada West Foundation.

ICHIRO TANIOKA

Ichiro Tanioka is president and professor of sociology at the Osaka University of Commerce in Osaka, Japan. Hi PhD is from the University of Southern California.

CONSTANTINA (DINA) TITUS

Dina Titus is a professor of political science at the University of Nevada, Las Vegas, and also a member of the United States Congress, 3rd district. She is the author of *Bombs in Their Backyards*. Her BA is from William and Mary, her MA from the University of Georgia, and her PhD from Florida State University.

ANDREW TOTTENHAM

Andrew Tottenham is the head of the gaming consultant firm Tottenham and Company, located in London. He has worked for many years in the casino industry. He is the coeditor of *International Casino Law*.

R. FRED WACKER

Fred Wacker has been a professor of history at Wayne State University and an adjunct professor in the Honors College at the University of Michigan. His BA is from Harvard, and his JD and PhD are from the University of Michigan.

SIDNEY WATSON

Sidney Watson is the former director of the Curriculum Materials Library of the University of Nevada, Las Vegas. She received her BA from the University of California, Santa Barbara, and her MA in public administration from the University of Nevada, Las Vegas.

MARIA WHITE

Maria White is the former director of circulations for the Lied Library at the University of Nevada, Las Vegas. She received her BA and MA degrees in public administration from the University of Nevada, Las Vegas.

BRADLEY WIMMER

Bradley Wimmer is an associate professor of economics at the University of Nevada, Las Vegas. He has served as an economist with the Federal Communications Commission. His BA is from Coe College and his PhD from the University of Kentucky.